899

An Historical Survey of Selected

LMS STATIONS

Volume Two

Layouts and Illustrations

Frequent trains to all parts. As a Fairburn 2-6-4T makes a spirited departure from platform 9, and passes Southport (Chapel St.) 'up' main east line starting signal, No. 54, columns of smoke in the distance reveal plenty of further activity. Steam billows out from the overall roof by Nos. 2 & 3 platforms, a locomotive blows off in No. 6 platform, and smoke drifts across the station from a further train in No. 8 platform. To the right, and separated from the running line by the Bradford Siding, a rake of stock occupies No. 1 road of the London St. excursion platforms. Further stock can be seen beyond that rake. For generations, this is what a busy city or seaside terminal was like. The date was July 1964 but, with stock some years older, it could have been decades previously. Today it is a scene from a vanished world.

An Historical Survey of Selected

LMS STATIONS

Layouts and Illustrations

Volume II

by
Dr. R. Preston Hendry MRCS LRCP BA (Cantab)
&
R. Powell Hendry LLB FCA

Oxford Publishing Co.

Typesetting by:
Aquarius Typesetting Services, New Milton, Hants.

Printed in Great Britain by:
Biddles Ltd.,
Guildford
Surrey

Published by:
Oxford Publishing Co.
Link House
West Street
POOLE, Dorset

Acknowledgements

Tribute is paid to the many railway officials, from regional Public Relations Officers and Engineers of the London Midland Region and Scottish Region, through District and Area Officers, to stationmasters, staff and signalmen. In many cases it is not possible to provide names and, in other cases, the passage of time has witnessed retirements or moves to other duties. To all of the railwaymen, whose co-operation was whole-heartedly given, we record our thanks. We are also indebted to many fellow enthusiasts, including Messrs M. Christensen, D. Collins, S. L. Jacobs, E. M. Bray, K. Grubb, G. Fox, M. G. D. Farr, J. P. Hooley, R. Dyer, H. Bostock, and the late C. E. Box. A special vote of thanks goes to Mrs Elaine Hendry, whose first hand experience of station waiting-rooms and car-parks could well provide material for a book in itself, for whilst many visits could be by train, others had to be by car, on account of the infrequency of many rural services.

Title Page: Having referred already to Seaton, we will take a preview of this most picturesque and typical LMS country junction, on lines, and in a county (Rutland) alas no more. In this view we look east towards Stamford and Uppingham.

Bibliography and Further Sources of Information

Sources consulted include the various standard or localised histories of the pre-group companies and the LMS, which are reasonably, although not fully, covered. The files of the Public Record Office, formerly at Ashridge, latterly at Kew, have also been inspected, whilst the local press is a useful source, particularly for events prior to 1870. Public and working timetables, sectional and general appendices, and Engineer's and signalling plans provide a further important source of data. Bradshaw's *Shareholder's Manual* is another valuable research tool, as are the various official returns of the Board of Trade and the railway companies themselves. In a few cases, where conclusions differ from other published works, detailed reference is made to sources; for example Seaton.

Amendments to Volume One

page 63 — Dingwall; illustration 'looking south' printed mirror image.

page 79 — Four Oaks; signal from bay to read No. 5.

page 125 — Marton; illustration selectively enlarged showing many items to larger size, but delete last 1½ lines in caption as not shown.

page 143 — Stamford; for 'Above' (left caption) read 'Below'; for 'Below' (right caption) read 'Above'.

Contents

Preface

In this second volume of LMS Stations, we have covered a further 67 passenger stations, junctions or other locations, ranging in size from Hulme End, on the much lamented Leek & Manifold Valley Light Railway, with its three or four trains a day, to Manchester (Victoria) nerve centre of the busy Lancashire & Yorkshire Railway. Adjoining Victoria was the LNWR station, Exchange and, under the LMS, so close did working become that they are best considered as one unit. In the Victoria/Exchange portrait, pride of place has been given to rare contemporary views of the 1928/9 LMS resignalling, which, as well as showing this busy station, give an insight into the complexity of such a task. At Birmingham (New St.) we see the cramped hub of the LNWR and Midland systems in the West Midlands, buried in a man-made canyon of roads, bridges and buildings. Elsewhere, we see the more tranquil face of railways, as at Upton-on-Severn, where a one coach local waits time.

The LMS was, by far, the largest of the Grouped companies, and through the empire building habits of the Midland and LNWR, its tentacles were spread wide. We visit Kensington (Addison Rd.) on the busy West London line, a vital cross-Thames link, in which the LMS, GWR and Southern all had an interest, and into which LT trains ran, all these movements being controlled from classic LNWR signal boxes. In Scotland, we see Inverness, one time headquarters of the Highland Railway, and still open today. Less fortunate is Glasgow (St. Enoch), headquarters of the Glasgow & South Western Railway, and long gone. We visit the station in G&SWR and LMS days, and recall the pioneer 1898 power signalling system, so strange that it appeared to turn normal signalling 'on its head' at times, and which the LMS replaced in 1933. In Wales, we look at Llandudno and Llandudno Junction, both important stations on the North Wales Coast. Travelling across country, we arrive at Lenwade, an LMS outpost

in East Anglia, which entered the fold as a result of MR involvement in the Midland & Great Northern Joint Railway.

In *Volume One* of this series, we portrayed a variety of stations from the principal constituents, the LNWR, Midland and LYR, but also gave prominence to two very different single track routes, the cross-country Stratford-upon-Avon & Midland Junction, and 'further north' line of the Highland. Company histories necessarily concentrate on the broad issues. If a survey such as this confines itself to local factors, the relationship of a specific station to broad strategic issues and inter-company rivalry can be overlooked. A third of the locations covered here fall within the strategic heartland of North Cheshire and Lancashire, an area of massive industrial capacity, and the cradle of the Liverpool & Manchester Railway, and other proud concerns. We study two important L&M stations, and locations associated with the Warrington & Newton, Bolton & Preston, North Union, Lancaster & Preston Junction, and Lancaster & Carlisle railways, to see the build-up of the West Coast Main Line.

The fierce rivalries within the constituents of the LYR come to the fore, with the Liverpool, Crosby & Southport, Liverpool, Ormskirk & Preston and East Lancashire railways. Macclesfield recalls the sometimes prickly relationship between the LNWR and 'Knotty'. A chain of stations, running more or less north-west, from Oxford to Birkenhead, recalls the border skirmishes with the Great Western, and the victories and defeats of both the LNWR and Midland.

Important though these issues are, we have not overlooked that the station existed for a purpose, and the yardstick frequently given in *Volume One* has been used once more, stopping passenger services, which give some measure of the station's ability to generate traffic.

Introductory Review

In *Volume One* of this series, we discussed the three broad phases of railway station design, an awareness of which is crucial to understanding any given station. For new readers, they merit brief mention. The first period, or 'Age of Grandeur', lasted from 1825 to about 1875, during which time the basic network was created. There were no guidelines to follow, and features were tried, proven or discarded. Early stations made extensive use of locomotive coach and wagon turntables. Platforms were low, and with short trains, even major stations were compact. Of the leading stations, many of the earliest examples had classical or Regency overtones. At wayside stations, after a period when areas of levelled gravel, and the use of a nearby inn, was essayed, a hangover from the stagecoach era, grandeur became the order of the day. Tudor, Gothic, Jacobean, Italianate and other architectural styles flourished. Sandon, on the North Staffordshire Railway, and Oundle, on the LNWR, typify this period.

By the 1870s, the accent was on filling in the gaps with branch lines and cut-offs and, as traffic mushroomed, upon doubling and quadrupling. The 'Era of Consolidation' had begun. Old stations were swept away, to permit enlarged facilities, as at Seaton. Wagon turntables started to go out of fashion, although cost constraints ensured their survival in many places, as at Brackley. Coach turntables withered in the face of six-wheel, and later bogie, stock. Block working and interlocking of points and signals were championed by the Board of Trade, and were virtually universal by 1890. The exuberance which had given rise to stations such as Sandon, had been overtaken by a greater realism as to traffic prospects. Foremost in this attitude was the LNWR, under the chairmanship of the austere Sir Richard Moon. Long Buckby Station, of 1881, reflects this. Marsh Gibbon & Poundon, of 1880, gives an even more graphic recognition. Even the Midland Railway became more restrained, with its new Hellifield Station, planned in the 1870s; an admirable compromise. Glasgow (St. Enoch) and its associated hotel, opened during 1876-9, was a late flowering of the 'Age of Grandeur', with its massive train shed and Gothic facade. Glorified when new, the Gothic revival was already fading, and the critics soon closed in. The process of consolidation continued into the new century. Steam railcar halts made an appearance, as at Stewartby, and electrification was essayed, as with Aintree, to meet tramway competition. Often this involved new halts, as at Orrell Park. Glasgow (St. Enoch) was an early example of power working of signals (1898). Southport (Chapel St.) portrays a drastic enlargement to a station before and during World War I, with greatly improved power signalling.

Changes in underlying trends can rarely be attributed to a specific year. The Glasgow & South Western Railway withdrew one suburban service in 1902, for example, yet new suburban stations were being opened thiry years later, but the Grouping of 1923 so closely coincides with the emergence of motor competition as a serious threat, to warrant our taking 1923 as the dawn of the 'Years of Change'. There was still optimism, as with the quadruplings at Kibworth or Barnt Green, schemes inherited from the Midland Railway. The complete rebuilding of St. Anne's Station, on the Fylde Coast, during 1923/4, was another project taken over by the LMS. Integration became an important theme. Manchester's Victoria and Exchange stations were joined together, to provide the longest passenger platform in the British Isles, and one of the authors has run the entire length of that platform in pursuit of steam (!). A new signalling system, by Westinghouse, made the union complete.

Chill winds were blowing, however. Nuneaton (Abbey St.) lost its services to Ashby and Loughborough in 1931, although retaining other services. Hulme End on the Manifold succumbed in 1934, as did Harborne. One was a narrow gauge terminal amongst the fields, and the other an inner suburban branch.

On the trunk routes. *(Below):* The way in which a route was envisaged sometimes affected the type of station provided and, on occasions, small communities could find themselves regarded as more of a nuisance than anything else. Shilton, on the Trent Valley line of the LNWR, was such a station. The station was convenient to the village, indeed only yards from the church, yet it is not the station, but the main lines which stretch to the horizon which dominate the scene. A cavalcade of expresses and freights thundered through the station, shaking the decrepit brick and timber buildings, but gaps of many hours elapsed between humble stopping passenger services. The station closed to passengers the year after this 1956 scene.

terminus. Investment in the Wirral showed that the LMS was not opting out of suburban workings, with electrification and complete modernisation of stations, such as Hoylake and Leasowe, both making use of the most advanced reinforced-concrete technology. West Allerton, on the opposite bank of the Mersey, was a brand new LMS station, opened in 1939 to serve new housing. It relied upon advanced hardboard technology! The Luftwaffe took a hand in station design from 1939, Kensington (Addison Road) being an example of their work. The system emerged from the war run-down, and further closures followed, as at Sandon, in 1947. This process continued under BR, the pretty little wayside station of Upton-on-Severn becoming a terminus from 1952 until 1961. By the early 1960s, mounting deficits had led to the Beeching era, and a gamut of closures, as at Bicester, Evesham, and Oundle. Main line stations closed too, as at Glasgow (St. Enoch), or Blackwell. Others were altered out of all recognition, as with Birmingham (New St.), during electrification. 'Rationalisation' could at times produce bizarre results, as at Rock Ferry, whilst stations were trimmed in size, as with Southport (Chapel St.).

As with *Volume One*, we hope that there will be much to interest the railway modeller, whether selecting a specific station, or features to incorporate in his own layout. With mechanical signalling a dying art, we are glad to place further material on record, for much has gone beyond recall, much is threatened, and much is now in private hands, preserved thankfully, but not readily 'on file'. We hope that this will also be of value to the modeller, as correct signalling of model railways is a neglected, but absorbing, subject.

Tranquility. *Below:* The chimney stacks of Upton-on-Severn Station cast diffused shadows from a hazy sun in this placid 1953 study. With a train service which can be counted on the fingers of one hand, the station slumbers for much of the day. A cursory glance at the station offices and house reveals the sure hand of Derby behind the Tewkesbury & Malvern Railway, of which Upton-on-Severn formed a part. The line opened in 1864, at which time even minor stations could expect imposing buildings, although not quite as ornate as those of a decade or two earlier. Retired Midland goods vans — or sleepers — provided a cheap increase in storage capacity, if lacking in aesthetic merit!

Notes to the Layout Diagrams

1   The scale drawings are the 'A' plans. In a number of cases, two scale plans are provided.

2   The signalling diagrams are the 'B' plans, and are not to scale. Their prime function, as with an actual signal box diagram, is to display the signalling details, and proportion and scale are sometimes incompatible with clarity.

3   Other supporting drawings, maps, etc., are sometimes provided.

4   The scale of the 'A' plans is indicated, as is the date of approximate period of the plan where definitely known.

5   The 'B' plan dates relate to the official diagrams from which they originate, or to a known time at which the layout was shown. Signalling and pointwork for certain disconnected, disused or lifted lines is sometimes shown, the relevant work being indicated.

6   In using the 'A' scale plans, it is important to remember that a small scale drawing cannot be relied upon to give measurements to the nearest few inches. Even original 30ft. or 40ft. plans are not that reliable, and were not intended to be used for such purposes. One experienced 19th century railway engineer observed that the only reliable scale plan was an unmounted rolled drawing on paper. Folding, repeated use, or damping and mounting on linen (as was frequently done for strength) was detrimental to accuracy, and to this list, we must add storage for 100 years or more. Overall, the plans give a satisfactory and reliable impression of the station, but they were never intended to give exact sizes of items such as water columns or gates, to take an extreme example.

7   The 'B' signalling plans have, for the most part, been prepared from original material, and verified back to the same. Such diagrams are thought to be correct, although it is amusing to record that a few signal box diagram inaccuracies came to light during the preparation of the book. One MR diagram, hanging in the authors' darkroom, shows a crossover in such a manner that, no matter how the points were set, a train would have to run through one set of blades. Readers are referred to Glasgow (St. Enoch) for similar discrepancies.

8   Both minor and major changes in signalling at stations have occurred, without layouts having necessarily been altered. Signals have been renewed, sometimes in a different location and to a different configuration, and transfer of ground signals from one side of the line to the other is not uncommon. It is thus possible that the signalling shown may differ from information in other sources. This does not mean that either source is wrong — it may simply be the result of changes.

9   Certain signalling details should be mentioned, as being liable to trip the unwary. Ground signals are sometimes shown on SB diagrams as discs, other times as miniature arms. These indications have been followed in the 'B' plans (in the absence of clear evidence to the contrary), although it should be understood that they are frequently symbolic, rather than exact representations of the type of signal in situ. Thus official records may err.

Wherever possible, spares and spaces have been distinguished, and when both terms appear, are as given. Sometimes, however, official diagrams group spares and spaces under the overall heading of spare.

The selection of the term signal box or ground frame is usually straightforward, but in few cases the choice is not so simple, and we have adopted the view that if it looks and behaves like a signal box, it is shown as such. The subject is open to argument, and like the classic question of how to define the front and rear of a steam locomotive, is deceptively simple. Peculiarities such as the 'Fairlie' locomotive can play havoc with nice logical definitions, and provide a locomotive with a front at each end and a rear in the middle! Signal boxes and ground frames are similar.

Features of Signal Box Diagrams

The signal diagram below, is intended to depict a wide range of typical signalling features to be found at a passenger station of modest size in manual signalling days. A steep gradient and level crossing have been included, as these allow for further 'demonstration' features. The 'up' line signalling (against the gradient) is kept to a minimum, whilst the 'down' line is more comprehensively signalled, with no fewer than five stop signals as opposed to two in the other direction. Ordinarily, there would be a rough balance in both directions, but the need for braking distances or other factors could lead to such a result. The positioning of the distant signals is also dependent upon line speed, sighting and gradients, and is less on a rising grade than on a falling grade. A level crossing is added at the right-hand side of the diagram, both to show a typical crossing cabin, and to illustrate the slotting of signals, where boxes were relatively close. In the 'up' direction, the limited number of signals at the station, and reduced braking distances, obviate the need for such measures. In the 'down' direction two typical slots are shown. As signal 28 is well under half a mile in advance of the level crossing, it would not be possible to put the station distant on the 'down' side of the gates; therefore it must be placed on the same post as the home signal for the crossing box (the crossing box signals being shown in outline only). This signal is 'slotted' by level crossing box signal No. 3 (L3) by means of multiple counter weights, so that 29 will only clear when station box No. 29 is pulled and the crossing home, L3, is pulled. This is to avoid the confusing indication, which might otherwise arise of L3 at danger and 29 at clear. Although the crossing signalman does effectively share control of 29 with his neighbour, it is not technically his signal. As distant 29, even though it is located on the crossing home post L3, is only 790yds. from signal 28 on a falling grade, it is essential that there should be an outer distant, and this signal, No. 30, is combined with the crossing distant, L4. For No. 30 to clear, both boxes have to be able to pull the appropriate levers, so this signal is not only worked by both boxes, but 'belongs' to both. It is sometimes said that a distant indicates the position of the next 'home' signal. This is incorrect. A distant signal indicates that all the relevant running signals at a particular box are 'off', i.e. 1 is 'led' by 2 and 3; 29 is led by 28, 27, 26, 25 and 24. An outer distant is led by an inner distant (30 by 29). Where an Intermediate Block signal is installed, this has its own

'distant' (see 23 and R23). A distant is thus independent of an 'IB'. In certain cases (e.g. junction or single lines where special caution is required) distants may be fixed, as at Callander or Hest Bank.

In the demonstration layout, slotting is confined to distant signals, but where two or more boxes work one station, usually a large and complicated one, stop signals can also be slotted, so that two boxes share control over one signal. For examples of this, see Manchester (Victoria) or Llandudno Junction.

The numbering of the levers in the layout follows standard practice, with 'up' and 'down' signals grouped at opposite ends of the frames and other signals grouped by the relevant crossovers, e.g. 7, 8 and 9. Where facing point locks are required, these adjoin the point lever. Early signalling layouts sometimes grouped all 'up' running signals and then all 'up' shunt signals, followed by points, FPLs, etc. and the 'down' shunt and 'down' running signals, to give a red, black, red frame pattern. As points were widely separated from their appropriate signals, it had little to commend it. The layout is partially track circuited on the 'down' line. IB signals were always track circuited, whilst home or starting signals remote from the box tended to be so treated before other sections easily seen by the signalman. The fireman's plunger and D sign on signal 28 was an alternative and cheaper method of advising the signalman of the presence of a train. In the absence of either system, the fireman was required to go to the box to remind the signalman of his train, so that it would not be overlooked and another train accepted. Comprehensive track circuit layouts to modern standards are seen at Blackwell and Wellington. The exact opposite, working a busy station in early days, is shown at Victoria, pre-1904. Other signalling details are noted in the drawing itself, e.g. ground frame release, yellow shunt signals, co-acting arms, etc.

Further details of track circuit indications, different arrangements of slips, etc. are given in the signalling notes. As certain of the signalling plans show arrangements which have been out of fashion for many years, some mention is made of these, including the placing of running signals for different routes vertically on the same post, instead of on a bracket signal, as latterly. Locating 'up' and 'down' signals on the same post was also more common in the old days than in recent times, whilst a number of pre-group railways used ringed arms for slow lines, and added S to shunt signals, etc.

Plan devised to show many typical features, nomenclature, numbering, slotting, co-acting arms, I.B.s, etc.

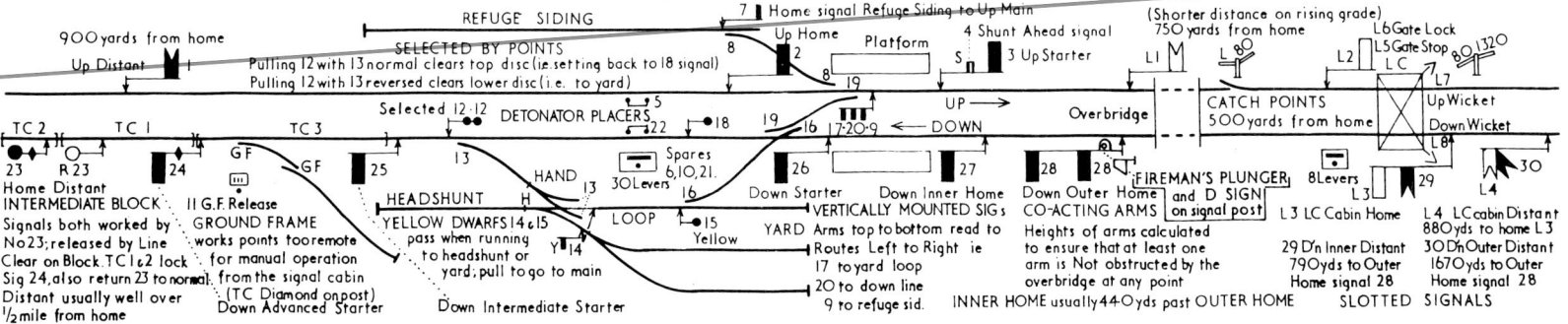

List of Stations and Facilities

Page	Station	Map Ref.	Facilities	Crane Tons Cwt	Notes
14	Aintree	A2	G P L H	1 10	LYR
18	Bamber Bridge	O2	G P L H	10 00	LYR
20	Barnt Green	C5	G P L H	—	Midland
22	Bay Horse	O3	G P F L H C	5 00	LNWR
23	Bicester	G2	G P F L H C	5 00	LNWR
26	Bidston	A1	P	—	Wirral (GC — P)
28	Birmingham (New St.)	D6	P F H C	—	LNWR & Midland
34	Blackrod	O1	G P L H	10 00	LYR
36	Blackwell	C5	G P	—	Midland
38	Brackley	G3	G P F L H C	5 00	LNWR
40	Bromsgrove	C5	G P F L H C	5 00	Midland
44	Callander (goods station)	Q16	G F L	6 00	Caledonian
45	Callander (Dreadnought passenger)	Q16	P H C	—	C&O
48	Coventry (Three Spires Junction)	F6	junc/private sidings		LNWR (opened 1914)
50	Earlestown	O1	G P L	5 00	LNWR (GWR — P)
54	East Langton	H7	G P L H	1 10	Midland
56	Evesham	D3	G P F L H C	5 00	Midland
159	Forder's Siding	L3	private siding	—	LNWR (Note A)
58	Formby	A4	G P L H	3 10	LYR (LNWR — P, H)
60	Freshfield	A4	G P	—	LYR (LNWR — P)
62	Glasgow (St. Enoch)	Q15	P F H C	—	G&SWR
68	Glasgow (Clyde Junction)	Q15	junction only		G&SWR
70	Harborne	D6	G P F L H C	5 00	Harborne Rly.
71	Hellifield	T11	G P L H	—	Midland (LYR — P, L, H)
74	Hest Bank	S11	G P L H	—	LNWR
76	Hoylake	S9	G P	5 00	Wirral (Birk — G)
78	Hulme End	U8	G P	—	L&MVLR
80	Inverness	Q19	G P F L H C	5 00	HR
84	Islip	G1	G P F L H C	—	LNWR
86	Kensington (Addison Road)	W5	P F H C	—	WL Jt. (GW/LNW)
86	Kensington (Addison Road)	W5	P H C	—	WLE (LSWR)
86	Kensington (Note B)	W5	P	—	WLE (LBSCR)
90	Kibworth	H7	G P F L H C	1 10	Midland
91	Kibworth North	H7	signal box only	—	Midland
93	Leasowe	A1	P	—	Wirral
94	Lenwade	Y8	G P F L H C	—	M&GN Jt.
96	Leyland	O2	G P F L H C	10 00	NU Jt.
99	Llandudno Junction	R9	G P F H C	—	LNWR
102	Llandudno	R9	G P F L H C	5 00	LNWR
106	Long Buckby	H5	G P F L H C	10 00	LNWR
111	Macclesfield (Central)	T9	P F L H C	—	GC&NS Jt.
109	Macclesfield Goods	T9	G F L H C	8 00	GC&NS Jt.
108	Macclesfield (Hibel Road)	T9	G P F L H C	10 00	LNW&NS Jt.
114	Manchester (Exchange)	T9	P F H C	—	LNWR (GW r.p.)
112	Manchester (Victoria)	T9	P F H C	—	LYR (LNWR/Midland r.p.)
122	Marsh Gibbon & Poundon	H2	G P L H	—	LNWR
124	Melton Mowbray	V8	G P F L H C	5 00	Midland
127	Melton Junction	V8	junction only	—	Midland
128	New Brighton	A1	G P	5 00	Wirral
130	Newton-le-Willows	O1	G P F L H C	5 00	LNWR (GW — P, H, C)
132	Nuneaton (Abbey St.)	F7	G P F L H C	5 00	Midland
136	Orrell Park	A2	P	—	LYR
137	Oundle	L7	G P F L H C	5 00	LNWR
138	Oxford (Rewley Road)	G1/V5	G P F L H C	10 00	LNWR
141	Rock Ferry	A0	G P	1 10	Birk Jt. (Mersey — P)
144	St. Annes-on-Sea	S10	G P F L H C	5 00	P&W Jt.
147	Sandon	U8	G P F L H C	—	NS (LNWR — P)
148	Seaton	K7	G P F L H C	—	LNWR (GNR — P, H, C)
150	Shilton	F6	G P L H	—	LNWR
152	Southport (Chapel St.)	A6	P H C	—	LYR (LNWR r.p.)
159	Stewartby	L3	P*	—	LNWR (Note C)
162	Tile Hill	E6	G P L H C	—	LNWR
164	Upton-on-Severn	B3	G P F L H C	5 00	Midland
166	Waterloo	A2	G P	5 00	LYR (LNW — P)
168	Wellington	T7	P F H C	—	S&W Jt. (LNW & GW)
169	Wellington (GWR Goods)	T7	G F L	8 00	GWR
169	Wellington (LNWR Goods)	T7	G F L	10 00	LNWR
171	West Allerton	A0	not open	—	Opened LMS (Note D)
172	Whitchurch	T8	G P F L H C	5 00	LNWR (Cambrian r.p.)
175	Winslow	J3	G P F L H C	5 00	LNWR
159	Wootton Broadmead	L3	P*	—	LNWR (Note E)

Note: *Station facilities given as in 1912/20 except for LMS opened stations, e.g. West Allerton.*

The owning company is given under notes; where other companies exercised running powers with all facilities, this is given thus (GWR r.p.); where such companies enjoyed partial facilities theses are indicated, e.g. (LYR — P, L, H).

G - Goods
P - Passenger & Parcel
P* - Passenger only
F - Furniture vans
L - Livestock
H - Horse-boxes
C - Carriages by passenger train

Note A: *Private siding, illustrated under Stewartby*
Note B: *Goods at two separate depots (GWR & LNWR)*
Note C: *Stewartby originally known as Wootton Pillinge Halt*
Note D: *West Allerton opened LMS 1939 — Facilities P*
Note E: *Railcar halt, illustrated under Stewartby*

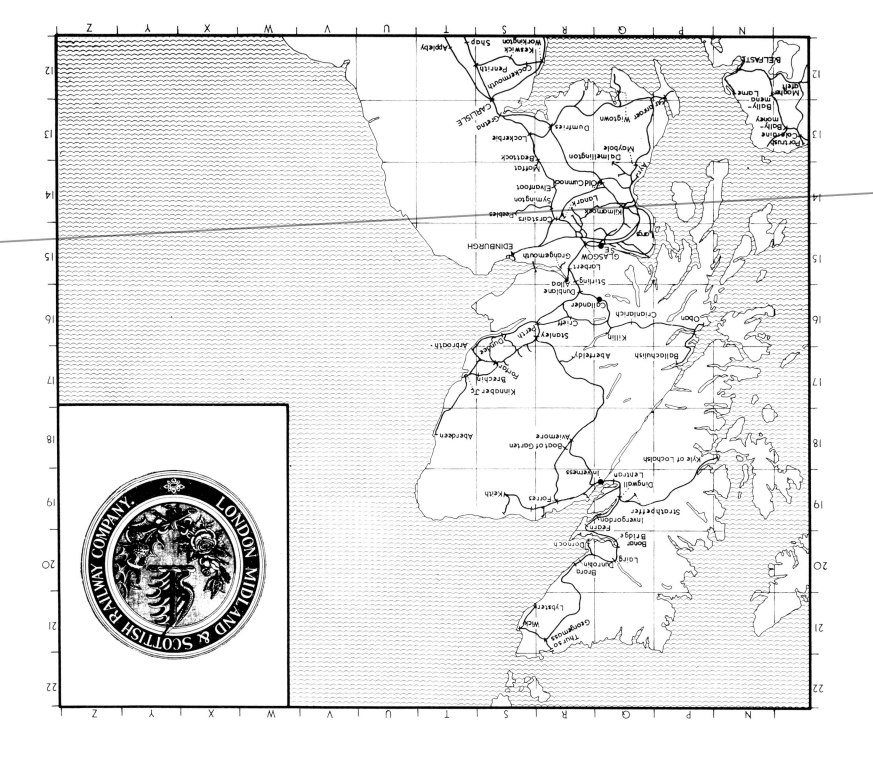

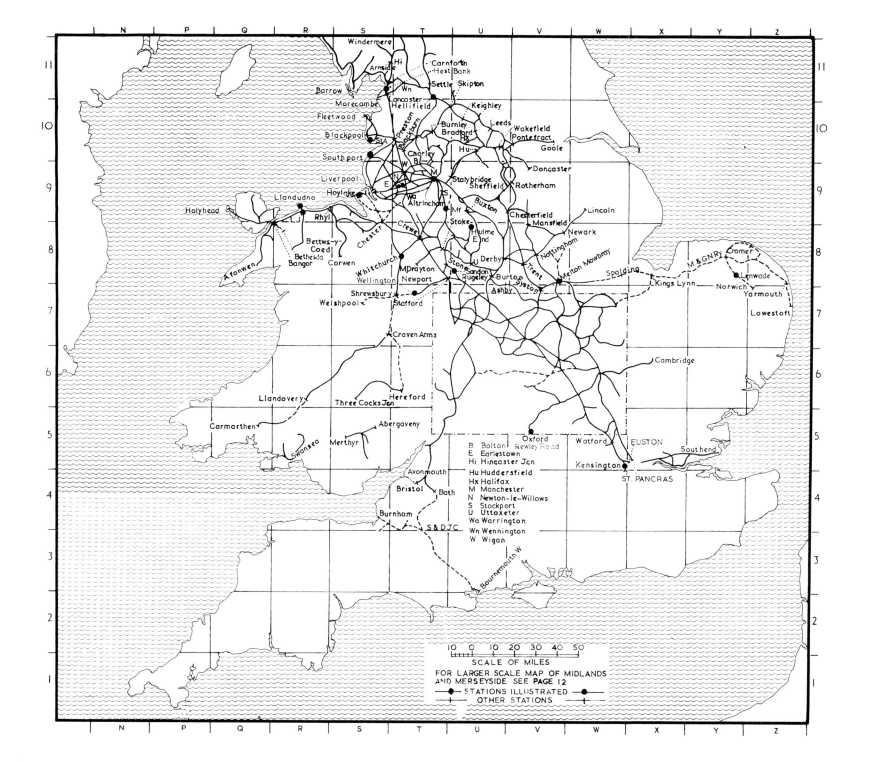

SCALE OF MILES

FOR LARGER SCALE MAP OF MIDLANDS
AND MERSEYSIDE SEE **PAGE 12**

B   Bolton
E   Earlestown
Hi Hincaster Jcn
Hu Huddersfield
Hx Halifax
M   Manchester
N   Newton-le-Willows
S   Stockport
U   Uttoxeter
Wa Warrington
Wn Wennington
W   Wigan

●—— STATIONS ILLUSTRATED ●
—┼— OTHER STATIONS ┼—

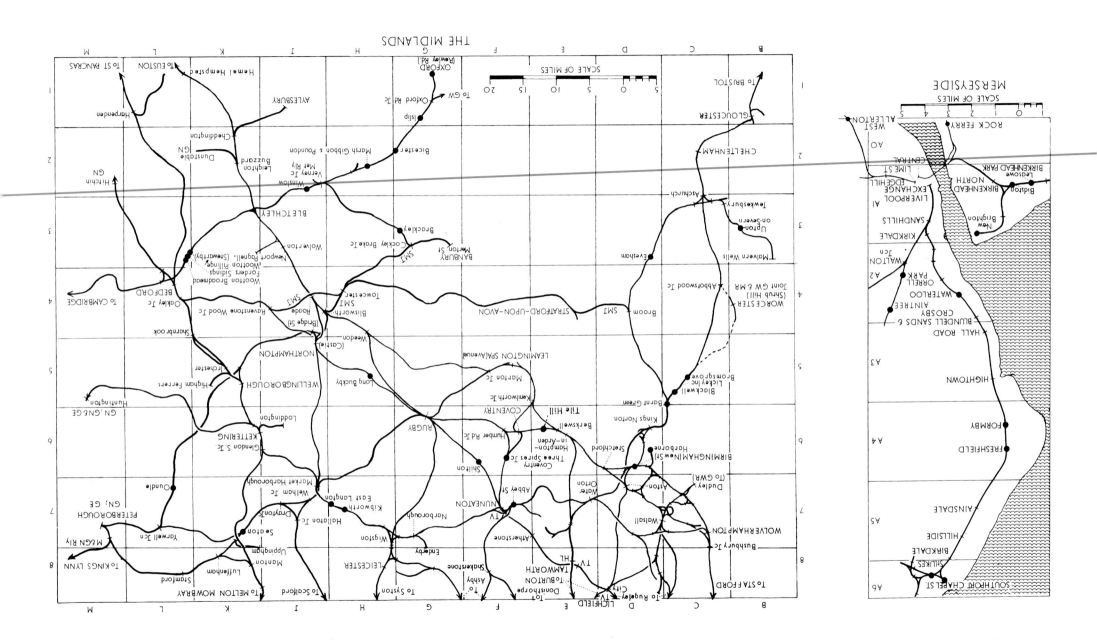

KEY TO THE SYMBOLS USED

on SCALE PLANS On SIGNAL CABIN DIAGRAMS

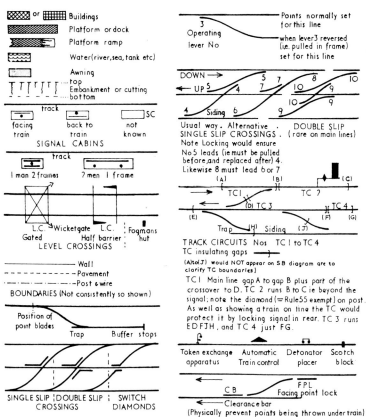

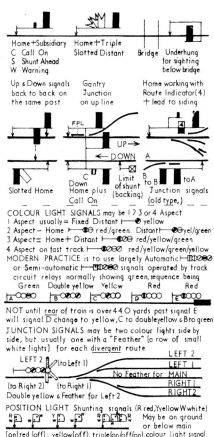

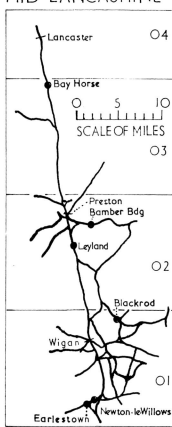

MID LANCASHIRE

SCALE OF MILES

ABBREVIATIONS

BH Booking hall	FB Footbridge	O Office	Tel Telegraph
BO Booking office	GF Ground frame	P, Po Porters room	W Water column
CD Cattle dock	GS Goods shed	PW Permanent way dept	WB Weigh bridge
Co Coal	H Hut	SB Station buildings	WC Lavatory
Cr Crane	LC Level crossing	SC Signal cabin	WO Weight office
CP Catch points	LG Loading gauge	SM Station Masters office	WR Waiting room
CS Carriage shed	LS Landing stage	SMH do do house	WS Waiting shelter
EL End loading dock	LWR Ladies waiting room	SP Signal post	WT Water tank
ES Engine shed	MB Main station buildings	Sw Subway	Y Yard
F Fogman's hut	MP Mile post	T Tank	

Above: A view looking towards Liverpool from the 'up' platform in 1982. The main station facilities were concentrated on the 'down' side, with only modest facilities, even in LYR days, on the 'up' platform. Aintree Station Junction box is visible above and beyond the overbridge.

AINTREE *(Map Ref. A2)*

Aintree, five miles north of Liverpool city centre, is best-known for the 'Grand National', but to generations of L&Y railwaymen, it was a key point in handling the mass of freight traffic to and from the Liverpool Docks and goods depots, whilst 'Grand National Day' provided a once-yearly invasion of 30,000 or more racegoers in a single morning. Aintree Station lies on the Liverpool, Ormskirk & Preston Railway, which was authorised in August 1846, from Walton Junction, on the Liverpool & Bury Railway to the outskirts of Preston. In 1846, the LO&P was merged into the East Lancashire Railway, and the Liverpool & Bury Railway became a part of the Manchester & Leeds Railway, itself to become the LYR in 1847. The ELR became a part of the LYR in 1859. The line, from Walton Junction to the vicinity of Preston, opened on 2nd April 1849, Aintree being 4¾ miles north of the old Tithebarn St. terminus — later Liverpool (Exchange).

As the Mersey Docks extended down river, freight access from the Wigan and Preston lines became increasingly difficult and, in May 1861, the LYR secured powers for its North Mersey freight branch, to run from Fazakerley Junction, on the Wigan line, to North Mersey goods depot, where connection was made with the Mersey Docks & Harbour Board lines. North-to-west curves were laid in from the LO&P at Aintree, and from the Southport line at Seaforth, and the North Mersey branch opened to goods on 27th August 1866. The LYR of the 1860s was a ram-shackle and inefficient concern; dividends were high, but traffic delays and congestion enormous. From 1875, a massive transformation took place, Aintree becoming one of the key points in the reformed system.

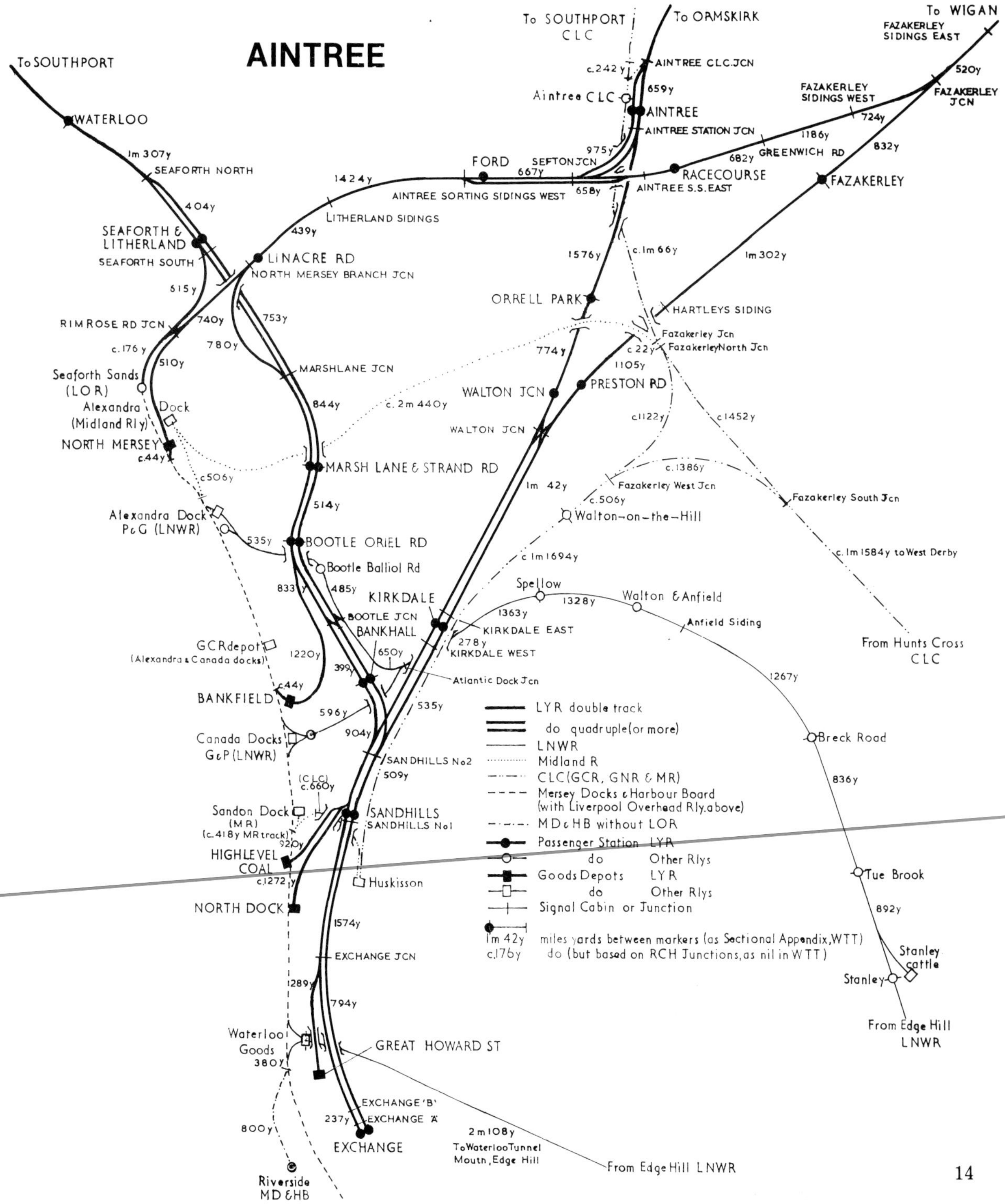

AINTREE

To SOUTHPORT

To SOUTHPORT CLC — To ORMSKIRK — To WIGAN

FAZAKERLEY SIDINGS EAST

WATERLOO

1m 307y
SEAFORTH NORTH

c.242y

AINTREE CLC.JCN

Aintree CLC

659y

AINTREE
AINTREE STATION JCN

FAZAKERLEY SIDINGS WEST

520y

FAZAKERLEY JCN

724y

FORD

SEFTON JCN

667y

975y

GREENWICH RD

682y

832y

1186y

RACECOURSE

AINTREE S.S. EAST

FAZAKERLEY

404y

1424y

AINTREE SORTING SIDINGS WEST

658y

439y

LITHERLAND SIDINGS

SEAFORTH & LITHERLAND

SEAFORTH SOUTH

LINACRE RD
NORTH MERSEY BRANCH JCN

1576y

c.1m 66y

1m 302y

615y

ORRELL PARK

HARTLEYS SIDING

RIMROSE RD JCN

740y

753y

c.22y

Fazakerley Jcn
Fazakerley North Jcn

c.176y

780y

774y

1105y

510y

MARSHLANE JCN

WALTON JCN

PRESTON RD

Seaforth Sands (LOR)

844y

c.2m 440y

c.1122y

c.1452y

Alexandra (Midland Rly)

Dock

WALTON JCN

NORTH MERSEY

c.44y

MARSH LANE & STRAND RD

1m 42y

c.1386y

Fazakerley West Jcn

c.506y

c.506y

Fazakerley South Jcn

Walton-on-the-Hill

Alexandra Dock P&G (LNWR)

514y

535y

BOOTLE ORIEL RD

c.1m 1694y

c.1m 1584y to West Derby

Bootle Balliol Rd

833y

485y

KIRKDALE

Spellow

1328y

Walton & Anfield

GCR depot
(Alexandra & Canada docks)

1220y

BOOTLE JCN

BANKHALL

650y

1363y

KIRKDALE EAST

278y
KIRKDALE WEST

Anfield Siding

From Hunts Cross CLC

BANKFIELD

399y

Atlantic Dock Jcn

1267y

c.44y

596y

535y

Breck Road

Canada Docks G&P (LNWR)

904y

SANDHILLS No2

836y

(CLC)
c.660y

509y

Sandon Dock (MR)
c.418y MR track

SANDHILLS
SANDHILLS No1

Tue Brook

920y

HIGHLEVEL COAL

c.1272y

Huskisson

892y

NORTH DOCK

1574y

Stanley cattle

Stanley

EXCHANGE JCN

1289y

794y

From Edge Hill LNWR

Waterloo Goods
380y

GREAT HOWARD ST

800y

237y

EXCHANGE 'B'
EXCHANGE 'A'

EXCHANGE

2m 108y
To Waterloo Tunnel Mouth, Edge Hill

From Edge Hill LNWR

Riverside MD&HB

─────	LYR double track
	do quadruple (or more)
───	LNWR
········	Midland R
─·─·─	CLC (GCR, GNR & MR)
─ ─ ─	Mersey Docks & Harbour Board (with Liverpool Overhead Rly. above)
─ ─ ─	MD&HB without LOR
●───●	Passenger Station LYR
○───○	do Other Rlys
■	Goods Depots LYR
□	do Other Rlys
─┼─	Signal Cabin or Junction
1m 42y	miles yards between markers (as Sectional Appendix, WTT)
c.176y	do (but based on RCH Junctions, as nil in WTT)

14

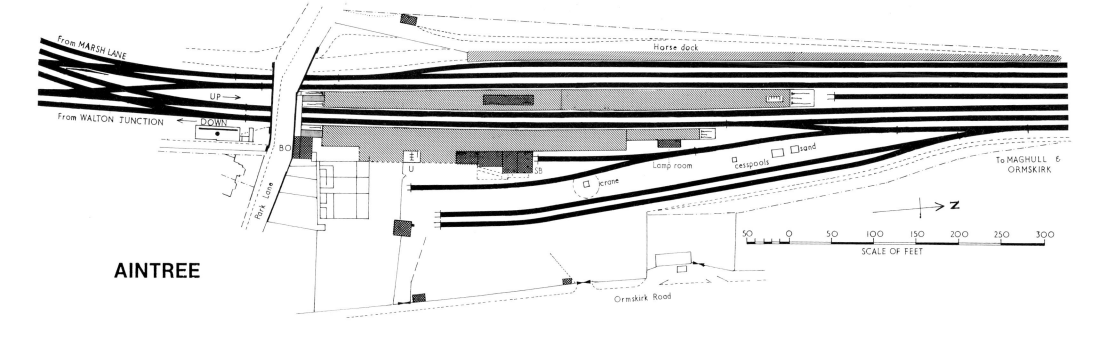

AINTREE

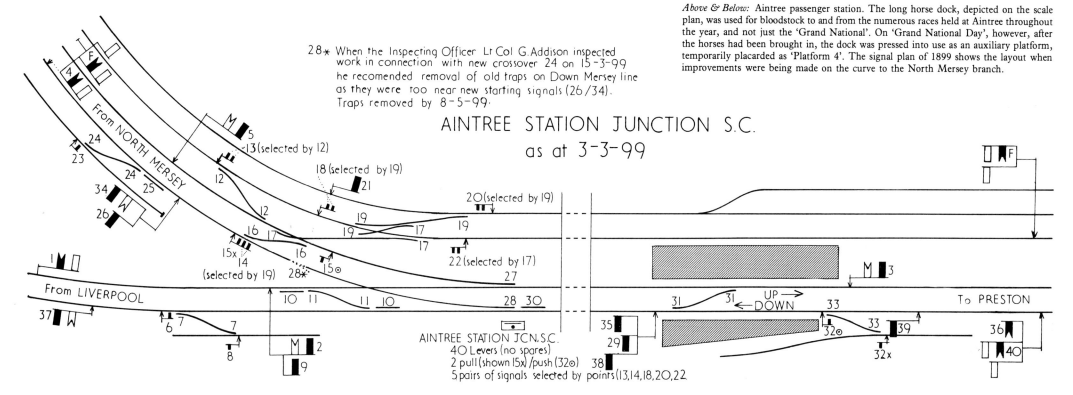

Above & Below: Aintree passenger station. The long horse dock, depicted on the scale plan, was used for bloodstock to and from the numerous races held at Aintree throughout the year, and not just the 'Grand National'. On 'Grand National Day', however, after the horses had been brought in, the dock was pressed into use as an auxiliary platform, temporarily placarded as 'Platform 4'. The signal plan of 1899 shows the layout when improvements were being made on the curve to the North Mersey branch.

28✳ When the Inspecting Officer Lt Col G. Addison inspected work in connection with new crossover 24 on 15-3-99 he recomended removal of old traps on Down Mersey line as they were too near new starting signals (26/34). Traps removed by 8-5-99.

AINTREE STATION JUNCTION S.C.
as at 3-3-99

AINTREE STATION JCN. S.C.
40 Levers (no spares)
2 pull (shown 15x) /push (32⊙)
5 pairs of signals selected by points (13,14,18,20,22

Although the North Mersey branch had provided a measure of relief in the 1860s, LYR operation in Liverpool was still chaotic, and, as a part of a system-wide rejuvenation, it was decided to route all freight into and out of Liverpool on to the North Mersey, and to provide sidings at Fazakerley Junction, and a massive marshalling yard on the North Mersey at Aintree. This was authorised in 1882. Construction began in 1885, the yard coming into use during the following year. To obviate light engine movements to and from Bank Hall Shed, a new locomotive depot was constructed in 1886, on a triangular plot of land (bought from the Cheshire Lines Committee) in the angle of the North Mersey and Aintree curve. The CLC passed within a few yards of the shed, but at a lower level. In the 1882 Act, powers were also granted for an east to south link, the Seaforth Connecting Line from the North Mersey to the Southport line facing towards Liverpool. This permitted direct access to the LYR freight depot at Bankfield.

The 'Aintree Iron', covering over 34 acres, and with 18 miles of track, became a part of Merseyside folklore. Three main line boxes controlled access to and from the North Mersey and five more boxes worked the yard. Inward freights stopped near the CLC bridge, the train engine running via the 'down' through road, Siding No. 11, to the shed. The wagons were then gravity-shunted to the arrival sidings, e.g. Great Howard St., (Siding 4), or Bankfield (Siding 8). Stock ex the Liverpool depots arrived from the North Mersey direction on the 'up' main, or 'up' loop and circular loop. Once again, the train stopped to the east of the CLC bridge where the brakevan was gravity-shunted to the brake siding (No. 23) in the arrival fan. The train was backed on to one of the three shunting necks, by No. 1 box, and then gravity-shunted into the 35 outward sidings. A second fan on the outward sidings permitted a final sorting, and then the completed train was propelled from the outward sidings to the departure sidings to await its engine. Sadly, the 'Aintree Iron' closed on 13th July 1964, a victim of changing freight patterns.

About 1890, a rudimentary station, Aintree Cinder Lane, (renamed Aintree Race Course in 1910) was opened east of the CLC bridge on the North Mersey line. This provided convenient access from the Wigan and Manchester direction for 'Grand National' traffic. By the turn of the century, the Liverpool

Overhead Railway, with its electric trains, had been in operation for several years, the Mersey Railway was being electrified, and the Liverpool Corporation tramways were commencing the spectacular growth which would make them one of the finest systems in the British Isles. The LYR, faced with increasing competition and traffic congestion, electrified the busy Liverpool to Southport route in 1904. It was an immediate success, with costs cut, service speeds and frequencies enhanced and traffic greatly increased. By this time, the Liverpool to Aintree service was feeling the effect of tramway competition, and the LYR decided to electrify both the North Mersey and Kirkdale routes to Aintree. As the North Mersey route could draw off existing sub-stations, electric services via the North Mersey began on 1st June 1906, with passenger stations opening at Linacre Rd. and Ford Halt. Direct services, via Kirkdale, began on 19th November 1906, when Aintree sub-station was ready. A steam railcar service ran from Aintree to Ormskirk from 1907. Electric services were extended to Maghull in 1909, Town Green in 1911, and Ormskirk in 1913.

The electric passenger service via the North Mersey branch was withdrawn on 2nd April 1951, and by the start of the 1980s, the North Mersey survived as a freight and p.w. link to Aintree and Fazakerley.

AINTREE

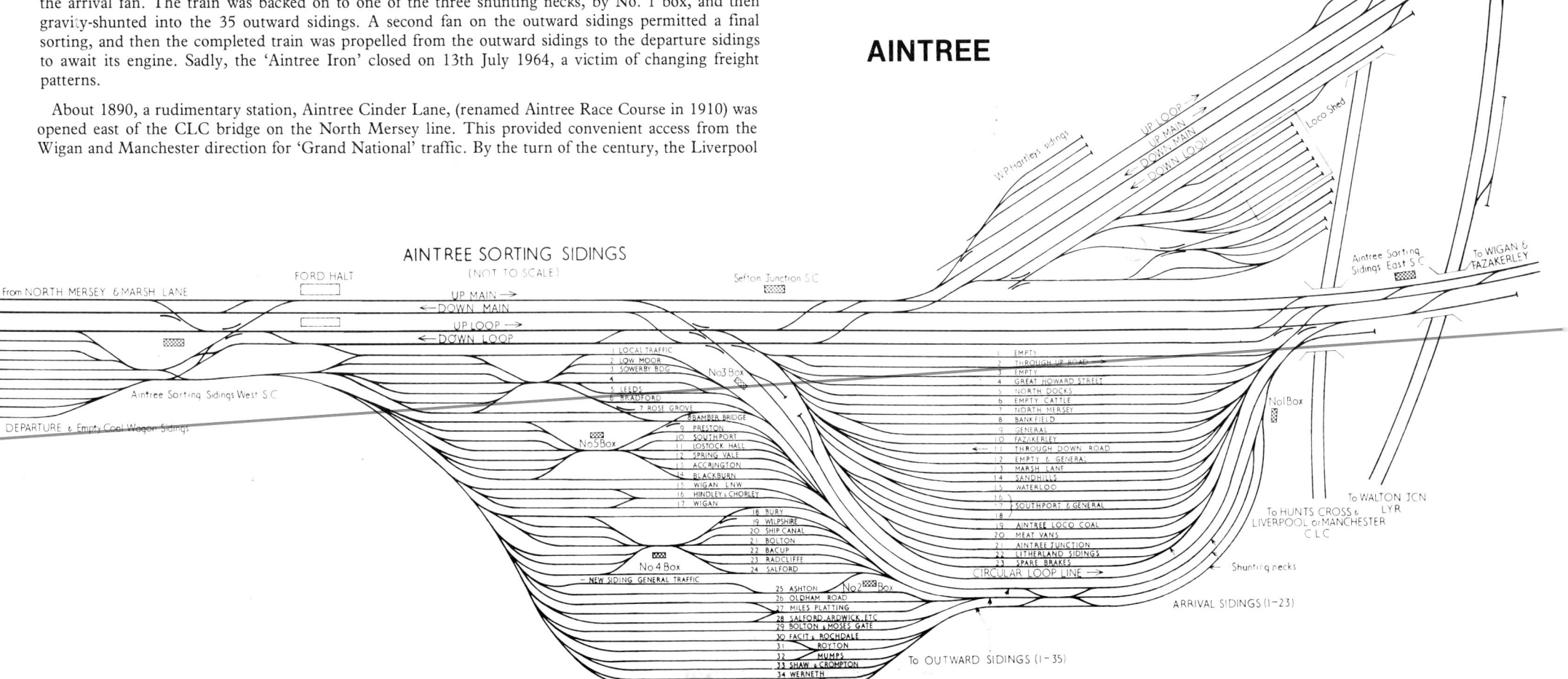

Above left: A neat but surprisingly small booking office fronted on to Park Lane. The use of yellow brick, with details in red brick, made an otherwise plain structure very pleasing. Leaving the booking hall, passengers could proceed down the stairs to the 'down' platform, or over a footbridge to the 'up' side. Substantial iron gates at the head of the 'up' platform stairs provided a further access to Park Lane.

Above centre: The platform starter at Aintree was a most unusual signal, its shape determined by the footbridge, overbridge and sighting problems, due to the canopy. The elimination of the signal arm, converting it to a species of colour light is a further peculiarity.

Below left: A view looking from the island platform towards Liverpool, with the horse landing on the right. On race days, the station not only saw LYR trains but through workings from the Liverpool Overhead Railway.

Above right: A view looking from the 'up' platform to the booking office, platform starter, Park Lane overbridge, and tall LYR Aintree Station Junction signal cabin beyond the bridge. The 'Grand National' course is on the east side of Ormskirk Road, i.e. to the left in this view. Reference to the scale survey will show that although the station fronts on to Park Lane, the LO&P runs parallel to the Ormskirk Road at this point.

AINTREE

Below right: Looking from the 'up' platform steps and entrance gate to Ormskirk. Such was the press of traffic on race days, that the LYR augmented its electric train carrying capacity, by coupling a driving motor car at each end of a rake of ten antiquated six-wheelers, with the control cables strung over the coach roofs. The LYR normal electric stock was replaced by LMS sets during the period 1938-40, the latter surviving until the late 1970s, and replacement of Exchange Station by the underground link line, with electric services to Southport and Ormskirk, and newly electrified services to Kirkby (ex-LYR) and Garston (ex-CLC).

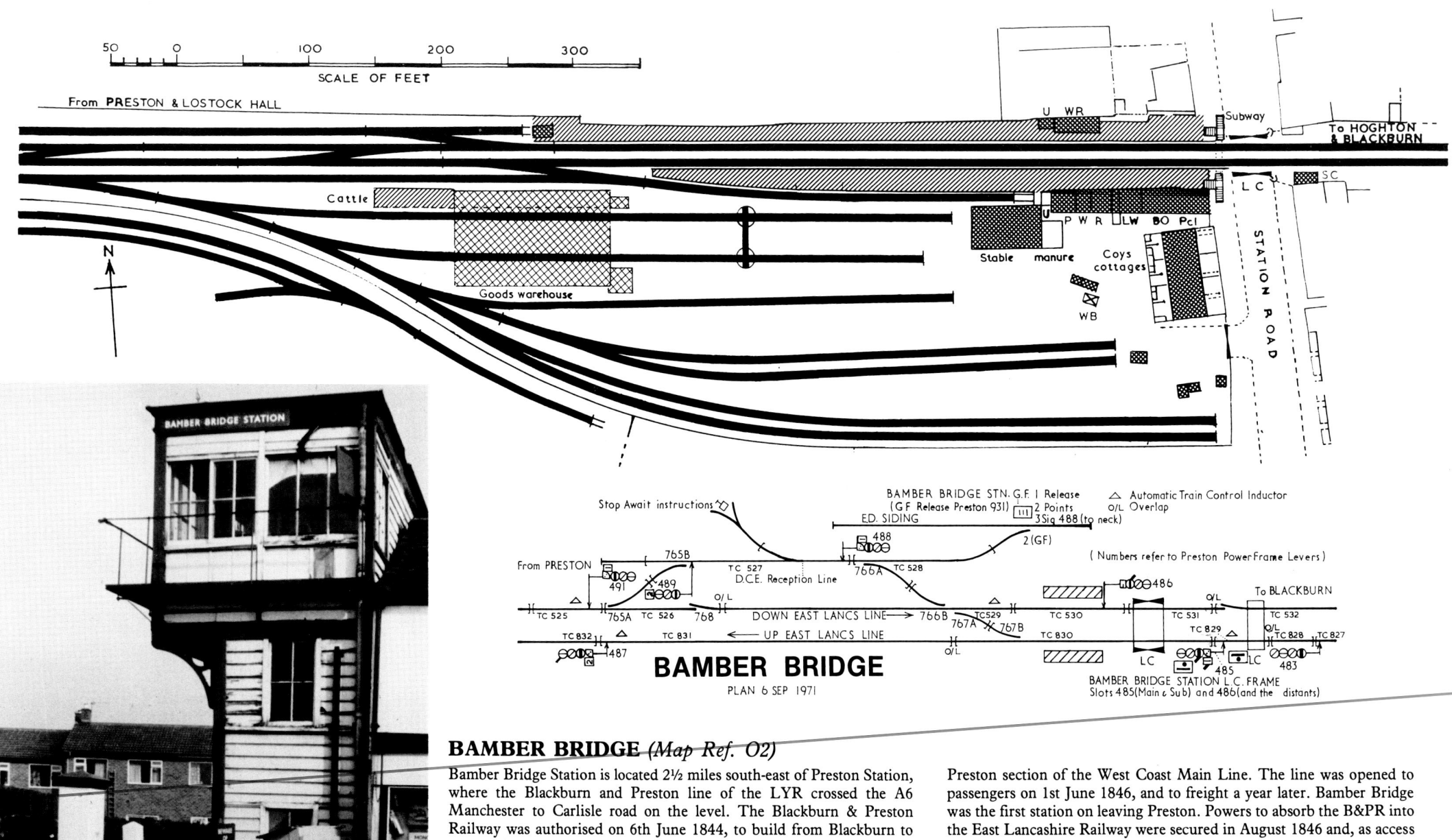

BAMBER BRIDGE *(Map Ref. O2)*

Bamber Bridge Station is located 2½ miles south-east of Preston Station, where the Blackburn and Preston line of the LYR crossed the A6 Manchester to Carlisle road on the level. The Blackburn & Preston Railway was authorised on 6th June 1844, to build from Blackburn to a north-facing junction at Farington, just over two miles south of Preston on the North Union Railway, which today comprises the Wigan to Preston section of the West Coast Main Line. The line was opened to passengers on 1st June 1846, and to freight a year later. Bamber Bridge was the first station on leaving Preston. Powers to absorb the B&PR into the East Lancashire Railway were secured in August 1846 and, as access to Preston over the NUR had proved unsatisfactory, the ELR secured a fresh Act of 22nd July 1847 to permit a new line, running more or less direct from Bamber Bridge to Preston Station, crossing the River Ribble en route. The north-facing junction to the NUR was abandoned, and a link was substituted to the Liverpool, Ormskirk & Preston Railway. The East Lancashire Railway was amalgamated into the LYR in 1859. Ultimately, direct access was possible from the Blackburn line to the West Coast Main Line facing north and south, to the LYR routes to Liverpool and Southport, and to Preston Docks.

Left: Bamber Bridge Station cabin, looking towards Blackburn from the A6 road. Cramped sites, such as this, could lead to curious structures, as in this case. The base is considerably narrower than the locking floor, which is carried on ornate spandrels. The proximity of the box, with its loud block bells and clashing frame, may not have enhanced the quality of repose in the upper storey of the adjoining shop. Repairs to the timber cladding of the box would hardly have been facilitated by the minimal gap!

Above: The 'down' platform waiting-room, looking towards Preston and the divergence of the Farington and Preston lines. The rough stone construction, invariably grey or grey black, contrasted with the lighter touch of the Midland or southern companies. A poster for the Isle of Man reminds us that, on summer Saturdays, routes such as this would carry a succession of excursions to the north-west resorts, Southport, Blackpool, Fleetwood, and on by sea to the Isle of Man. Wakes weeks in the mill towns to the east would see communities all but deserted.

Above: A view of the main station building on the 'up' platform, looking towards Blackburn. The low platform, near the door into the booking office, is a reminder of the antiquity of this structure. A further ramp carries the platform to a 'modern' height. The subway, with entrances to both platforms and the road, was found at a number of 'Lanky' stations. By the 1930s, 20-25 passenger trains called in each direction, with 8 or 9 on Sundays. Most were local services, but through trains between Morecambe and Blackpool to Colne, Accrington, etc. also called.

BAMBER BRIDGE

Below: With staffing costs rising, and vandalism an ever increasing problem, the basic railway concept came to Bamber Bridge, although mercifully not in the form of a 'bus shelter'. Instead, the windows, doors and other timber work were stripped out to create an open shelter, which we see on looking towards Blackburn.

Below: The entrance to the 'up' platform and subway. It will be noted that the old level crossing gates have been replaced by barriers, controlled from the box. Freight services ceased on 6th November 1967, but the station still handles passengers.

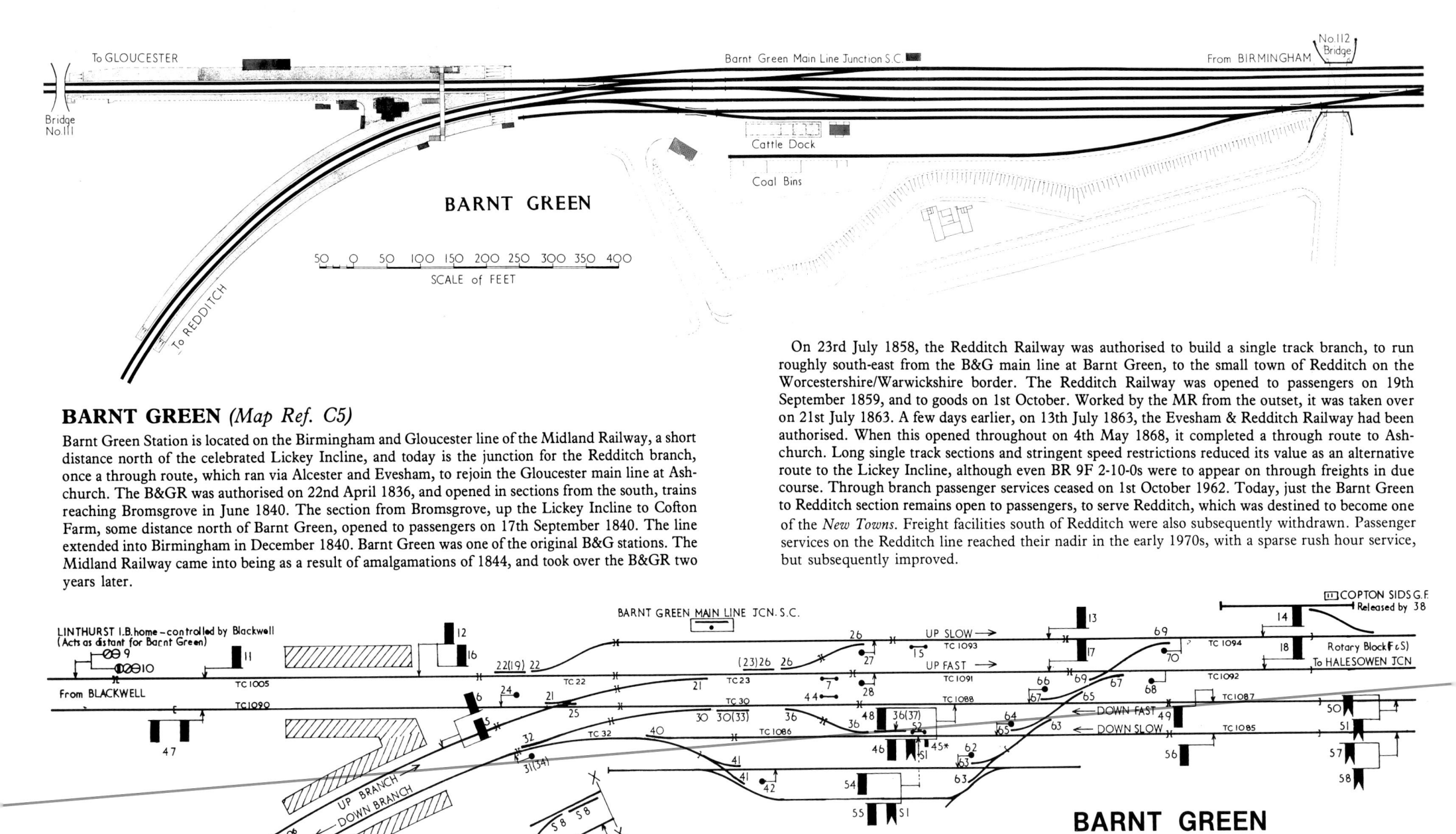

To GLOUCESTER

Barnt Green Main Line Junction S.C.

From BIRMINGHAM

No.112 Bridge

Bridge No.111

Cattle Dock

Coal Bins

BARNT GREEN

50 0 50 100 150 200 250 300 350 400
SCALE of FEET

To REDDITCH

BARNT GREEN (Map Ref. C5)

Barnt Green Station is located on the Birmingham and Gloucester line of the Midland Railway, a short distance north of the celebrated Lickey Incline, and today is the junction for the Redditch branch, once a through route, which ran via Alcester and Evesham, to rejoin the Gloucester main line at Ashchurch. The B&GR was authorised on 22nd April 1836, and opened in sections from the south, trains reaching Bromsgrove in June 1840. The section from Bromsgrove, up the Lickey Incline to Cofton Farm, some distance north of Barnt Green, opened to passengers on 17th September 1840. The line extended into Birmingham in December 1840. Barnt Green was one of the original B&G stations. The Midland Railway came into being as a result of amalgamations of 1844, and took over the B&GR two years later.

On 23rd July 1858, the Redditch Railway was authorised to build a single track branch, to run roughly south-east from the B&G main line at Barnt Green, to the small town of Redditch on the Worcestershire/Warwickshire border. The Redditch Railway was opened to passengers on 19th September 1859, and to goods on 1st October. Worked by the MR from the outset, it was taken over on 21st July 1863. A few days earlier, on 13th July 1863, the Evesham & Redditch Railway had been authorised. When this opened throughout on 4th May 1868, it completed a through route to Ashchurch. Long single track sections and stringent speed restrictions reduced its value as an alternative route to the Lickey Incline, although even BR 9F 2-10-0s were to appear on through freights in due course. Through branch passenger services ceased on 1st October 1962. Today, just the Barnt Green to Redditch section remains open to passengers, to serve Redditch, which was destined to become one of the *New Towns*. Freight facilities south of Redditch were also subsequently withdrawn. Passenger services on the Redditch line reached their nadir in the early 1970s, with a sparse rush hour service, but subsequently improved.

COPTON SIDS G.F.
Released by 38

BARNT GREEN MAIN LINE JCN. S.C.

LINTHURST I.B. home - controlled by Blackwell
(Acts as distant for Barnt Green)

UP SLOW →
UP FAST →

From BLACKWELL

To HALESOWEN JCN
Rotary Block F & S

UP BRANCH
DOWN BRANCH

← DOWN FAST
← DOWN SLOW

BARNT GREEN

From REDDITCH

BARNT GREEN SINGLE LINE JCN. S.C.
12 Levers M.R. Tumbler (shown thus S1-S12)
Spare 5, 6.
Box closed on 6-8 Sept 1969
Note to agree with Main Line Jcn S.C. this
frame is inverted

BARNT GREEN MAIN LINE JCN. S.C.
Opened 15 Sep 1929. Drawing as at Aug 1957. Closed 6-8 Sep 1969.
70 Lever Midland 4½" Frame
Spares 8, (19)(20)(23),29,(33)(34) 35(37)39, 43,53,59,60,61. Nos bracked used later (see below)
Levers 22 26 30 & 36 worked FPLs as well as cross-overs at first, later FPLs worked by 19 23 33 & 37
Single slip 21/25 replaced by trailing crossover (down/up) further to right (worked by 25)
Minor repositioning of crossings & signals (24→29,31→34) changed
Signal 45 was a subsidiary down fast to branch; later starter ex branch pfm.
By 1968 the lead to the slow line via 22 had gone
do   ladder of slips & shunting signals 62→70 and protecting signals 13,17 all removed
Sigs 14 & 18 taken out of use Feb 1969, and 9 10 11 & 47 taken over by Gloucester PSB also 1969
Down slow ex Halesowen TOU May 1969 (levers 36 37 & 54-58), 40 fixed normal
Before closure spares were 8-11, 13-15, 17-20, 22, 24, 27, 31, 35-37, 39, (40), 43, 47, 53-70.

Above: A view looking from the Redditch line towards the main line junction and Birmingham. Junction stations where the passenger platforms diverged so sharply were relatively uncommon, and Arnside *(see Volume One in this series)* makes an interesting comparison.

Above: A view looking along the main line towards Gloucester, and to Redditch on the left. With the introduction of MAS working, controlled from Saltley power box, the impressively-titled 'Barnt Green Main Line Junction' signal box was replaced by a small ground frame, to control movements to the sidings retained on the east side of the line for engineering purposes, general freight facilities having been withdrawn on 6th July 1964.

BARNT GREEN

Barnt Green Station, 10½ miles from Birmingham (New St.) was the southern extremity of the Midland Railway's suburban service, and traffic workings were complicated. In the 1930s, about a dozen local or semi-fast through services on the Birmingham to Gloucester section called in each direction. At the Birmingham end of the line, these were supplemented by the suburban workings, which either took the Selly Oak route, or the King's Heath route, ex-New St. The two lines merged near King's Norton, where most of the King's Heath workings terminated. About thirty suburban workings continued on to Barnt Green, some being third class only, and sixteen to eighteen of these workings ran on to Redditch. South of Redditch, the branch carried seven through services to Alcester, Evesham and Ashchurch.

Even today, Barnt Green remains a small community, and its significance as the terminal point for such an extensive suburban service, is more on account of the railway facilities available, than the traffic potential of the station. Quadrupling was carried out by the LMS, north of Barnt Green, a 70 lever LMS box replacing the 28 lever Main Line box on 15th September 1929. Prior to quadrupling, the 'up' platform had been north of the junction.

Left: A study of the Redditch platforms and substantial footbridge, which had to span both B&G main lines, the two platform roads of the Redditch line, and the central platform.

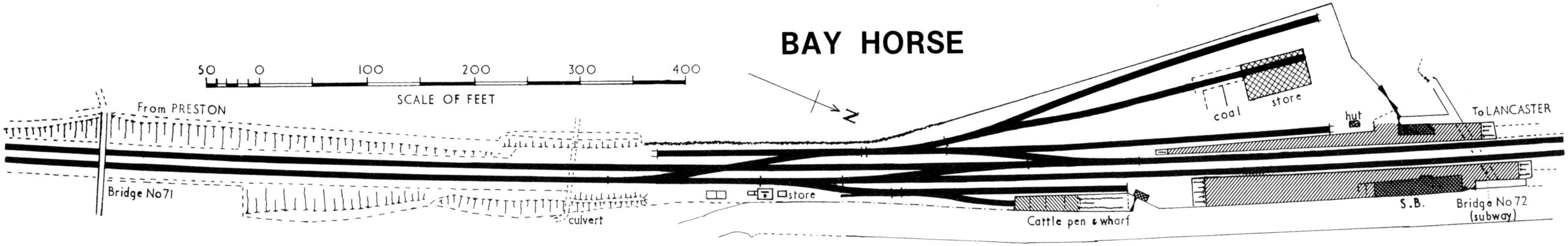

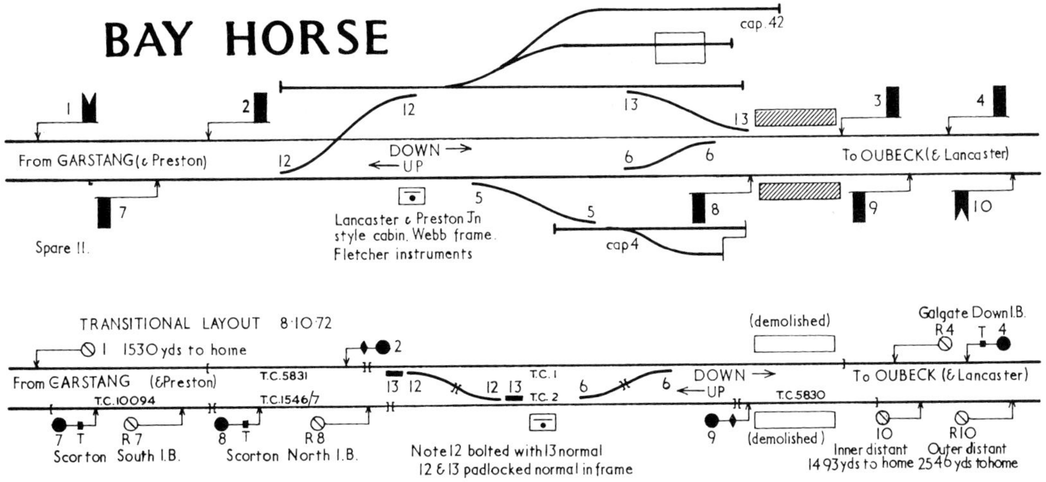

BAY HORSE

SCALE OF FEET
50 0 100 200 300 400

N

From PRESTON   To LANCASTER

coal   store   hut

Bridge No 71   culvert   store   Cattle pen & wharf   S.B.   Bridge No 72 (subway)

BAY HORSE

cap. 42

1   2   12   13   13   3   4

From GARSTANG (& Preston)   12   DOWN →   ← UP   6   6   To OUBECK (& Lancaster)

7   5   5   8   9   10

Spare !!   Lancaster & Preston Jn style cabin, Webb frame. Fletcher instruments   cap 4

TRANSITIONAL LAYOUT 8·10·72

(demolished)   Galgate Down I.B.   R4   T 4

1 1530 yds to home   2

From GARSTANG (& Preston)   T.C.5831   13 12   12 13   T.C.1   6   6   DOWN →   ← UP   T.C.5830   To OUBECK (& Lancaster)
T.C.10094   T.C.1546/7   T.C.2

7 T   R 7   8 T   R 8   9   (demolished)   10   R10
Scorton South I.B.   Scorton North I.B.   Note 12 bolted with 13 normal   Inner distant   Outer distant
12 & 13 padlocked normal in frame   1493 yds to home 2546 yds to home

---

Below: It was only in 1869 that the LNWR began to adopt the absolute block system, requiring a massive resignalling operation, the Northern Division of the LNWR adopting an all brick cabin for a time, of which Bay Horse was a late survivor.

A view from the signal cabin, looking towards Lancaster.

Below: Commissioning of Preston power box led to the LNWR box being replaced by a BR emegency ground frame of LNWR design.

BAY HORSE *(Map Ref. O3)*

Bay Horse Station, which was named after a nearby inn, rather than a community, was located on the Lancaster & Preston Junction Railway, now a part of the West Coast Main Line. The L&PJ was authorised with high hopes in 1837, and formally opened on 25th June 1840, by which time reality had set in. The L&PJ was constructed on an ultra-economy basis, although it substantially exceeded the estimate of the usually meticulous Joseph Locke. Bay Horse was one of the original 'stations', although a 3 foot wide platform 40yds. in length was not authorised until 1841. Within a fortnight of opening, a train had charged the level crossing gates then provided. In 1842 the L&PJ was leased by the Lancaster Canal Company, whose boats were more comfortable than L&PJ trains! With the completion of the Lancaster & Carlisle Railway in 1846, the L&PJ became a part of a trunk route and, despite the canal lease, fell under a kind of L&C rule. Matters were brought to a head when an Anglo-Scottish express ran into the rear of a northbound L&PJ local train at Bay Horse in 1848, the inspector castigating the single red flag which sufficed as a signalling system. The line came more firmly under L&C control from 1849, but was not amalgamated into the L&C until 1859, and that in turn into the LNWR. Bay Horse remained a tiny and primitive station, closing to passengers on 13th June 1960, and to goods on 18th May 1964. Today, the goods yard houses a sub-station for the 25kV West Coast Main Line electrification.

BAY HORSE NORTH
EMERGENCY FRAME

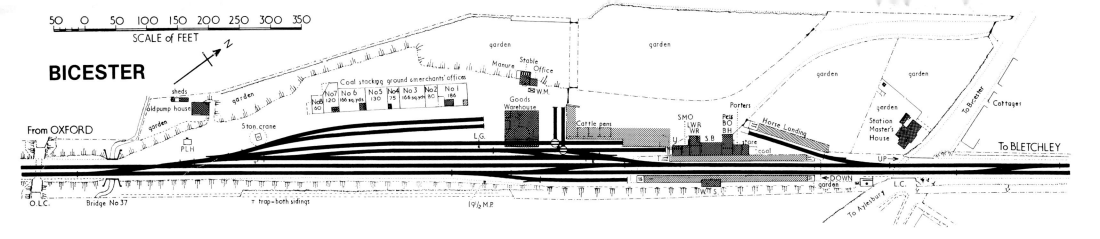

BICESTER

SCALE of FEET

50 0 50 100 150 200 250 300 350

From OXFORD

To BLETCHLEY

Below: One of the characteristics of the branch line era was that stations frequently altered little, if at all, from the introduction of block working and interlocking of signals and points; a process virtually complete by 1890, through to the Beeching era. Except for a slight raising of the platforms, and the most trivial of details, different chimney pots, lamps or fencing, etc., Bicester Station had hardly changed since Victorian times, when this February 1967 photograph was taken. In this view, looking towards Oxford, one can see the main buildings on the 'up' platform. The yard is still well-filled with the traditional four-wheel wagon. It is a curious thought that generations of travellers could have passed through Bicester, with the station hardly altering, and then, within a few years, Bicester, along with thousands of other stations, was swept into oblivion. The waiting-room and ladies' room/WCs, are located beneath the far gable. Next comes the circulating area, open on the platform side to the elements, and the booking office and parcel office occupy the near gable section. A porters' room, lamp room and stores take up the near block.

BICESTER *(Map Ref. G2)*

Bicester is a market town with a population of 4,200, and was served by the LNWR's Bletchley to Oxford branch, and from 1910, by the GWR Aynho cut-off. The LNWR station was opened as a part of the nominally independent Buckinghamshire Railway on 1st October 1850. The BR was an amalgam of two earlier schemes, the Oxford & Bletchley Junction Railway, and the Buckingham & Brackley Junction Railway, both of which were fostered by local landowners in the LNWR camp. The desire to keep the GWR out of the area, and if possible thwart its plans to extend northwards from Didcot to Worcester and the West Midlands, were at least as important as any traffic the area might offer. Bicester acted as a temporary terminus of the branch from October 1850 until 2nd December 1850, when the line was extended west towards Oxford. The completion of the line was the cause of much rejoicing, but the joy was to be muted within the year when a derailment in Bicester Station claimed six lives. Originally single, the Oxford line was doubled in the 1860s. The main buildings were on the 'up' side, in a light grey limestone to typical 'Bucks' style, with a paved and roofed circulating area, open to the platform where the booking hall would normally be. The railway crossed the Aylesbury to Bicester road to the east of the station, and a standard LNWR box was installed by 1882. Yard connections were worked from the box, and from a ground frame near bridge No. 37. In 1940, construction of a vast military base, with its own rail system, commenced. The junction for this was controlled by an 'ARP' box, Bicester No. 2, 950yds. west of the station box, which became No. 1. At its World War II peak, the Bicester Military Railway totalled over 70 miles of track. The wartime box was eventually replaced by a 6-lever ground frame and, after lying derelict for many years, was demolished in 1980.

BICESTER

Traditionally, the area was prime hunting country and, in the days when the gentry and their horses moved by rail, facilities at Bicester were barely adequate. On 12th February 1883, William Cawkwell, who had retired as General Manager of the LNWR, but occupied a curious position between the Chairman, Richard Moon, and the Manager, George Findlay, informed the Board of Trade that the LNWR had been approached, by 'noblemen and gentlemen accustomed to hunt the country around Bicester, to provide more accommodation for embarking and disembarking horses'. In an otherwise already fully-used site, the only space for a landing was at the Bletchley end of the station. Such a site would interfere 'in some slight degree with the use of the level crossing at the station'. By 1883, this was contrary to BOT guidelines, and Cawkwell adroitly passed this 'hot potato' to the BOT, with the observation 'if the Board of Trade will sanction the construction, the Directors would undertake to incur the necessary expense'. With Cawkwell able to divert the wrath of the nobility upon the heads of its political masters, the BOT graciously consented, and Col. Rich was sent to inspect the siding in May.

In 1883, seven services, including an express, called at Bicester in each direction. By 1909, there were five or six stopping trains, and three semi-fasts. These were augmented, between Bicester and Oxford, by six steam railcar trips, a facility which commenced in 1905. Under the LMS, the through services survived but the railcars succumbed. Passenger services ceased on 1st January 1968.

Above left: The main buildings, pictured looking towards Bletchley in February 1967. In 1958, the western extremity of the Oxford to Bletchley branch passed into Western Region hands, in one of those inter-regional transfers based upon geography rather than cohesive routes. The Western Region's chocolate and cream paint proclaimed the new 'owner'. The small notice 'London Road' fixed to the 'Hawkseye' LMS nameboard was a BR addition, to distinguish the station from the GW Bicester North Station.

Above right: A view looking towards Bletchley, with No. 1 box seen in the distance. The 'down' platform, and modest shelter, did not long survive the ending of passenger services, both succumbing in December 1969. The signal box and 'up' buildings were retained.

Below: This was the view from the 'down' platform, looking towards Oxford in February 1967. The pile of splintered timbers to the left of the mineral wagon record the site, and demise, of the goods shed. Barrow-ways were provided at both ends of the station and passengers were asked to 'Look before crossing the Line'. During World War II, forces' late-leave specials were common, and many were worked into Bicester by LMS engines, and taken on to the camp by WD engines and crews. No. 2 box is just visible in the far distance, on the right of the running lines.

BICESTER

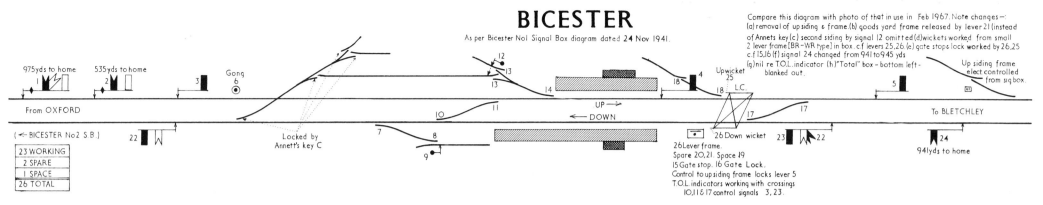

As per Bicester No1 Signal Box diagram dated 24 Nov 1941.

Compare this diagram with photo of that in use in Feb 1967. Note changes—:
(a) removal of up siding & frame.(b) goods yard frame released by lever 21 (instead of Annets key (c) second siding by signal 12 omitted (d) wickets worked from small 2 lever frame [BR–WR type] in box. c.f levers 25,26. (e) gate stop & lock worked by 26,25 c.f 15,16 (f) signal 24 changed from 941 to 945 yds (g) nil re T.O.L. indicator (h) "Total" box - bottom left - blanked out.

975 yds to home   535 yds to home   Gong   Up siding frame elect. controlled from sig box.

From OXFORD

To BLETCHLEY

(← BICESTER No2 S.B.)

| 23 WORKING |
| 2 SPARE |
| 1 SPACE |
| 26 TOTAL |

Locked by Annett's key C

26 Lever frame.
Spare 20,21. Space 19
15 Gate stop. 16 Gate Lock.
Control to up siding frame locks lever 5
T.O.L. indicators working with crossings
10,11 & 17 control signals 3, 23.

94 yds to home

Above: The November 1941 signal box diagram shows the layout upon the opening of the Military Railway (worked by No. 2 box) whilst an 'up' siding, for the nearby RAF base, existed to the east of Bicester. This was electrically-released from No. 1 box.

Below: The RAF siding was removed shortly after the war, and a new LMS diagram was prepared. This was updated by the Western Region up to 1967. An electric release lever has replaced the Annett's key for the yard ground frame, but of greatest interest is the arrival of a small 2-lever frame to work the wickets. This was a common GWR habit, but is a bizarre piece of 'Westernisation', as the wickets were already worked from the LNWR frame, and it merely created two spares in the frame!

Right: 'No Western Region signal box should be without one' — the two lever wicket frame installed to do what the LNWR had done for decades already!

Lower right: The LNWR frame, gate wheel and Western Region addition in 1967. There is an LNWR frame support gap between 16 and 17; 19/20 are spaces 21 (short-top) — electric.

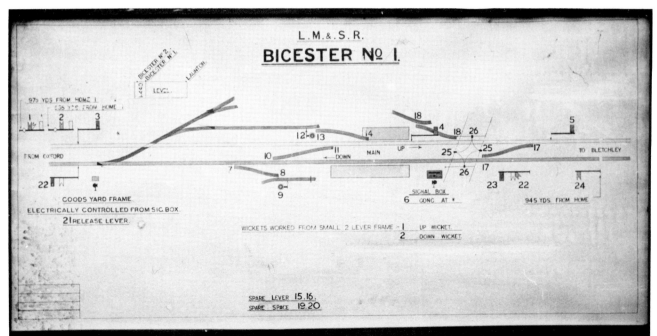

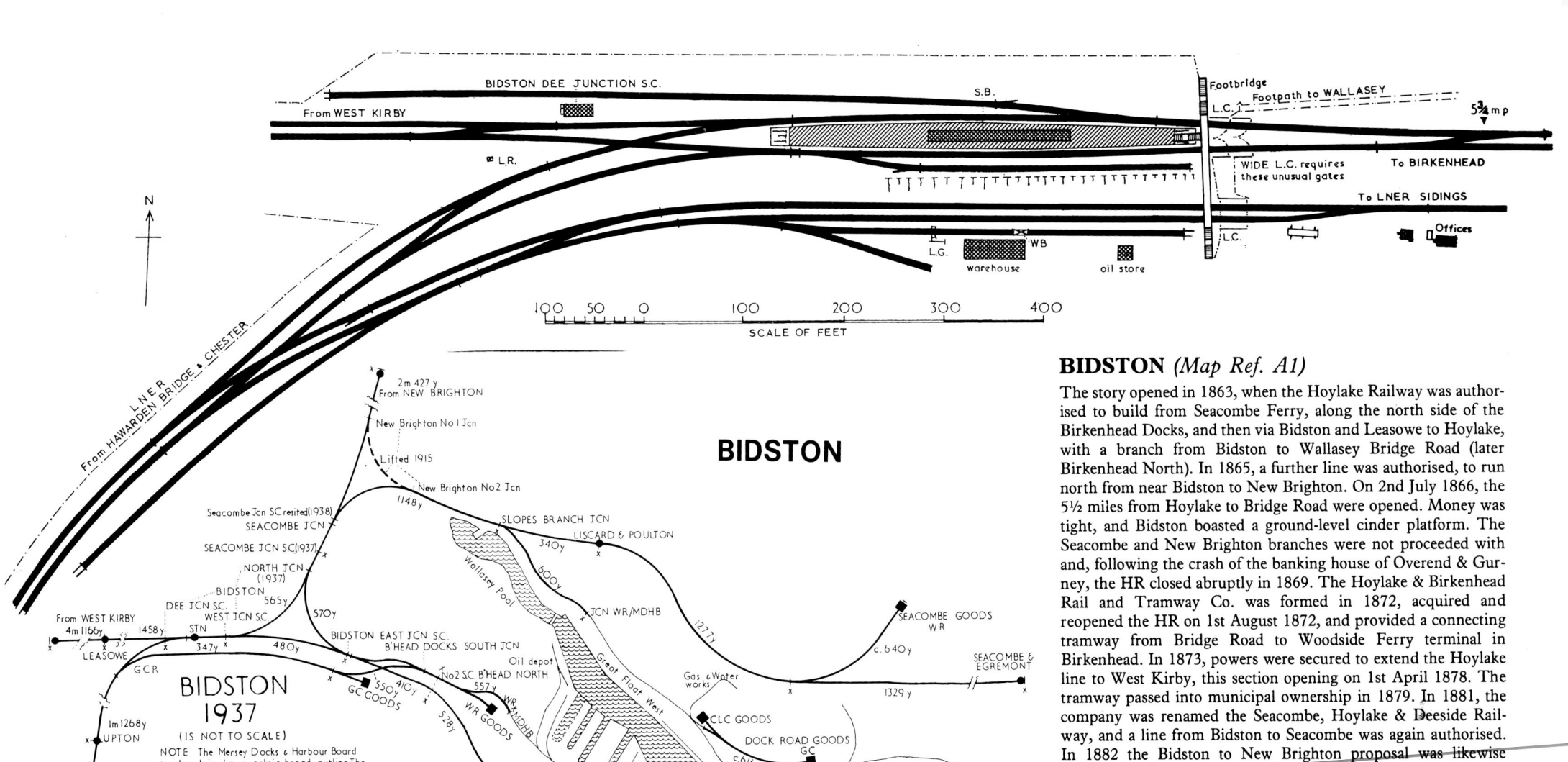

BIDSTON DEE JUNCTION S.C.

From WEST KIRBY

S.B.

Footbridge
Footpath to WALLASEY

L.C.

5¾ m p

L.R.

WIDE L.C. requires
these unusual gates

To BIRKENHEAD

To LNER SIDINGS

L.G.

WB

L.C.

Offices

warehouse

oil store

100 50 0   100   200   300   400

SCALE OF FEET

BIDSTON

LNER From HAWARDEN BRIDGE & CHESTER

2m 427y
From NEW BRIGHTON

New Brighton No 1 Jcn

Lifted 1915

New Brighton No2 Jcn

1148y

SLOPES BRANCH JCN

LISCARD & POULTON

340y

600y

JCN WR/MDHB

SEACOMBE GOODS
W R

Seacombe Jcn SC resited (1938)
SEACOMBE JCN

SEACOMBE JCN S.C.(1937)

NORTH JCN
(1937)

BIDSTON
565y

DEE JCN S.C.
WEST JCN S.C.

570y

480y

From WEST KIRBY
4m 1166y   1458y

STN

LEASOWE
347y

G.C.R.

BIDSTON EAST JCN S.C.
B'HEAD DOCKS SOUTH JCN

Oil depot

No2 SC. B'HEAD NORTH

557y

WR GOODS

528y

c.640y

1329y

SEACOMBE &
EGREMONT

Wallasey Pool

1277y

Gas & Water
works

CLC GOODS

DOCK ROAD GOODS
GC

c.616y

Great Float West

Great Float East

**BIDSTON
1937**
(IS NOT TO SCALE)

1m 1268y
UPTON

12m 981y
HAWARDEN BRIDGE
G.C.R.

NOTE The Mersey Docks & Harbour Board
trackwork is shown only in broad outline. The
coal loading facilities (right lower) are notable

550y
GC GOODS

410y

No I S.C
BIRKENHEAD NORTH
(ex 'BIRKENHEAD DOCKS')

WR/MDHB

Duke Street Bdg

Vittoria Dock

CH2

Wirral Foundry

1542y

LMS/GWR

CH 3

MCH1

MCH MDHB

CC

CT

Cavendish
wharf

coal sids. Duke St wharf

CC Coal conveyors
CH3 Coal hoists No3 cc
C T Coal tips
MCH Movable coal hoist

BIRKENHEAD PARK
(WR/ Mersey Ry Jt)

To LIVERPOOL CENTRAL   3m 10y

Above: The desolate area of Bidston Moss, lying just to the west of the Birkenhead
Docks, is the key to unravelling the complex pattern of lines which made up the Wirral
Railway, and which, although boasting just 13¾ route miles, possessed four major
terminating stations, and ten principal junctions, all of the latter in close proximity to
Bidston. The map shows the web of routes created by the Wirral Railway, the Great
Central, Mersey Railway, and Mersey Docks & Harbour Board. It functioned as an
independent company up to 1923, and since 1938, as an electrified suburban service, with
limited contacts with the rest of BR, has retained much of its character. The MDHB lines
repay study; note the coal hoists, movable hoists, coal tips and conveyors.

BIDSTON *(Map Ref. A1)*

The story opened in 1863, when the Hoylake Railway was authorised to build from Seacombe Ferry, along the north side of the
Birkenhead Docks, and then via Bidston and Leasowe to Hoylake,
with a branch from Bidston to Wallasey Bridge Road (later
Birkenhead North). In 1865, a further line was authorised, to run
north from near Bidston to New Brighton. On 2nd July 1866, the
5½ miles from Hoylake to Bridge Road were opened. Money was
tight, and Bidston boasted a ground-level cinder platform. The
Seacombe and New Brighton branches were not proceeded with
and, following the crash of the banking house of Overend & Gur-
ney, the HR closed abruptly in 1869. The Hoylake & Birkenhead
Rail and Tramway Co. was formed in 1872, acquired and
reopened the HR on 1st August 1872, and provided a connecting
tramway from Bridge Road to Woodside Ferry terminal in
Birkenhead. In 1873, powers were secured to extend the Hoylake
line to West Kirby, this section opening on 1st April 1878. The
tramway passed into municipal ownership in 1879. In 1881, the
company was renamed the Seacombe, Hoylake & Deeside Railway, and a line from Bidston to Seacombe was again authorised.
In 1882 the Bidston to New Brighton proposal was likewise
resurrected.

In 1883, a Wirral Railway was incorporated, by Board of Trade
certificate, to build from the Mersey Railway (then under construction) to Bridge Road, and from Bidston through the Wirral
peninsula to the MS&L near Hawarden Bridge. It will be seen
that Bidston featured in virtually every plan, successful or otherwise. In 1884, a non-statutory Wirral Railways Co. Ltd. was
formed, to buy the shares of the SH&D and the 1883 Wirral
Railway Co., a proceeding authorised by Act of 11th June 1891,
to create a third 'Wirral Railway Co.'. On 2nd January 1888, the
Mersey Railway opened to Birkenhead Park and, on the same day,
the Wirral factions opened the Park to Bridge Road section (by
now known as Birkenhead Docks, and latterly Birkenhead North)
and the New Brighton branch, as far as Wallasey. The line was
completed to New Brighton in March. The Seacombe branch
opened on 1st June 1895.

Above: Bidston Dee Junction signal cabin, an LMS standard box built to control the junction of the GCR 'Dee' line and the West Junction curve. The bricked-up windows to the locking room were common on boxes in urban areas, and were usually an Air Raid Precaution to protect the interlocking from the Luftwaffe. Today they provide protection from vandals.

Involved though this was, there were still several loose ends, for the Wirral companies had not been able to raise funds for the Bidston to Hawarden Bridge line, and powers for this had passed to the MS&LR in 1889. This would provide that company with access to the Birkenhead Docks, whilst it already enjoyed access to the Liverpool Docks via the CLC. The central Wirral line opened to goods on 16th May 1896, and to passengers on 18th May. From 1898 GC trains ran through to Seacombe.

During this period, Birkenhead had expanded dramatically, as had the Wirral coast towns, which became high-class residential suburbs for Liverpool. In the 1860s, three to six trains had been provided on the Hoylake line; by the late 1870s, over a dozen were running, and by the 1880s, it was up to twenty trains. By 1888, Bidston, Moreton and Hoylake were passing places, but doubling of the West Kirby line began in 1894, and was completed out to Hoylake by 1895. With doubling, service frequencies continued to increase. From 1888, through workings had taken place with the Mersey Railway, engines being changed at Birkenhead Park Station, but with the deplorable conditions in the tunnel sections, the Mersey traffic had been faltering, a trend hardly helped by the completion of the Wirral branch to Seacombe Ferry in 1895. In 1900, the Mersey Railway obtained powers to electrify, commencing electric services in 1903. The Wirral obtained powers, but did not exercise them, and through workings thus ceased.

When the LMS took over in 1923, it inherited a compact but antiquated suburban network. Some stations had been rebuilt, but others, including Bidston, were woefully inadequate. Signalling had also stagnated for many years. A substantial new signal box of LMS 'standard' design (a hybrid of LNWR and Midland features) appeared at Bidston Station, replacing the old Dee and West Junction boxes in preparation for the 1938 LMS electrification. Several stations (*see Hoylake and Leasowe*) received typically 1930s' concrete and glass structures, but Bidston was not so blessed. Although the station was extremely busy, with trains every few minutes to West Kirby, its location in the middle of Bidston Moss, with few houses in the immediate vicinity, limited its traffic potential. The Seacombe branch was not electrified, and closed to passengers in 1960. As will be seen from the scale plan, the GC had a small freight yard at Bidston, which closed on 29th July 1968. By this date, there was a limited passenger service down the GC line, and a high-frequency electric service to West Kirby. New Brighton trains use the 'East to North' curve.

BIDSTON

Below: A view looking from the station footbridge towards West Kirby, in October 1965. A 2-car diesel multiple unit signalled for Hawarden Bridge, makes a change from the more plentiful electric sets. The GC freight tracks are seen in the foreground.

Below: Bidston West Junction (to the east of Bidston Station) in October 1965, looking towards Birkenhead Docks, with its cranes and coal elevators visible on the skyline. With power-working of points, many junction signal boxes were dispensed with, as was the case with the former West Junction box. The line to the left, to Bidston North Junction, provides access from the GC to the North Docks, Seacombe and New Brighton. The East Junction to North Junction formation is on the skyline. The lines in the centre are to Birkenhead Park, and on the right is the GC freight branch.

BIRMINGHAM (New St.) *(Map Ref. D6)*

Birmingham's prosperity as 'Workshop to the World' stemmed from the Industrial Revolution, but the city's history stretched back centuries before that, and indeed the oldest building in the city, the church of St. Martin's in the Bull Ring, stands close to New St. Station. New St. was not a part of the original railway network of the city, but to understand the station and its history, it is necessary to look back to the dawn of the railway age in Birmingham, and the authorisation of the Grand Junction Railway, from Warrington to the city, and of the London & Birmingham Railway, both on 6th May 1833. On 22nd April 1836, the Birmingham & Gloucester Railway was authorised, to join the L&B east of Curzon St., and to use the yet unbuilt L&B terminus, 'or any future terminus of that company'. In May 1836, the Birmingham & Derby Junction Railway was authorised, making the city a crossroads of trunk routes from Bristol to Derby and York, and London to Wolverhampton, and the north-west. The GJR opened to a temporary terminus at Vauxhall on 4th July 1837, with the L&B opening to Curzon St. on 9th April 1838. The GJR extended from Vauxhall to a terminus alongside the L&B on 1st January 1839. On 17th August 1841, the Birmingham & Gloucester Railway, which had opened in sections from the south, linked up with the L&B, and began to use Curzon St., which was already hopelessly inadequate for the traffic. The Birmingham & Derby Junction Railway had planned to feed into the L&B at Stechford, east of the city, but relations with the L&B were cool, and opened instead to its own terminus, Lawley St., on 10th February 1842.

In 1844, the B&DJ became a part of the Midland Railway, acquiring the B&G from under the nose of the Great Western two years later. That same year, the L&B and GJR merged to form the LNWR. By this time, the gauge war was at its height, with a GW thrust to Birmingham, Wolverhampton and the Mersey. A string of Bills came before Parliament, including the GWR-backed Shrewsbury & Birmingham Railway, and the GJR-endorsed Shropshire Union Railway & Canal Co. Compromise was possible between these lines *(see Wellington)* but a deeper feud erupted over a more direct rail route between Wolverhampton and Birmingham than was provided by the Grand Junction, via Vauxhall, Aston and Bescot. It led to one of the most celebrated battles in railway history.

The L&B, in its last months, backed two Bills, both authorised on 3rd August 1846. The L&B (Birmingham Extension) Act, to which Robert Stephenson was Engineer, approved a line of less than one mile in length, from near Curzon St. to a new station in Navigation St. (or New St.). The Birmingham, Wolverhampton & Stour Valley Railway would run direct from Birmingham, through Oldbury to the GJR beyond Wolverhampton. This was also approved, shattering the hopes of the Shrewsbury & Birmingham Railway to build south. Instead, provided the S&B did not merge with the GWR, they were later granted running powers over the Stour Valley, which was leased by the LNWR long before completion. By late 1850, the Stour Valley was virtually complete, but the LNWR was in no hurry to open it, for they already possessed the GJR route, and unless S&B was amalgamated with the GWR, it would give this GW ally a route into Birmingham. Move and countermove followed, with the Board of Trade embroiled in the dispute. Opening was sanctioned in November 1851 by the Board of Trade from a temporary platform at Navigation St., Birmingham, to Wolverhampton and Bushbury, but postponed by the LNWR on safety grounds, to thwart an S&B demand to use their running powers. The Stour Valley finally opened to LNWR passenger services on 1st July 1852, trains being timed not to connect with S&B services at Wolverhampton. A series of law suits resulted in S&B trains reaching New St. from the north on 4th February 1854.

Construction of the Birmingham Extension line from Curzon St. had been painfully slow, and costly, with numerous properties to demolish, and several streets and lanes to block up, amongst them Peck Lane and The Froggary. The most important thoroughfare, King St., prompted Parliament to demand a pedestrian right of way, crossing the station at right-angles. LNWR passenger services were switched from Curzon St. to New St. on 1st June 1854, Midland trains moving a month later, although some excursions continued until 1893. It is sometimes said that the LNWR allowed the Midland Railway to use New St. in gratitude for 'saving' the Birmingham & Gloucester from the GWR. In fact, the MR secured its rights under the B&GR Act.

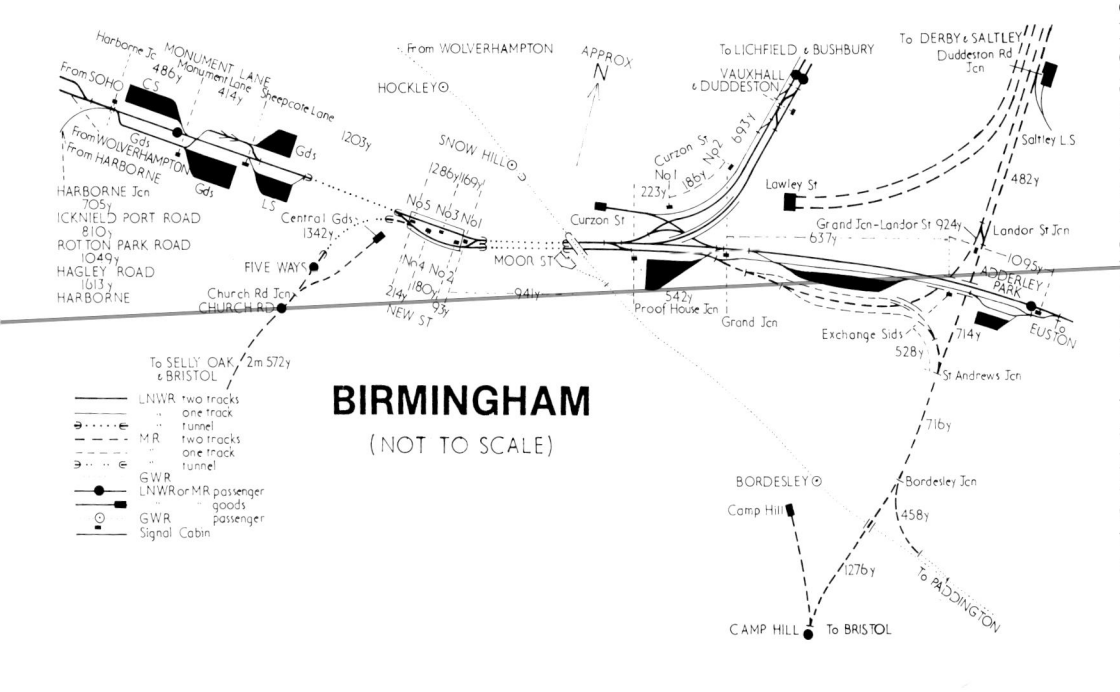

BIRMINGHAM

(NOT TO SCALE)

LNWR two tracks / one track / tunnel
MR two tracks / one track / tunnel
GWR
LNWR or MR passenger / goods
GWR passenger
Signal Cabin

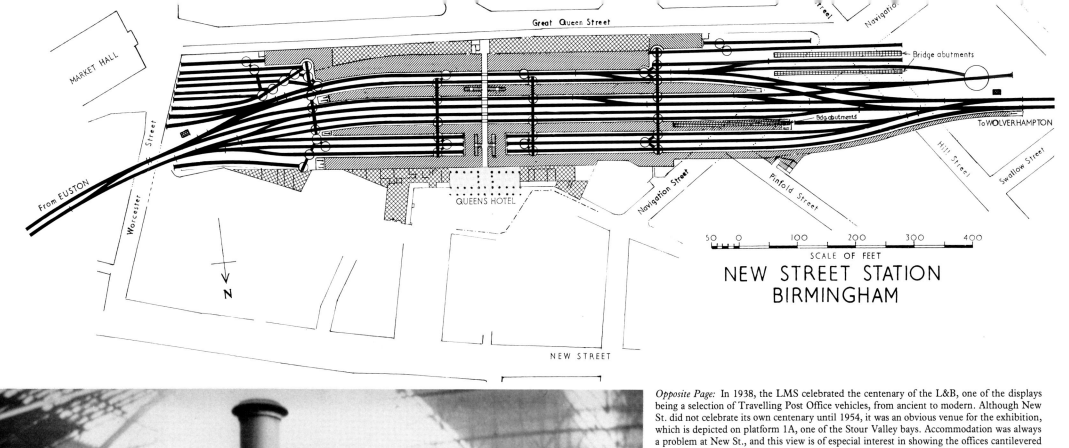

Great Queen Street

← Bridge abutments

Bdg. abutments

To WOLVERHAMPTON

From EUSTON

Worcester Street

Navigation Street

Pinfold Street

Hill Street

Swallow Street

MARKET HALL

QUEENS HOTEL

NEW STREET

N

50 0   100   200   300   400
SCALE OF FEET

NEW STREET STATION
BIRMINGHAM

Opposite Page: In 1938, the LMS celebrated the centenary of the L&B, one of the displays being a selection of Travelling Post Office vehicles, from ancient to modern. Although New St. did not celebrate its own centenary until 1954, it was an obvious venue for the exhibition, which is depicted on platform 1A, one of the Stour Valley bays. Accommodation was always a problem at New St., and this view is of especial interest in showing the offices cantilevered out from the back of the LNWR-owned Queen's Hotel, over platform 1A. The footbridge is visible in the right distance, whilst the details of the train shed roof, a 212ft. span, by 840ft., repay study. At one time it was the largest single span roof in the world.

Survey: The New St. Station of the 1850s comprised four through passenger lines, and two sets of bays, connected via over forty carriage turntables to carriage sidings at both ends of the station. The size of these turntables necessitated the triangular or staggered configuration, where it was desired to serve adjoining tracks. LNWR expresses arrived and departed normally, but at this time, as both MR routes entered New St. from the east, MR Derby to Gloucester expresses calling at Birmingham had to reverse; a time consuming procedure.

Left: Although dating from the LMS era, this 1920s portrait of a Webb 6ft. 6in. 'Precedent', No. 5000 *Princess Beatrice*, carrying express headlamps at No. 4 platform, recalls pre-grouping days. Perched above the footbridge, and reached by a ladder, is the quaint No. 3 signal box, with its open lever frame, and instrument house reminiscent of the wheel house of a ship! The box was removed before the war.

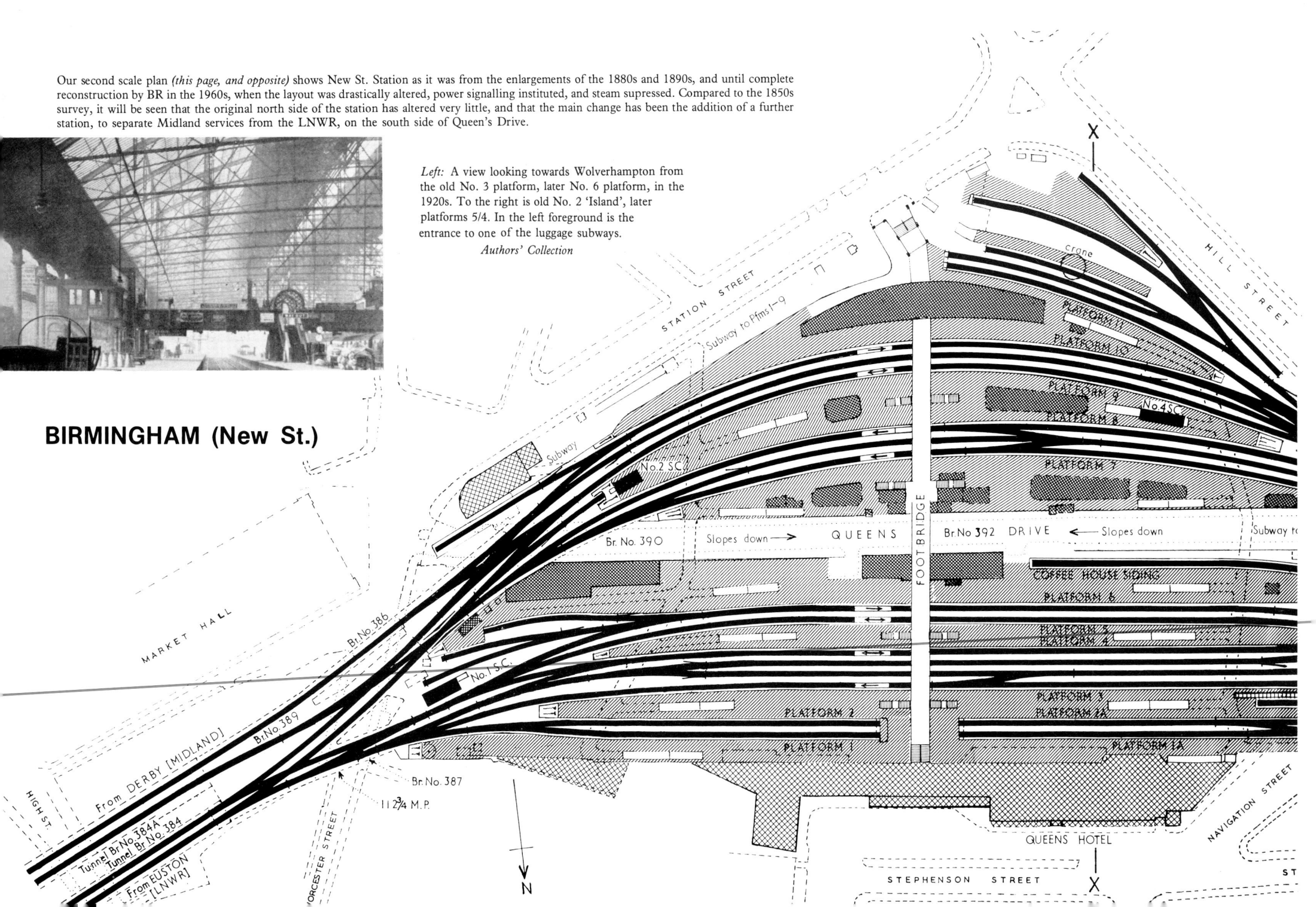

Our second scale plan *(this page, and opposite)* shows New St. Station as it was from the enlargements of the 1880s and 1890s, and until complete reconstruction by BR in the 1960s, when the layout was drastically altered, power signalling instituted, and steam supressed. Compared to the 1850s survey, it will be seen that the original north side of the station has altered very little, and that the main change has been the addition of a further station, to separate Midland services from the LNWR, on the south side of Queen's Drive.

Left: A view looking towards Wolverhampton from the old No. 3 platform, later No. 6 platform, in the 1920s. To the right is old No. 2 'Island', later platforms 5/4. In the left foreground is the entrance to one of the luggage subways.

Authors' Collection

BIRMINGHAM (New St.)

STATION STREET

Subway to Pfms 1–9

Subway

No.2 S.C.

crane

PLATFORM 11

PLATFORM 10

PLATFORM 9

No.4 S.C.

PLATFORM 8

PLATFORM 7

Br. No. 390

Slopes down →

QUEENS

FOOTBRIDGE

Br.No. 392 DRIVE

← Slopes down

Subway to

COFFEE HOUSE SIDING

PLATFORM 6

MARKET HALL

Br. No. 386

Br. No. 389

No.1 S.C.

PLATFORM 5
PLATFORM 4

PLATFORM 3
PLATFORM 1A

PLATFORM 2

PLATFORM 1

PLATFORM 1A

Br. No. 387

112¾ M.P.

N

HIGH ST.

From DERBY [MIDLAND]

Tunnel Br.No. 384A
Tunnel Br.No. 384

From EUSTON [LNWR]

WORCESTER STREET

QUEENS HOTEL

STEPHENSON STREET

NAVIGATION STREET

HILL STREET

The 1854 station was a great advance on Curzon St., but increasing frequency of main line services over both the Midland Railway and the LNWR, plus additional routes, saw the station working to capacity, surprisingly quickly. On 2nd June 1862, the LNWR Aston to Sutton Coldfield branch was opened, and a heavy suburban traffic evolved. The line was extended to Lichfield in 1884. In 1874, the Harborne Railway, worked by the LNWR, came into use, and on 1st April 1889, the Soho to Perry Barr connection opened to passenger traffic. LNWR suburban services ran east, along the main line to Coventry; west over the Stour Valley to Wolverhampton; via Aston, or via Soho, to Walsall; via Aston to Sutton Coldfield; and over the Harborne branch. In 1859, the Redditch Railway, operated by the MR, first contributed its quota of trains. In 1864 a direct connection was provided between Landor St. Junction on the B&DJ, and St. Andrew's Junction on the B&G, but MR expresses still required to call at New St. and reverse. The solution to this problem came in a roundabout way. A single track independent line, the Birmingham West Suburban Railway, was authorised in 1871 from Lifford on the B&G to an isolated terminus in Birmingham. This was taken over by the MR in 1875, and opened in 1876. On 18th July 1881, the MR secured powers to double the BWSR and extend the line to come in at the West end of New St. The LNWR undertook to double the size of New St. Station, with four through platforms, bays and parcels sidings on the south side of Great Queen St., which remained a public thoroughfare, but was effectively converted into a central carriage drive for the station. The new platforms, largely given over to Midland trains, came into use on 8th February 1885 and, on 1st July, the Birmingham West Suburban line was extended to New St. Other work delayed diversion of MR expresses to the BWS line until 1st October 1885.

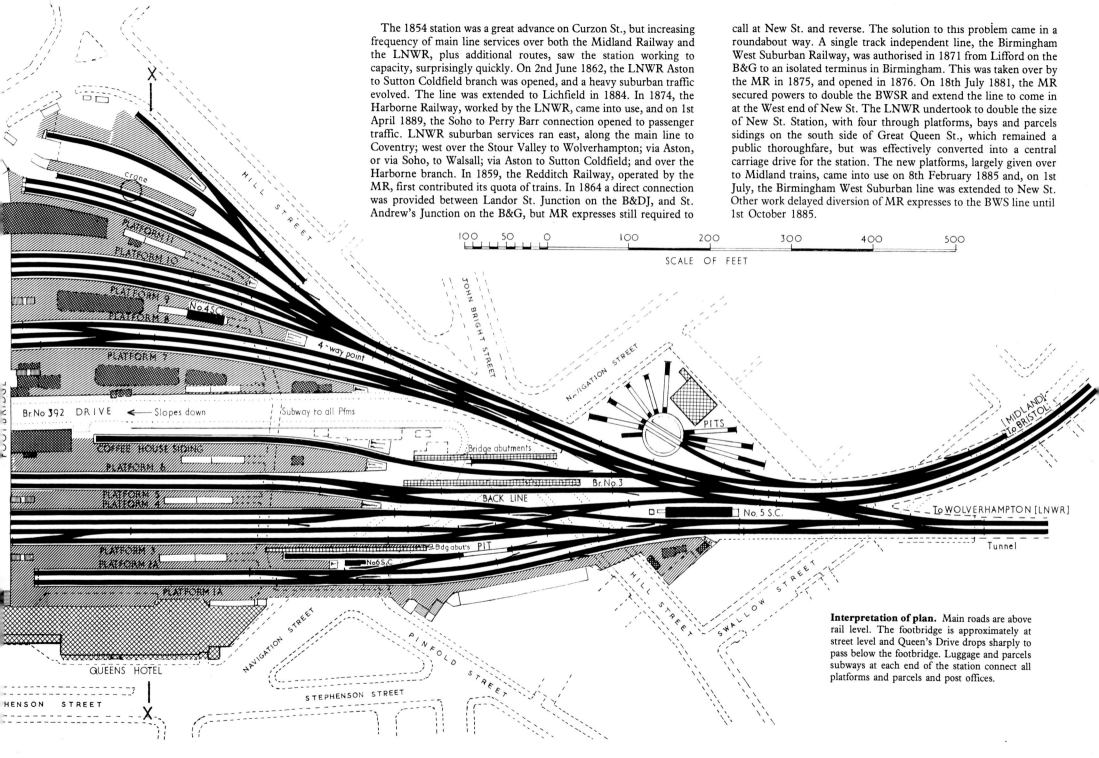

Interpretation of plan. Main roads are above rail level. The footbridge is approximately at street level and Queen's Drive drops sharply to pass below the footbridge. Luggage and parcels subways at each end of the station connect all platforms and parcels and post offices.

Above: The removal of the 1854 overall roof in 1947 drastically altered the look of the LNWR platforms, and made the surroundings properties more apparent, as seen in this 1950s' study of No. 45681 *Aboukir* leaving No. 4 platform with empty coaching stock.

Below: A view looking across the LNWR platforms from the Queen's Hotel steps, prior to 1914. At this time each 'Island' platform was given one number, thus what later became platform faces 4/5 was then No. 2, and 1, 1A, 2, 2A and 3 were platform 1.

Authors' Collection

Above: The Queen's Hotel and entrance to New St. from Stephenson Place, showing the building as designed by J. W. Livock, and prior to the addition of two extra floors in 1911. The kiosk and railings were later removed.

Authors' Collection

BIRMINGHAM (New St.)

Below: The Midland side of New St., looking towards Derby. This side of the station was built under the LNWR (Additional Powers) Act of 1881, the extension footbridge being one legal requirement. 'Island 4' to the left later became platform 7, and 'Island 5' to the right, platforms 8 and 9.

Authors' Collection

With eight through platforms instead of four, the enlargements of 1885 eased congestion at New St., but highlighted a further problem. West of the station, LNWR trains used the Stour Valley line, whilst the Midland services were carried on the Birmingham West suburban metals. To the east, all the LNWR and Midland workings had to be shoe-horned through the double track approach from Proof House Junction to the 1854 tunnel, just outside New St. The LNWR (New Railways) Act, of 27th June 1892 tackled this bottleneck. A new double track tunnel was bored on the south side of the existing double track tunnel, and widenings provided four lines as far as Grand Junction, where the connections to the MR bulged to the south to make room for exchange sidings. Instead of the original flat crossing from the B&DJ on to the L&B, a fruitful source of delay, the link line now burrowed under the L&B, so that Derby and L&B services no longer impeded one another. On 15th June 1892, the Midland and LNWR concluded a far-reaching agreement that 'New St. Station, Birmingham, and the southern approaches thereto are to be placed under the Management of the Joint Committee of the two Companies constituted under the L&NWR Railway (Ashby & Nuneaton Lines) Act 1867 with a standing arbitrator'. As the Midland Railway would benefit from the improved connections, their contribution was settled at 42½ per cent. The agreement was confirmed in the LNWR Act of 27th July 1893, which provided that New St. Station should remain vested solely in the LNWR, but that it should be managed jointly. The quadruple track approach to New St., and the new south tunnel came into use on 17th May 1896, and New St. assumed full 'joint' status from 1st April 1897.

From 1885, when the new platforms were opened, until 1889, southbound Midland expresses used the MR side of the station, and northbound services the LNWR side, but pressure on the LNWR platforms ended this. A method of working evolved which endured for decades, and using the later platform numbering, platforms 1 and 2 became the South Stafford bays, platforms 1A and 2A the Stour Valley bays, platform 3 was the principal London express departure line, whilst platform 4, which was dual-directional, handled many of the Sutton Coldfield workings. Platform 6 was the usual northbound express departure point. Collectively, this became known as 'New St. Old Station'. The Midland side, commonly known as the 'Extension' or 'New Station' boasted two 'up' and two 'down' platforms, No. 9 later being made dual-directional, and short bay. The station covered an area of 12 acres, of which over 8 acres was enclosed — there being 5¾ acres of glass in the LNWR single span, and twin span Midland roofs. The height to the top of the arched rib of the 1854 LNWR roof was 73ft., and the glass alone weighed 115 tons, with 1,050 tons of ironwork. Following the collapse of Charing Cross Station roof, the New St. roof was carefully inspected, and supplementary tie bars added another 216 tons of metal in 1906. As with the painting of the Forth Bridge, maintenance work was continuous and, in 1947, the LMS replaced the LNWR train shed by individual platform awnings, although the Midland train sheds, which were much younger, survived.

Quartered by a road and a public right of way, with inadequate gas lighting, platforms all but devoid of seating and shelters, and with a venerable 4-acre train shed over half the station, New St. had its critics, even in LMS days. Rebuilding of the LMR 'Western Lines' for 25 kV electric services saw a complete transformation at New St. Authority was finally secured to dispense with Queen's Drive and the footbridge. The four bays were converted into through platforms and, working from south to north, the station was progressively rebuilt, with twelve through platforms and three through roads. No. 3 signal box, on the footbridge, went before the war, the other boxes going in January/February 1966, as stages 1 and 2 of the commissioning of New St. power box, which was roughly on the site of the old turntable. Work began in 1964, and was largely completed by March 1967.

Above: The view from platform 4, looking towards Worcester St. bridge and Euston in the 1950s. One of the SR prototype diesels, No. 10203, which spent some years on the London Midland Region, is about to depart from platform 3 with an express. After the removal of the 1854 LNWR canopy, the North Western side of the station received individual platform awnings of utilitarian appearance. Visible beyond the Worcester St. bridge is the tunnel mouth for the North Western lines. To the right of the bridge is New St. No. 1 box, and to the right of that the girders straddling the approach tracks to the Midland side of the station. A facing point locking bar was usually fitted to the fixed rail, short of the blades. In Platform 4 space was at a premium, and the bar is seen on the moving blade, with increased maintenance and effort in pulling.

Right: The view from platform 1, looking towards the Worcester St. bridge in 1966. Urban redevelopment coincided with station renewal, and there is little in common with the 1950s scene pictured above. The Worcester St. properties have gone, as has the bridge itself, a new pre-stressed concrete structure carrying the roadway. The spire of the 13th century St. Martin's church stands revealed amongst demolition and reconstruction.

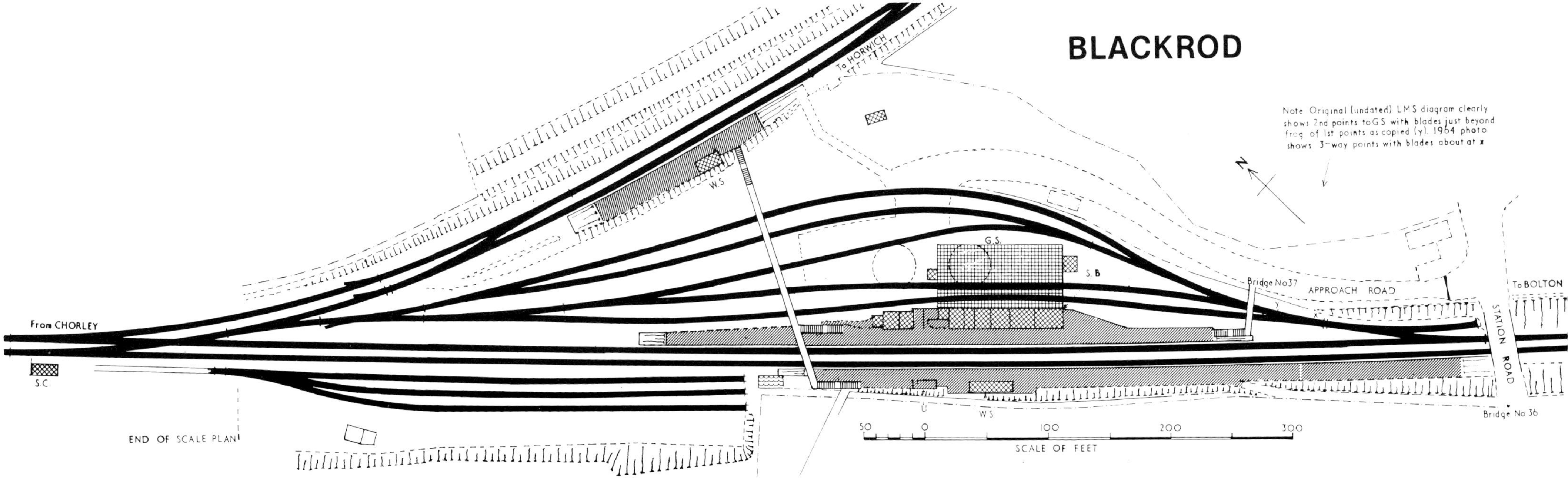

BLACKROD

Note Original (undated) LMS diagram clearly
shows 2nd points to GS with blades just beyond
frog of 1st points as copied (y). 1964 photo
shows 3-way points with blades about at x

To HORWICH

To BOLTON

From CHORLEY

APPROACH ROAD

To Bolton

STATION ROAD

Bridge No 37

Bridge No 36

G.S.

S.B.

W.S.

S.C.

U
W.S.

END OF SCALE PLAN

| 50 | 0 | 100 | 200 | 300 |

SCALE OF FEET

BLACKROD *(Map Ref. O1)*

Blackrod Station is located roughly midway between Bolton and Chorley, on the LYR Bolton & Preston line, and is about one mile south-west of the LYR's Horwich Works. The Bolton & Preston Railway was authorised in 1837 to provide a direct link between its 'named' towns. It was to make an end-on junction with the Manchester & Bolton Railway, and to join the North Union Railway south of Preston, the junction point being a cause of acrimony at first. The B&PR was opened from Bolton to near Adlington, a village south of Chorley, on 4th February 1841, to Chorley on 24th December 1841, and to the agreed junction with the North Union Railway at Euxton Junction in 1843. Blackrod was on the first section of the B&PR to open, and was a small community some distance to the west and north of the station, which was positioned where the Blackrod to Horwich road crossed the line. Indeed, the station was initially known as 'Horwich & Blackrod'. Friction between the NUR and B&PR led to proposals for a B&P line to parallel the NUR into Preston, but were resolved by merging both concerns into an enlarged North Union Railway in 1844. Two years later, the new concern was taken over by the LNWR/LYR, and the line remained joint until partition in the 1880s, when the former B&PR passed to the LYR.

Right: The view from the station footbridge, looking towards Bolton, in 1964. The splitting distants refer (left) to Bolton, and (right) to Wigan, the divergence being controlled by Horwich Fork Junction, which also controlled the curve from the south on to the Horwich branch.

Below: Blackrod eventually came under the control of Preston power box, the old LYR cabin being retained for local connections only, as per the signalling plan.

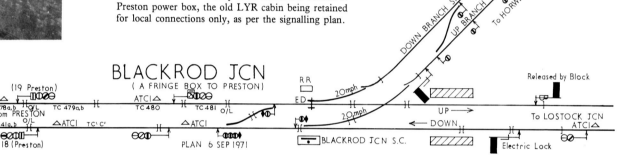

BLACKROD

Above left: Looking from the footpath to Station Road bridge towards Chorley and Preston, in 1964. The capacious 2-road goods shed butts on to the station buildings which it dwarfs. The yard had closed some months earlier, on 1st August 1963, although private siding traffic continued for some time. The photograph and scale plan reveal several unusual features. Firstly, a 2-track goods shed, with one line having no access to the unloading platform is most unusual — indeed unprototypical! The siding which curves so closely round the back of the goods shed is equally improbable, for ordinarily this area would be given over to road vehicle access, whilst the absence of any dead-end sidings is exceptional. It is a thoroughly unlikely layout! It will also be noted that the scale plan and photograph do not agree regarding the access at the south end of the goods shed. The picture shows a 3-way point, and indeed it is questionable if anything else would fit. The scale plan, prepared from an LMS survey, postulated two separate points.

Above right: A view from the northbound platform, looking towards the junction with the Horwich branch, opposite Blackrod signal box. The footbridge in the distance connects the two platforms, and continues over all five through sidings to the single Horwich branch platform. The right-hand section of this footbridge can be seen through the open doorway of the goods shed. Timber footbridges of this type, given a periodic coat of pitch, were to be found at many 'Lanky' stations, and were a hangover from the 'prehistoric' era of the LYR, so graphically described by E. L. Ahrons. Reading Ahrons' accounts, it is conceivable that passengers of those days achieved a greater velocity upon LYR footbridges than on certain of the company's trains! Whatever they may have lacked in aesthetic appeal, the timber footbridges made up for it in economy and longevity, so may still serve as an example to today!

In the 1860s, the B&PR was the focus of a hard-fought battle between the LYR and LNWR, with the North Western backing a line from near Blackburn to Wigan, via Chorley. The LYR response involved use of part of the B&PR near Chorley, and this succeeded as a joint line, whilst in the same Bill, the LYR had sought and won powers for a junction from their Liverpool & Bury line, just east of Wigan, to the B&PR, south of Blackrod. A further line, from the small town of Horwich, with a population of around 3,000, to a north-facing junction with the B&PR, was also approved, on 25th July 1864. The LYR line from Hindley, on the Bury line, to Red Moss Junction, on the B&PR opened in 1868, but the Horwich branch did not open to passengers until 14th February 1870. Horwich & Blackrod was thereupon renamed Horwich Junction, and renamed yet again, in 1873, Blackrod & Horwich Junction! On 16th April 1888, it finally became Blackrod.

By the early 1880s, the LYR was emerging from the stagnation described by Ahrons, and with Miles Platting Works hopelessly inadequate, was seeking an open field site for a new works. The fortuitous offering by auction of an estate at Horwich clinched matters in 1884, and construction of the new works began in 1885. To facilitate locomotive movements to and from the LYR system, largely to the south, a south-facing connection on to the B&PR was authorised in 1885. This connection left the Horwich branch just east of Blackrod Station, and joined the B&PR south of the station, the 1868 Bury line connection being rerouted from Red Moss Junction to the same location, which became Horwich Fork Junction. Between 1881 and 1891, the population rose from less than 4,000 to over 12,000. The branch fell victim to Beeching cuts on 27th September 1965. The B&PR continues to carry passenger services, so the wheel has virtually come full circle.

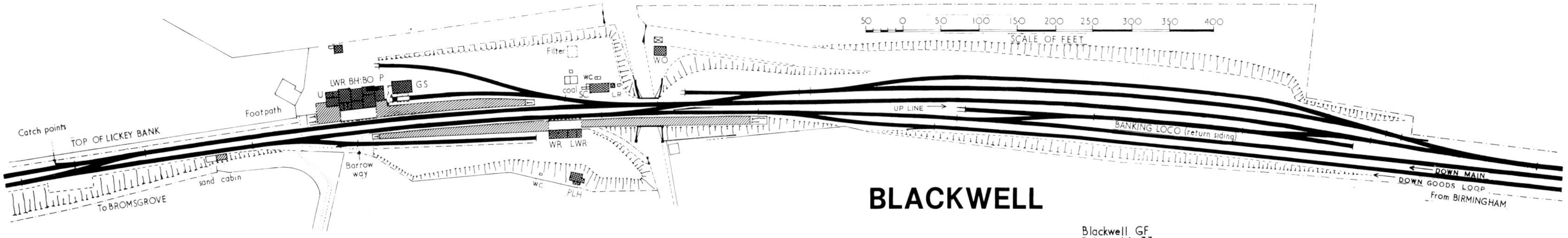

BLACKWELL

Diagram labels (scale plan, top):

SCALE OF FEET — 50 0 50 100 150 200 250 300 350 400

Catch points — TOP OF LICKEY BANK — Footpath — LWR BH:BO P — GS — Filter — WO — coal — WC — SC — LR — UP LINE → — BANKING LOCO (return siding) — sand cabin — Barrow way — WR LWR — WC — PLH — DOWN MAIN — DOWN GOODS LOOP — From BIRMINGHAM — To BROMSGROVE

BLACKWELL

Signalling diagram labels:

Data by Mike Christensen

BLACKWELL S.C. Total 55. Space 5,13,15,16,37,45,46. Spare 1-4,6-11, 14,28-32.

UP LIE BY — UP MAIN → — ENGINE LIE BY — Blackwell GF Released by 33 /415yd — 1230yd (Green by BarntGreen) LINTHURST I.B.

2366yd R12 — 2016yd 12 — 764yd 17 — 263yd 23 — 18 19 — 27yd 24 — 20 — 48 — TC 1274 — 21/R22 — 22

From BROMSGROVE STATION S.C. — TC 1276 — TC 1271 — TC 1272 — 26 — TC 1273 — 25 — 38 — 27 — 47 — 51 52 — 49 50 — 53 — TC 1275 — Motor — TC 1276 — To BARNT GREEN MAIN LINE JCN.S.C.

TC 418 — TC 417 — TC 406 — 34 — 34 35 — 42 216yd — TC 1829 — 54 — 54 TC1466 — TC 1465 (200yds)

40 39 — 41 203yd — (Abolished on 24-7-66) — 49 — ← DOWN MAIN — 43 680yd — 44 1538yd

36 143yd — 55 — ← DOWN LOOP

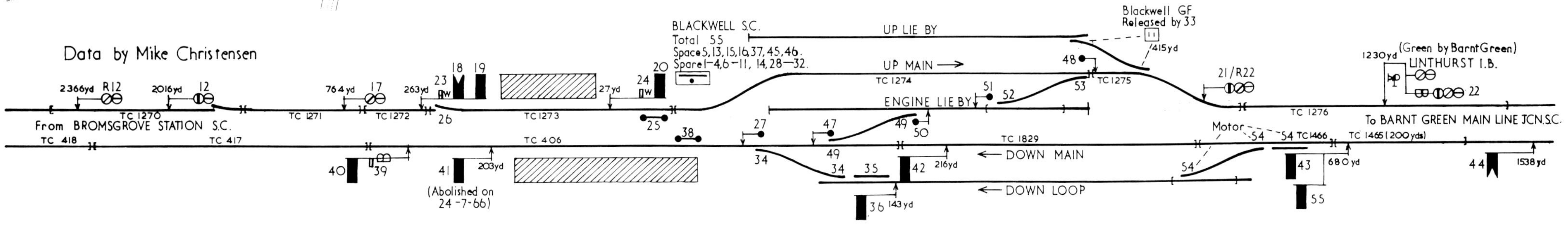

Top & Above: The scale plan and signalling at Blackwell. A comparison will show that many connections had been lifted latterly. Signals 40/41 are unusually close together, whilst the distant, R12 for the 'Lickey Signal', 12 is only 350yds. out, but on the 1 in 37 gradient that would suffice! Blackwell's second distant, 17, is only 501yds. from the home, but with trains moving very slowly . . . ! Five 'up' distants are controlled by Blackwell; R12, 17, 18, 21 and 22.

BLACKWELL *(Map Ref. C5)*

To railway enthusiasts, the names of Bromsgrove and Blackwell are synonomous with the legendary Lickey Incline. Today dieselisation has robbed the Lickey of its appeal, and Blackwell Station is no more, but both live on in our memories. Blackwell is situated on the Birmingham & Gloucester line of the Midland Railway, an outline history appearing under Barnt Green. The B&GR was authorised in 1836, opened from the south to Bromsgrove in June 1840, and up the Lickey to Cofton Farm, near Barnt Green, on 17th September 1840. Blackwell was the first station north of Bromsgrove, and marked the end of a killing 1 in 37 gradient, although the line continues to climb, much more gently for a short distance beyond Blackwell. The incline presented a formidable challenge to enginemen throughout steam days. Banking engines varied from the puny machines of early times, through the familiar 'Jinties', to the massive Midland 0-10-0, No. 2290, the LNER Garratt, and BR 9F No. 92079. At Blackwell, it was a common sight to see strings of bankers, having dropped off their trains, waiting in the centre engine siding for a path down to Bromsgrove. Engines frequently returned in multiples of 2, 3 or 4, or even 6!

To the working patterns of a minor wayside station were added the complexities of bank engine working, with the extensive engine handling facilities. Another peculiarity of the signalling system was Linthurst IB. The IB home, 22, shows a red aspect when lever 22 is normal. When pulled, the two yellow aspects are given, as the signal also serves as a splitting distant for Barnt Green Main Line Junction SB. When a train is signalled through by Barnt Green to the main or slow lines, north of the station, the appropriate green will clear, the other aspect remaining at yellow.

Left: No. 73031 approaches Blackwell with a 'down' local from Birmingham in 1963. The unequal length of the platforms, with the 'down' side being almost twice the length of the 'up', is apparent from the scale plan and this illustration.

BLACKWELL

The Lickey Incline is seen as a handicap to northbound trains, but southbound or 'down' trains were also affected. 'Down' freights used to come to a stand at the head of the incline for the crew to test brakes, and for the guard or incline brakesman to pin down a sufficient number of brakes on unfitted trains. With piped or fitted freights, comprehensive instructions were laid down, detailing the proportion of vehicles requiring to be braked, and if there were too few braked vehicles, bank engines had to be attached in front of the train to provide additional brake power down the incline.

At the turn of the century, 10-12 stopping trains called in each direction, including some semi-fasts. By 1946, there were 9 southbound and 8 northbound workings. One reason for the decline may be that, until 1941, even passenger trains had to come to a stand for brake testing, and there was little benefit in avoiding a booked station stop. The rule provided 'The driver of every 'down' passenger train, not booked to stop at Blackwell for traffic purposes, must bring his train to a stand at Blackwell 'down' main line home signal, and must not proceed until he has received permission from the brakesman, or the guard of the train when a brakesman is not on duty, to descend the incline'. Banking, and incline working generally, add much interest to railway operation, and are seldom portrayed by the modeller, which is a great pity.

BRACKLEY

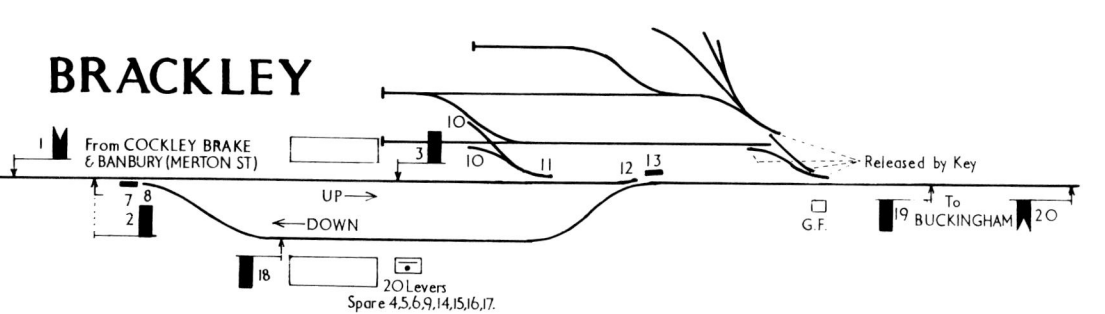

(Buildings shown thus on original plan!)

From BANBURY · MB · UP→ · ←DOWN · Horse Landing · Scotch · To Works · W.S.

Scale of Feet: 40 0 40 80 120 160 200

To BLETCHLEY

BRACKLEY *(Map Ref. G3)*

Located on the Northamptonshire/Oxfordshire/Buckinghamshire borders is Brackley, an attractive rural community with a population of 2,300, and at a distance of 7½ miles from Buckingham and 10 miles from Banbury. The headwaters of the Ouse, which empties into the Wash, arise near the town. It was situated on two different lines, now both closed. The earliest, the LNWR's Banbury to Verney Junction branch, opened on 1st May 1850. The second was the much lamented London Extension of the GCR, of 1899. The LNWR branch was created under the auspices of the Buckinghamshire Railway, a London & Birmingham/LNWR satellite, which arose out of L&BR plans of 1846, for lines from Bletchley to Oxford, and Tring to Banbury. These would protect the flanks of the L&BR, and pose a threat to the Great Western. The Oxford & Bletchley Junction was authorised, as was a line from Brackley to a point on the Oxford line, later to become Verney Junction. In 1847, the two concerns were amalgamated as the Buckinghamshire Railway and powers were secured to carry the Brackley line on to Banbury. Construction pressed ahead during 1847/8. The weather was exceptionally bad, and a local poet recorded of one bridge, 'But owing to the wet, the crowns fell in'. As these words are being written during the exceptionally wet summer of 1985, one can appreciate the feelings of those involved all the more! The Buckinghamshire Railway was little more than an appendage of the LNWR, and was leased in 1851, and absorbed in 1878.

BRACKLEY

From COCKLEY BRAKE & BANBURY (MERTON ST) · UP→ · ←DOWN · Released by Key · G.F. · To BUCKINGHAM · 20 Levers · Spare 4,5,6,9,14,15,16,17.

Above: The introduction of full signalling, with LNWR standard equipment, led to the 'down' loop being cut back in 1883 to finish just north of the platforms, to bring the loop points within working distance of the box. Thereafter, except for removal of the square crossing through the running lines, Brackley was to alter little until BR days as per the signalling plan. Points 11 and 12 are, in fact, very close, but as point 11 is on the 'up' line (just) and is trailed, it does not require a facing point lock, in contrast to point 12, which is on the single track section. The signal diagram exaggerates the separation for clarity. Where both points are traversed by passenger trains as facing points, both would be locked; sometimes by one lever and sometimes by two.

Below: The 'up' platform and remains of the wagon turntable visible on the 19th century scale plan. The wagon turntable gave access to the goods shed on the right-hand side of the line, cutting through the road serving the cattle landing (right).

Below: The 'down' platform, shelter, and 1880s LNWR box, looking towards Bletchley.

Left: A view, looking north towards Banbury, with a permanent way trolley in the right foreground. The 'down' shelter with its three arches, heavy hipped roof and indeterminate architectural style, between Classical and Regency, is a curiosity, and in marked contrast to the main building on the 'up' platform, which was to the standard 'Bucks' style. The horse-landing is visible on the extreme right. The goods yard, at the south end of the station closed on 2nd December 1963, but enjoyed a further lease of life as a scrap yard, wherein many rail vehicles perished. The original horse-landing, replaced by that shown above, was on the 'down' loop beyond the signal box, a most peculiar location. If reproduced on a model, it would be ridiculed as unprototypical! The archaic 32in. platforms are a reminder of the antiquity of this delightful station. After closure, the site was razed, and the road bridge, carrying the Northampton to Oxford road, demolished, the road slashing straight across the one-time trackbed.

BRACKLEY

Right: The 'up' buildings, looking towards Banbury. Although to typical 'Bucks' style, with an open circulating area/booking hall, individuality was given to each station by use of local stone, the Brackley buildings being to a creamy-grey stone, even differing from that used in much of the town! In 1895, five passenger trains called in each direction, one continuing on to Banbury on Thursdays only. The 1915 service was similar, and even in 1938, other than for certain short workings, there had been little change. The station, on the Buckingham to Banbury section of the Buckinghamshire Railway, witnessed an attempt by BR to reprieve the line from 1956 by use of two single unit diesel railcars, but losses continued, despite a marked increase in traffic, and the last trains ran on 31st December 1960. Brackley Borough Council, not wishing to see rail services end, sought, unsuccessfully, to lease or buy the line from Brackley to Buckingham. A municipal railway would have been rather nice!

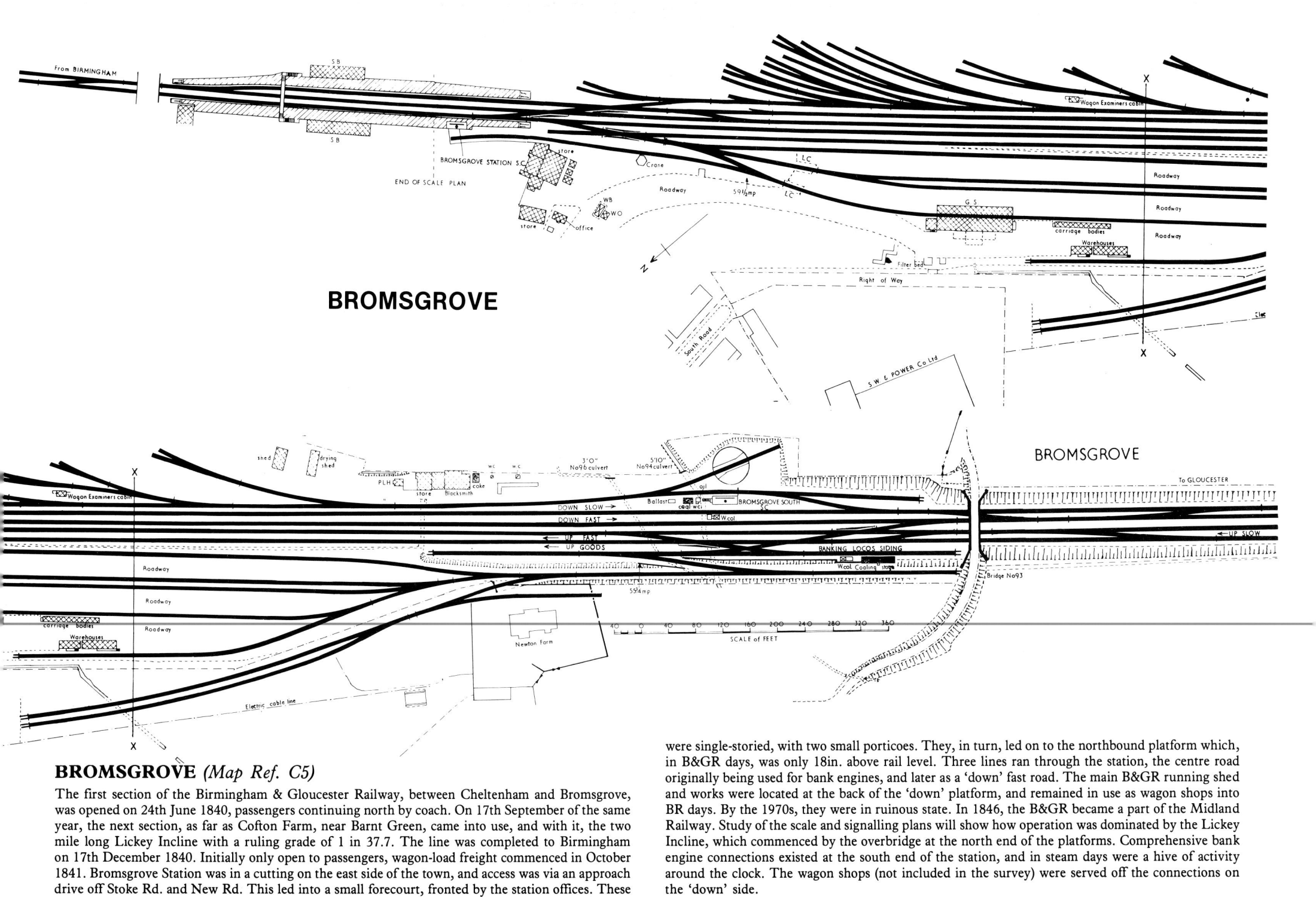

BROMSGROVE

From BIRMINGHAM

S B

S B

BROMSGROVE STATION S.C

END OF SCALE PLAN

store

store

office

WB
WO

Crane

Roadway

59½mp

LC

LC

Wagon Examiners cabin

Roadway

G.S

carriage bodies

Roadway

Warehouses

Roadway

Filter bed

Right of Way

South Road

S.W & POWER Co Ltd

Elec

BROMSGROVE

shed

drying shed

PLH
T.C

store
Blacksmith

coke

w c

w c

3'O"
No 96 culvert

5'10"
No 94 culvert

Ballast
coal wc i

oil

Wagon Examiners cabin

DOWN SLOW →

DOWN FAST →

BROMSGROVE SOUTH
S.C

To GLOUCESTER

← UP FAST

← UP SLOW

← UP GOODS

BANKING LOCOS SIDING

Wcol Coaling stage

Roadway

59 4 mp

Wcol

Bridge No 93

Roadway

40 0   40   80   120 160 200 240 280 320 360

carriage bodies

Warehouses

Roadway

Newton Farm

SCALE of FEET

Electric cable line

X

X

X

X

BROMSGROVE *(Map Ref. C5)*

The first section of the Birmingham & Gloucester Railway, between Cheltenham and Bromsgrove, was opened on 24th June 1840, passengers continuing north by coach. On 17th September of the same year, the next section, as far as Cofton Farm, near Barnt Green, came into use, and with it, the two mile long Lickey Incline with a ruling grade of 1 in 37.7. The line was completed to Birmingham on 17th December 1840. Initially only open to passengers, wagon-load freight commenced in October 1841. Bromsgrove Station was in a cutting on the east side of the town, and access was via an approach drive off Stoke Rd. and New Rd. This led into a small forecourt, fronted by the station offices. These were single-storied, with two small porticoes. They, in turn, led on to the northbound platform which, in B&GR days, was only 18in. above rail level. Three lines ran through the station, the centre road originally being used for bank engines, and later as a 'down' fast road. The main B&GR running shed and works were located at the back of the 'down' platform, and remained in use as wagon shops into BR days. By the 1970s, they were in ruinous state. In 1846, the B&GR became a part of the Midland Railway. Study of the scale and signalling plans will show how operation was dominated by the Lickey Incline, which commenced by the overbridge at the north end of the platforms. Comprehensive bank engine connections existed at the south end of the station, and in steam days were a hive of activity around the clock. The wagon shops (not included in the survey) were served off the connections on the 'down' side.

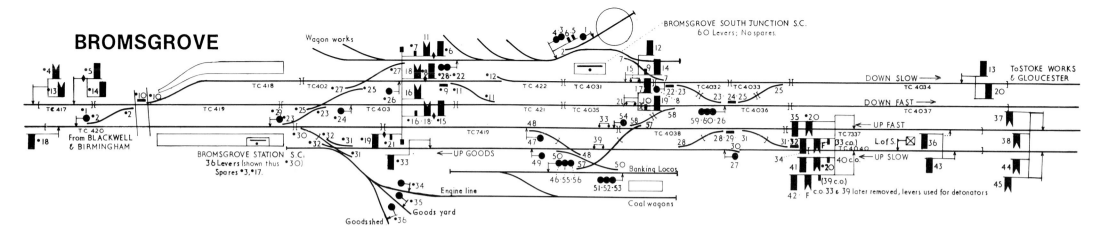

BROMSGROVE

Wagon works

BROMSGROVE SOUTH JUNCTION S.C.
60 Levers; No spares.

BROMSGROVE STATION S.C.
36 Levers (shown thus •30)
Spares •3, •17.

To STOKE WORKS & GLOUCESTER

DOWN SLOW →

DOWN FAST →

From BLACKWELL & BIRMINGHAM

← UP GOODS

← UP FAST

← UP SLOW

L. of S.

Banking Locos

Coal wagons

Engine line

Goods yard

Goods shed

c.o. 33 & 39 later removed, levers used for detonators

Below: Bromsgrove Station, looking north, in July 1963, with the foot of the Lickey Incline visible in the right distance. The signal box was located on the platform, set forward from the building line of the station offices to provide visibility along the 'up' platform. Had the box been of normal height, visibility in the 'up' direction would have been severely curtailed by the road bridge but, with such a low box, a train in the platform obstructed a view of the 'down' side of the station; a typical example of the problems and compromises in signal box siting. Although not immediately obvious, Bromsgrove's passenger station is on an ascending gradient of 1 in 300, whilst the yard and bank sidings are mostly on a 1 in 100 ascent, so that engines have had to work before they faced the really gruelling part of the climb. As the gradient was at its most benevolent in the platform, in the early days it was the practice for trains to stop in the platform for bank engines to be attached. In LMS days, no train was permitted to tackle the Lickey Incline without a bank engine, other than freight trains equal to not more than eight wagons, and passenger trains equal to not more than six vehicles.

Below: One of the problems of the Lickey, compared to many inclines, was that the ascent ran northwards, with all the woes that entailed for photographers. Indeed one photographer suggested the incline ought to have run the other way, although this might have caused geographical problems! This scene at Bromsgrove, looking south, recalls the photographers' problems. The promise of future excitement was in that direction, and here we can see a freight engine brewing up near the gantry, prior to tackling the climb, whilst more smoke hangs over the turntable and bank engine sidings. It is well worth sparing a few moments to identify the signals on the gantry from the signal plan. The low arm to the right of the gantry is in fact not a part of that structure at all, but signal 33 ex the 'up' goods. After the end of steam, Bromsgrove suffered from severe 'rationalisation', in which the 'down' platform was closed, and a facing lead installed on the bank, to allow one of the infrequent 'down' stopping trains to cross to the 'up' line, so as to use the 'up' platform. After its station stop, the train would run 'wrong road' for a short distance to another crossover. General freight facilities were withdrawn on 5th June 1967.

As was illustrated on the previous page, goods trains customarily paused on the 'up' goods loop, to prepare for the ascent of the Lickey Incline, and to pick up banker(s). In the case of passenger trains booked to stop for traffic purposes, bankers were added during the station stop. Prior to 1914, even expresses had to come to a stand in the platform if requiring a banker. Apart from the operating inconvenience of unadvertised station stops, there was the added drawback of a standing start on to the 1 in 37 gradient and, in 1914, the connections at the South box were modified to allow bank engines to attach to passenger trains stopped outside the station. This permitted a run on the 1/100 and 1/300 sections before coming to the Lickey Incline proper, as well as avoiding the unwanted station stop. An indicator, illuminated at night, was provided at which enginemen would stop, to enable the banker to run forward off the bank road and on to the train. LMS instructions noted that if the train exceeded twelve bogie vehicles, enginemen should use their descretion to draw past the board. In pre-grouping days, quadruple track ran from the station box to the south box, but this was extended as far as Stoke Works by the LMS.

Above: A view looking from the station approach, across the forecourt to the 'up' building, with its twin porticoes. The Station signal box is visible on the extreme right-hand side, and the driveway provides access to a carriage landing. Bromsgrove was graded a 'first class station' when the B&GR was opened, and the buildings housed the Secretary and Resident Engineer as well as usual station facilities.

Right lower: Bromsgrove Wagon Works in July 1963, looking east. The Cowans, Sheldon traverser (of 1954) in the foreground, draws power from the electric overhead system, so is a form of electrified ultra-broad gauge! The works originated as the B&GR locomotive works and running shed, and the near structure shows evidence of many changes.

Passenger trains were required to take not less than five minutes to descend, and goods trains twelve minutes, giving speeds of 27 and 11m.p.h. respectively. 'Down' passenger trains not booked to call were restricted to 10m.p.h. through Bromsgrove, whether routed via the platform or through roads. 'Down' freights came to a stand between the Station and South boxes to unpin brakes, and detach any bankers added for braking control.

Below: The scene from the 'down' platform, at the commencement of the 1 in 37 bank, in September 1956. Any sizeable station required living quarters for senior staff, stationmaster, inspectors, etc., and frequently for more junior grades as well, so that a station often became a railway colony with its own social hierarchy. Residences for stationmasters (or above) as in this case, were frequently imposing.

BROMSGROVE

Above: A Hughes-Fowler 'Crab' No. 42790, gets under way with a northbound express in September 1956. Smoke from the banker(s) drifts across from the left-hand side of the view. Loaded platform trolleys give an air of bustle to the station.

Above: A pair of 'Jinties', Nos. 47305 and 47502, are hard at work as a northbound express clears the 'up' platform, in 1956. This view shows the end of the 'down' platform, which, most unusually, extends as far as the main line points, so that a train reaching to the end of the platform would in fact be fouling the 'down' through line as well as the platform line. Although there are only ten coaches, two bankers have been assigned to the train!

BROMSGROVE

Below: A trio of LMS 'Jinties' return from banking duties, and swing over on to the 'down' platform road in this pleasing 1950 scene. The nearest engine, No. 47276, bears a non-standard BR numbering and LMS lettering on the tanks. The second engine, No. 47301, carries the early 'lion and wheel' emblem, whilst the third engine is lettered 'BRITISH RAILWAYS'. The splitting 'down' home signal is visible through the bridge. This signal was modified on a number of occasions, both as a structure, and as to precedence of the through and platform arms.

Below: A Fowler 4F, No. 44213, makes a cautious entry into the 'down' platform road with a partially-fitted freight in 1956. On the right is the wagon works, the old B&GR running sheds, and workshops. After nationalisation, the Lickey Incline passed to the Western Region for a time, and whilst train engines tended to be LMS or BR Standards, a batch of 94XX pannier tanks was drafted in to replace the 'Jinties', adding an improbable 'Western' touch to a traditionally Midland outpost.

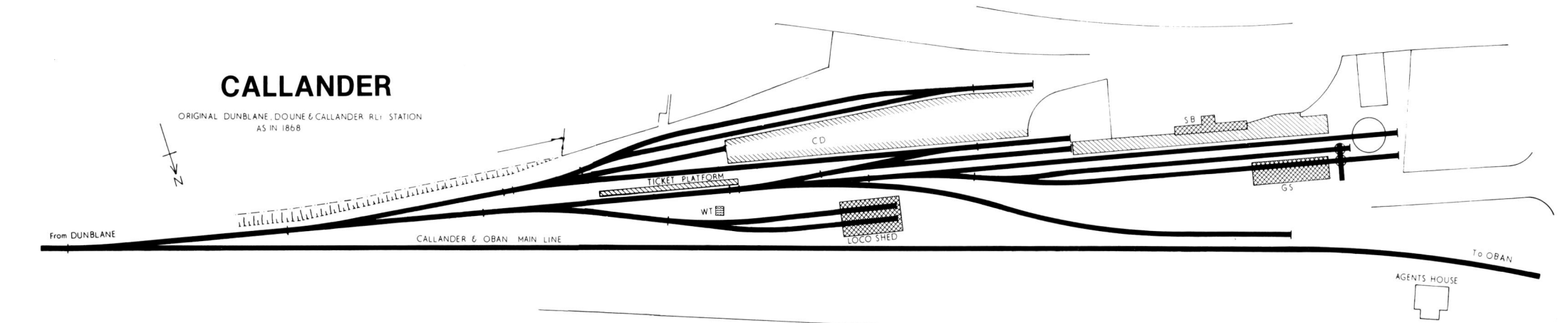

CALLANDER

ORIGINAL DUNBLANE, DOUNE & CALLANDER RLʸ STATION
AS IN 1868

From DUNBLANE

CALLANDER & OBAN MAIN LINE

TICKET PLATFORM

WT

LOCO SHED

CD

SB

GS

To OBAN

AGENTS HOUSE

N

Above: The original Dunblane, Doune & Callander Railway terminus of 1858, shortly after construction of the Oban extension began. Typical, but long-forgotten features include a narrow ticket platform, just short of the station proper. Wagon turntables by the goods shed permit loaded or empty wagons to be moved in or out of either end of the goods shed. With its short trains, diminutive locomotives and four-wheel carriages, the terminus would make a highly original model, whilst the contractor's line, worked no doubt by the contractor's own motive power, would add a most unusual feature.

CALLANDER *(Map Ref. Q16)*

For centuries before the railways came to Central Scotland, the low-lying valley of the Allan, slashing through the Ochil Hills to the east and the Perthshire Highlands to the west, provided a natural route for traders, ordinary travellers, and even armies of conquest. At the southern end of this natural corridor lies Stirling, its castle the backdrop to grim deeds in Scottish history. Forty five miles to the north-east, Perth stands sentinel over the Tay, as Stirling does to the Forth. The bleak uplands to the west were home to *Rob Roy*, and a host of other figures famed in fact or legend. When railways did come to Central Scotland, it was no surprise that the valley of the Allan would assume strategic importance, and the Scottish Central Railway secured this promising route in 1845, opening in 1848. Connections with the Caledonian, south of Stirling, and on to Aberdeen, assured success. The lowlands extended ten miles west of the SCR at Dunblane, to the village of Callander, described by one Victorian writer as 'interesting to the tourist as the first place going north at which he will hear Gaelic spoken'. It was a convenient starting point for touring country made famous by Sir Walter Scott in *Rob Roy, Lady of the Lake,* etc. A separate company, the Dunblane, Doune & Callander Railway, was authorised in 1846, but failed to raise sufficient funds, and a new act was secured on 21st July 1856, and the 10½ mile branch opened on 1st July 1858, with five trains in summer and two in winter. By an Act of 29th June 1865, the DD&CR was taken over by the SCR. Unusually for a branch, shareholders did quite well, receiving £75 of SCR stock, guaranteed by the Caledonian Railway, for every £100 DD&CR stock.

Left: A view looking east from the C&O towards Dunblane. The facing siding in the middle distance is a safety siding to stop 'up' trains running away.

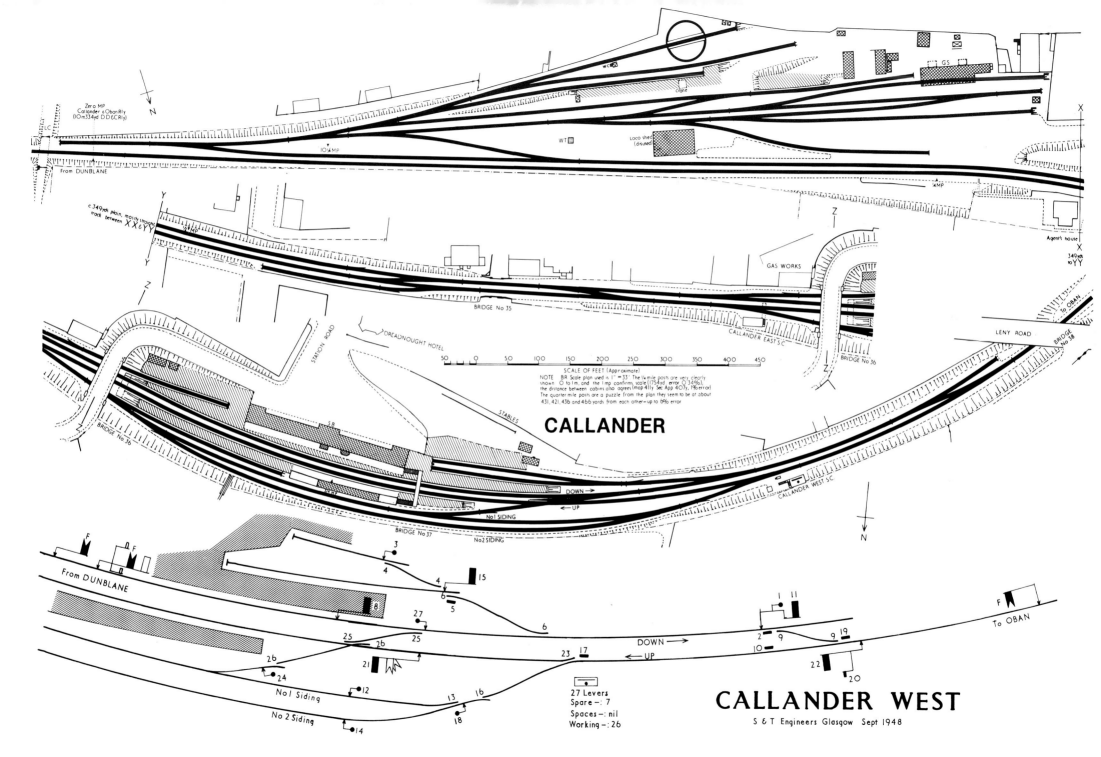

Zero MP
Callander & Oban Rly
(10m 334yd D.D &CRly)

LC

From DUNBLANE

10¼ MP

WT

Loco shed
(disused)

wc

crane

GS

X

¼ MP

X

N

c. 349 yrd plain, mostly straight
track between XX & YY

Y

¼ MP

Y

Z

Agent's house

349 yrd
to YY

X

GAS WORKS

Z

BRIDGE No 35

CALLANDER EAST S.C

To OBAN

Z

LENY ROAD

BRIDGE No 36

BRIDGE No 36

STATION ROAD

DREADNOUGHT HOTEL

SCALE OF FEET (Approximate)

50   0   50   100   150   200   250   300   350   400   450

NOTE   BR Scale plan used is 1" = 33'. The ¼ mile posts are very clearly
shown O to 1m, and the 1 mp confirm, scale (1754 yd, error O 34%),
the distance between cabins also agrees (map 4 lly Sec App 407y, 1% error).
The quarter mile posts are a puzzle from the plan they seem to be at about
431, 421, 436 and 466 yards from each other – up to 6% error

STABLES

CALLANDER

SB

BRIDGE No 38

DOWN →

← UP

CALLANDER WEST S.C

No1 SIDING

N

BRIDGE No 37

No2 SIDING

F

F

From DUNBLANE

3

4

4

15

6

5

8

27

6

F

1   11

To OBAN

25

26

25

2   9

9   19

DOWN →

10

26

23   17

← UP

22

24

21

20

12

13   16

27 Levers

Spare –: 7

Spaces –: nil

Working – 26

18

14

No1 Siding

No 2 Siding

CALLANDER WEST

S & T Engineers Glasgow Sept 1948

CALLANDER

Above: The main buildings were located on the 'down' platform, and were approached from a modest, but adequate, forecourt. Although timber was widely used in smaller structures, its use in a station of this size and quality is noteworthy. Although cheap, it did pose fire risks, and more than a few stations had to be hurriedly rebuilt. Beyond the station, the ground rose up steeply, offering an attractive wooded backdrop. Although photographed in the 1950s. the scene hardly differed from the station known to Victorian days, a part of the permanence of the railway scene which was to be ended so abruptly. Passenger services were seasonal, with seven through workings in summer and four in winter by the mid-1890s. The through services were augmented by trains terminating at Callander from Dunblane or Stirling. In the halcyon days before World War I, sleeping cars operated from Oban to London, day through stock operated and, as a finishing touch, a Pullman observation car, *Maid of Morven*, commenced running in August 1914, and reappeared for a time after the war. Out of season, the line took on a family nature, with regular travellers and staff known to one another. By 1938, four or five trains traversed the whole route each weekday, with a single Sunday working into Oban (Sunday services had commenced in the 1920s, but were not popular in this remote and traditional part of Scotland). Wednesday and Saturday trains complicated the picture east of Callander. This section was served by some nine to twelve trains each way. From 1894, the C&O made a right-angle junction at Crianlarich with the North British West Highland line. There was no exchange of traffic for the first three years over the curve, as the C&O viewed such ideas with little enthusiasm, as they would tend to abstract traffic from the eastern half of the C&O.

Seventy miles to the west, in far off Argyll, and separated from the peaceful lowlands of Callander by the bleak Perth and Argyll Highlands, lay Oban, fishing port and gateway to the Western Isles. Steamers plied up and down the west coast. Coaches clattered out of the town towards Loch Lomond and Fort William, but the mountains between Callander and Oban were devoids of visitors. With the promotion of fisheries, the highlands and tourism, objects dear to the Victorian heart, this could not be allowed. In 1864, local landowners joined forces to promote the Callander & Oban Railway, a name to become legendary in railway history. Alas, population was scant, no more than 4,000 over the whole route, and fund-raising was difficult. The local promoters realised that it was vital to tap one of the major Scottish companies, and approached all, seeking funds in return for a say in the line. The Caledonian was lukewarm, but the Scottish Central was interested, and outbid the opposition, offering £200,000, in return for 5 seats on a 9-man Board, if the promoters raised £400,000. The Callander & Oban Act was passed in July 1865. The 1860s had, however, been a period of amalgamation for the Scottish railways, with many well-established names passing into the 'Caley' or North British nets, and in the same session, the takeover of the SCR by the Caledonian was approved, coming into effect on 1st August 1865. Safeguards precluded outright abandonment of the C&O, but the 'Caley' was lukewarm in contrast to the enthusiasm of the SCR. Indeed 'Caley' men hoped that the local promoters would not be able to raise their £400,000. It was decided to proceed by sections, with the contract for the first 17½ miles, from Callander to Killin, being let in 1866. This section was opened on 1st June 1870, the C&O diverging from the DD&CR just short of the old terminus, which became a goods depot. Construction of the seventeen miles from Killin to Tyndrum began in October 1871, with the line opening on 1st August 1873. By this time, Caledonian interests had secured an Abandonment Act for the remainder of the line to Oban, and a fresh Act was required in 1874, with the Tyndrum to Dalmally section opening on 1st May 1877, and to Oban on 30th June 1880. The C&O, although worked by the Caledonian, as heirs to the SCR, from the outset, retained nominal independence, with an Oban office from 1880 until the Grouping. This office was closed by the LMS in 1924, a move which prompted forebodings as to the effect of control from afar.

By the 1960s, losses on the Scottish Regions of British Railways were steadily mounting, and retrenchment was in the air. At one time, both the Callander & Oban and the West Highland appeared to be under threat, but it was decided to retain the ex-NBR line in toto, and to keep the C&O west of Crianlarich, Oban trains leaving Glasgow via the NB route, and diverting on to the C&O via the little-used curve of the 1890s. Closure notices for the eastern section of the C&O, between Crianlarich and Callander, and also for the Callander to Dunblane section, appeared during 1965, the closure date being 1st November 1965. In the event, fate was to play a hand, and a landslip blocked the line in Glen Ogle, between Callander and Killin, on 27th September 1965. With threat of substantial further slippage, the Callander to Crianlarich section was closed, and a diesel multiple unit service was instituted between Glasgow and Callander until the scheduled closure date.

CALLANDER

Left: A view from bridge No. 36, looking towards Oban, showing the short 'up' bay with a three-coach corridor set, the sharp curve, and rising ground on the north side of the line. The slopes of Ben Ledi, 2,873ft., are largely obscured by the distant mist of a 'soft' Highland day.

Below: From the 'down' platform looking towards Dunblane, the detail enthusiast may care to dwell upon the antique luggage barrow beneath the footbridge stairs on the 'up' side, and the gangway end door against the footbridge.

Operationally, the station is of considerable interest. Initially, a junction between the DD&CR and the C&O was made a short distance east of the original terminus of 1858, which became a goods depot when the line was opened throughout. Double-track working existed through the station, and in 1903, the section from the C&O junction to the station was doubled, and worked from a small box, named C&O Junction. Latterly C&O Junction was taken out of use, and access to the yard was gained via the former 'down' line, which became a very long headshunt from the East box. The line each side of Callander was single, and worked by the electric token system, St. Bride's Crossing being the block post to the west, and Drumvaich to the east. In both cases, round brass tokens were in use. St. Bride's could be switched out, and long section working to Strathyre implemented, square aluminium tokens being utilised for the Strathyre to Callander West section. Propelling of freight trains between C&O Junction and Cambusmore Siding (between Callander and Drumvaich) was authorised, an interesting working not often reproduced in model form. Trains would be running slowly at Callander Station, but at C&O Junction, a Manson tablet 'snatcher' was installed to collect the token from 'down' trains. Train loads were limited to 14 six-wheelers, or 10 bogie vehicles, between Oban and Dunblane and, owing to restricted clearances, twelve-wheeled bogie stock, other than regularly-rostered equipment, was not permitted west of Callander. Study of the scale plan will reveal the Dreadnought Hotel by the C&O station. This was one of two principal hotels in the village, and gave its name to the station, both in 'Caley' official books and the 'Junction' books produced by Airey for the Railway Clearing House!

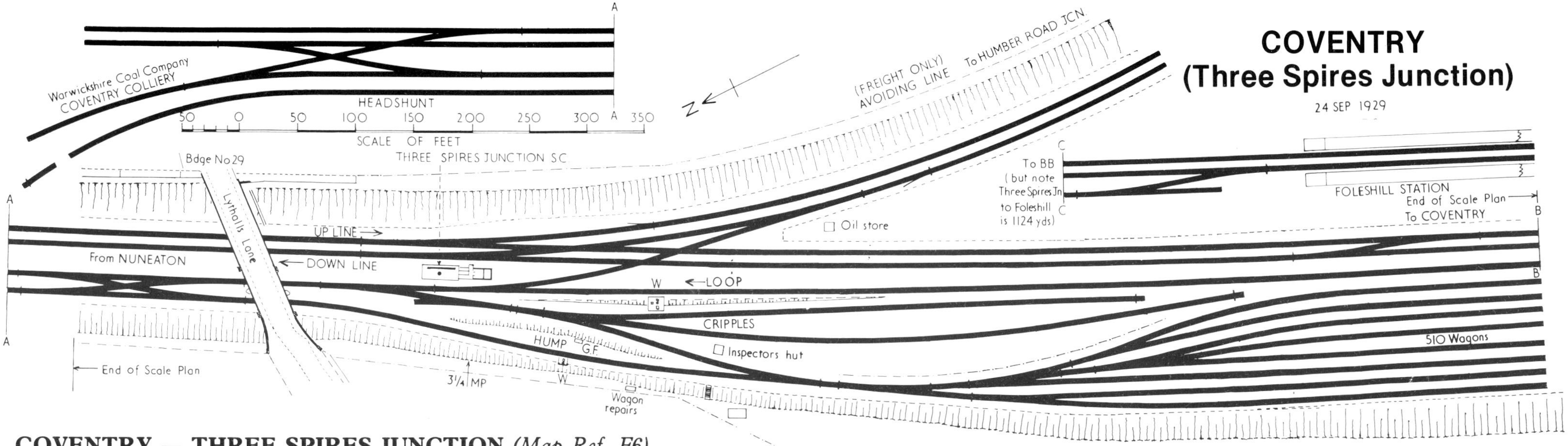

Diagram labels:

Warwickshire Coal Company
COVENTRY COLLIERY

HEADSHUNT

SCALE OF FEET
THREE SPIRES JUNCTION S.C.

Bdge No 29

(FREIGHT ONLY)
AVOIDING LINE   To HUMBER ROAD JCN

Lythalls Lane

UP LINE →

From NUNEATON

← DOWN LINE

Oil store

To BB
(but note
Three Spires Jn
to Foleshill
is 1124 yds)

FOLESHILL STATION
End of Scale Plan
To COVENTRY

W ← LOOP

CRIPPLES

Inspectors hut

End of Scale Plan

510 Wagons

HUMP GF

3¼ MP

W

Wagon
repairs

COVENTRY — THREE SPIRES JUNCTION *(Map Ref. F6)*

Three Spires Junction was located on the Coventry to Nuneaton branch of the LNWR within the northern outskirts of Coventry, and took its name from the 'Three Spires' for which the city was famed. The Coventry & Nuneaton branch was authorised on 3rd August 1846, and opened on 2nd September 1850. By the turn of the century, considerable industrialisation had taken place around Coventry, and this, coupled with the need for a freight avoiding line, prompted the LNWR to secure powers for a 3½ mile loop line, to run from Three Spires Junction, just north of Foleshill Station on the Coventry & Nuneaton line, to Pinley Junction (later renamed Humber Road Junction) on the London & Birmingham line, both junctions facing away from Coventry. Pinley Junction opened for construction traffic in May 1913, and Three Spires box opened on 28th June 1914, although the loop line did not come into use until 10th August 1914. Public goods depots existed at Bell Green and Gosford Green, and private sidings elsewhere. The line was not completed to passenger standards, and was indeed worked on the 'no block or bell' system, traffic primarily being to/from factories along the loop line or the C&N. At the north end of Three Spires Junction, through sidings curved off to the west to the Warwickshire Coal Com-

pany's Coventry Colliery. A hump shunting yard, with a capacity for 510 wagons, existed on the 'down' side, the hump being a few yards from the signal box. On 10th November 1963, the loop line was severed at Humber Road Junction, prior to the commissioning of Coventry power box, and the line was worked as a dead-end freight branch from the north. Passenger services ceased on the C&N on 18th January 1965, and public freight facilities ceased at Bell Green in July 1965. Suggestions were advanced that the formation of the loop line would make a splendid urban motorway. In 1970, Gosford Green, at the south end of the loop, found a new lease of life as a rail depot for motor trade car distribution to and from Scotland. Bell Green was later reopened, and by the mid 1970s one functioned for British Leyland, and the other for Chrysler. Meanwhile, the Foleshill Railway, owned by Courtaulds, and feeding into the loop, was ailing and closed in 1972 and, within a decade, the motor vehicle, having saved the loop, was to doom it, with urban roadway proposals to the fore. For many months after traffic ceased, the metals lay silent and rusty.

Above: Three Spires, looking north, with the Coventry Colliery curve to the left. Bedlam Crossing is visible in the distance on the Nuneaton line. Signals 16, 22/23, 25/24/7 visible.

Above: Three Spires, looking north, from the divergence of the loop line, with the lines from Coventry in the left foreground and the loop in the right foreground.

COVENTRY (Three Spires Junction)

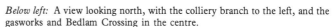

Above left: Coventry Colliery Sidings, with the exit sidings on the left, and inwards lines on the right. Extensive freight traffic made Three Spires a busy box in its heyday, as indeed was the C&N and the loop.

Above right: A study of the departure signal, 22, ex the 'down' loop, with the miniature fixed distant arm (for Bedlam Crossing) and dwarf signal, 23, into the Colliery. Running signals ex-freight lines are frequently smaller than those ex-passenger lines, but rarely boast a distant arm as well, making the small distant a rarity.

Below left: A view looking north, with the colliery branch to the left, and the gasworks and Bedlam Crossing in the centre.

Below right: Bedlam Gates and Crossing frame. The triple home signal is slotted by Bedlam and Three Spires, reading right to left, to the loop, Coventry and the yard.

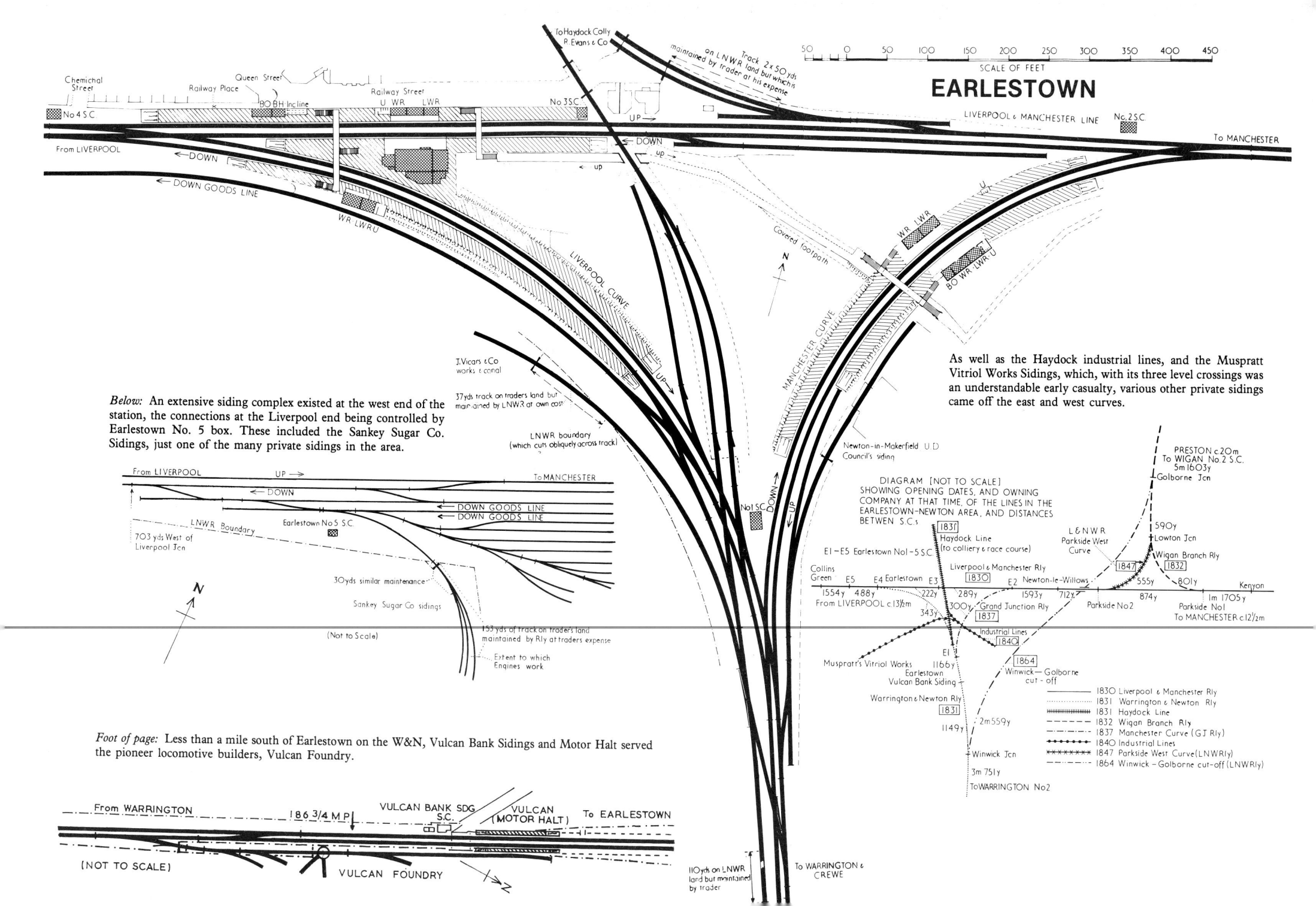

EARLESTOWN

Chemichal Street

Railway Place

Queen Street

Railway Street

No 4 S.C.

BO BH Incline

U WR LWR

No 3 S.C.

No. 2 S.C.

LIVERPOOL & MANCHESTER LINE

To Haydock Colly R. Evans & Co

Track 2 x 50 yds on LNWR land but which is maintained by trader at his expense

SCALE OF FEET

50   0   50   100   150   200   250   300   350   400   450

From LIVERPOOL

DOWN

UP

DOWN

To MANCHESTER

DOWN GOODS LINE

up

WR. LWR U

LIVERPOOL CURVE

UP

up

Covered footpath

N

W.R. LWR

BO WR. LWR. U

MANCHESTER CURVE

J. Vicars & Co works & canal

37 yds track on traders land but maintained by LNWR at own cost

LNWR boundary (which cuts obliquely across track)

No1 S.C.

DOWN UP

Newton-in-Makerfield U.D Council's siding

As well as the Haydock industrial lines, and the Muspratt Vitriol Works Sidings, which, with its three level crossings was an understandable early casualty, various other private sidings came off the east and west curves.

Below: An extensive siding complex existed at the west end of the station, the connections at the Liverpool end being controlled by Earlestown No. 5 box. These included the Sankey Sugar Co. Sidings, just one of the many private sidings in the area.

From LIVERPOOL   UP →

DOWN

DOWN GOODS LINE

DOWN GOODS LINE

To MANCHESTER

LNWR Boundary

Earlestown No 5 S.C.

703 yds West of Liverpool Jcn

30 yds similar maintenance

Sankey Sugar Co sidings

153 yds of track on traders land maintained by Rly at traders expense

Extent to which Engines work

N

(Not to Scale)

DIAGRAM [NOT TO SCALE] SHOWING OPENING DATES, AND OWNING COMPANY AT THAT TIME, OF THE LINES IN THE EARLESTOWN–NEWTON AREA, AND DISTANCES BETWEN S.C.s

E1–E5 Earlestown No1–5 S.C.

PRESTON c.20m
To WIGAN No.2 S.C.
5m 1603y
Golborne Jcn

590y
Lowton Jcn

L & N W R Parkside West Curve

Wigan Branch Rly

|1831|

|1847|

|1832|

Haydock Line (to colliery & race course)

Collins Green

E5

E4 Earlestown

E3

Liverpool & Manchester Rly

|1830|

E2 Newton-le-Willows

555y

80 1y

Kenyon

1554y   488y   222y   289y   1593y   712y   874y   1m 1705y

From LIVERPOOL c.13½m

343y   300y   Grand Junction Rly

|1837|

Parkside No2

Parkside No1

To MANCHESTER c.12½m

Industrial Lines

|1840|

E1

|1864|

Winwick – Golborne cut-off

Muspratt's Vitriol Works

1166y   Earlestown Vulcan Bank Siding

Warrington & Newton Rly

|1831|

1149y

2m 559y

Winwick Jcn

3m 751y

To WARRINGTON No2

1830 Liverpool & Manchester Rly
1831 Warrington & Newton Rly
1831 Haydock Line
1832 Wigan Branch Rly
1837 Manchester Curve (GJ Rly)
1840 Industrial Lines
1847 Parkside West Curve (LNWRly)
1864 Winwick – Golborne cut-off (LNWRly)

Foot of page: Less than a mile south of Earlestown on the W&N, Vulcan Bank Sidings and Motor Halt served the pioneer locomotive builders, Vulcan Foundry.

From WARRINGTON

186 3/4 M P

VULCAN BANK SDG. S.C.

VULCAN (MOTOR HALT)

To EARLESTOWN

[NOT TO SCALE]

VULCAN FOUNDRY

N

110 yds on LNWR land but maintained by trader

To WARRINGTON & CREWE

EARLESTOWN *(Map Ref. O1)*

Earlestown Station is located on the Liverpool & Manchester Railway, about 15 miles east of Liverpool (Edge Hill), and became the junction of the L&MR and the Grand Junction Railway, although its duration as a part of the West Coast Main Line was brief, due to completion of a cut-off. The Liverpool & Manchester Railway opened on 15th September 1830, and Parkside, the site of the tragic accident to William Huskisson, lies a short distance to the east of Earlestown, then still known as Newton. Early wayside stopping places on the L&MR were extremely basic, and it was the coming of the Warrington & Newton Railway, in 1831, which bestowed importance upon Newton Junction. In the scale plan and map, a connection from Haydock Colliery joins the L&MR from the north, the first part of the colliery connections opening in May 1831. The W&N, which had been authorised in 1829, was opened to an end-junction with the Haydock line in June 1831, in time for the Haydock Park races. The industrial line crossed the L&MR on the level, a source of much anxiety and, in due course, several accidents. On 25th July, Newton West Curve was laid in, permitting through working from the W&N towards Liverpool. In 1830, powers were obtained for lines, roughly on the site of the 1864 cut-off, to join the L&MR, facing towards Manchester and the Wigan Branch Railway, but this fell through.

Earlestown No. 2 box on the L&MR, looking towards Manchester. An express swings on to the Manchester Curve 'up' platform line.

The Manchester Curve platforms, looking towards Warrington. A BR Standard locomotive is entering the station with a local train. Note the check rail on this very tight curve.

Meanwhile, the London & Birmingham and Grand Junction Railways had been seeking Parliamentary sanction, and these two companies would link London with Warrington, and via the W&N, provide connection to the L&MR. In 1835, the GJR took over the W&N. The GJR opened as a through route in 1837, a south to east chord, the Manchester Curve, being opened at Newton on 4th July. Trains combined and split at Newton Junction, and the station soon achieved critical importance to the smooth working of the L&MR and GJR. With freight trains appearing off the Haydock branch, and other movements to a vitriol works, accidents and near misses were common. By the 1840s, the station building, in the divergence of the L&MR and Liverpool Curve, was surrounded by a complex, if primitive, signalling system of lights, chequer boards and arrows. The signals today are MAS colour light, but happily much of the original structure survives. The Wigan Branch Railway, with a junction facing only towards Manchester, had been opened in 1832, and provided the stepping stone to Preston and Carlisle. The creation of the LNWR in 1846 brought all these lines under common control, and a west curve was laid in at Parkside, in 1847, permitting through working of

The booking hall and inclined entrance from Queen St. to the 'up' L&MR platform, looking towards Liverpool.

A view from the 'up' platform, looking towards Liverpool, showing the venerable 'down' side buildings with their short canopy. On the extreme left, a fence separates the platform from the footpath to the Manchester Curve platforms. This once ran in a covered way, and burrowed beneath the Haydock branch, but now follows a surface route, and is open to the elements.

The scene from the footbridge, looking towards Manchester. A 'bus stop' structure graces the 'up' platform. The Haydock line crossed almost at right-angles beyond the platforms, and in the tiny triangle between the square crossing and the curve on to the L&MR, three railway houses once nestled — the closest one was likely to get to the 1950s' tune 'The Railroad runs through the middle of the House'!

EARLESTOWN

The Manchester curve, looking north. Electrification masts have banished steam. Platform 4 is seen on the left, platform 5 on the right (formerly Nos. 5 & 6).

Above left: From the 'up' L&MR platform, this view shows the 'up' booking office, main buildings and the remains of the Liverpool Curve.

Above: A study of the footbridge and station buildings.

Below: A detail portrait of the 'down' L&MR buildings and their quaint canopy; an attractive challenge for the modeller.

EARLESTOWN

Anglo-Scottish services. The funnelling of the West Coast traffic on to a 1½ mile section of the L&MR inevitably created congestion, and in 1864, a direct chord was made, from the old W&N south of Newton, to the Wigan line north of Parkside. Other than for diversion working, the Manchester Curve declined in significance, as most LNWR expresses were routed via the Manchester & Birmingham Railway, or 'Knotty', and Anglo-Scottish services over the Winwick cut-off.

In July 1852, Newton Junction was renamed Warrington Junction. In 1853, the LNWR began construction of a new wagon works, under the eye of veteran LNWR Director, Sir Hardman Earle, an early opponent, and then Director of the L&MR. The works and associated housing was named Earlestown, an honour more common in the USA than in the UK. Warrington Junction was renamed Earlestown Junction in November 1861, the 'Junction' suffix being dropped 99 years later.

Today, the Haydock lines are but a memory, as is the square crossing at which L&MR expresses were wont to ram coal trains which had imprudently strayed into their path. The L&MR still carries a passenger service, and this part of the station is little altered. The Manchester Curve platforms are also in use, and indeed electrified as a diversion route for the West Coast Main Line and for local services, but the buildings have been swept away. The Liverpool Curve lost its passenger service on 6th July 1964, and is now singled and for freight only.

EAST LANGTON

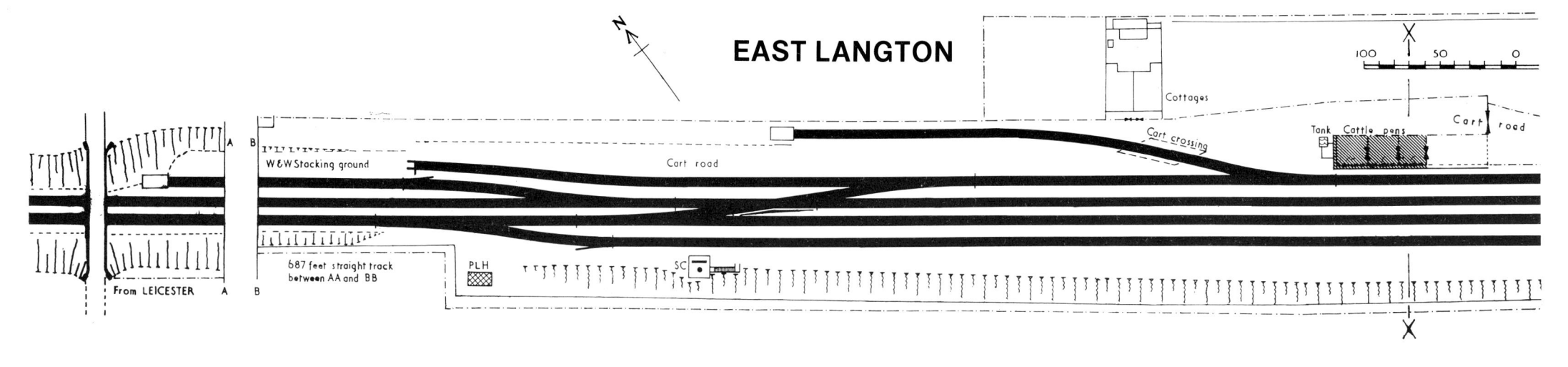

N

100 50 0

Cottages

Cart road

Tank Cattle pens

Cart crossing

W & W Stacking ground

Cart road

From LEICESTER   A   B

687 feet straight track
between AA and BB

PLH   SC

Above & Below: The survey of East Langton Station portrays an almost classical example of the wayside station. The line is carried by a small overbridge over a road, the station approach coming off that road. The principal station offices are concentrated on one side of the line, with a rudimentary shelter on the other platform. Access between platforms is by barrow-way at the northern end of the station. Had the station been built in later years, or substantially rebuilt, Board of Trade requirements would have compelled the MR to provide an overbridge, and the survival of barrow-way access on a fast and busy main line is thus interesting. Freight facilities are concentrated at the northern end of the station, the box being positioned adjacent to the majority of those connections. Refuge sidings, holding 33 and 40-wagon freights respectively, are provided on the 'up' and 'down' sides. Rather short for latter-day operations, this was a typical load for an 0-6-0 in Victorian times. Details worthy of note include the stationmaster's house, fronting on to the road, with steps down to the station forecourt, and the manner in which the 'down' refuge siding diverges away from the running line to clear the platform, providing accommodation for an extra two or three wagons.

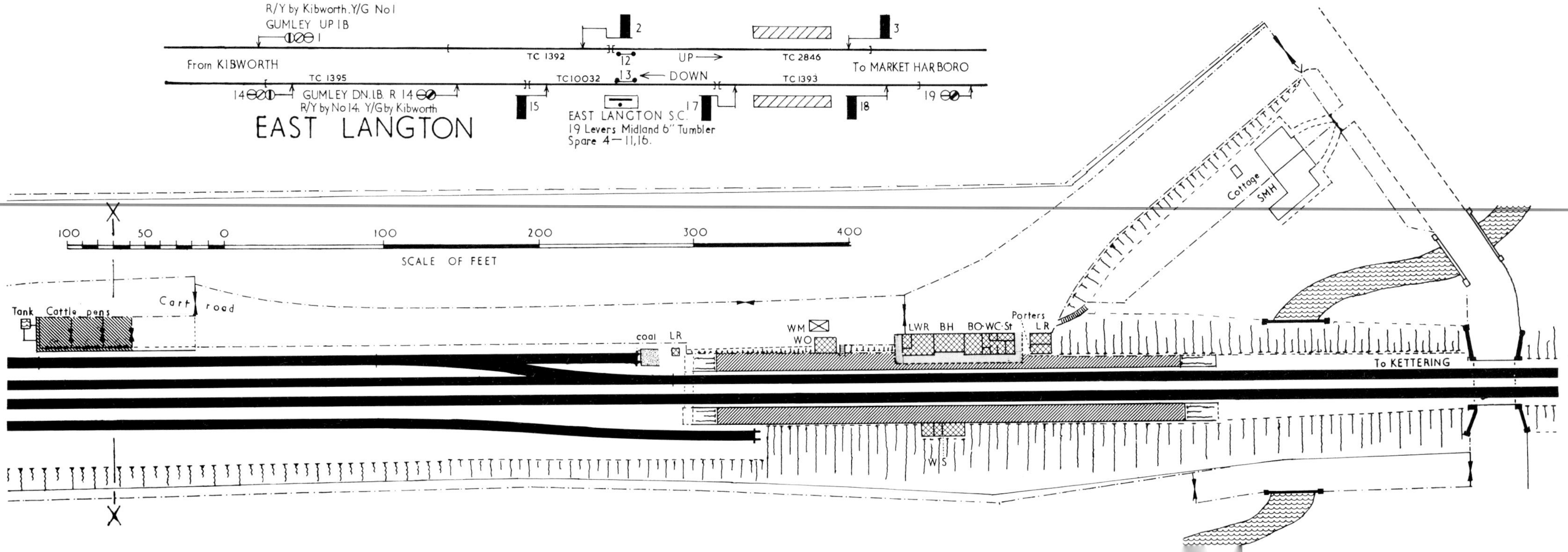

R/Y by Kibworth.Y/G No1
GUMLEY UP 1B   2   3

From KIBWORTH   TC 1392   12   UP →   TC 2846
                                         13 ← DOWN
                      TC 1395   TC10032   TC 1393   To MARKET HARBORO
14 GUMLEY DN.1B. R 14   19
R/Y by No14. Y/G by Kibworth   15   17   18

EAST LANGTON
                                    EAST LANGTON S.C.
                                    19 Levers Midland 6" Tumbler
                                    Spare 4—11,16.

100 50 0   100   200   300   400

SCALE OF FEET

Cottage   SMH

Tank Cattle pens   Cart road

coal LR   WM   WO   LWR BH BO-WC-St   Porters LR   To KETTERING

WS

EAST LANGTON *(Map Ref. H7)*

East Langton Station was on the MR Leicester-Bedford-Hitchin line, a few miles south-east of Leicester. When the Midland Railway came into being in 1844, it was dependent upon the outlets provided by its constituents to the LNWR at Birmingham, Hampton, and particularly at Rugby. Proposals had been advanced for a connection further to the south, but had fallen through. A Leicester & Bedford Railway was proposed under independent auspices during the 'Railway Mania', and authorised as an MR route in 1847, but powers were allowed to lapse. Local interest remained strong, and when a merger between the MR and LNWR was rejected by Parliament in 1853, powers were promptly obtained for a 63 mile line from Leicester, through Market Harborough and Wellingborough, to Bedford and Hitchin, where it joined the Great Northern main line to London. This would provide the Midland with a fresh outlet to the south, avoiding the bottleneck which had developed on the LNWR south of Rugby, and which was causing friction. Money was tight, and the MR engineers were told they had to build the line for £15,000 per mile, adopting an undulating course to minimise earthworks. The new route opened to coal traffic on 15th April, to goods on 4th May, and to passengers on 8th May 1857.

East Langton was a neat wayside station with picturesque timber buildings, and was known as Langton until 1st May 1891. Drivers of 'up' trains routed to the LNWR's Northampton route at Market Harborough gave three whistles on passing the box. In 1942, six trains called at East Langton in each direction, including certain semi-fast workings. Freight facilities were withdrawn on 2nd March 1964 and the station closed to passengers on 1st January 1968.

Above: East Langton box, looking towards Leicester, with the 'up' home signal visible on the left. The box was 'switched out' as many minor boxes could be regularly. It was taken out of use, but following a fire at nearby Kibworth Station box, caused by over-enthusiastic stoking of the stove, was temporarily reopened until Kibworth was made inhabitable once more!

EAST LANGTON

Below: Whereas the LNWR preferred plain, almost severe, timber waiting shelters, the Midland opted for diagonal, horizontal and vertical panelling, and sundry flourishes.

Below: A view from the 'down' platform, looking towards Leicester, in April 1967. The main buildings have seen better days, as evidenced by the missing ridge tiles and canopy valance. The building is flanked at both ends by venerable MR van bodies.

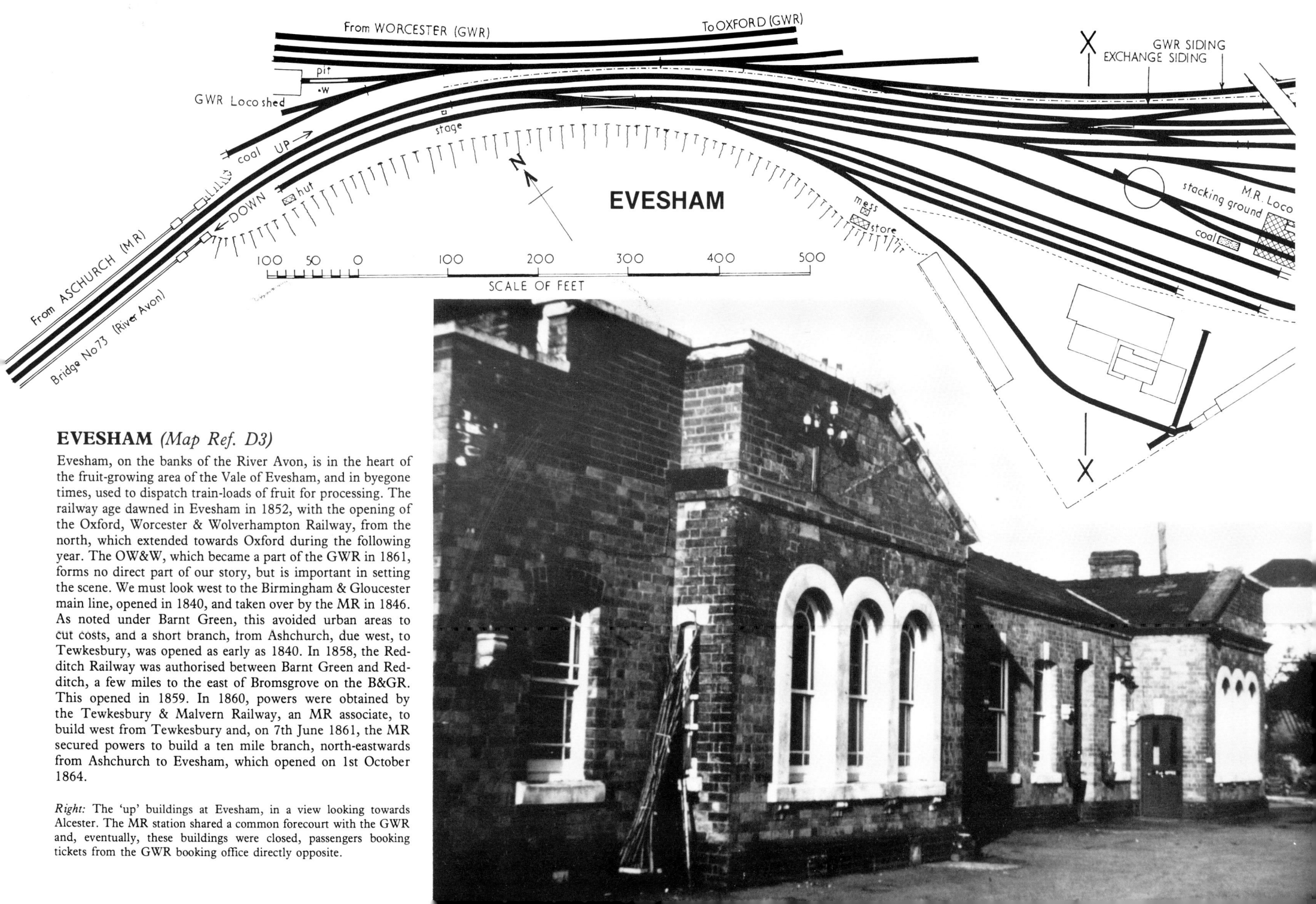

From WORCESTER (GWR)   To OXFORD (GWR)

GWR SIDING
EXCHANGE SIDING

GWR Loco shed

pit
·w

coal UP →

stage

DOWN   hut

From ASCHURCH (MR)

Bridge No 73 (River Avon)

N

EVESHAM

mess
store

stacking ground   M.R. Loco

coal

100 50 0   100   200   300   400   500

SCALE OF FEET

EVESHAM *(Map Ref. D3)*

Evesham, on the banks of the River Avon, is in the heart of
the fruit-growing area of the Vale of Evesham, and in byegone
times, used to dispatch train-loads of fruit for processing. The
railway age dawned in Evesham in 1852, with the opening of
the Oxford, Worcester & Wolverhampton Railway, from the
north, which extended towards Oxford during the following
year. The OW&W, which became a part of the GWR in 1861,
forms no direct part of our story, but is important in setting
the scene. We must look west to the Birmingham & Gloucester
main line, opened in 1840, and taken over by the MR in 1846.
As noted under Barnt Green, this avoided urban areas to
cut costs, and a short branch, from Ashchurch, due west, to
Tewkesbury, was opened as early as 1840. In 1858, the Redditch Railway was authorised between Barnt Green and Redditch, a few miles to the east of Bromsgrove on the B&GR.
This opened in 1859. In 1860, powers were obtained by
the Tewkesbury & Malvern Railway, an MR associate, to
build west from Tewkesbury and, on 7th June 1861, the MR
secured powers to build a ten mile branch, north-eastwards
from Ashchurch to Evesham, which opened on 1st October
1864.

Right: The 'up' buildings at Evesham, in a view looking towards
Alcester. The MR station shared a common forecourt with the GWR
and, eventually, these buildings were closed, passengers booking
tickets from the GWR booking office directly opposite.

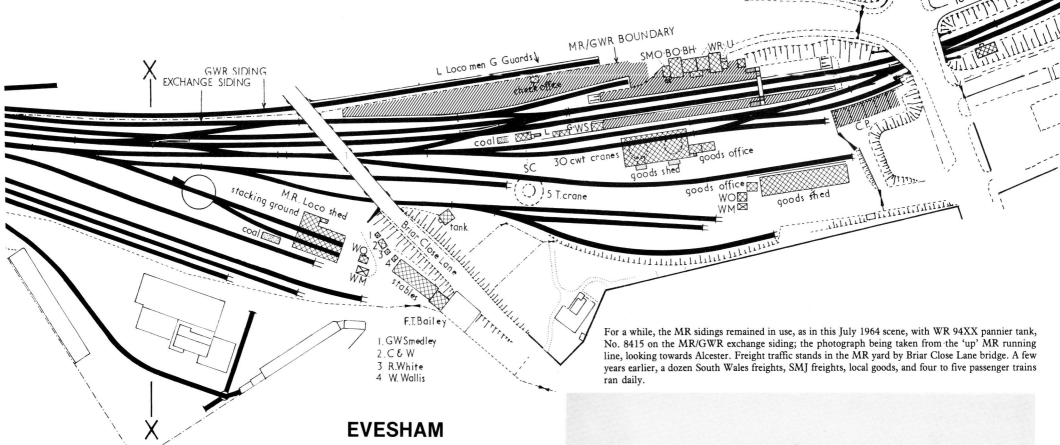

GWR SIDING
EXCHANGE SIDING

MR/GWR BOUNDARY

L Loco men G Guards↓

SMO·BO·BH   WR·U

check office

coal   L G WS

M.R. Loco shed

stacking ground

coal

SC   30 cwt cranes   goods office

goods shed

5 T.crane

goods office
WO
WM   goods shed

CP

tank

Briar Close Lane

WO
2
3
4
WM

stables

F.T.Bailey

1. GW Smedley
2. C & W
3. R.White
4. W.Wallis

To ALCESTER

EVESHAM

For a while, the MR sidings remained in use, as in this July 1964 scene, with WR 94XX pannier tank, No. 8415 on the MR/GWR exchange siding; the photograph being taken from the 'up' MR running line, looking towards Alcester. Freight traffic stands in the MR yard by Briar Close Lane bridge. A few years earlier, a dozen South Wales freights, SMJ freights, local goods, and four to five passenger trains ran daily.

Passengers travelling to Birmingham and the north by the GWR had to change, or face a roundabout journey, and Evesham interests, with MR backing, formed the Evesham & Redditch Railway on 13th July 1863, to bridge the 17¼ mile gap to Redditch. This opened as a single line to Alcester on 17th September 1866, and to Redditch on 4th May 1868. The E&R, which was worked by the MR, was vested in the Midland in 1882, and dissolved four years later. The line was single from Barnt Green to Evesham, with crossing facilities at Redditch, Studley, Alcester, Broom and Harvington. In MR days, there were two signal boxes at Evesham, the North box controlling the single line junction. Both boxes were replaced by an LMS standard hybrid box at the Ashchurch end of the platforms. South of Evesham, the line was double. As late as 1889, the 7 mile section from Evesham south to Beckford was worked on the 'time interval' system, with Beckford to Ashchurch on the old telegraph system, not Absolute Block. In LMS days, the Evesham line carried freights ex the SMJ route from Broom Junction, but these were rerouted by BR, and diversionary use away from the Lickey Incline also curtailed. The Alcester to Evesham section was closed to all traffic on 1st October 1962, and the Evesham to Ashchurch passenger service ceased on 17th June 1963. The Evesham to Ashchurch section had been used for through freights ex the OW&W line between Oxford and South Wales. These were rerouted in September.

FORMBY

From LIVERPOOL & HIGHTOWN

Old S.C.

DOWN →

← UP

Old L.C.

B.H.

W.R.

W.R.

→ N

50 0 50 100 150 200 250 300 350

Scale of Feet

X

New S.C.

To FRESHFIELD & SOUTHPORT

FORMBY *(Map Ref. A4)*

Formby Station is situated between Hightown and Freshfield on the LYR Liverpool to Southport line. The Liverpool, Crosby & Southport Railway was authorised in July 1847, and opened from Waterloo, in north Liverpool, to the outskirts of Southport, on 24th July 1848. Initially single, the line was doubled by 1852. Formby, one of the original stations, is 11¼ miles north of Liverpool (Exchange) Station, and was 23½ minutes from Exchange, and 13 minutes from Southport under the early electric schedules. Together with Freshfield (q.v.) it serves the community in the area to the east of the low-lying Formby Hills, the principal residential area between Crosby and the outskirts of Southport.

Left: The 'down' line platform and waiting-room at Formby, looking towards Southport.

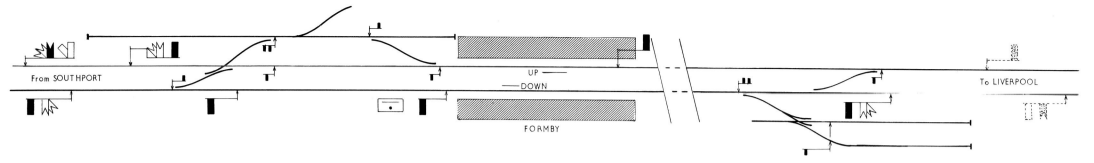

From SOUTHPORT

UP ——

—— DOWN

FORMBY

To LIVERPOOL

Below: The 'up' platform and waiting-room, looking towards Liverpool (Exchange). The main buildings, erected when the original level crossing was replaced by an overbridge, are visible in the distance, along with the ticket collectors' booths. A small goods yard formerly existed on the 'down' side of the line beyond the bridge. 'Up' sidings were also provided.

FORMBY

Being relatively undeveloped in the early 1900s, and on account of its more or less central location, Formby was selected as the site for the LYR generating station for the pioneer Southport electrification, and the power house was established about ⅓ mile south of the station near the River Alt. It was situated on the east side of the line, and rakes of high-capacity coal hoppers were a common sight. The plant contained sixteen massive coal-fired boilers, generating steam to drive reciprocating cross-compound steam engines. These in turn worked four generators of 1,500kW, and one of 750kW capacity, and produced current at 7,500 volts for transmission via feeders to rotary sub-stations near Bank Hall, Seaforth, Formby and Birkdale, for conversion to 625 volt line power. Peaks in demand were such that battery sub-stations were added at Southport St. Lukes, Freshfield, Hall Road and Liverpool, in September 1905. These smoothed load variation, and reduced coal consumption to 0.412lb. per ton mile. The power-station, with its compound reciprocating plant was soon obsolete, but gave good service until 1946 when the LMS took power from outside. The buildings survive in industrial use, but are not rail-connected. One well-remembered peculiarity was that a train running in the vicinity of a station, and particularly upon starting, caused the station lights to dim markedly.

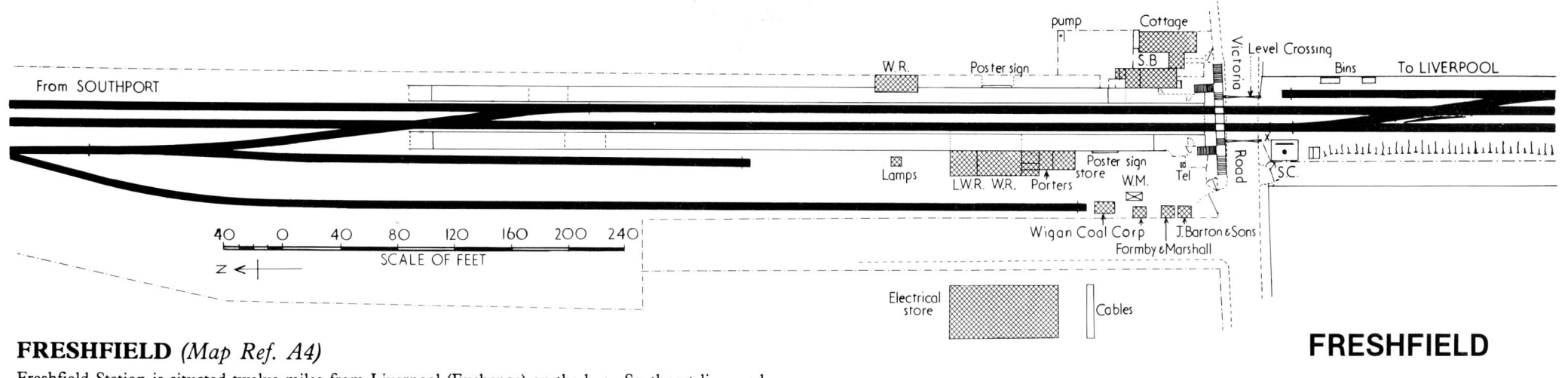

On the diagram: From SOUTHPORT / To LIVERPOOL / pump / Cottage / Level Crossing / S.B. / Victoria / Bins / W.R. / Poster sign / Lamps / L.W.R. W.R. Porters / Poster sign store / W.M. / Tel / Road / S.C. / Wigan Coal Corp / J. Barton & Sons / Formby & Marshall / Electrical store / Cables

40 0 40 80 120 160 200 240
SCALE OF FEET
z ←

FRESHFIELD *(Map Ref. A4)*

FRESHFIELD

Freshfield Station is situated twelve miles from Liverpool (Exchange) on the busy Southport line, and opened in 1854, six years after the first section of the LC&S was completed. The buildings were quite unlike any others on the line, and with their ornate windows, and 'beam and plaster' finish, give a passable impression of what a Shakespearian railway station might have been like, had railways been around at that time. A battery sub-station was installed on the west side of the line to the north of the station in September 1905 (further details of the pioneer LYR electrical system appear under Formby). Colour light emergency signals were provided north of the station near Woodvale aerodrome. They were normally unlit but, in the event of an aircraft crashing, with possible obstruction of the line, they could be controlled from the airfield. Wickey Dale 'up' IB signal, 1 mile 560yds. from Freshfield box, also had an airfield control.

Below left: A view from the footbridge, looking north towards Southport. The main building and waiting-room on the right-hand side are separated by no more than 140ft., a somewhat extravagant provision of buildings. The drumhead clock, on the near building, is a reminder that clocks visible from the platforms were a Board of Trade requirement.

Below right: The waiting-room, at first sight similar to the main building, differs markedly in this view, looking towards Liverpool. Compare, for example, the windows, window frames, door lintels, gable or pitched roof, or even the general style of panelling.

Above: The waiting-room on the northbound platform offered yet more contrast, and was the only brick structure for public use.

Below: The booking office and station cottage. The diminutive porch over the ticket hatch would hardly bring much joy to passengers queueing to book tickets on a wet day. Note the low-height platform in front of the building, and hinged gate closing the barrow-way to passengers, for safety reasons.

Above: The footbridge and level crossing gates, looking towards Liverpool. Note the very short timber guard planks protecting the ends of the third rail.

Below: Freshfield signal cabin and gates.

FRESHFIELD

Above: The handsome viaduct over the River Clyde, with Clyde Junction signal box on the right, and Clyde signals 98/95 and 91/88/85.

(Clyde Junction)

Right: A G&SWR official engraving of St. Enoch Station and hotel prior to enlargement from 1898. In the right foreground is St. Enoch Square, with the station approach incline rising up towards the entrance to the cab road (right distance). To the left is North Approach, whilst a horse and carriage is pictured on the slope up from Maxwell St., which burrows under the station, to North Approach.

GLASGOW (St. Enoch) *(Map Ref. Q15)*

Third in size of the Scottish railway companies, with almost 600 route miles owned or part-owned, the Glasgow & South Western Railway was in the shape of a letter A, with Glasgow at the apex, and Stranraer and Carlisle as the feet. One of its primitive constituents, the Kilmarnock & Troon, was authorised in 1808. The main line of the Glasgow, Paisley, Kilmarnock & Ayr Railway was completed from a terminus south of the River Clyde in 1840. In 1850, amalgamation with the Glasgow, Dumfries & Carlisle Railway led to the Glasgow & South Western Railway. From its Bridge St. terminus, trains radiated out across Renfrew and Ayr but, as with London, the major commercial districts lay to the north of the river. The idea of a north bank terminus evolved in the 1840s, but opposition from other companies, Glasgow Corporation, and the river authorities, frustrated progress. Other than via the lines to the south and east of Glasgow, owned by that 'Sou' West' enemy, the Caledonian, the G&SWR had no communication to the Edinburgh & Glasgow Railway, or other lines north of the Clyde.

In 1864, the G&SWR and Edinburgh & Glasgow Railway joined forces to promote the City of Glasgow Union Railway, to provide a link between the two, and an imposing passenger terminal — to be open to allcomers — on the north bank of the Clyde. In 1865, the E&G became a part of the North British Railway, whilst the 'Caley' preferred to build its own river crossing. The main line of the CGU began at Pollok Junction, on the Glasgow & Paisley Joint line, ran east to the Gorbals, and then turned north to cross the Clyde on a two track viaduct. North of the river, the through route turned east and north, to join the NBR's Sighthill branch, and the NB line from Coatbridge. Just north of the river, the line forked, at Clyde Junction, and ran westwards to the new north bank terminal station, fronting on to St. Enoch Square. At one time it was proposed that St. Enoch should be a through station, bridging the square, and running west to new docks at Stobcross. As opposition to bringing the railway into St. Enoch

Above: A comprehensive train information board was installed on the concourse beneath the train shed, spanning platforms 1-6. Despite tramway competition, we see the variety of services provided before 1914.

Authors' Collection

Left: Looking from the station hotel along the six-track train shed, with platform 1 on the left. A pair of 'Sou' West' 4-4-0s recall the elegance of this delightful railway which blended English and Scottish features. The horse-cab adds a nice period touch.

Authors' Collection

GLASGOW (St. Enoch)

Square was fierce enough, and led to a six year delay in completing St. Enoch Station, it is hardly surprising that the extension withered before the storm! The Clyde viaduct was opened on 2nd June 1870, and a temporary station, Dunlop Street, opened on 12th December 1870. It was not until 1874 that most of the property had been acquired. Work was pushed ahead rapidly, for with the MR Settle to Carlisle line nearing completion, the G&SWR at long last had a partner in its dreams of an Anglo-Scottish service. Although work was still in progress, the first train from St. Pancras, drew into St. Enoch on 1st May 1876, the day that the 'Long Drag' opened. A ceremonial opening followed, by the Prince and Princess of Wales, on 17th October.

As at St. Pancras, to which it formed a fitting Scottish counterpart, high Victorian Gothic prevailed, but in the eleven years between the passage of the Bill in 1865, and completion of the station, the Gothic trend had begun to falter, and the station, despite its splendour, was to gain more critics than admirers. As at St. Pancras, the frontage was dominated by a station hotel, although this was not ready until 3rd July 1879. With over 200 bedrooms, it was the largest hotel in Scotland, and was the creation of a London architect, Thomas Willson, and a Glaswegian, Miles Gibson. It could best be described as 'Scottish Gothic'. Initially, the station was provided with six platforms, and boasted a train shed roof similar to that at St. Pancras, although somewhat smaller.

As well as passenger services to the south, the G&SWR also wished to operate services to its North British partner, and a curve, serving the two northernmost platforms at St. Enoch, permitted services to Saltmarket. The station was immediately popular and, between 1880 and 1900, passenger bookings more than doubled, many being inner suburban commuters. A heavy traffic also built up to the Ayrshire Coast resorts. Even in the 1880s, 140 trains had used St. Enoch daily, and with congestion increasing, a comprehensive resignalling, using W. R. Sykes equipment, came into use in July 1898. This was part

of a phased plan for which powers had just been obtained, and which included quadrupling the CGU from Port Eglinton Junction, across the Clyde and into St. Enoch itself, where an additional six platforms were added on the south side of the line. Roof extension, partly with a train shed, and partly with individual platform awnings, served to emphasise this division between old and new, and work continued until 1904.

Until 1896, the CGU had remained nominally separate from the G&SWR or NBR, but on 7th August, it was partitioned, the G&SWR taking over the lines south of the Clyde, St. Enoch, and the connecting link as far as College West Junction. As a result, the G&SWR headquarters were finally in a station owned by the company! The extensions had come too late to benefit the 'Sou' West' however, for in 1898, the first sections of the extensive Glasgow Corporation Tramways were electrified. Within a few years, a fleet of over 1,000 Standard 'Caurs' had decimated the inner suburban traffic. The G&SWR admitted defeat as early as 1902, with the cessation of its Springburn passenger service. It was only the success of the Ayrshire resorts which brought relief.

In 1923, St. Enoch fell into the hands of the LMS, which north of the border, meant control by the hated Caledonian. By the mid-1930s, 'Sou' West' steam had been slaughtered, to make way for 'Caley' or MR types, and St. Enoch, with little money made available by the 'Caley' overlords, was declining in importance. Nationalisation hastened the process, and St. Enoch became steadily dingier. Finally, on 27th June 1966, St. Enoch closed down, passenger trains switching to the Caledonian's Central Station. Other than for resignalling by the LMS in 1933, as the Sykes system, a pioneer power installation, was hopelessly outdated, the station had altered little since its enlargement at the turn of the century. The station hotel lasted until 1974. Within a few years, the site had been swept bare of railway reminders. The CGU cross-river line survives as a valuable freight link.

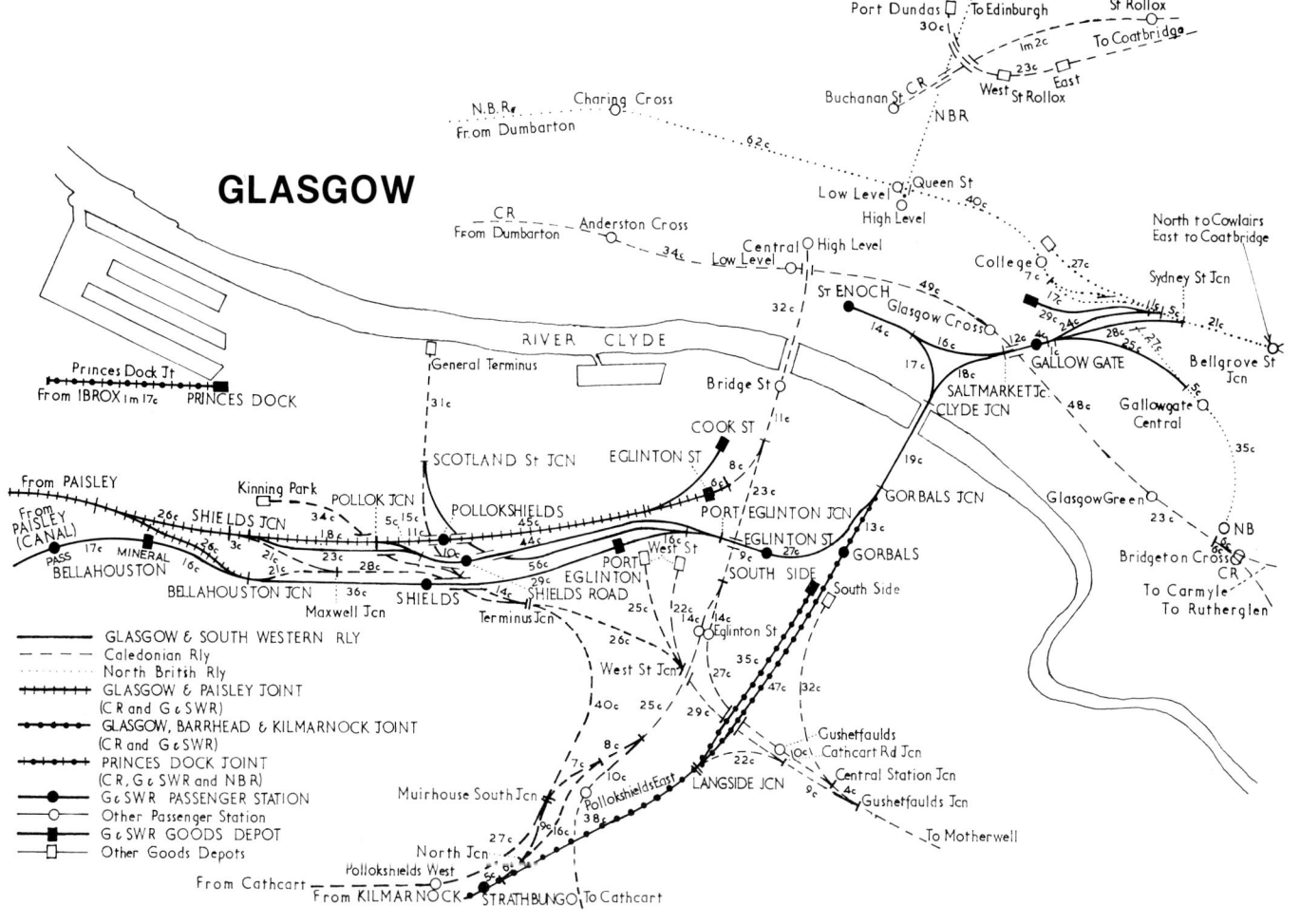

GLASGOW

Legend:
—————— GLASGOW & SOUTH WESTERN RLY
– – – – Caledonian Rly
············· North British Rly
+++++++ GLASGOW & PAISLEY JOINT (CR and G&SWR)
•—•—•—• GLASGOW, BARRHEAD & KILMARNOCK JOINT (CR and G&SWR)
•+••+••+• PRINCES DOCK JOINT (CR, G&SWR and NBR)
—●— G&SWR PASSENGER STATION
—○— Other Passenger Station
—■— G&SWR GOODS DEPOT
—□— Other Goods Depots

This position map shows the complex web of routes and mass of stations in the heart of Glasgow. It is interesting that of the four principal routes ex-St. Enoch, three make connections with other companies or joint lines, and only the Bellahouston line to the west is purely Glasgow & South Western. As the Edinburgh & Glasgow (later the North British) and the 'Sou' West did not seriously impinge upon one another, relations with NBR were generally good, and for many years the G&SWR and NBR shared ownership of St. Enoch. Given the bitter feud between the 'Sou'

West' and its 'Caley' neighbour, it is curious that the two joint lines to the south are in association with the 'Caley'. The map shows the City of Glasgow Union after partition between the G&SWR and NBR, and indeed the inner Glasgow network at its peak. Tramway competition, the bus, the motor car, and a massive clearance of the tenements of the Gorbals, have reduced the market for rail transport more drastically than virtually any comparable inner-city area in the British Isles.

Below: A view looking from platform 6 to the locomotive shed, with a G&SWR wing tank brewing up, in 1931. Compared to the pre-1914 study of the signal bridge, the out-of-use crosses have gone, and an extra outgoing low signal has been provided, as have label boxes, ex-Middle Sidings 1/2 and between posts 1/2 and 3/4 for the existing but undesignated banners.

Glasgow (St. Enoch) was a remarkable example of a very early electro-mechanical signalling system devised by W. R. Sykes, a company more commonly associated with the constituents of the Southern. A trial installation came into use at St. Enoch in July 1898, and expanded to work the whole of the enlarged station area and adjoining boxes. The points were controlled mechanically from a normal frame, and the signals from miniature slides mounted above the main frame. Linking the points and signals were the route levers in the mechanical frame. These stood normal in mid-position, and were pulled (X) or pushed (⊙) to prove mechanically that the route had been set correctly, and to release electrically the relevant signal levers. Once the signals were pulled, the route lever was locked, so holding the road. All points were detected, and facing points locked electrically. Before pulling a point or route lever, the signalman had to press a foot pedal, and unless every relevant blade and point lock was proved, the lever remained locked. Sykes 'Lock and Block' provided a further safeguard, as starting signals could not be cleared until 'Line Clear' had been obtained from the box in advance, and 'Train out of Section' could not be given until the train had passed over a treadle releasing the block instrument. As the signal slides were at 2in. centres, and above the mechanical levers, at 5¼in. centres, frames were very compact. At Clyde Junction, a 100 lever frame, of which levers 1-30 were mechanical, occupied just 12ft. 8¼in. At St. Enoch, worked by three men, levers 1-88 were mechanical, and 89-488 electrical.

The main running signals were semaphores, operated by motors placed inside the lattice posts. Signal lamps were also within the posts, and on the signal bridge, one lamp would serve two back-to-back arms. Banner shunting signals, with a red arm and opal background, were provided, being fully illuminated by night. These signals were balanced, working by electro-magnetic coils. Most dropped to the left when pulled, but forty were double-acting, e.g. 464/1 and 456/1, by crossover 82 in platform 11. These dropped left for the left-handed route, or right, for the right-handed route. Thus 82 and 464/1 were needed to go over the crossover into platform 12, or 82 normal and 456/1 pulled to run into platform 11. Adding to the complexity, 464 or 456 in position 2 cleared the left-hand shunt signal by 79 crossover, leading to 464/1, etc. In the diagram, dual-direction signals were shown as a cross, but were of course a single red banner, dropping left or right. All signals show their lever number, and also the route lever required to release them, e.g. route lever 72 X (i.e. pulled), releases signal 468 ex-platform 12.

Route levers were mostly bi-directional, e.g. 72 (push) was either from the 'down' line to platform 12, or from platform 12 shunting out wrong road to the 'down' line. Lever 72 (pull) worked from platform 12 to the 'up' line or vice versa. It was impossible to route trains from two lines to a given platform simultaneously, and all main arrival/departure routes were so fitted. However, route levers for the turntable (9) engine sidings (35) or dead end sidings (36, 37, 38, 47, 66, 73, 74) were uni-directional, but from numerous starting points to a given destination. Lever 74 pull for example, could release 481/2 ex-platform 11, or 483 ex-platform 12, both to dead end No. 3! With

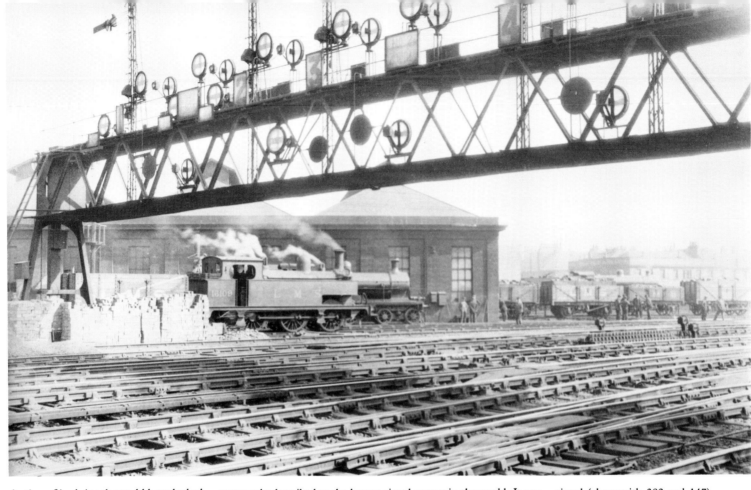

GLASGOW
(St. Enoch)

bi-directional route levers, selection of 'up' signals would have locked 'down' signals, or vice versa.

The two 4-arm 6-route bracket shunt signals, noted 'A' and 'B' on the diagram, merit study. The signals are beyond the points they refer to, and in some cases, more than one route is available, e.g. the second signal on 'A' gives the same indication to platform 6, whether worked by 245 (46 push from the 'down' line, or by 343 (46 pull) from the 'up'). Lever 323 works signals on bracket 'A' or 'B', both being 'up' line to platform 4, but via points 33 or 30/31.

The signalling at St. Enoch was most unusual, and at times, even basic principles were inverted. The general rule, that a signal relates to a train in a specific place, and tells a driver where he is routed to, was sometimes ignored, and in interpreting the system, it helps to remember that, on occasions, a signal may tell a driver where he has come from, but not where he is going, or by which sub-route.

The principal feature was the signal bridge, with 66 separate arms, making it larger than the better-known LNWR gantry at Rugby,

commonly described as the largest signal gantry in the world. It was a massive structure, with twelve main posts, each carrying the inward and outward arms for their respective platforms. An inset diagram shows the signals on the platform 10 post. Most posts were the same, but in some cases there were additional routes whilst Nos. 1 and 2 Middle Sidings merited their own low posts. There was a multiplicity of starting signals, with as many as five ex-platform 9, 436 on the bridge, 443 about 20yds. away, a second 443 at the awning end, and two No. 444s along the platform! The total distance was about 240yds.

With this plethora of signals, the bracket ex-platform 1 is strange. The left-hand (tall) arm is shown on original drawings as 122 (6 pull) and 260 (39 pull). If this were so, the same signal would apply ex-platform 1 to Saltmarket, or the 'up' main. The right-hand arm is labelled 302 (41 pull) and 147 ('No route circuit through points') the former being platform 2 to 'up' main. It is likely that the original was wrong, and that 260 (39 pull) should have applied to the right-hand

signal (along with 302 and 147).

Occasionally, no route lever was needed, e.g. three shunt signals 394 ex-platform 9. 'No route circuit through points' — e.g. '147 NRC' — can apply to main running signals, as well as shunt arms, and weakens the whole route lever concept. In emergency, a signal lever could be partially replaced in the frame, throwing the signal to danger, but the lever would not go back fully until normal clearance was completed, so holding the road. In the St. Enoch Station diagram, it will be noted that the main and canal line crossings are worked by Clyde Junction, and are therefore not numbered in the St. Enoch plan. The only connection available to St. Enoch box between the six old platforms Nos. 1-6 and the new side, platforms 7-12, was via No. 2 dead end road. Train routeing on to the Canal or main lines had to be done at Clyde Junction.

The St. Enoch installation vanished in 1933; it was archaic years before, and few published accounts survive in readily available form. The details merit wider access as a pioneer power system.

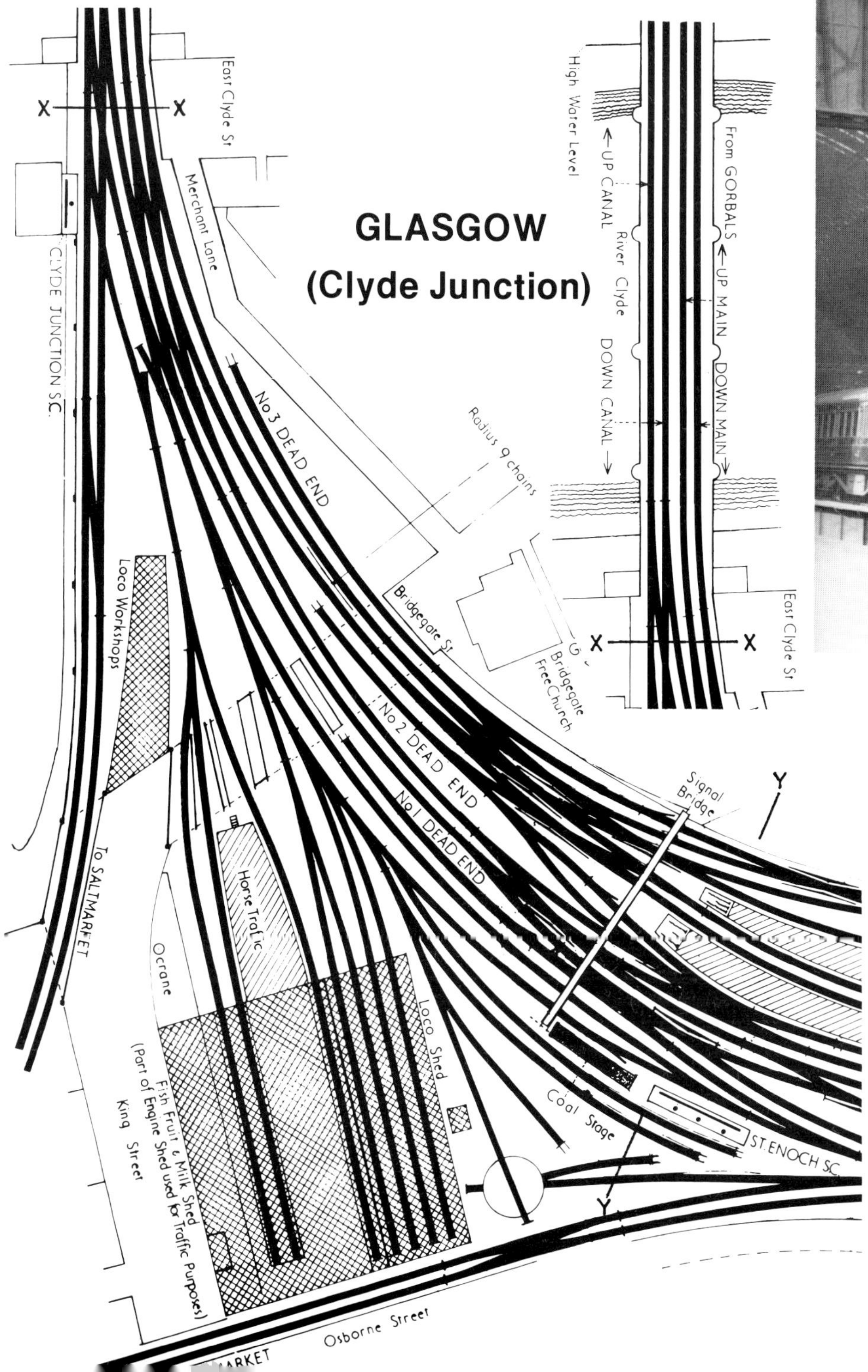

GLASGOW
(Clyde Junction)

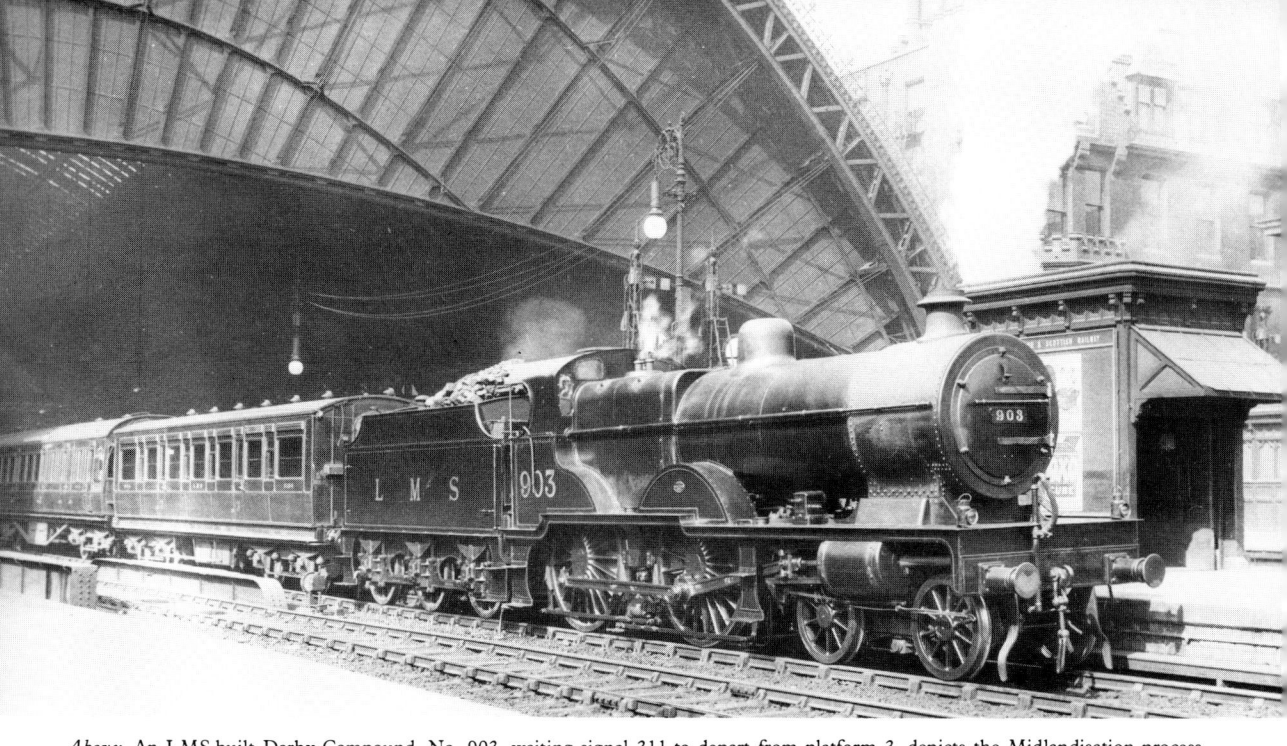

Above: An LMS-built Derby Compound, No. 903, waiting signal 311 to depart from platform 3, depicts the Midlandisation process. The luggage lift is to the right of the Compound. The girder on the left bridges Dunlop St., whilst the ground signal is variously worked by 319, 318, 224 or 180!

The method of working was fascinating, taking for example a train ex the 'down canal' to platforms 7-12. Clyde Junction would obtain 'Line Clear' from St. Enoch on the 7-12 platforms 'down' block instrument; next he would pull point/point lock 28 and point 27, i.e. 'down canal' to 'down' main; 26 and other conflicting routes would have to be normal. Route lever 20 (pull) would prove the route and lock it mechanically, freeing signals 92, 91 and distant 93 electrically. Signal 91 was slotted by St. Enoch, and would only clear when St. Enoch 370 was pulled. St. Enoch would select the platform, say No. 11, requiring points 76 and 81, and route lever 71 'push'. Signal 403 on the signal bridge, and the slotted signal 370 could be cleared. If platform 11 was not clear to the stops, the signalman waited until the train had nearly halted at the signal bridge and then cleared the subsidiary (call-on) arm 404.

For inwards shunting moves, it was inconvenient to have the shunt signals high in the air, and a subsidiary repeater signal, for groups of routes, was provided low in the girder work of the signal bridge. One such repeater was provided covering the six subsidiary signals ex the 'down' main to platforms 7-12, and one for the six signals ex the 'up' main to platforms 7-12. The same principle with added complications applied for platforms 1-6 and Middle Sidings 1 and 2. There was an additional 'up' line between platforms 1/2 and the 'up' Canal road. As the signal bridge was so far from the points it 'protected', remote shunting signals were provided for each of the five approach lines, e.g. the banners below both 418 signals, both 251 and 249. They were worked by no fewer than 31 levers, one number higher on the out roads, and one lower on in roads than the corresponding signals on the signal bridge.

The original diagram postulates that the platform escape crossovers 'are worked from one lever ground frames, electrically released from the signal box', e.g. 410/1 for platforms 11/12. Four signal indications are possible, which could have been selected via the points, except that this is specifically ruled out.

With 'Lock and Block', the Clyde Junction slots, 35-37, 41-43, and 45, were controlled by the 'Line Clear' on the block from the next box, Gorbals Junction. To permit shunting moves at St. Enoch, 'shunt-by' discs, controlled by Clyde Junction (47-54) and St. Enoch, were provided. Advance starters 38 and 46 at Clyde Junction would be block-released in any normal system, but block release of inner starters was a peculiarity of the Sykes system.

The signals ex-platform 1 to the turntable are strange, most notably the 3-banner bracket between points 3 and 4. An engine stopping here would foul the incoming line ex-Saltmarket, and there is only one route open to the driver — all the signals do is to remind him where he has come from. Paradoxically, upon leaving the turntable, the driver had three possible routes, which shared a solitary signal.

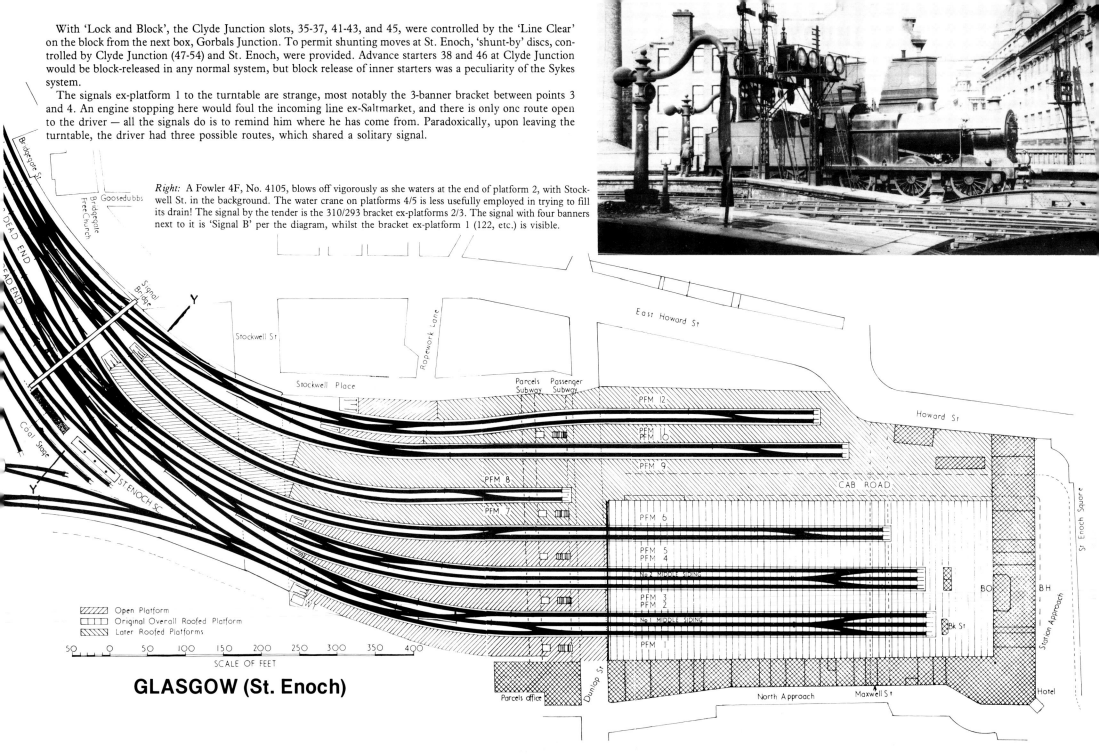

Right: A Fowler 4F, No. 4105, blows off vigorously as she waters at the end of platform 2, with Stockwell St. in the background. The water crane on platforms 4/5 is less usefully employed in trying to fill its drain! The signal by the tender is the 310/293 bracket ex-platforms 2/3. The signal with four banners next to it is 'Signal B' per the diagram, whilst the bracket ex-platform 1 (122, etc.) is visible.

GLASGOW (St. Enoch)

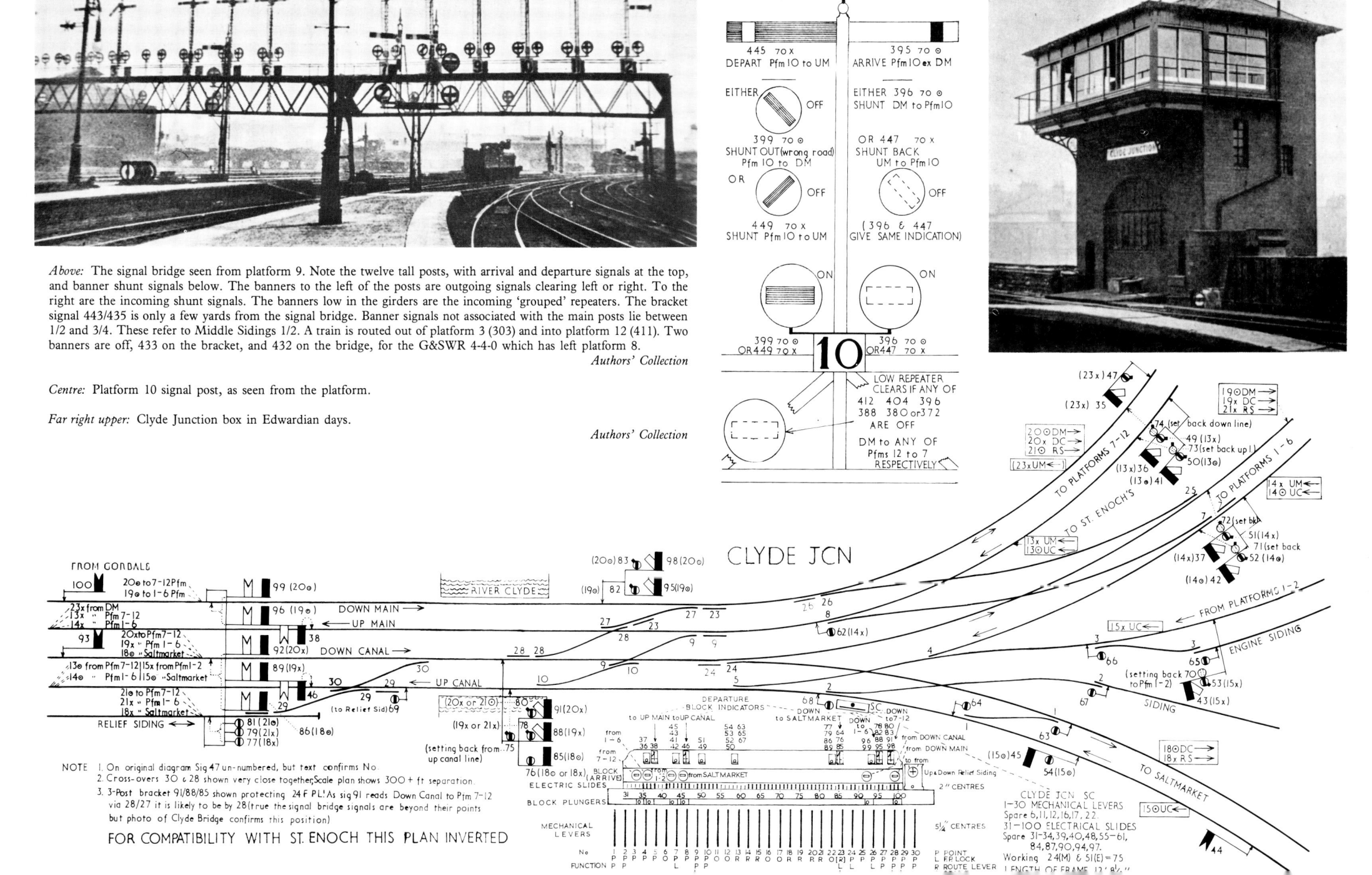

Above: The signal bridge seen from platform 9. Note the twelve tall posts, with arrival and departure signals at the top, and banner shunt signals below. The banners to the left of the posts are outgoing signals clearing left or right. To the right are the incoming shunt signals. The banners low in the girders are the grouped 'grouped' repeaters. The bracket signal 443/435 is only a few yards from the signal bridge. Banner signals not associated with the main posts lie between 1/2 and 3/4. These refer to Middle Sidings 1/2. A train is routed out of platform 3 (303) and into platform 12 (411). Two banners are off, 433 on the bracket, and 432 on the bridge, for the G&SWR 4-4-0 which has left platform 8.

Authors' Collection

Centre: Platform 10 signal post, as seen from the platform.

Far right upper: Clyde Junction box in Edwardian days.

Authors' Collection

CLYDE JCN

FOR COMPATIBILITY WITH ST. ENOCH THIS PLAN INVERTED

NOTE 1. On original diagram Sig 47 un-numbered, but text confirms No.
2. Cross-overs 30 & 28 shown very close together. Scale plan shows 300 + ft separation.
3. 3-Post bracket 91/88/85 shown protecting 24 F.P.L.!As sig 91 reads Down Canal to Pfm 7-12 via 28/27 it is likely to be by 28 (true the signal bridge signals are beyond their points but photo of Clyde Bridge confirms this position)

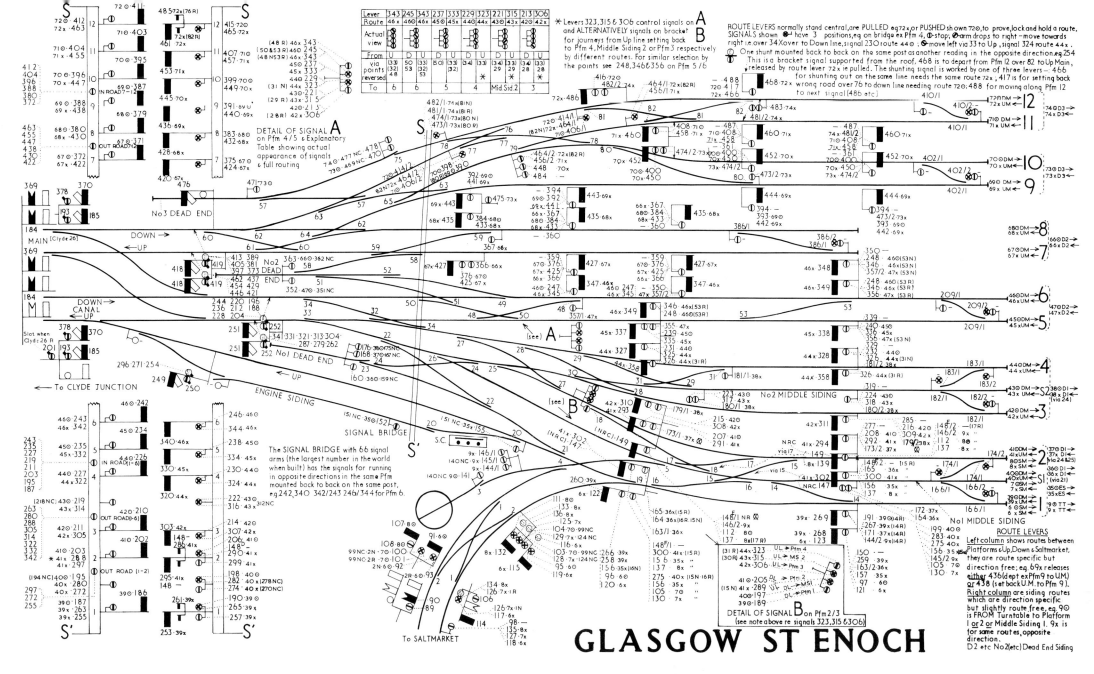

GLASGOW ST ENOCH

St. Enoch box comprised mechanical levers 1-88, and electrical levers 89-488. Points 1-5; 14-18; 20-34; 48-53; 57-65; 75-82; Route levers 6-9; 35-47 and 66-74, i.e. 26 in all, or with push-pull facility, 52 routes. Spares 10-13, 19, 54-56, 83-88. Of the electrical signal slides, some were spare, many operated two or three signals, and No. 148 worked four signals. In other cases several levers operated a single signal — as many as seven or eight.

HARBORNE (Map Ref. D6)

Just a short distance south-west of Birmingham's busy city centre lie the pleasant residential suburbs of Harborne and Edgbaston. The Harborne Railway diverged southwards from the LNWR's Birmingham to Wolverhampton line, 1 mile 3 furlongs west of New St., and ran for nearly 2½ miles to Harborne, with three intermediate stations. In the original Bill, there was also to have been a junction with the GWR, and an extension to the GWR at Halesowen, but these were discarded. The HR was incorporated in 1866 with a capital of £100,000, and five years to build this short line with no major engineering works. Progress was painfully slow, and the line only opened to passengers on 10th August 1874, and to goods on 1st October 1874. From the outset, the HR was worked by the LNWR for 50 per cent of gross receipts. At first the line was single throughout, worked by 'one engine in steam', with six trains each way on weekdays. Despite the 22,000 population of Harborne, a receiver had to be called in, in 1879, a situation not resolved for 21 years. 'Staff and ticket' working was instituted in 1882, and 'Electric Train Staff' in 1892. Finally, a passing loop was added at Rotton Park Road Station in 1903, reflecting the steady growth of suburban traffic. A second platform was added adjacent to the run-round at Harborne in 1901 but, with electrification of the Birmingham Tramways, was never used, and was removed in 1911, and carriage sidings added. The footbridge in the illustration leads in fact to a housing estate. By 1897, twenty trains ran each way, and twenty nine by 1910, handled by Webb 2-4-2T or 0-6-2T locomotives. Tram and bus competition eroded traffic in LMS days but, at the date of closure in 1934, there were still nineteen workings. After passenger closure, 'one engine in steam' working returned, branch freights handling domestic coal and brewery traffic. Freight services ceased on 4th November 1963.

An SLS special, hauled by Webb 2-4-2T No,. 46757, on 3rd June 1950.

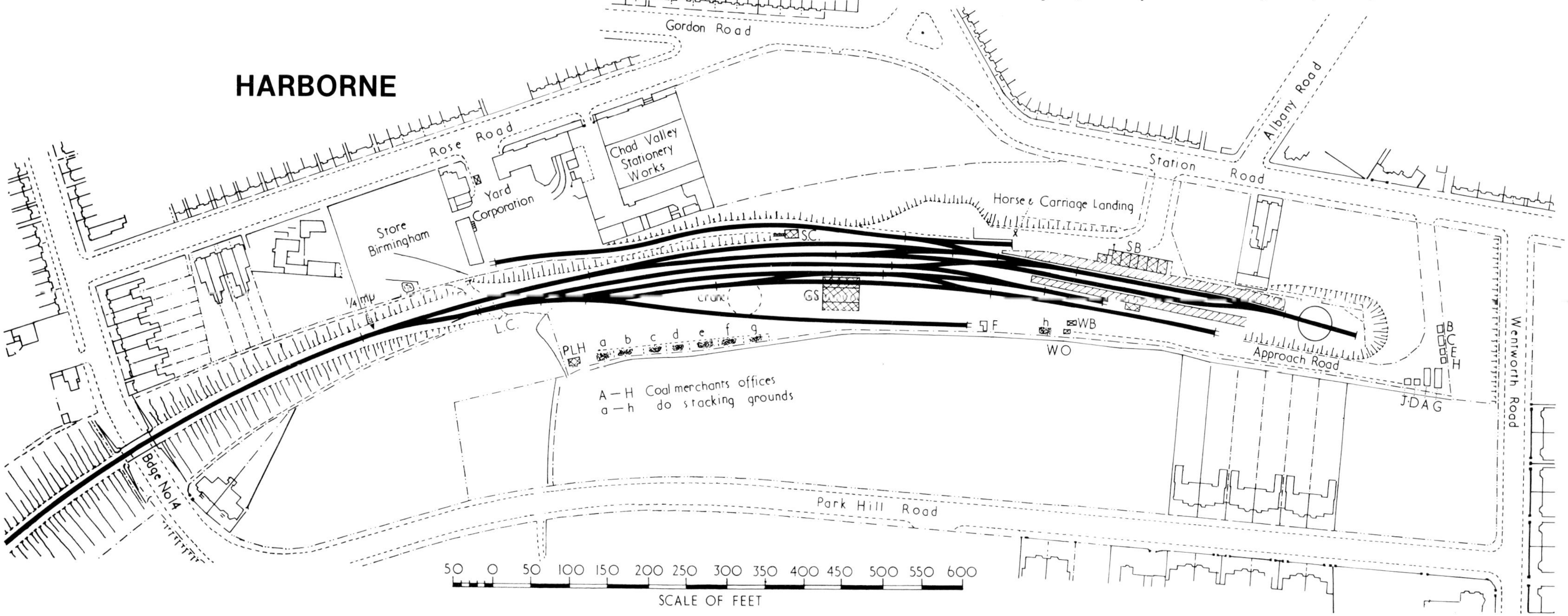

HARBORNE

Gordon Road

Rose Road

Chad Valley Stationery Works

Yard Corporation

Store Birmingham

Horse & Carriage Landing

Station Road

Albany Road

SC

SB

GS

F   h   WB

A – H Coal merchants offices
a – h   do stacking grounds

PLH   a b c d e f g

WO

Approach Road

B
C
F
H

J.D.A.G

L.C.

¼mp

Bdge No 14

Park Hill Road

Wentworth Road

50 0   50 100 150 200 250 300 350 400 450 500 550 600

SCALE OF FEET

HELLIFIELD *(Map Ref. T11)*

Hellifield Station, located less than five miles south-east of Settle, the starting point for the legendary Settle to Carlisle line, is one of the paradoxes of railway history. Its status, and its role as the locomotive depot for the 'Long Drag', makes it a part of the Settle to Carlisle line, yet it predates that line by a quarter of a century. Its form is seen as determined by the Settle to Carlisle line, yet the largely neglected LYR branch from Blackburn, determined its location and facilities.

During 1844/5, an untapped area of countryside, between Lancaster on the west coast, and Skipton, north-east of Leeds and Bradford, and close to the Lancashire/Yorkshire border, beckoned. A company, soon to be known as the 'Little North Western Railway', to distinguish it from the mighty LNWR (so named in 1846) was formed, and secured an Act on 26th June 1846, to build from Skipton to Lancaster, and towards Tebay. The line from Skipton to Ingleton was opened on 30th July 1849, the through route to Lancaster being completed on 1st June 1850. Hellifield was one of the lesser stations, the stationmaster not rating as highly as nearby Gargrave or Bell Busk. Initially single, the 'Little North Western' was doubled west of Hellifield in 1850, and eastwards in 1852. The 'Little North Western' served as a bridge for Anglo-Scottish traffic between the Midland and the Lancaster & Carlisle railways, the latter to become part of the LNWR. Any small company sandwiched between such giants was destined for an eventful life. In 1851, it nearly fell into the hands of the Great Northern, but the Midland prevailed, working the line from 1852. The MR was an expansionist company, looking to extend south to London, and north to Scotland. Collapse of negotiations over use of the Lancaster & Carlisle route prompted the MR to secure powers for the Settle to Carlisle route in 1866. Soon, the Midland was to recoil from the cost, and fight a costly abandonment battle, which failed in 1869. Construction began, with the S&C opening to freight in August 1875 and to passengers on 1st May 1876. It had cost almost £3 million, and came close to ruining the MR.

Meanwhile, the Lancashire & Yorkshire Railway had been considering the Anglo-Scottish traffic, and obtained powers in 1870 to build north-east from the northern limits of LYR territory, round Blackburn and Burnley, to Hellifield, the junction facing towards Scotland. The LYR was to join the Midland just north of the old 'Little North Western' station, and a new joint station was agreed in 1872. Extensive exchange sidings, between the MR and LYR, came into use on 1st March 1880, and the line was opened to passengers on 1st June 1880. The new station, yards and locomotive depot, cost the MR over £20,000,

Above: A view from the 'up' platform, looking to the locomotive shed and repair shop.

HELLIFIELD

Below left: Passengers approached the station by an inclined ramp from a tiny station approach on the south side of the line. Inspectors' and ticket collectors' booths were sited at the head of the inclined approach.

Below: The 'down' platform, looking towards Skipton, and providing an opportunity to study the canopy construction.

HELLIFIELD

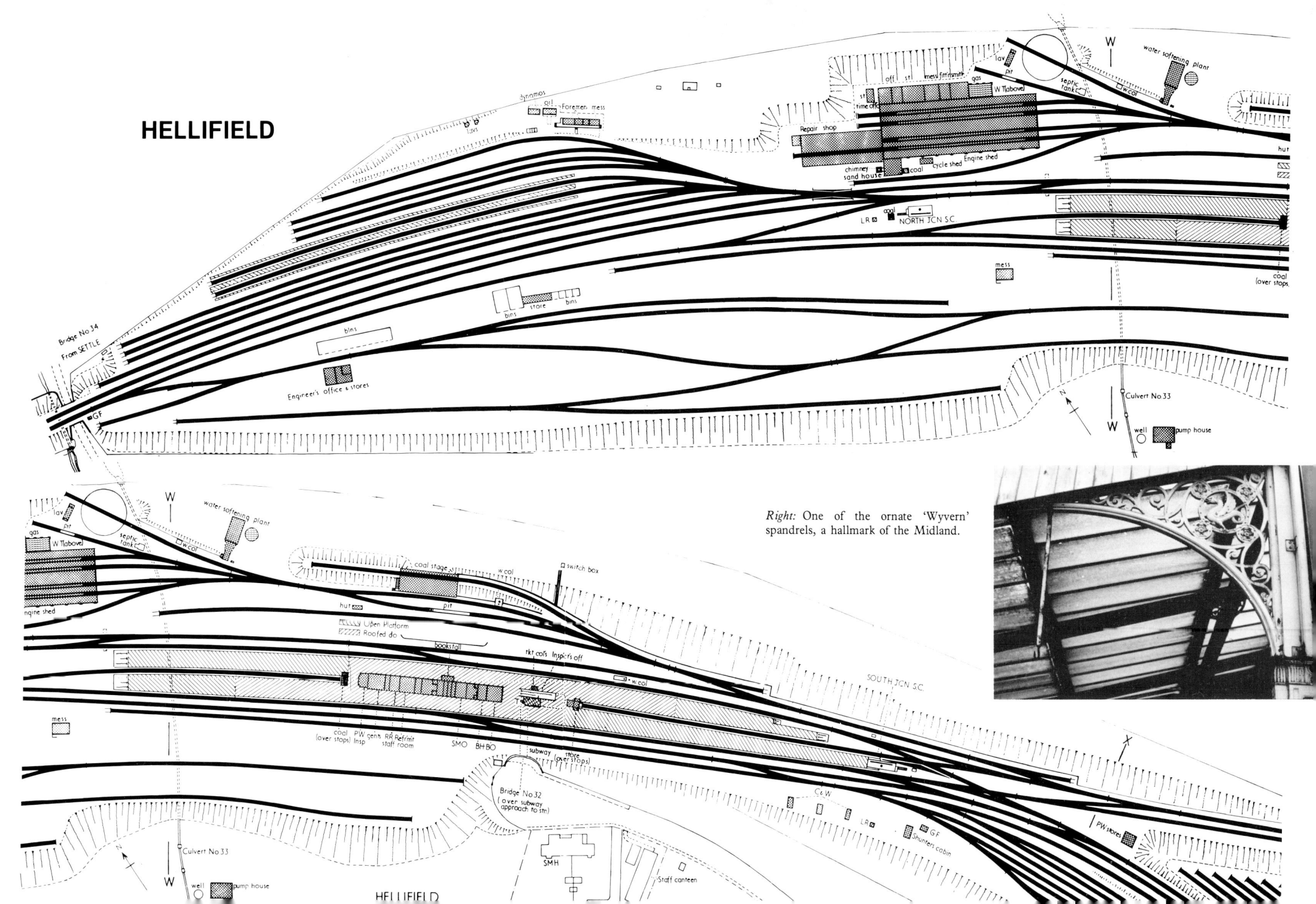

dynamos
oil
Foremen mess
Lavs

off st mess fittrsmith gas
st time offc W Tlabove lav pit
Repair shop
W col septic tank
water softening plant
chimney coal cycle shed Engine shed
sand house
hut

LR coal
NORTH JCN S.C.

mess

coal (over stops)

bins store bins

bins

Bridge No.34
From SETTLE

N
Culvert No 33
W
well pump house

Engineer's office & stores

GF

Right: One of the ornate 'Wyvern' spandrels, a hallmark of the Midland.

W
water softening plant
lav pit
gas
septic tank
W Tlabove
W col
engine shed

coal stage
switch box
w.col

hut pit

SOUTH JCN S.C.

Open Platform
Roofed do

bookgstall

tkt cols Inspr's off

w col

mess

coal PW genn RR Refrmt
(over stops) Insp staff room SMO BH BO

subway
store
(over stops)

Bridge No.32
(over subway
approach to stn)

C&W

LR GF
Shunters cabin

PW stores

Culvert No 33
W well pump house

SMH

Staff canteen

HELLIFIELD

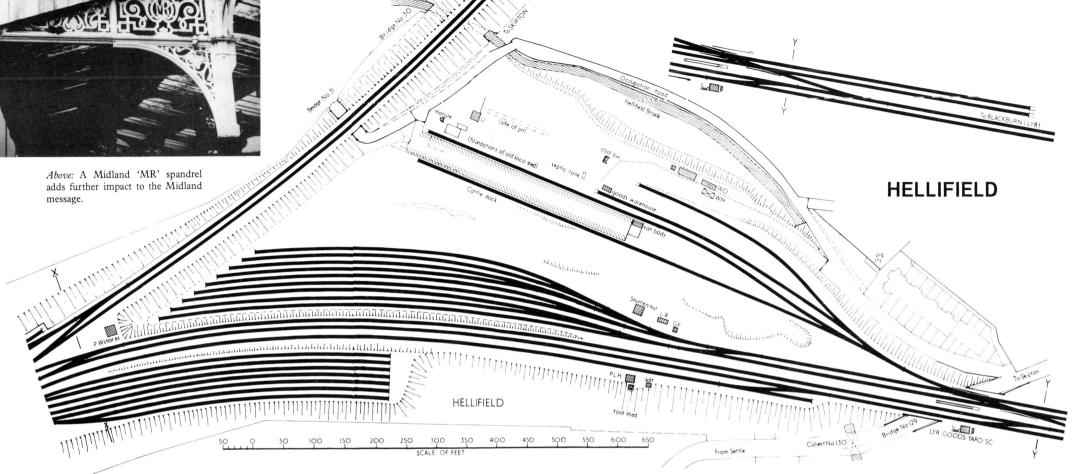

Above: A Midland 'MR' spandrel adds further impact to the Midland message.

HELLIFIELD

HELLIFIELD

50 0 50 100 150 200 250 300 350 400 450 500 550 600 650
SCALE OF FEET

the LYR paying a rental. The locomotive depot was to gain fame as home to the hardy engine crews working the 'Long Drag'. Had an 1882 proposal come to fruition, the railway map would have been more complex, for the North Yorkshire & Lancashire Railway proposed a line to strike north-east from Hellifield to the long NER branch at Fingall, in Wensleydale.

By the outbreak of war in 1914, Hellifield was served by some 90 passenger trains daily, over the Leeds-Settle-Carlisle route, over the LYR, and via the Midland, to Lancaster and Carnforth. A total of 200,000 wagons a year passed through the exchange sidings, and 28 locomotives were kept busy. In 1918, proposals were advanced under the Light Railways Act for a branch from the LNWR at Longridge (north-east of Preston) to Hellifield, but these fell through. On 17th June 1963, Hellifield motive power depot was closed, although used as a store for a period for the official collection of locomotives. The Blackburn to Hellifield branch had lost its passenger service on 10th September 1962, although remains open to goods. Local freight services at Hellifield ended on 20th April 1964. The shed, bays, and most sidings were lifted over the next few years. Recurrent threats to the Settle to Carlisle Railway make for a precarious existence, even though the Carnforth route also survives.

The 'down' platform looking towards Settle, with its truly imposing canopies and station buildings.

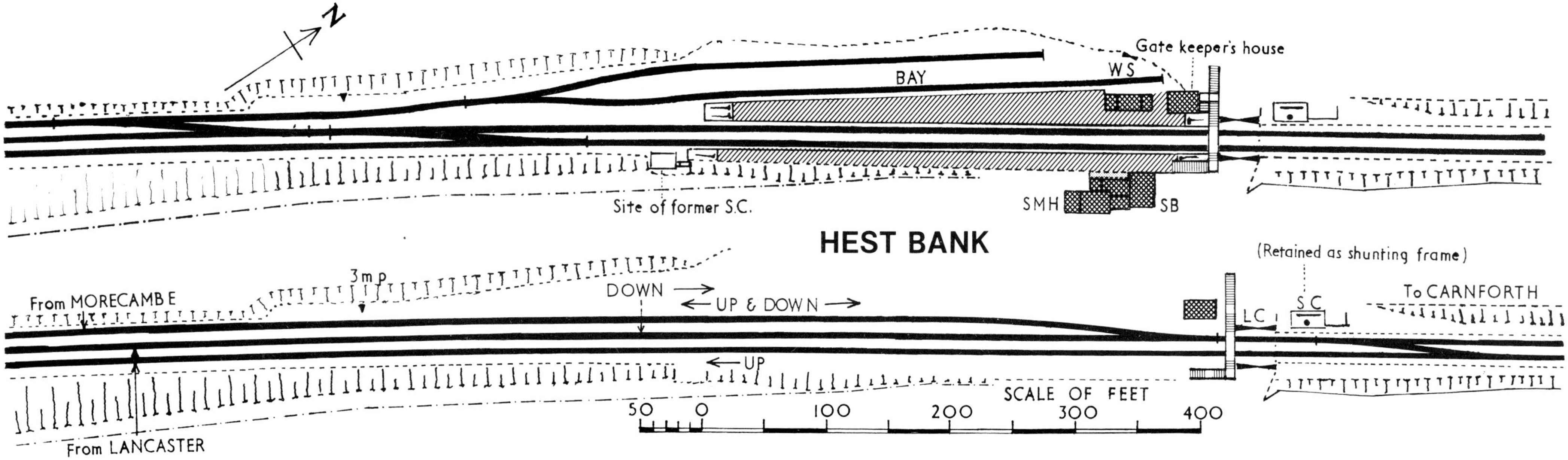

Gate keeper's house

BAY WS

Site of former S.C.

SMH SB

HEST BANK

(Retained as shunting frame)

From MORECAMBE 3mp

DOWN ←UP & DOWN→

←UP

To CARNFORTH

LC SC

From LANCASTER

SCALE OF FEET
50 0 100 200 300 400

Above: The two scale plans show Hest Bank as a passenger station with the old LNWR signal cabin near the junction, and after the removal of the platforms and construction of a new signal box. This box was used as a block post until Preston power box was commissioned, and then as a 'shunting' frame to supervise the gates, and a direction lever working to Bare Lane.

Below left: The station buildings and stationmaster's house (on the left). Rugged construction characterised the early L&C section stations and, in many cases, station houses outlived their stations.

Below: The gates, footbridge and gatekeeper's house.

HEST BANK *(Map Ref. S11)*

Hest Bank Station was located on the West Coast Main Line, a short distance north of Lancaster and, paradoxically, is the only station in sight of and in close proximity to the coast in the entire length of the West Coast Main Line. As is recorded elsewhere in this volume, creation of the West Coast route was piecemeal. By 1841, the London & Birmingham, Grand Junction, North Union and other lines provided a rail route from Euston to Fleetwood, where passengers embarked on a coastal steamer to Ardrossan for Glasgow. A Royal Commission in 1841 advocated the West Coast as the one route to Scotland, and planning began to strike north from Lancaster to Carlisle. The L&CR was authorised on 6th June 1844, and opened to Oxenholme on 23rd September 1846, and to Carlisle in December. A station had been proposed for Hest Bank in 1845, and was duly provided. Meanwhile, the 'Little North Western Railway' had been formed to build across country from Skipton to Lancaster, and concluded an alliance with the Morecambe Bay & Harbour Railway, retitled Morecambe Harbour & Railway in its Act. One branch was to run approximately north-east from Morecambe, to join the L&CR at Hest Bank. In the event, this line was abandoned, to the chagrin of the L&CR. In the 1850s, the L&CR hoped to develop an export trade in coke and other minerals from the north-east via Morecambe and, on 13th August 1859, powers were obtained for a branch from Hest Bank to Morecambe. A month later, the L&CR accepted a working lease by the LNWR. The Morecambe branch was thus built by the LNWR, and opened as a double track route on 8th August 1864.

Mineral traffic did not develop, and the line was subsequently singled. As Morecambe developed as a tourist resort, the need for a south-facing connection to the LNWR arose, and a short south curve was laid in during 1888. Most LNWR passenger trains took this route, and beyond Bare Lane Station on the branch, where the old and new lines joined, was redoubled. The section from Bare Lane to Hest Bank remained single.

Hest Bank Station gained renown between the wars as the only station between Preston and Carlisle to be electrically lit, the brainchild of an inventive member of staff! A small goods yard, reached off the Morecambe branch, existed on the 'down' side of the line. This closed on 2nd December 1963. As with many other goods yards, the track was put to good use; camping coaches being located here, to cash in on the proximity to the seaside. Passenger services ceased on 3rd February 1969.

Looking south towards Lancaster and Morecambe in the 1950s, as a BR 'Britannia' Pacific, No. 70052, *Firth of Tay* heads an northbound express through the station. To the left is the LNWR signal box and, to the right, the bay, the goods yard tracks and branch connection. Two sidings exist in the yard, whilst the running connections have been moved closer to the station, compared to the earlier survey.

HEST BANK

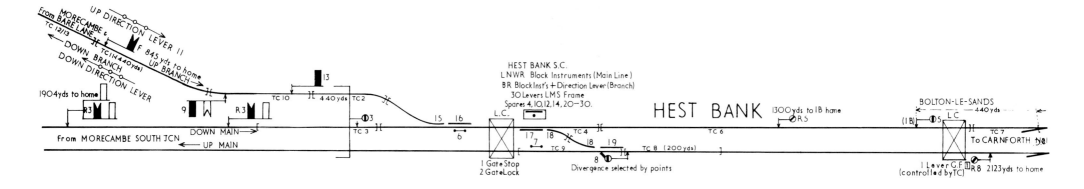

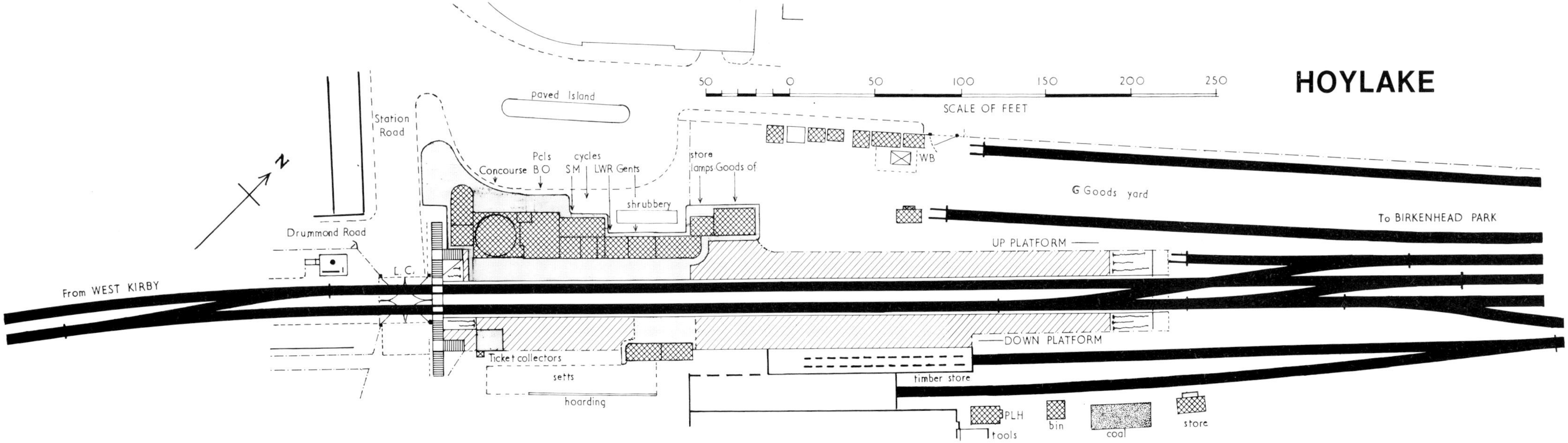

HOYLAKE

SCALE OF FEET

50   0   50   100   150   200   250

Station Road

paved Island

Drummond Road

Concourse   B O   SM   LWR Gents

Pcls   cycles

store lamps Goods of

shrubbery

WB

G Goods yard

To BIRKENHEAD PARK

UP PLATFORM

From WEST KIRBY

L.C.

Ticket collectors

setts

hoarding

DOWN PLATFORM

timber store

PLH   bin   coal   store

tools

Below: A view looking towards Birkenhead, from the 'up' platform. One advantage of the cantilever beam construction, with the reinforcing beams above the roof, is that it avoids the need for intermediate pillars, or for a broken roof line. Lighting can be arranged much more easily, with fewer areas left dark where passengers could stumble over obstructions.

Below: Looking from the 'down' platform at Hoylake, towards West Kirby, with the old Wirral signal box contrasting with the 1930s' LMS footbridge. Signal boxes of very similar appearance were built over a long period by Saxby & Farmer, the Railway Signal Co., and the LYR signalling department, and were therefore common in the north of England.

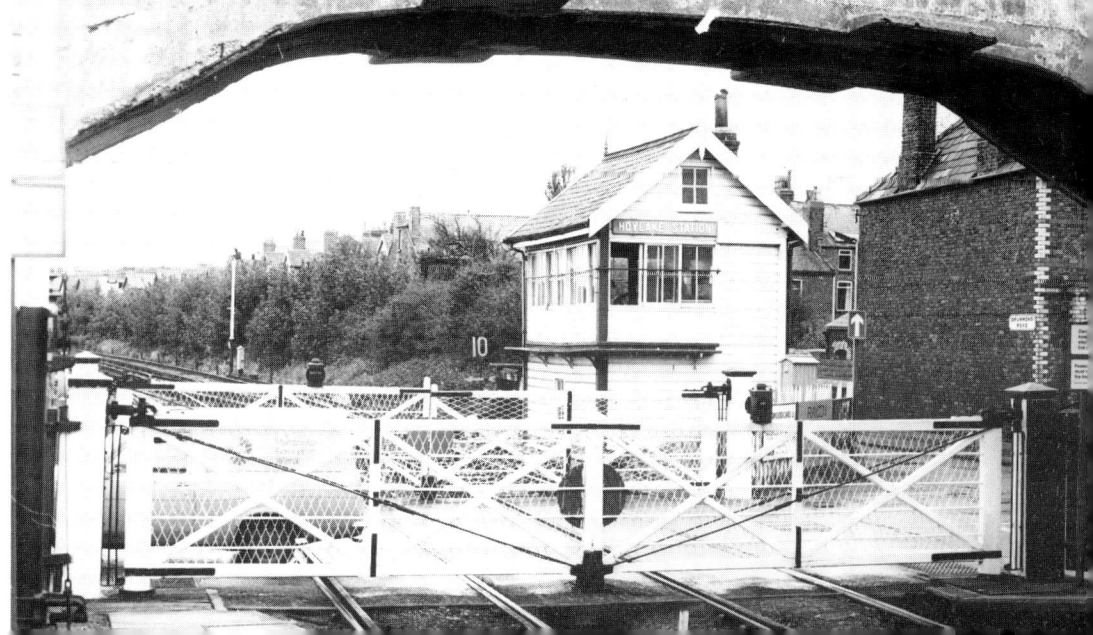

HOYLAKE *(Map Ref. S9)*

Hoylake Station was the original western terminus of the Hoylake Railway, which opened to Birkenhead on 2nd July 1866. The line closed in 1869, reopened on 1st August 1872, and was extended south and west to West Kirby on 1st April 1878, eventually becoming a part of the Wirral Railway. An extended historical perspective is given under 'Bidston'. When one sees the intensive suburban service carried on this route today, and recalls that, in the 1880s, as many as twenty trains were scheduled each way daily, it comes as a surprise to discover that this line was operated on the 'time interval' system well into the 1880s. Until 1887, the whole of the Seacombe Hoylake & Deeside Railway (all 6½ miles) was single track, operated on the 'train staff and ticket' system, without block telegraph. In 1888, the Birkenhead Park to Birkenhead North section opened, as did the New Brighton branch, which was double, and worked on 'absolute block' from the outset but, until 1889, when block working was instituted on the West Kirby section, this remained 'time interval'. During 1895, a second line was brought into use between Bidston and Hoylake, and extended to West Kirby during the following year.

Above: The station approach and footbridge, as seen from the north, with BR and Merseyside PTE logos. By the 1930s, Hoylake was a sizeable community, and although the 'down' building was simple, the 'up' building was more commodious, with a circular upper floor. The curving motif, also to be found in many other 1930s' buildings, is emphasised by the curved projection of the canopy by Station Road and the forecourt. The whole structure is redolent of mid-1930s concrete styling.

Below: The 'up' platform buildings looking towards Birkenhead. The footbridge visible in these plates was a part of the 1930s' modernisation. Its cracked and stained appearance compares ill with more antiquated building materials.

HOYLAKE

Below: A view looking towards Birkenhead Park. The old SH&D station was replaced by the LMS in 1938 by concrete-framed buildings with brick infilling and metal-framed windows. The platform awnings were supported by reinforced-concrete cantilever beams from above; a striking new development at that time. This is clearly visible on the 'down' shelter (right). Note the extensive provision of advert hoardings.

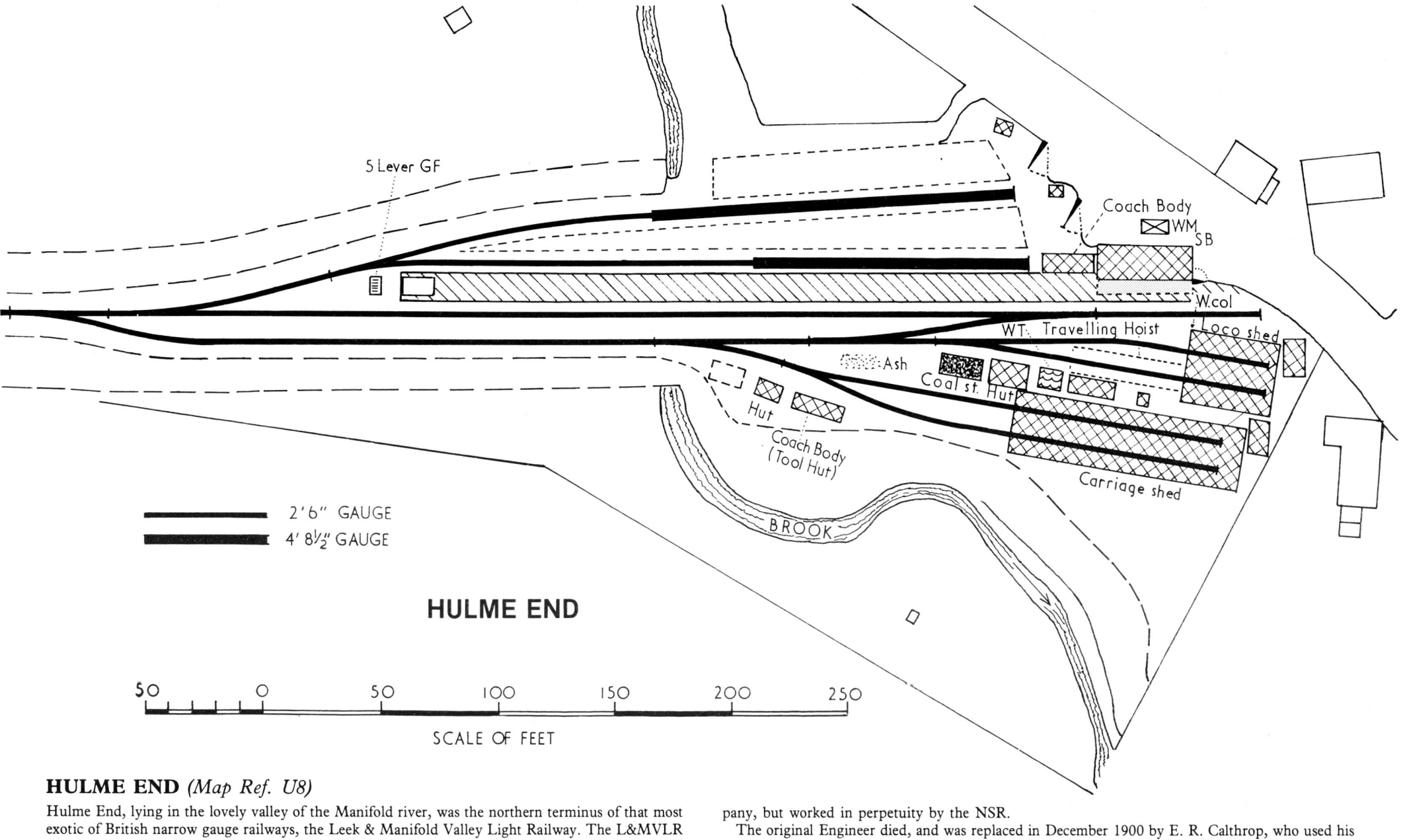

5 Lever GF

Coach Body

WM SB

W.col

Loco shed

WT Travelling Hoist

Ash

Coal st. Hut

Carriage shed

Hut

Coach Body
(Tool Hut)

BROOK

HULME END

——— 2'6" GAUGE

▬▬▬ 4' 8½" GAUGE

50   0   50   100   150   200   250

SCALE OF FEET

HULME END (Map Ref. U8)

Hulme End, lying in the lovely valley of the Manifold river, was the northern terminus of that most exotic of British narrow gauge railways, the Leek & Manifold Valley Light Railway. The L&MVLR was a product of the Light Railways Act of 1896, which permitted the construction of secondary rural railways, without the cost of a full Parliamentary Bill, and imposed less costly standards for construction or operation. The L&MVLR was one of four sections of line, three standard gauge, approved by the Leek, Caldon Low and Hartington Light Railways Order of 1898. A standard gauge branch was to run from the NSR Churnet Valley line to Waterhouses, a distance of 9½ miles, to be constructed and worked by the North Staffordshire Railway, where it would make end-on connection with the 8 mile-long 2ft. 6in. gauge Leek & Manifold Valley Light Railway, to be built by a separate company, but worked in perpetuity by the NSR.

The original Engineer died, and was replaced in December 1900 by E. R. Calthrop, who used his work for the Barsi Light Railway in India, as the basis of the new line, providing engines with massive lamp houses, double tropical roofs, etc. Construction began in 1902, with the line opening on 27th June 1904. Facilities at Waterhouses, where the L&MVLR connected with the NSR, comprised just a few sidings and run-round facilities, and locomotive and carriage sheds and workshops were located at Hulme End. The L&MVLR was taken over by the LMS in 1923, and all services ceased from Monday, 12th March 1934. Demolition took place in 1937, much of the track bed becoming a public footpath.

Above left: Station facilities at Hulme End comprised a timber station building at the extremity of the line, supplemented by an old standard gauge coach body, mounted upon timber staging to preserve it from ground damp. In the foreground are the 2ft. 6in. metals of the L&MVLR. Calthrop was a pioneer of the transporter wagon, which permitted standard gauge wagons to be worked through to their destination, and, rather than tie up transporter wagons whilst wagons awaited load, isolated sections of standard gauge were provided at stations. The end of one such siding, terminating by the coach body, is visible above.

Above right: One of the benefits of the Light Railways Act was the relaxation of normal construction standards and, with limited traffic, this was quite sensible. Train movements at Hulme End were controlled from an open 5-lever ground frame beyond the end of the platform. Conventional signalling would have entailed the expense of a 15 to 20-lever signal box, with block telegraph, etc. The object on the end of the platform, described in some works as 'signal box', was a very crude toilet.

HULME END

Right: A detailed study of the station building and ancient coach body, and also of the timber-facing to the platform. In this, and the other general view of the station, one of the transporter wagons can be seen in use, carrying an open wagon. The limited traffic potential of the L&MVLR, three to four trains a day, is emphasised by the rural nature of Hulme End, the largest community en route!

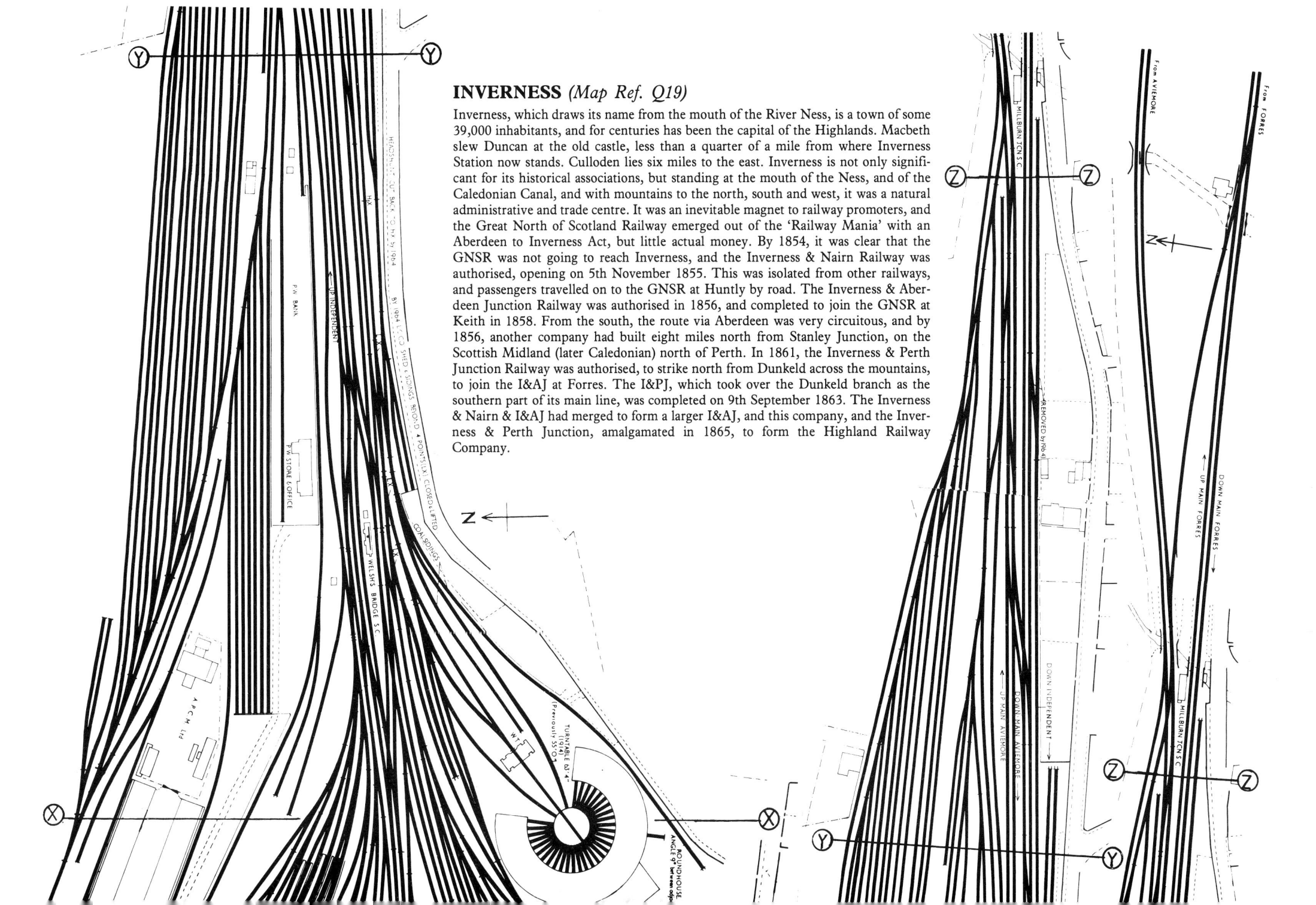

INVERNESS *(Map Ref. Q19)*

Inverness, which draws its name from the mouth of the River Ness, is a town of some 39,000 inhabitants, and for centuries has been the capital of the Highlands. Macbeth slew Duncan at the old castle, less than a quarter of a mile from where Inverness Station now stands. Culloden lies six miles to the east. Inverness is not only significant for its historical associations, but standing at the mouth of the Ness, and of the Caledonian Canal, and with mountains to the north, south and west, it was a natural administrative and trade centre. It was an inevitable magnet to railway promoters, and the Great North of Scotland Railway emerged out of the 'Railway Mania' with an Aberdeen to Inverness Act, but little actual money. By 1854, it was clear that the GNSR was not going to reach Inverness, and the Inverness & Nairn Railway was authorised, opening on 5th November 1855. This was isolated from other railways, and passengers travelled on to the GNSR at Huntly by road. The Inverness & Aberdeen Junction Railway was authorised in 1856, and completed to join the GNSR at Keith in 1858. From the south, the route via Aberdeen was very circuitous, and by 1856, another company had built eight miles north from Stanley Junction, on the Scottish Midland (later Caledonian) north of Perth. In 1861, the Inverness & Perth Junction Railway was authorised, to strike north from Dunkeld across the mountains, to join the I&AJ at Forres. The I&PJ, which took over the Dunkeld branch as the southern part of its main line, was completed on 9th September 1863. The Inverness & Nairn & I&AJ had merged to form a larger I&AJ, and this company, and the Inverness & Perth Junction, amalgamated in 1865, to form the Highland Railway Company.

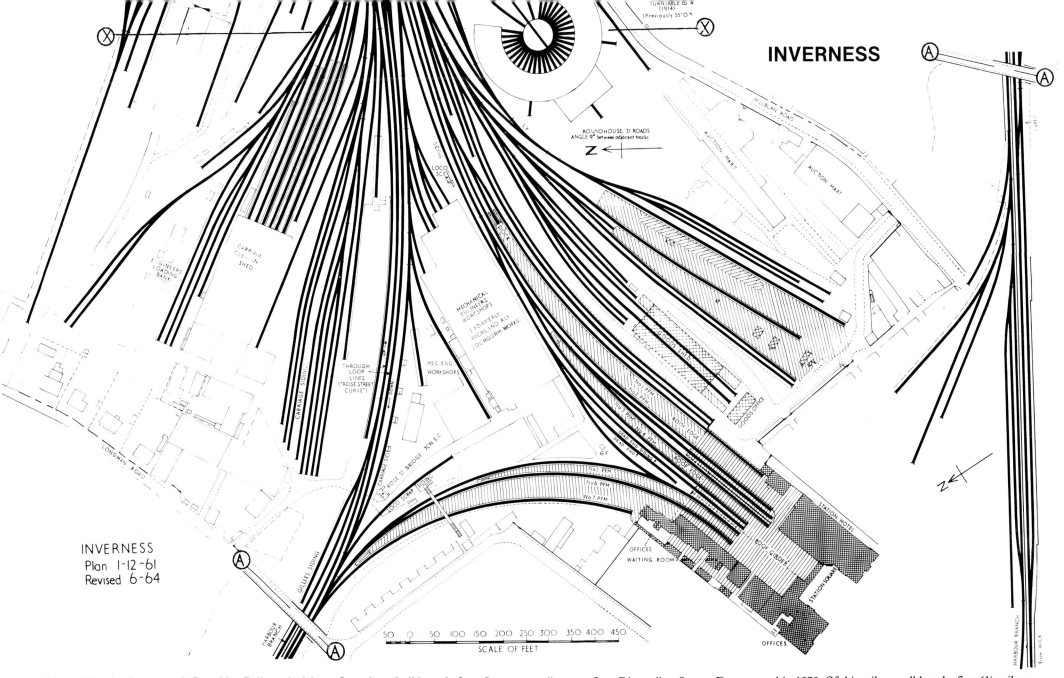

INVERNESS

ROUNDHOUSE. 31 ROADS
ANGLE 9° between adjacent tracks

TURNTABLE 63' 4"
(1914)
(Previously 55'0")

MILBURN ROAD

AUCTION MART

AUCTION MART

GOODS SHED

GOODS OFFICE

No1 PFM
No2 PFM
No3 PFM
No4 PFM
DOCK
ROOF EDGE
ROOF EDGE

DEAD END SIDING
DEAD END
GF

No5 PFM
No6 PFM
No7 PFM
OFFICES
WAITING ROOM
ROOF GIRDER
STATION HOTEL
STATION SQUARE
OFFICES

ENGINEERS
LOADING
BANK

CARRIAGE
CLEANING
SHED

MECHANICAL
ENGINEERS
WORK SHOPS
(FORMERLY
HIGHLAND RLY
LOCHGORM WORKS)

MEC ENG
WORKSHOPS

CARRIAGE SIDINGS

THROUGH
LOOP
LINES
("ROSE STREET
CURVE")

DOWN
UP

CARRIAGE SIDING
ROSE ST BRIDGE JCN S C
LOCO SCRAP SIDING

LONGMAN ROAD

INVERNESS
Plan 1-12-61
Revised 6-64

GILLIES SIDING

HARBOUR BRANCH

HARBOUR BRANCH

from WICK

50 0 50 100 150 200 250 300 350 400 450
SCALE OF FEET

Meanwhile, the Inverness & Rossshire Railway had been formed, to build north from Inverness, opening to Dingwall on 11th June 1862. A series of further companies, all of which finally came into the Highland orbit, carried metals to Bonar Bridge by 1864, Golspie by 1868, and Thurso in 1874. The line west from Dingwall to Strome Ferry opened in 1870. Of this mileage, all but the first 6¾ miles ex-Inverness on the Aberdeen line were single. By the 1880s, the existing route from the south, which joined the Aberdeen line 24 miles east of the town, was itself regarded as circuitous and, following NBR adven-

Above: An ex-G&SWR 'Pug', No. 16040, shunts on the harbour branch by Rose St. Bridge Junction in 1930. The shorter semaphore signal by Rose St. box (extreme right) is for the barrow-crossing, one of the principal accesses into the HR works!

Above right: The scene from the northern platforms, Nos. 7 (left) and 6/5 (right), looking towards the Rose St. curve. The harbour branch descends between the railings and Gillies Siding on the right. Both the near signal, ex-platforms 5/6, and the bracket by the bridge, would appear to be beyond the clearing point of the junctions which they 'protect'. Note also the steps on the near bracket platform, and the 'X' shunt arms.

Below: The extreme width of the island platform between platforms 6 and 7 is heightened by the narrowness of platform 5/6. In the background is the stepped train shed of this most curious station. The goods shed is visible on the far left-hand side.

INVERNESS

tures, the HR secured their own act for a direct Aviemore to Inverness line in 1884. This was opened to Millburn Junction, just outside Inverness, on 1st November 1898, the last few miles into Inverness being double.

The I&AJ station was on a south-westerly axis, with a short branch running past the station on the north side to the docks. When the Ross line from the north arrived, additional platforms were added on the north-west side of the old station, the harbour branch completing a triangle. Eventually, three platforms existed on the north side, and four on the south. The Highland Railway's Lochgorm Works were established within the triangle.

The approach to Inverness from the south and east was controlled by two boxes, Millburn Junction, and Welsh's Bridge. To avoid geographical confusion, it should be noted that the Aviemore line is carried over the Forres line beyond the limits of the scale plan.

Normal passenger services terminated at Inverness and, to facilitate connections between the north and south lines, trains from the north mostly took the Rose St. curve, and backed into the south platform, for cross-platform interchange. Trains from the south, likewise, backed into the north platforms and trains from the east ran straight in. Inverness remains an important railway centre today, the routes surviving primarily through social need, especially in winter.

INVERNESS

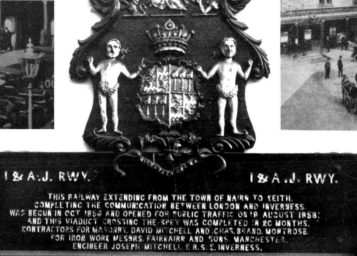

Below: This imposing plaque records the importance attached to the completion of rail communication with London, with the opening of the I&AJ Railway.

Above: The former Highland Railway Company head offices and station frontage, looking across the square in the mid-1920s. What a fine selection of cars are in view.

Authors' Collection

Above: The station hotel and entrance, seen from the HR offices prior to World War I. Compare the road vehicles with those opposite.

Authors' Collection

Below: A view looking past the coal sidings near Welsh's Bridge box, circa 1930. To the left is the coal stage and, in the centre, 'Jones Goods' No. 17921. To the right is an HR brake.

Below: No. 5121, a Class 24 diesel, double-heads No. 5342, a Class 26, in platform 2, with a Perth express. In the background is the station canopy and, to the right, Lochgorm Works.

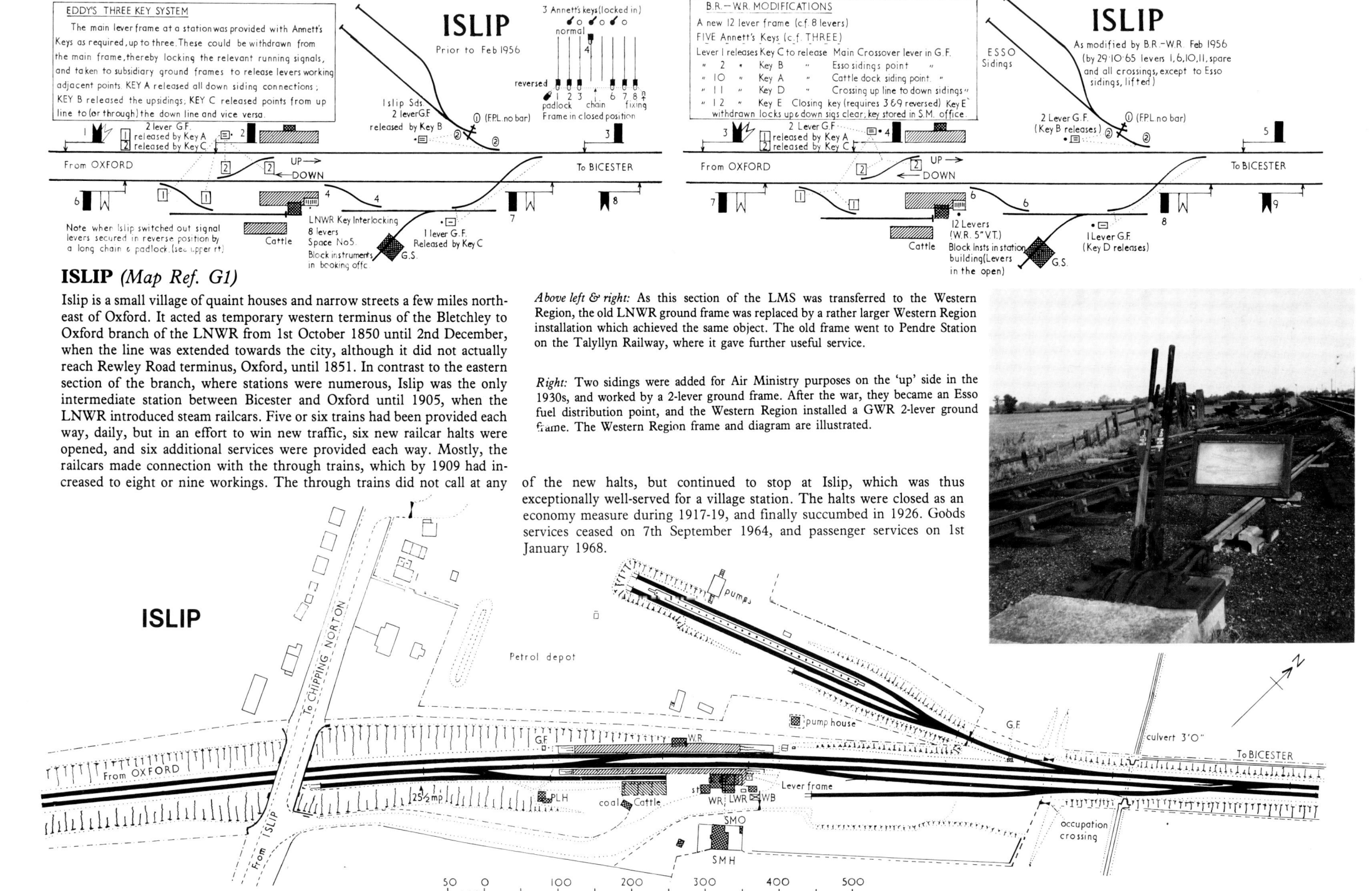

Diagram annotations (top left)

EDDY'S THREE KEY SYSTEM

The main lever frame at a station was provided with Annett's Keys as required, up to three. These could be withdrawn from the main frame, thereby locking the relevant running signals, and taken to subsidiary ground frames to release levers working adjacent points. KEY A released all down siding connections; KEY B released the up sidings; KEY C released points from up line to (or through) the down line and vice versa.

ISLIP

Prior to Feb 1956

3 Annett's keys (locked in)
normal
reversed
padlock chain fixing
Frame in closed position

Islip Sds
2 lever G.F.
released by Key B

① (F.P.L. no bar)

2 lever G.F.
① released by Key A
② released by Key C

From OXFORD

UP →
← DOWN

To BICESTER

Note when Islip switched out signal levers secured in reverse position by a long chain & padlock (see upper rt.)

Cattle

LNWR Key Interlocking
8 levers
Space No.5.
Block instruments in booking offc.

1 lever G.F.
Released by Key C

G.S.

Diagram annotations (top right)

B.R. — W.R. MODIFICATIONS

A new 12 lever frame (c.f. 8 levers)
FIVE Annett's Keys (c.f. THREE.)
Lever 1 releases Key C to release Main Crossover lever in G.F.
" 2 " Key B " Esso sidings point "
" 10 " Key A " Cattle dock siding point. "
" 11 " Key D " Crossing up line to down sidings"
" 12 " Key E Closing key (requires 3 & 9 reversed) Key E withdrawn locks up & down sigs clear; key stored in S.M. office.

ISLIP

As modified by B.R.-W.R. Feb 1956
(by 29·10·65 levers 1,6,10,11, spare and all crossings, except to Esso sidings, lifted.)

ESSO Sidings

2 Lever G.F.
(Key B releases)

① (F.P.L. no bar)

From OXFORD

UP →
← DOWN

To BICESTER

Cattle

12 Levers
(W.R. 5" V.T.)
Block Insts in station building (Levers in the open)

1 Lever G.F.
(Key D releases)

G.S.

ISLIP (Map Ref. G1)

Islip is a small village of quaint houses and narrow streets a few miles northeast of Oxford. It acted as temporary western terminus of the Bletchley to Oxford branch of the LNWR from 1st October 1850 until 2nd December, when the line was extended towards the city, although it did not actually reach Rewley Road terminus, Oxford, until 1851. In contrast to the eastern section of the branch, where stations were numerous, Islip was the only intermediate station between Bicester and Oxford until 1905, when the LNWR introduced steam railcars. Five or six trains had been provided each way, daily, but in an effort to win new traffic, six new railcar halts were opened, and six additional services were provided each way. Mostly, the railcars made connection with the through trains, which by 1909 had increased to eight or nine workings. The through trains did not call at any

Above left & right: As this section of the LMS was transferred to the Western Region, the old LNWR ground frame was replaced by a rather larger Western Region installation which achieved the same object. The old frame went to Pendre Station on the Talyllyn Railway, where it gave further useful service.

Right: Two sidings were added for Air Ministry purposes on the 'up' side in the 1930s, and worked by a 2-lever ground frame. After the war, they became an Esso fuel distribution point, and the Western Region installed a GWR 2-lever ground frame. The Western Region frame and diagram are illustrated.

of the new halts, but continued to stop at Islip, which was thus exceptionally well-served for a village station. The halts were closed as an economy measure during 1917-19, and finally succumbed in 1926. Goods services ceased on 7th September 1964, and passenger services on 1st January 1968.

Map (bottom)

ISLIP

To CHIPPING NORTON

From ISLIP

From OXFORD

Petrol depot

pump

pump house

G.F.

25½ mp

PLH

coal Cattle

WR LWR WB

SMO

SMH

WR

G.F.

To BICESTER

culvert 3'0"

occupation crossing

50 0 100 200 300 400 500

ISLIP

Above: The waiting shelter on the 'up' platform, in this view looking towards Bicester on 29th October 1965. Timber-built platforms of this type were to be found at many wayside LNWR stations, generally dating from the late 1870s or early 1880s, at which time a prefabricated shelter with a gently sloping roof, extended outwards to provide a small awning, was favoured. Western Region chocolate and cream paint has been applied, but does not disguise the lines of a 1930s LMS 'Hawkseye' sign. Passenger access to the 'up' platform was via a pedestrian/barrow-way at the Bicester end of the station.

Below: Looking from the 'up' side towards Bicester, in 1965, as a BR Standard locomotive approaches down the long straight at the east end of the station. The main building on the 'down' side is a replacement for the original structure, which disintegrated during a blizzard in January 1881! The remains of a small cattle dock can be seen at the extreme right-hand edge of the picture. The station ground frame can just be seen to the immediate left of the station buildings. Islip was a block post, open for part of the day, the block instruments being located in the buildings. When closed, the levers were 'locked' in position by means of a long chain and padlock. The Western Region installed a closing lever which was locked by Annett's Key. The signalling at Islip, despite its renewal by the Western Region in 1956, was a remarkable survival of a system adopted by E. M. G. Eddy to hasten, and economise on, interlocking in the 1880s. Eddy was then a District Officer of the LNWR, later to become Chief Commissioner of Railways for New South Wales. When inspecting stations of the Buckinghamshire branch, Eddy realised that an extended use of Annett's Key working was feasible and cheap, the latter in accord with the Chairman, Sir Richard Moon's, dictat. His plan was to use three keys controlling subsidiary ground frames from a main running ground frame. The signal department at Crewe perfected the idea, and Annett's Key (A) released 'down' sidings at such installations, Key (B) released 'up' sidings, and Key (C) all connections affecting both 'up' and 'down' lines. In the case of Islip, this resulted in a main frame and three subsidiary key-locked frames. Installations of this type, although common on the LNWR, proliferated in the colonies, where economy of construction was even more vital. Some signal manufacturers not only offered extensive key locking systems, but point locks which could be run through in the wrong direction without causing immense damage; an important saving where inexperienced native staff were used! At Islip, such exotic creations were hardly necessary. The Western Region resignalling of 1956 took five keys to accomplish what Crewe managed with three and a padlock.

Below: The Western Region lever frame, showing the locking lever, No. 12.

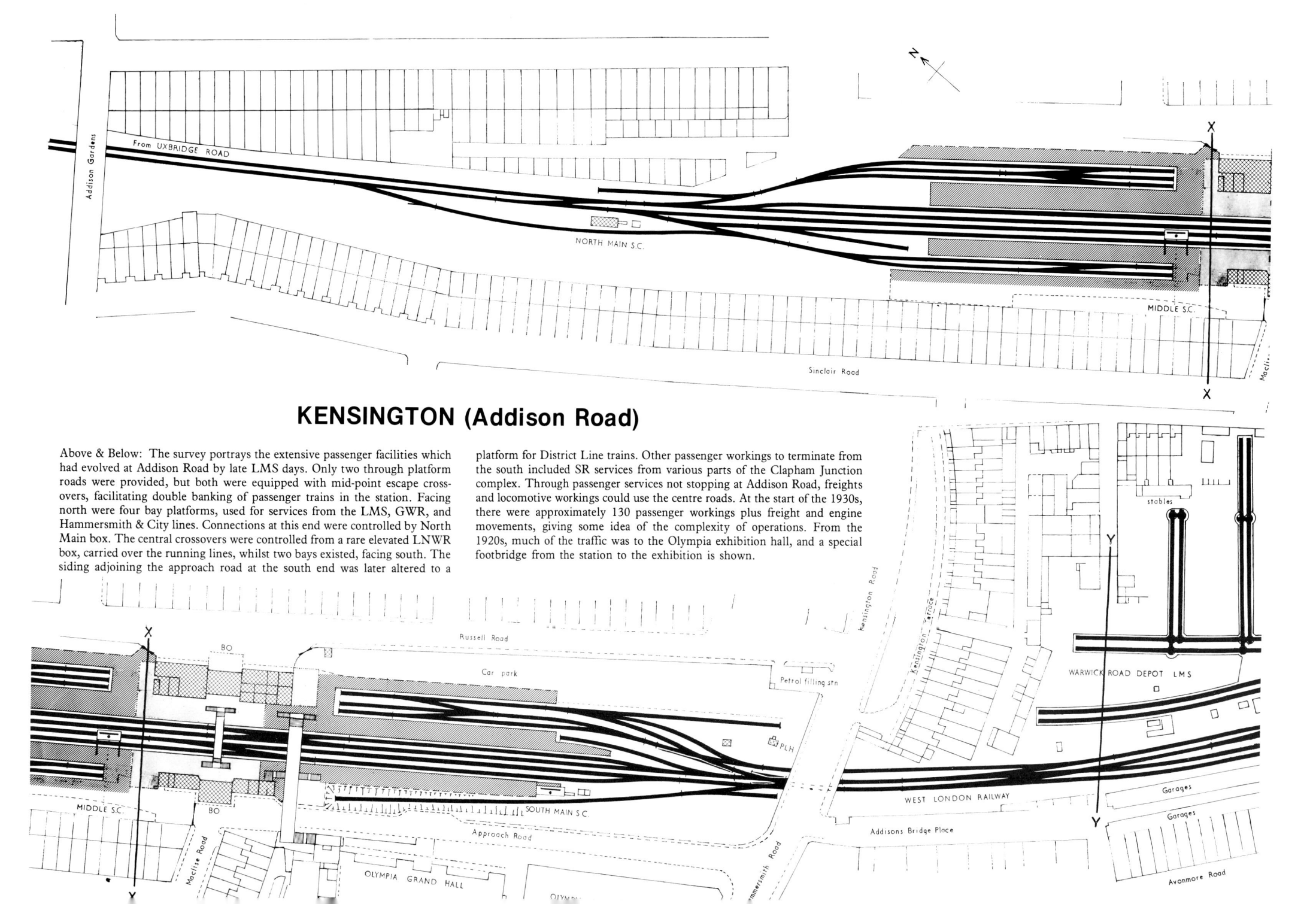

KENSINGTON (Addison Road)

Above & Below: The survey portrays the extensive passenger facilities which had evolved at Addison Road by late LMS days. Only two through platform roads were provided, but both were equipped with mid-point escape cross-overs, facilitating double banking of passenger trains in the station. Facing north were four bay platforms, used for services from the LMS, GWR, and Hammersmith & City lines. Connections at this end were controlled by North Main box. The central crossovers were controlled from a rare elevated LNWR box, carried over the running lines, whilst two bays existed, facing south. The siding adjoining the approach road at the south end was later altered to a platform for District Line trains. Other passenger workings to terminate from the south included SR services from various parts of the Clapham Junction complex. Through passenger services not stopping at Addison Road, freights and locomotive workings could use the centre roads. At the start of the 1930s, there were approximately 130 passenger workings plus freight and engine movements, giving some idea of the complexity of operations. From the 1920s, much of the traffic was to the Olympia exhibition hall, and a special footbridge from the station to the exhibition is shown.

KENSINGTON ADDISON ROAD

Left: Kensington North Main box, looking south towards Clapham Junction.

Above: The separate GWR and LMS freight depots to the south of Addison Road Station, the separation of the goods and passenger lines, the junction with the Metropolitan District Railway to Earl's Court, and the connection from the MDR Lillie Bridge Depot.

KENSINGTON (Addison Road) *(Map Ref. W5)*

The origins of Kensington (Addison Road) were anything but promising, and in marked contrast to the phenomenal traffic to be handled by the station at its peak. In the 1830s, Kensington was a small village still surrounded by fields. In 1837, the London & Birmingham Railway cut through to the north, near Willesden, to be followed a year later by the Great Western, again to the north, near Mitre Bridge, and the London & Southampton Railway, later to become the LSWR, south of the Thames. On 21st June 1836, the Birmingham, Bristol & Thames Junction Railway Company was authorised, to build a line three miles in length, from the L&B to Kensington, and to acquire a canal. Mercifully the company changed its name in 1840 to the West London Railway. In less than seven years, on 27th May 1844, it was ready to open as a 3-mile single track branch, boasting mixed gauge from its junction point with the GWR. As the station, on Hammersmith Road, was a mile distant from habi-

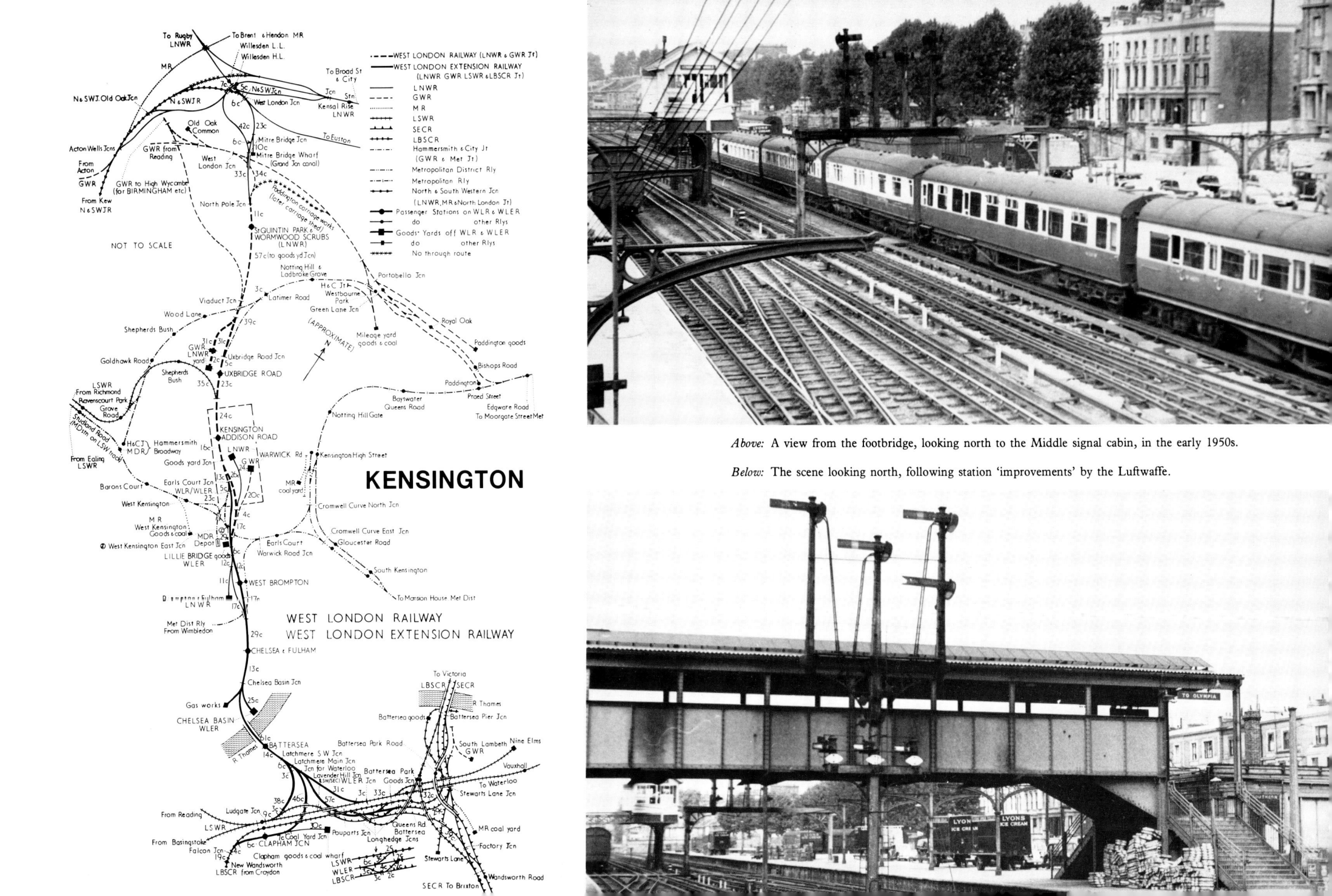

Key / Legend (right of the Kensington map):

- ═ ═ ═ WEST LONDON RAILWAY (LNWR & GWR Jt)
- ──── WEST LONDON EXTENSION RAILWAY
  (LNWR GWR LSWR & LBSCR Jt)
- ──── LNWR
- ─ ─ ─ GWR
- ········ MR
- ─┼─┼─ LSWR
- ─╫─╫─ SECR
- ─✕─✕─ LBSCR
- ─··─··─ Hammersmith & City Jt
  (GWR & Met Jt)
- ─ ·─ ·─ Metropolitan District Rly
- ─··─··─ Metropolitan Rly
- ─◆─◆─ North & South Western Jcn
  (LNWR, MR & North London Jt)
- ●─── Passenger Stations on WLR & WLER
- ●─── do   other Rlys
- ■─── Goods' Yards off WLR & WLER
- ■─── do   other Rlys
- ✕✕✕✕✕ No through route

KENSINGTON

WEST LONDON RAILWAY
WEST LONDON EXTENSION RAILWAY

NOT TO SCALE

Above: A view from the footbridge, looking north to the Middle signal cabin, in the early 1950s.

Below: The scene looking north, following station 'improvements' by the Luftwaffe.

tation, passenger and freight traffic was sparse. The line took almost seven years to build, and less than six months to close; the last train running on 30th November 1844. From 1845, a spasmodic goods service was resumed and, in 1846, the GWR and LNWR leased the WLR, the line being vested in the two companies in 1854. Three factors were to save the WLR from total ignominy. London was expanding dramatically, and close-packed housing was replacing the green fields. There was a need for a through north to south route to connect the LNWR and GWR with the companies south of the Thames, and finally the success of the Great Exhibition of 1851 guaranteed future similar events.

In 1859, the GWR, LNWR, LSWR and LB&SCR jointly secured powers for the West London Extension Railway, which would run south from Kensington, cross the Thames near Battersea, and join the LSWR and LB&SCR at Clapham Junction. In 1862, an international exhibition opened near Kensington (roughly on the site of the Science Museum). It caused much congestion on the trunk lines from the north, and was a factor in the creation of the all Midland route to St. Pancras; locally it prompted the LNWR/GWR to resume passenger services over the WLR, on 2nd June 1862. The West London Extension Railway which, like most of the WLR, was largely mixed gauge, opened on 2nd March 1863, conferring a new significance to the line. In 1869, the Metropolitan District opened to Earl's Court Junction, just south of Kensington and, initially steam-worked, this became a part of the London Transport Underground. Very naturally, the original 1844 station had been unsuitable for enlargement, and a new station, slightly to the north of Hammersmith Road bridge, was opened in 1862. At first, facilities were concentrated on the east side of the line, and northbound trains had to reverse into the platform, but the west side was added in 1869-72. From 1868, when the Metropolitan's Kensington (High St.) Station opened, the station became Kensington (Addison Road). The Olympia exhibition hall opened in 1886 and, from 1924, the station was known as 'Kensington, (Addison Rd.) for Olympia'. By 1946, Olympia was better known than the roadway, which disappeared from the title. From 1965, the station became the London terminal of the BR Motorail, by which time suburban traffic had declined due to the car and bus, although exhibition traffic remained heavy. LMS, GWR, Southern and LT stock could be seen in profusion, and celebrated workings included the LNWR/LBSCR 'Sunny South Special', just one of many through trains or carriage services to traverse the WLR/WLER.

Above left: Prior to the construction of the additional bay at the South-eastern side of the station, services ex the Metropolitan District ('District') terminated in the main northbound platform. A southbound BR train is seen on the 'down' through road.

KENSINGTON (Addison Road)

Above: A 57XX pannier tank, No. 9751, trundles along the 'down' through road on an 'engine and brake' working; a classical piece of steam railway working which, alas, is no more.

Below: A view looking south from the 'up' platform towards Earl's Court Junction. What would the promoters of the 1830s have said?

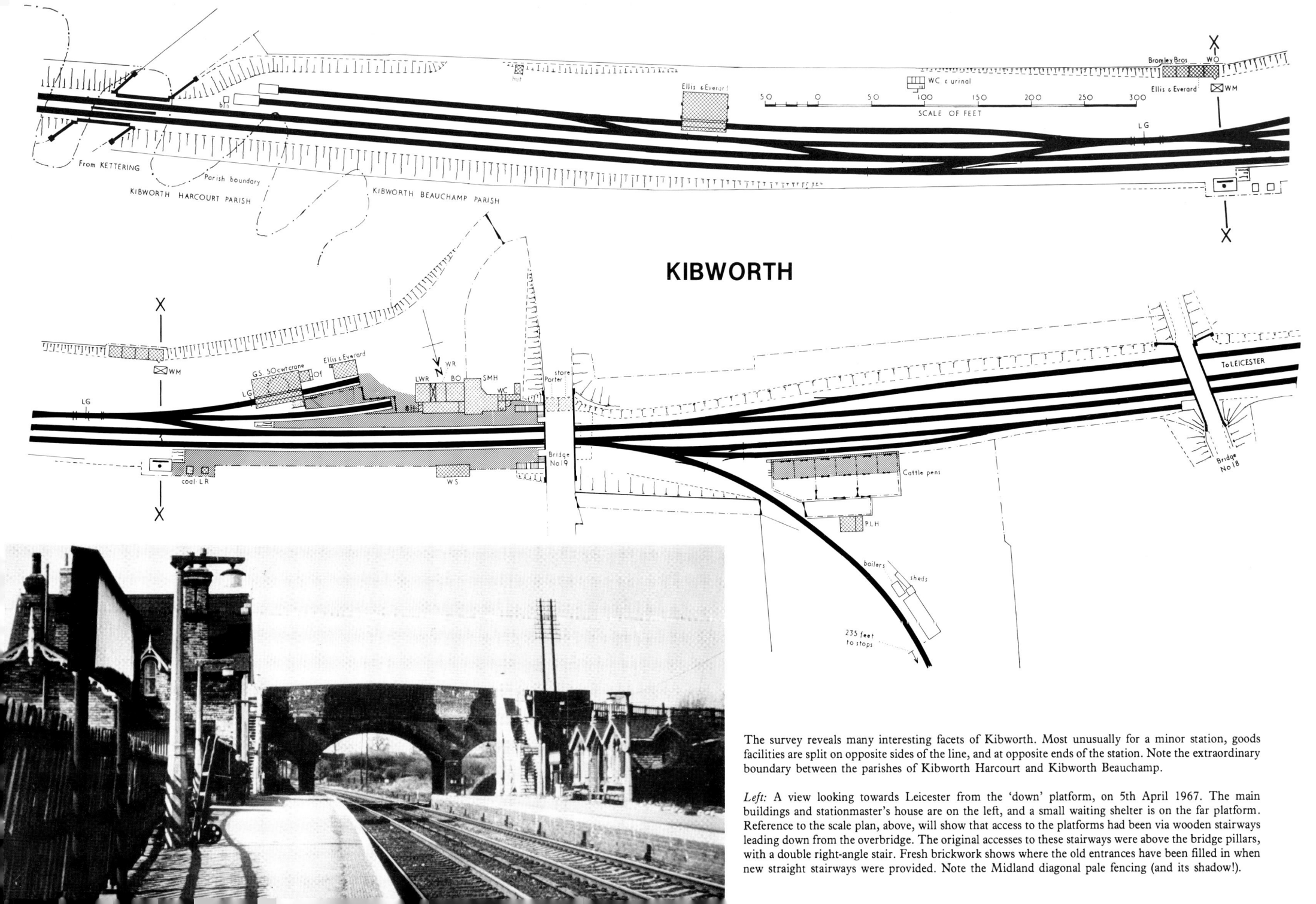

KIBWORTH

From KETTERING

Parish boundary

KIBWORTH HARCOURT PARISH

KIBWORTH BEAUCHAMP PARISH

Bromley Bros

Ellis & Everard

WC & urinal

50 0 50 100 150 200 250 300
SCALE OF FEET

hut

Ellis & Everard

WM

LG

WM

GS 50cwt crane

Ellis & Everard

LG

LWR WR BO SMH

WC

store

Porter

To LEICESTER

LG

Bridge No18

coal LR

Bridge No19

WS

Cattle pens

PLH

boilers sheds

235 feet to stops

The survey reveals many interesting facets of Kibworth. Most unusually for a minor station, goods facilities are split on opposite sides of the line, and at opposite ends of the station. Note the extraordinary boundary between the parishes of Kibworth Harcourt and Kibworth Beauchamp.

Left: A view looking towards Leicester from the 'down' platform, on 5th April 1967. The main buildings and stationmaster's house are on the left, and a small waiting shelter is on the far platform. Reference to the scale plan, above, will show that access to the platforms had been via wooden stairways leading down from the overbridge. The original accesses to these stairways were above the bridge pillars, with a double right-angle stair. Fresh brickwork shows where the old entrances have been filled in when new straight stairways were provided. Note the Midland diagonal pale fencing (and its shadow!).

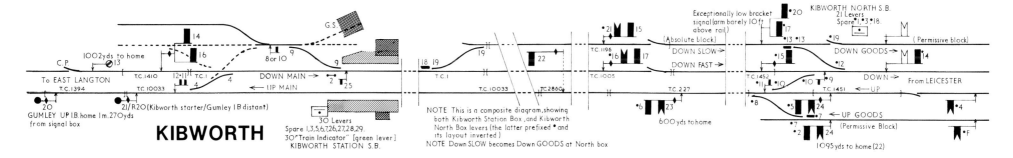

KIBWORTH

Spare 1,3,5,6,7,26,27,28,29.
30″Train Indicator″ [green lever]
KIBWORTH STATION S.B.

30 Levers

1002yds to home
C.P.
To EAST LANGTON
T.C.1394
GUMLEY UP I.B.home 1m.27Oyds
from signal box
20   21/R20 (Kibworth starter/Gumley I B distant)
T.C.1410   T.C.10033   T.C.1
DOWN MAIN →
← UP MAIN
G.S.
8 or 10

NOTE This is a composite diagram,showing
both Kibworth Station Box ,and Kibworth
North Box levers (the latter prefixed ● and
its layout inverted)
NOTE Down SLOW becomes Down GOODS at North box

KIBWORTH NORTH S.B.
21 Levers
Spare ●1, ●3, ●18.

Exceptionally low bracket
signal(arm barely 10 ft
above rail)
(Absolute block)
(Permissive block)
DOWN SLOW →
DOWN FAST →
DOWN GOODS → M
DOWN →
From LEICESTER
← UP
← UP GOODS
(Permissive Block)
600 yds to home
1095 yds to home (22)

KIBWORTH *(Map Ref. H7)*

Kibworth Station was on the Midland main line, between Leicester and Market Harborough, and was a short distance east of Kibworth Summit, the most northerly of the three summits on the Leicester-Bedford-Hitchin line. The historical backdrop to the construction of this route is given under 'East Langton', and this important section of the MR was opened to coal traffic on 15th April 1857, to goods on 4th May, and to passengers on 8th May. Although built to avoid a bottleneck on the LNWR, south of Rugby, traffic soon built up to such an extent that the new line itself became congested. Traffic delays on the GN main line, south of Hitchin, added to problems, resolved once again by means of a new main line, all the way to St. Pancras. Eventually the whole section from St. Pancras to Glendon Junction (north of Kettering) was quadrupled. At Glendon, Midland trains could continue north, via Leicester, or take the Nottingham direct line through Manton. North of Glendon, therefore, traffic was not quite so heavy and refuge sidings, as at East Langton (q.v.) or goods loops, as at Kibworth, sufficed, A 'down' slow line was provided from just beyond Kibworth Station to Kibworth North (1,510yds.) with quadruple track, two passenger and two goods lines running on to Wistow (1,332yds.). The Kibworth loops, although planned by the MR, only received Parliamentary sanction in 1923, and were built by the LMS.

These additional loops enabled slow goods trains to be routed out of the way of the St. Pancras to Leicester passenger services which, with the Midland small train policy, were frequent. South of Kibworth, the next box was Gumley, later replaced by IB signals. The signalling plan shows the station layout after the installation of the Gumley IB. All train movements through the platforms, whether running or shunting, required the use of the 'train indicator to platform' lever, No. 30. Runaway catchpoints on the 'down' lines, between the Station and North boxes, guarded against freight trains becoming divided and running back in the last few yards of the ascent to Kibworth Summit. Permissive block working, permitting more than one freight train into a section, existed between North Box and Wistow. Freight services were withdrawn on 4th July 1966, and the station closed to passengers on 1st January 1968. The station buildings were in the familiar Midland Ecclesiastical/Gothic style, and Kibworth handled the occasional semi-fast or express, as well as local services. In 1942, for example, the 1.24p.m. Nottingham to St. Pancras express was scheduled to call.

Below left: The scene from the 'up' platform steps, looking south. The yard was in use for engineering purposes in April 1967.

Below right: The station approach and stationmaster's house. The architect was C. A. Driver.

KIBWORTH

Above: The waiting shelter on the 'up' platform, with its ridge and furrow frontage, matched the main buildings. Neat little end gables, leaded lights, and the attractive floral displays produced an eyecatching ensemble, characteristic of the Midland Railway.

Below: A view looking towards Kibworth North box, with the 'down' slow signals, Nos. 20/17, in the foreground. The exceptionally low post is accounted for by the cutting, and the need to accord the main line signal (No. 15) height precedence.

Above: Kibworth Station signal cabin. The low brick base is most unusual for a Midland box, as all-timber construction was the rule, unlike the LNWR which favoured brick bases. The MR policy was cheaper, and permitted boxes to be assembled quickly, or replaced easily when traffic warranted a larger box. On the other hand, rot was a persistent enemy.

Below: A panorama of Kibworth loops, with the North box on the right. The distants below signals 2 and 5 are for Kibworth Station. The low overbridge, cutting and need to accord priority to No. 15, explain the dwarf bracket for Nos. 20/17.

KIBWORTH NORTH

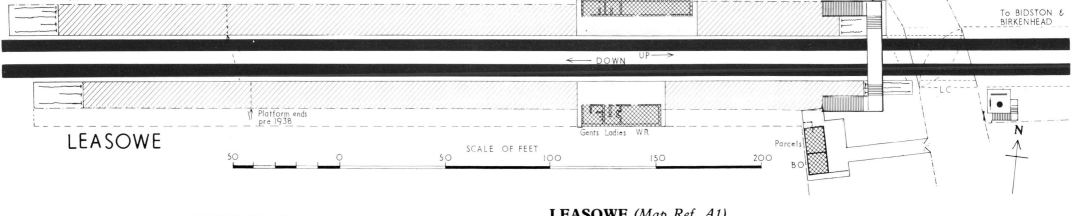

To BIDSTON &
BIRKENHEAD

LEASOWE

↑ Platform ends
pre 1938

Gents Ladies W.R.

SCALE OF FEET

50   0   50   100   150   200

Parcels

N

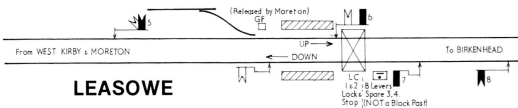

(Released by Moreton)

GF

5

M   6

From WEST KIRBY & MORETON

UP

DOWN

To BIRKENHEAD

LC
1 & 2 8 Levers
Lock & Spare 3, 4.
Stop (NOT a Block Post)

7

8

LEASOWE

LEASOWE *(Map Ref. A1)*

When the Hoylake Railway opened between Birkenhead and Hoylake in 1866, the north Wirral communities were small, and Leasowe was not judged worthy of even one of the ultra-economy gravel clearings which the Hoylake Railway saw fit to describe as stations. Roughly two miles separated Bidston from the next station to the west, Moreton, and in June 1894, whilst doubling was in progress on the Bidston to Hoylake section, the Wirral Railway decided to remedy this omission, and provided a couple of brick platforms and corrugated-iron huts at what had been a hitherto inconspicuous level crossing. Today, it is easy to forget how easily such facilities could be provided, for the brickwork could be laid in quickly, and the Engineer to any of the more impecunious railways would have catalogues of firms such as Hill & Smith, A. & J. Main, or Francis Morton (the latter just across the river at Garston). They could supply anything in corrugated iron, from a waiting shelter to a tea warehouse, hospital or church!

Below left: When LMS Divisional Officers from the LNWR or Midland saw Leasowe for the first time, with its corrugated-iron hutches, and hand-worked gates, they may well have shuddered, but they left well alone. With electrification in 1938, it must have seemed too incongruous to permit the nice new electric sets to frequent such an outmoded station, and two concrete framed buildings, similar in style to Hoylake, made their appearance, with a separate booking office on the approach path. In this illustration, looking towards West Kirby, the support beams cantilevered out above the roof slabs are clearly seen.

Below right: The LMS decided it was time to replace the hand-operated gates with a set of four gates controlled from a diminutive 10ft. long standard signal cabin, located on the Bidston side of the road crossing. As this was sufficiently far from Birkenhead Docks to make a raid by the Luftwaffe unlikely, it was not deemed necessary to brick in the windows of the locking room. The gate wheel can be seen through the windows of the box.

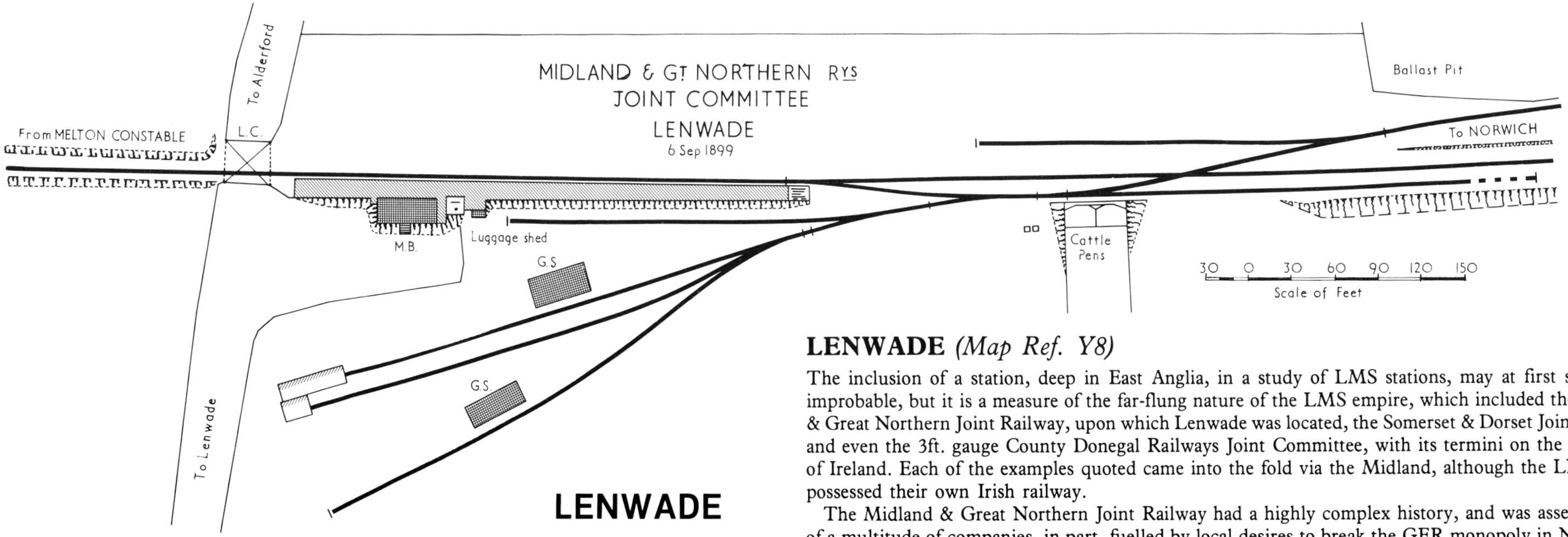

MIDLAND & GT NORTHERN RYS
JOINT COMMITTEE
LENWADE
6 Sep 1899

From MELTON CONSTABLE

To Alderford

L.C.

Ballast Pit

To NORWICH

M.B.

Luggage shed

G.S.

G.S.

Cattle Pens

To Lenwade

30 0 30 60 90 120 150
Scale of Feet

LENWADE

LENWADE *(Map Ref. Y8)*

The inclusion of a station, deep in East Anglia, in a study of LMS stations, may at first sight seem improbable, but it is a measure of the far-flung nature of the LMS empire, which included the Midland & Great Northern Joint Railway, upon which Lenwade was located, the Somerset & Dorset Joint Railway, and even the 3ft. gauge County Donegal Railways Joint Committee, with its termini on the west coast of Ireland. Each of the examples quoted came into the fold via the Midland, although the LNWR also possessed their own Irish railway.

The Midland & Great Northern Joint Railway had a highly complex history, and was assembled out of a multitude of companies, in part, fuelled by local desires to break the GER monopoly in North Norfolk and, in part, as a result of boardroom politics of the big companies. It stretched from Little Bytham on the Midland Railway, (east of Melton Mowbray and the Midland Railway's Manton to Nottingham route) to the Norfolk resorts of Cromer, Yarmouth and Lowestoft. A further connection ran from the GNR and MR at Peterborough, to join the Little Bytham line west of King's Lynn.

Below left: Looking from the station approach towards Norwich, the station building, although hardly ornate is of pleasing design with attractive shaped bargeboards. A small luggage shed was provided for parcels, etc. In the scale and signal plans of 1899, it will be noted that the signal box was shown on the platform, but a more normal location, by the level crossing, was later adopted. The problem encountered by railway engineers was to secure good visibility for the signalman, convenient access to a level crossing where applicable, as gates could only conveniently be worked by the signalman if the box was adjacent, and to keep all points within working distances permitted by the Board of Trade.

Below: A view looking along the platform towards Norwich, with the goods yard in the distance. The crossed pailings were a characteristic form of fencing on the M&GN, as typical as the diagonal fencing on the Midland Railway. Similar buildings were to be found at a number of Joint line stations.

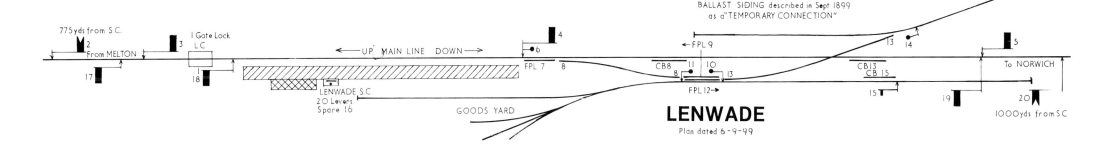

BALLAST SIDING described in Sept 1899 as a "TEMPORARY CONNECTION"

775yds from S.C.

From MELTON

I Gate Lock LC

← UP MAIN LINE DOWN →

←FPL 9

GOODS YARD

LENWADE

Plan dated 6-9-99

LENWADE S.C.
20 Levers
Spare 16

To NORWICH

1000yds from S.C.

Below left: The level crossing, signal box, and tall platform starter, in a view looking towards Norwich. One of the goods sheds is visible to the right of the signal cabin. In the early 1900s, the basic passenger service over the Norwich line was six trains each way, of which four or five called at Lenwade. By 1938, six trains called in each direction, and by 1947, there were seven northbound and eight southbound workings. The level crossing gates with their unusual vertical tie rods, were a feature of the M&GN, as was the ornamental barge boarding to the signal cabin.

Below right: A view looking towards Melton Constable a few years later, after the signal box had gone. The platform has been commandeered by the permanent way men, to serve as a material stacking ground, and is none too tidily stacked at that! The flat nature of the North Norfolk countryside will be evident from these views of Lenwade, in marked contrast to some of the other locations covered, such as Callander. In studying the signal and scale plans, it may initially seem strange that a ballast siding on the east side of the line came off the yard headshunt on the west side of the track, and cut through the running line by a diamond crossing, but this was in response to the Board of Trade's dislike of more facing points than was absolutely necessary, itself a legacy of the days prior to facing point locks and interlocking. The use of facing point locks in the yard is, however, unusual, as these are normally associated with passenger running lines.

The M&GN established its locomotive works deep in the heart of the Norfolk countryside, about twenty miles north-west of Norwich, at the village of Melton Constable. This became a railway crossroads, with branches striking north from the M&GN main line to the seaside resort of Cromer, and south to Norwich. Lenwade Station was located on the latter route which opened from Melton Constable to Lenwade on 1st July 1882, and into Norwich City Station on 2nd December 1882. Lenwade lost its passenger services during the slaughter of the Joint line on 2nd March 1959, but the Melton Constable to Norwich section remained open for general goods, private siding traffic, and coal into Norwich City. General freight facilities were withdrawn from Lenwade on 31st October 1966. As freight for Norwich City Station had to travel over fifty miles from Norwich GE to the M&GN station, about fifty times the direct distance, a connecting curve was laid in from the GER County School to Wroxham branch to the 'Joint', just north of Lenwade. As the GE line through Aylsham was still open to freight, this permitted the closure of over twenty miles of the M&GN, concentrated all freight on to the one route, and cut the mileage to Norwich City. Even so, the journey was still too long, and the Norwich service ceased, leaving Lenwade as the only former M&GN station to handle freight, at private sidings south of the station. These boasted their own industrial locomotives, and an oil terminal gave some promise for the future, well into the 1970s. Sadly, the winds of change have continued to bite.

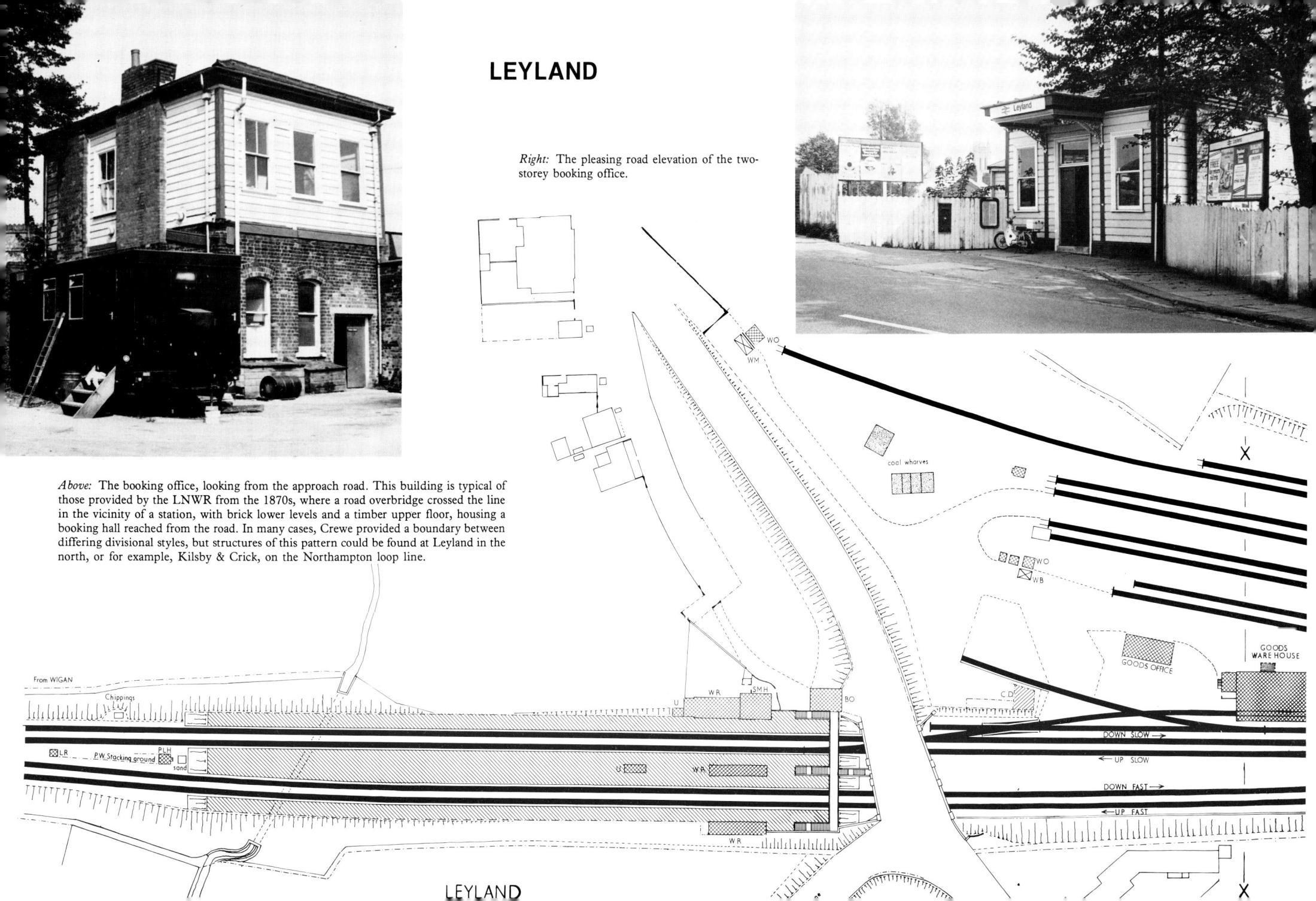

LEYLAND

Right: The pleasing road elevation of the two-storey booking office.

Above: The booking office, looking from the approach road. This building is typical of those provided by the LNWR from the 1870s, where a road overbridge crossed the line in the vicinity of a station, with brick lower levels and a timber upper floor, housing a booking hall reached from the road. In many cases, Crewe provided a boundary between differing divisional styles, but structures of this pattern could be found at Leyland in the north, or for example, Kilsby & Crick, on the Northampton loop line.

From WIGAN

Chippings

LR   P.W. Stacking ground   PLH
                              sand

U   W R   SMH
                      BO
U   W R

WR

WO
WM

coal wharves

WO
WB

GOODS OFFICE

GOODS WAREHOUSE

C D

DOWN SLOW →

← UP SLOW

DOWN FAST →

← UP FAST

LEYLAND

LEYLAND *Map Ref. O2)*

Leyland Station is located on the North Union Railway, 3¾ miles south of Preston. The NUR was an amalgamation of the Preston & Wigan Railway, authorised in 1831, and the Wigan Branch Railway, and opened between Wigan and Preston on 31st October 1838, one of the original stations being Golden Hill, renamed Leyland within a few months, although the old name persisted for a time. In June 1843, the Bolton & Preston Railway joined the NUR at Euxton Junction, 5¼ miles south of Preston. In 1844, the NUR and B&PR merged under the NUR title, and from 1st January 1846, the NUR was leased by the

Grand Junction Railway (incorporated into the LNWR in 1846) and the Manchester & Leeds Railway (LYR from 1847).

With the LYR feeding in from the Manchester direction, for Blackpool and Preston, and the west coast traffic of the LNWR, the section from Euxton Junction to Preston was very congested and, in the LNWR Act of 1875, powers were obtained for quadrupling. This was completed on 1st August 1880. Technically, the NUR was still in existence but, in 1888, the company was dissolved, and in 1889 the Bolton & Preston Railway passed into LYR ownership, and the original NUR, south of Euxton Junction, into LNWR hands. The section from Euxton Junction to Preston, including Leyland, remained joint, although largely administered by the LNWR.

On 2nd June 1898, a Blackpool to Manchester excursion of the LYR had drawn to a stand at the 'up' fast home signal north of the station. This was in accordance with station instructions that trains not booked to call were to be held at the home signal, rather than allowed forward to the platform starter. Within four minutes, another LYR excursion, from Morecambe, had run through the signals at the next box to the north and into the standing train, causing two immediate fatalities and many injuries. The collision occurred midway between the signal box and bridge No. 72. As well as showing how close headways were on this busy route, the accident recalls the use made by the LYR of its free-running 0-6-0 goods engines on excursions in high season.

At the time this accident took place, other developments in Leyland were to lead to a marked reduction in railway traffic, for it was from this small community that the mighty Leyland bus and truck concern took its title; the works being served by their own private sidings. Leyland remains open to passengers, but general freight facilities were withdrawn in 1968, and the signal box made way for Preston power box in 1972.

Above: The station house, island platform and, beyond the overbridge, Leyland signal box, looking towards Preston.

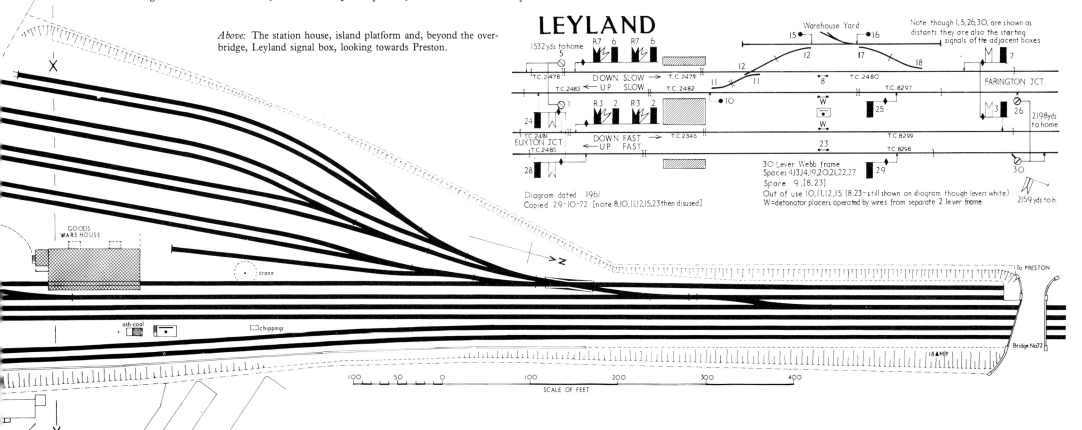

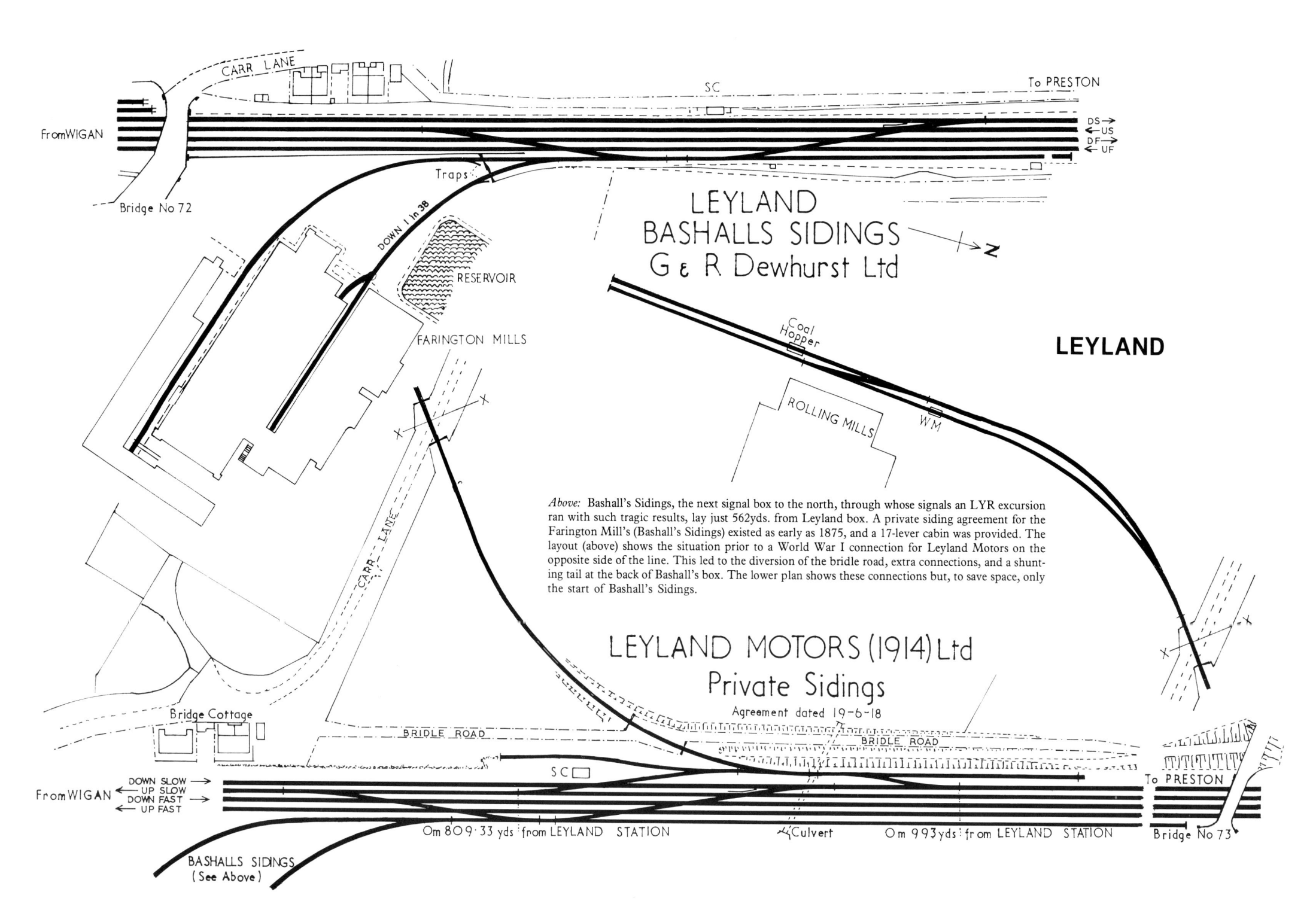

CARR LANE

SC

To PRESTON

DS →
← US
DF →
← UF

From WIGAN

Traps

Bridge No 72

DOWN 1 in 38

RESERVOIR

LEYLAND
BASHALLS SIDINGS
G & R Dewhurst Ltd

N

FARINGTON MILLS

Coal
Hopper

LEYLAND

ROLLING MILLS

WM

Above: Bashall's Sidings, the next signal box to the north, through whose signals an LYR excursion ran with such tragic results, lay just 562yds. from Leyland box. A private siding agreement for the Farington Mill's (Bashall's Sidings) existed as early as 1875, and a 17-lever cabin was provided. The layout (above) shows the situation prior to a World War I connection for Leyland Motors on the opposite side of the line. This led to the diversion of the bridle road, extra connections, and a shunting tail at the back of Bashall's box. The lower plan shows these connections but, to save space, only the start of Bashall's Sidings.

CARR LANE

Bridge Cottage

LEYLAND MOTORS (1914) Ltd
Private Sidings
Agreement dated 19-6-18

BRIDLE ROAD

BRIDLE ROAD

SC

From WIGAN

DOWN SLOW
UP SLOW
DOWN FAST
← UP FAST

To PRESTON

0m 809·33 yds from LEYLAND STATION

Culvert

0m 993 yds from LEYLAND STATION

Bridge No 73

BASHALLS SIDINGS
(See Above)

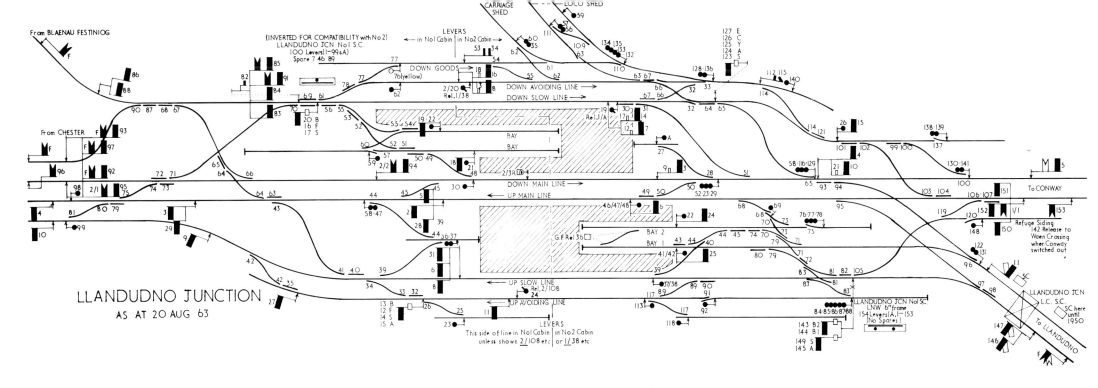

LLANDUDNO JUNCTION
AS AT 20 AUG 63

Above: A composite signalling diagram of Llandudno Nos. 1 and 2 boxes, which show how the 1890s' station, depicted under construction in the scale plan, was signalled. Upgrading of the goods lines as passenger avoiding lines produced some anomalies in the signalling, and some of the connections serve little useful purpose, as, for example, the three connections from the 'down' slow to the 'down' main at the Conway end. Two would have covered all normal requirements. The inclusion of extra levers — 'A' in both boxes — was an LNWR habit. Compared to the photograph opposite, it will be seen that the bay 1 and 2 platform starters sported subsidiary arms at that time, whilst No. 6, and the selected shunt signal, 46/47/48 are, somewhat surprisingly, separated by some yards, an undesirable feature as an engine must pass one or other at danger. The better practice is to place such signals side by side.

LLANDUDNO JUNCTION

Llandudno Junction Station, looking towards Chester from a train (headed by a Fowler 2P locomotive) entering the 'up' slow platform. The two tracks in the foreground lead into bays 1 and 2, the former being occupied. To the right are the main lines, and beyond that, the 'down' slow.

LLANDUDNO JUNCTION (Map Ref. R9)

As related under Llandudno, the Chester & Holyhead Railway was one of a number of competing schemes to proposed different ports for the Irish Mail and passenger traffic. The St. George's Harbour scheme, to Llandudno, is there detailed. A second scheme would have commenced at Shrewsbury, and run inland to Port Dynllaen on the south-west Caernarvonshire coast. At the behest of the Chester & Crewe Railway, the Stephensons became involved in a Chester & Holyhead project which, with substantial backing from the London & Birmingham and Grand Junction railways, was authorised in July 1844. The line was opened as far west as Bangor on 1st May 1848. What was to become Llandudno Junction was a windswept spot on the east bank of the River Conway, where the Llandudno road and Telford's Holyhead road split, the latter projecting out along a narrow spit to the Conway suspension bridge of 1826. The C&HR followed this route closely, with its twin tubular bridge just to the south. In 1853, the St. George's Harbour and Railway was sanctioned, and the Llandudno branch finally came into use in October 1858. Initially, Llandudno branch trains reversed into Conway Station, across the river, but

Llandudno Junction was operational by November 1858. It was located by the road junction, on a site barely 250ft. wide at its maximum. In 1860, the Conway & Llanrwst Railway was authorised to build the first section of what became the LNWR's Blaenau Ffestiniog branch. This opened on 17th June 1863, was extended to Bettws-y-Coed on 6th April 1868, and to Blaenau Ffestiniog on 22nd July 1879. The branch joined the main line at the east end of the station, hugging the east bank of the River Conway. A small locomotive depot was established parallel to the branch. The layout is shown below, as in 1888. By the 1890s, these facilities were hopelessly inadequate to cope with traffic on the Chester & Holyhead and Llandudno routes, and powers were secured for a new station, some 1,200ft. to the east of the existing one, where land was available, for four through passenger roads and dead-end bays. The second plan, of 1896 shows the relationship of the two. The old station was closed to passengers on 1st October 1897, at which time the new station came into use.

Centre left: Two large new signal boxes were constructed to work the new station, Llandudno No. 1 at the east end and No. 2 at the west end. Rationalisation has seen the station latterly reduced to a single box, formerly No. 2.

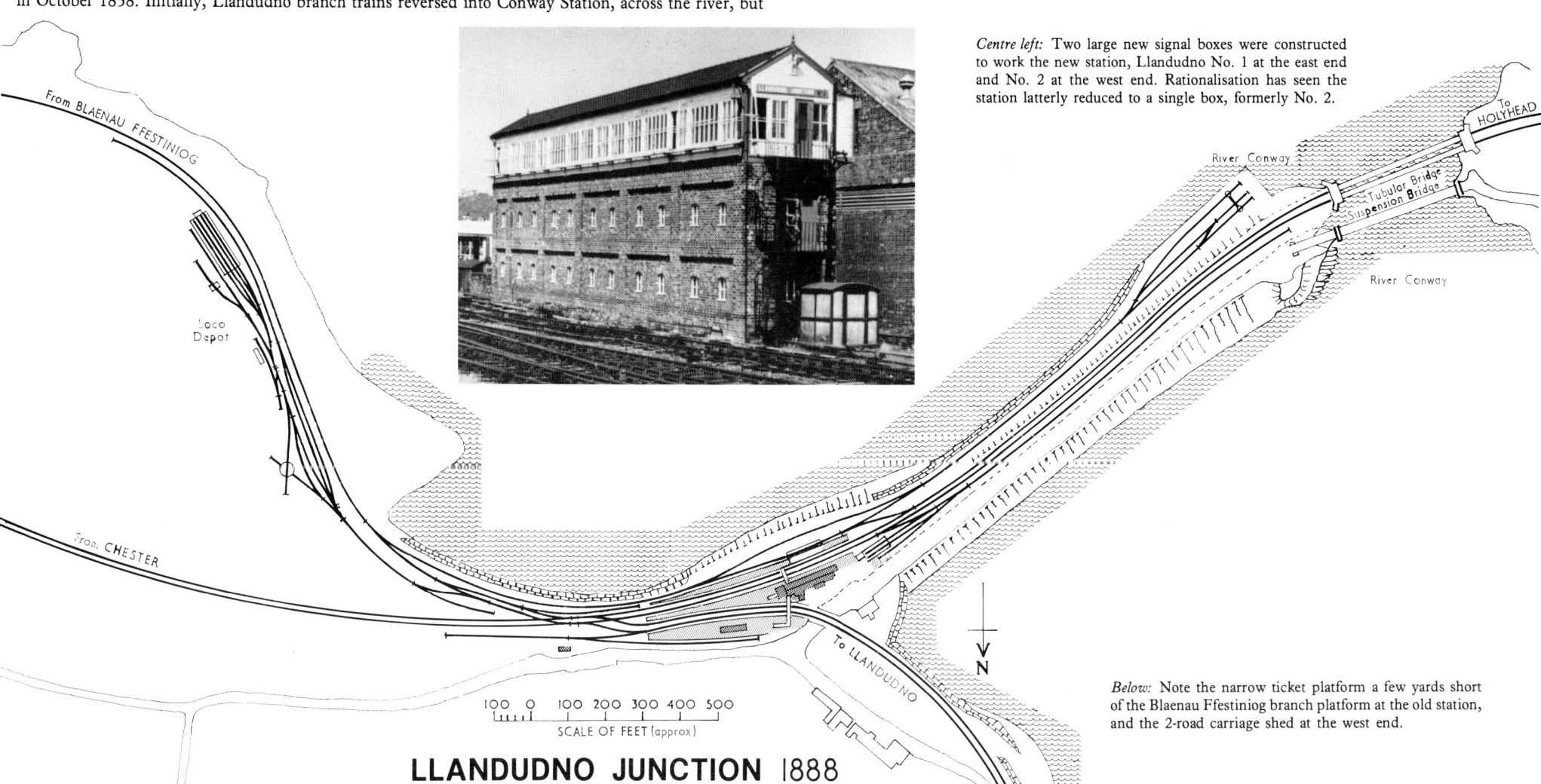

SCALE OF FEET (approx)

LLANDUDNO JUNCTION 1888

Below: Note the narrow ticket platform a few yards short of the Blaenau Ffestiniog branch platform at the old station, and the 2-road carriage shed at the west end.

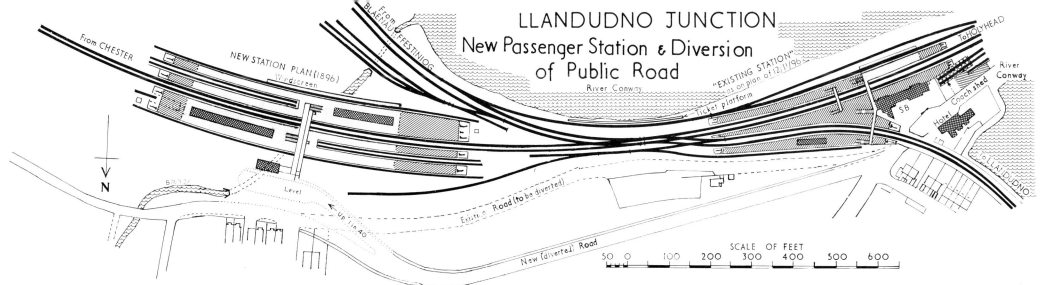

LLANDUDNO JUNCTION
New Passenger Station & Diversion of Public Road

From CHESTER

NEW STATION PLAN (1896)
Windscreen

From BLAENAU FFESTINIOG

River Conway

"EXISTING STATION"
as on plan of 12/11/96

Ticket platform

To HOLYHEAD

River Conway

S.B.

Hotel

Coach shed

To LLANDUDNO

N

BROOK

Level

Up 1 in 40

Existing Road (to be diverted)

New (diverted) Road

SCALE OF FEET

50 0   100   200   300   400   500   600

Above: Access from both branches was necessarily modified for the new station. The road north of the line was diverted, and the Llandudno branch was provided with direct access to the west end bays or through roads. The Ffestiniog branch would completely miss the station on its riverbank route, and was diverted inland on a new alignment, to approach the new station from the east, with access to the bays, etc. The old formation was severed where the new line joined it, and the riverside formation provided access to greatly-enlarged carriage and locomotive stabling facilities. With Llandudno alone handling eighty trains on a peak Saturday, they were very welcome. The old station was used for freight until July 1903, when the new facilities came into use.

Below left: Llandudno Junction Station, looking towards Holyhead in the 1950s. On the far left are the goods and 'down' loop platform, followed by the two Ffestiniog bays, the two through platforms, the short road depicted on the plan, and the 'up' loop. The C&HR was much busier east of the junction, than to the west, largely due to the Llandudno traffic. As a result, much of the route between Chester and Llandudno Junction was quadrupled, the quadruple track ending at the junction.

Below right: A view looking from the west end of the station towards Conway Castle, the Telford suspension bridge and Stephenson tubular bridges. The photograph is taken approximately from the site of the 1858 station. Note the sidings to the left.

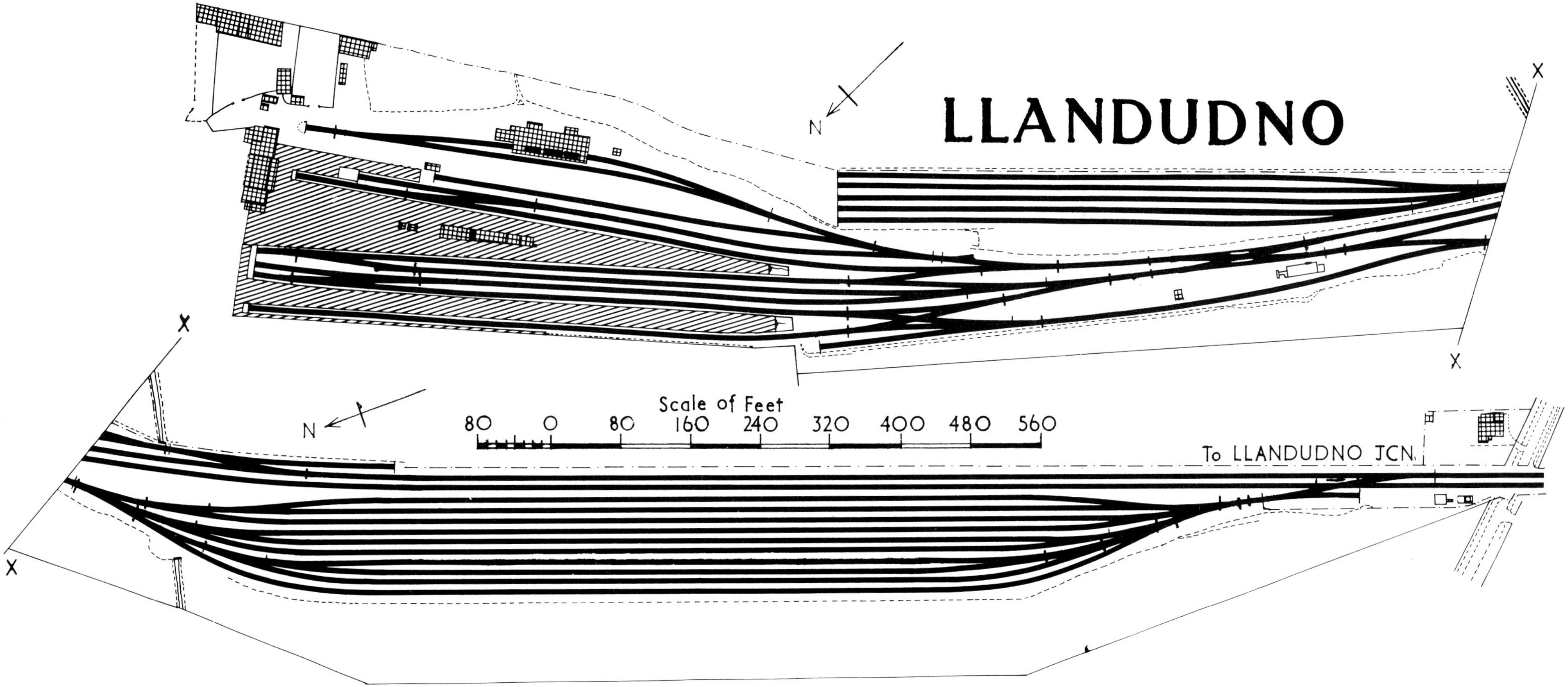

LLANDUDNO

Scale of Feet
80 0 80 160 240 320 400 480 560

To LLANDUDNO JCN.

Above: Llandudno is a classic example of Victorian development of a seaside town. In 1888, the station possessed four platforms, a small goods yard and five carriage sidings on the east side of the line. By 1891, the date of the first scale plan, ten more carriage sidings had been installed on the west of the line, and even then, G. P. Neele, the LNWR Superintendent of the line was to comment, 'the accommodation for visitors to that attractive watering-place having been sadly below the required standard'. During the summer peak, the two westernmost platforms were used for excursions, and the two eastern platforms for regular services. When a special had unloaded, it was propelled into the new sidings by the train engine, which then ran light to Llandudno Junction for stabling. On its return, the train engine used the connections at the outer, or No. 1 box, and coupled to the front of its train, which it then propelled into the platforms, saving much station work.

Right: A view looking northwards past Llandudno No. 1 box to the terminus. The 1891 fan of carriage loops is to the left of the running lines. The coal wagon and turntable sidings were a subsequent addition.

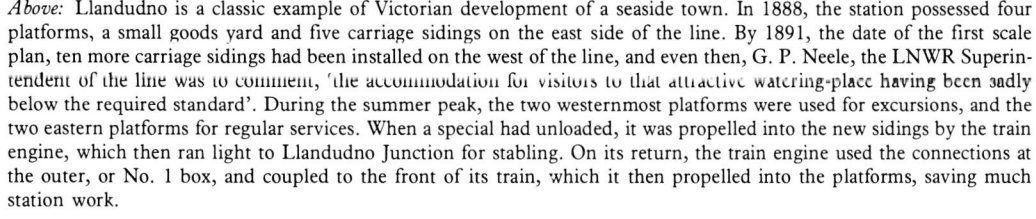

Below: The carriage and foot passengers' exits, looking from the concourse to Madoc Street and the seafront.

Below right: The ticket barriers to platform 1. Stations such as Llandudno, which might handle only a limited traffic for much of the year, had to be spacious to cope with the summer Saturday crush.

LLANDUDNO
F Foreman's office
Ha Harness room
man manure
o.sh open shed
Mews
Builders yard
Contractors yard
Corporation yard
Slaughter house
Lav
MOH
Builders yard
Ice factory
BUILDERS STREET
OXFORD ROAD
MASONS YARD
BUILDERS YARD
COAL YARD
Ha STABLES
man
coal wharf
c w
o.sh
c w
S
Carriage Landing
Cattle Road
GOODS APPROACH ROAD
stores
VAUGHAN ST
WM
C&Wstore
C&Woffice
Mess
Guards
Tktcol
Goods' Warehouse
30cwt cranes
Cloak room & pcls
W.R
Luggage
Linen
shed
5 ton crane
Yard
Gas Works siding
incinerator
store
CARRIAGE SIDINGS
Neville Hotel
Ticket col's off above steps
PLATFORM 1
PLATFORM 2
Carriage Road
PLATFORM 3
PLATFORM 4
PLATFORM 5
LWR
Lav
W.R
Tea
Book stall
Enquiries
Pcls
FSMO
Gents
Dairy
Bakery
Stable
shed
Roof end
Cottages
Stable
Laundry
Jubilee Passage
Mineral water factory
MADOC STREET
JUBILEE STREET
TRINITY STREET
ash-coal
No2SC
oil
PLH
meter
Gas tank
Advertisment Hoarding
Rocket apparatus
grass
garden
Builders yard
X
X

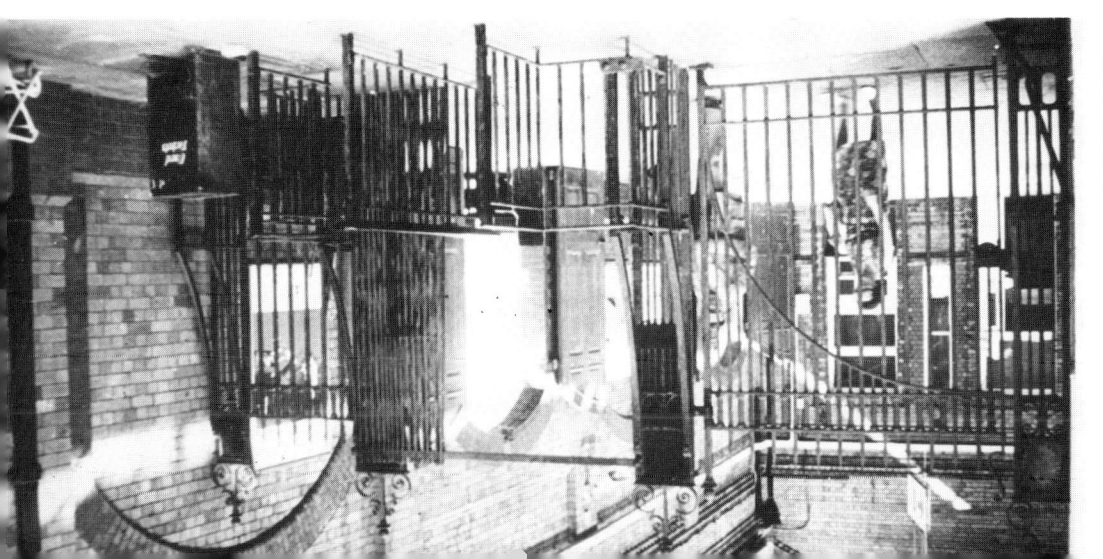

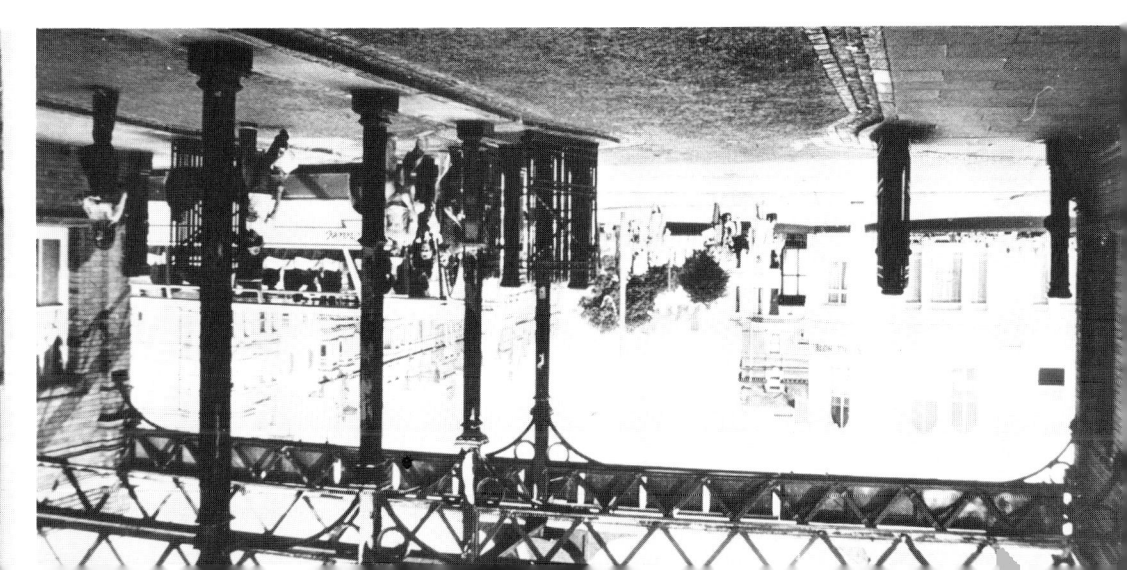

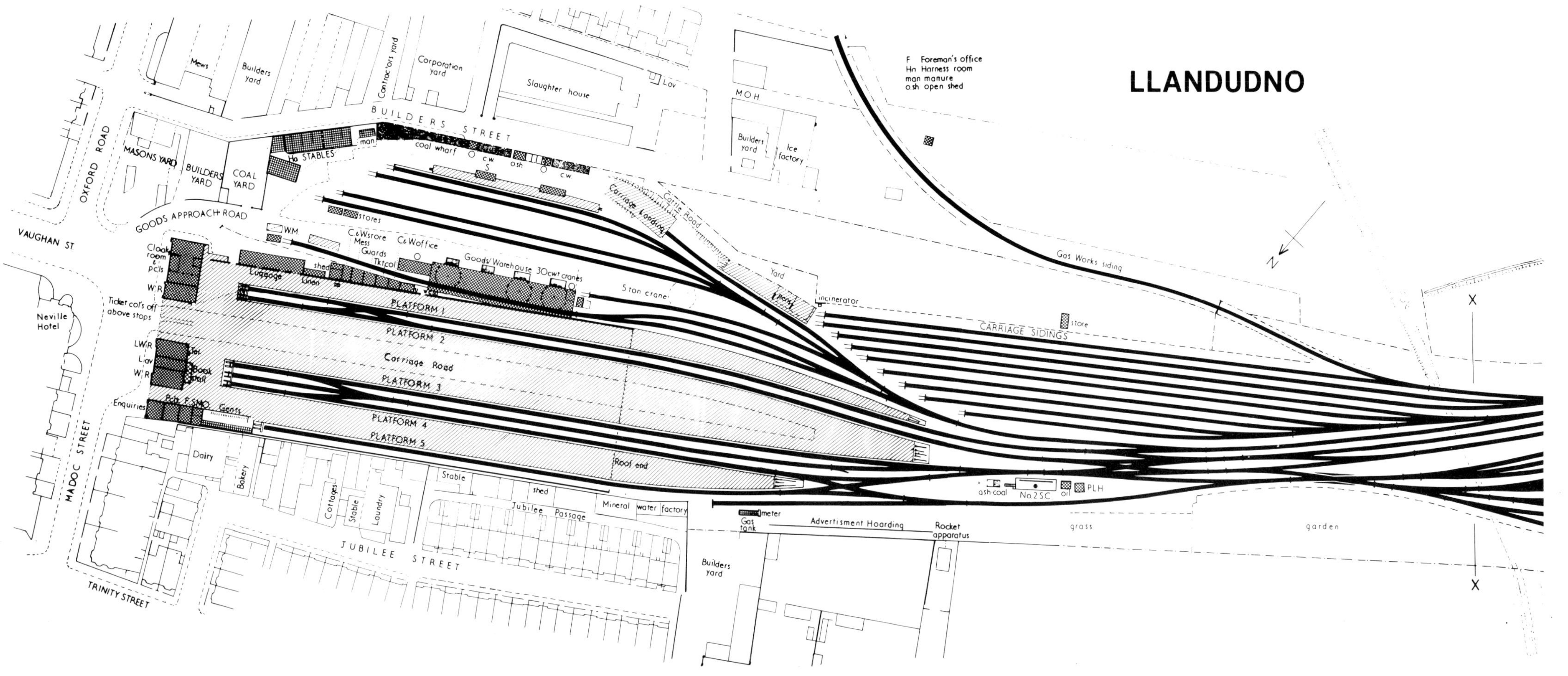

LLANDUDNO

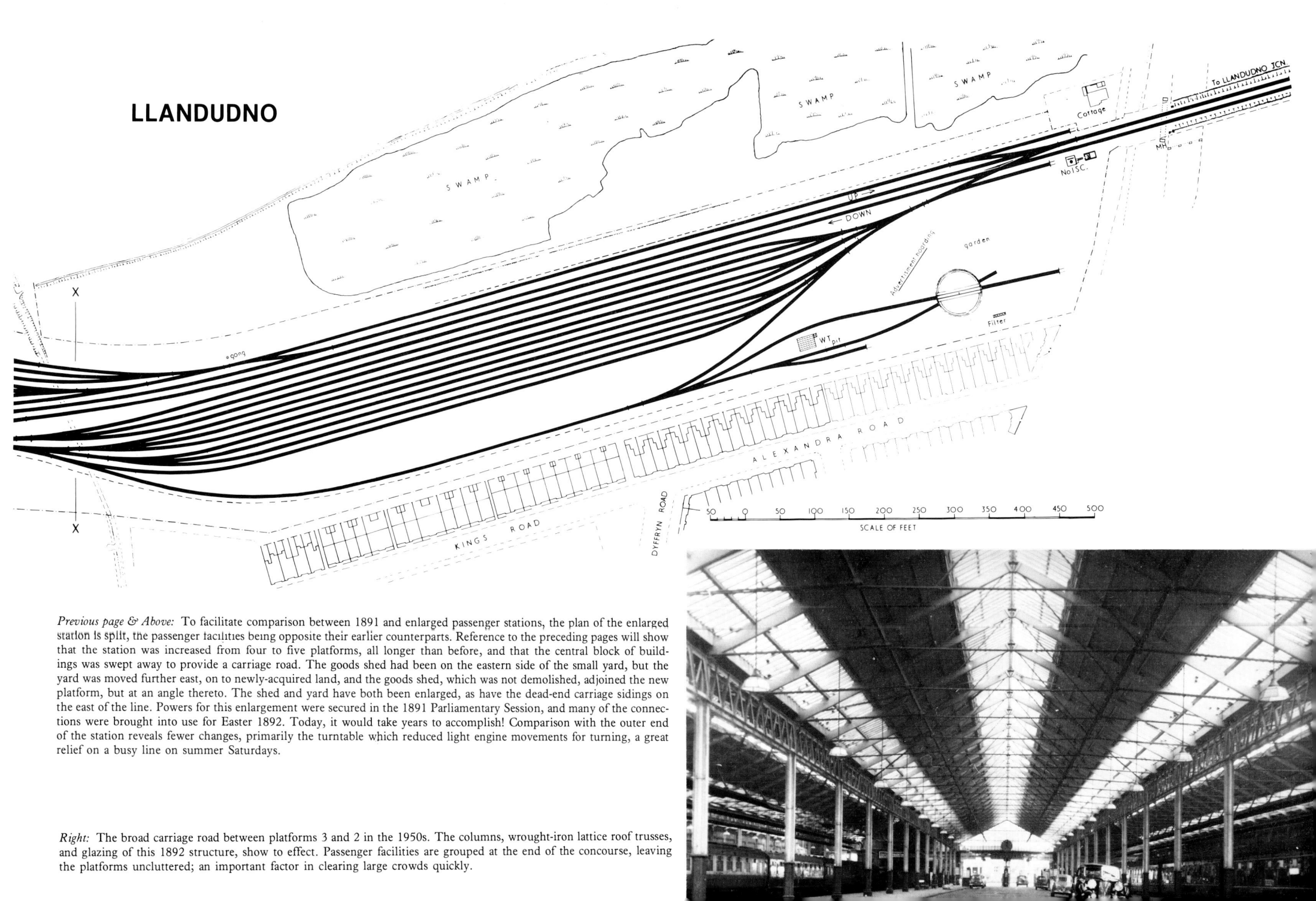

Previous page & Above: To facilitate comparison between 1891 and enlarged passenger stations, the plan of the enlarged station is split, the passenger facilities being opposite their earlier counterparts. Reference to the preceding pages will show that the station was increased from four to five platforms, all longer than before, and that the central block of buildings was swept away to provide a carriage road. The goods shed had been on the eastern side of the small yard, but the yard was moved further east, on to newly-acquired land, and the goods shed, which was not demolished, adjoined the new platform, but at an angle thereto. The shed and yard have both been enlarged, as have the dead-end carriage sidings on the east of the line. Powers for this enlargement were secured in the 1891 Parliamentary Session, and many of the connections were brought into use for Easter 1892. Today, it would take years to accomplish! Comparison with the outer end of the station reveals fewer changes, primarily the turntable which reduced light engine movements for turning, a great relief on a busy line on summer Saturdays.

Right: The broad carriage road between platforms 3 and 2 in the 1950s. The columns, wrought-iron lattice roof trusses, and glazing of this 1892 structure, show to effect. Passenger facilities are grouped at the end of the concourse, leaving the platforms uncluttered; an important factor in clearing large crowds quickly.

LLANDUDNO (Map Ref. R9)

Today, Llandudno is one of the premier holiday resorts of North Wales, but railway connection was first proposed for an entirely different purpose. Following unrest in Ireland in the 1790s, the Act of Union of 1800 merged the Dublin Parliament with Westminster, bringing Irish MPs into the Imperial Parliament, but subjecting them to tiresome journeys. As a result, convenient communication between London and Dublin became a pressing political issue, an early outcome being Telford's Holyhead road. By the 1830s, MPs were anxious for better travel facilities and, whilst Telford's suspension bridge carried the road across the Menai Straits, a railway bridge was seen as prohibitively costly. With steam ships replacing the sailing packets, Llandudno, commonly called Ormeshead, was seen as a suitable mail port for Dublin. John Jenkins, Engineer to the St. George's Harbour and Chester Railway, prepared an elegant plan for a line striking north-west from Chester, and terminating at a harbour at the foot of the Great Orme, protected by a vast L-shaped breakwater, 4,500ft. in length. Such a plan failed to find favour in the 1837 Parliamentary Session and, in the end, a Stephenson route triumphed, the legendary Chester & Holyhead Railway. This was opened between 1846 and 1850.

John Jenkins continued to press his scheme for some time, but it was not until 1853 that a 3¼ mile branch, the St. George's Harbour & Railway Company, was authorised. This opened in October 1858 and, instead of Llandudno becoming the mail packet port for Dublin, it was destined to become one of the leading seaside resorts of the United Kingdom. The St. George's company was absorbed into the LNWR in 1861, predeceasing the Chester & Holyhead Railway by eighteen years, but as these lines were firmly within the LNWR orbit, such dates had little practical effect.

As holidays by the seaside became fashionable in late Victorian times, traffic repeatedly outstripped facilities, as commented earlier. By the mid-1890s, the station had passenger facilities which would have done credit to a sizeable city, although the lack of goods accommodation, or indeed of passenger waiting-rooms, revealed the function of this layout. By 1930, at which date the station would handle over eighty specials on an August Bank Holiday Saturday, there were five platforms, a 10-road carriage fan on the west, with 2,459yds. of stabling, a further 1,577yds. of stabling on the east, a 98-wagon yard, and a small open-air locomotive yard and 60ft. turntable.

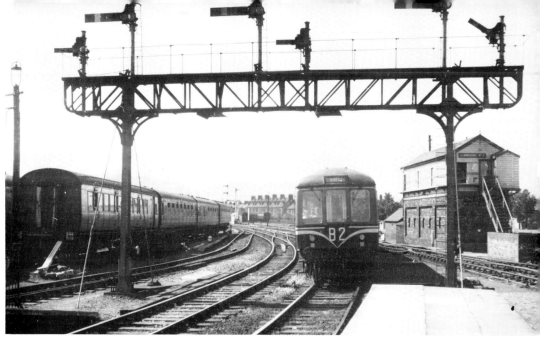

Above: An early BR diesel multiple unit enters platform 2, as a shunting move is set up ex-platform 3 to the 'down' carriage sidings, visible in the centre distance. The 'up' sidings are also well-filled.

Below left: A panoramic view of the station, complete with palm tree, looking from platform 1 towards the 4-bay LNWR 'Euston' roof of 1892.

Below right: The station frontage from Madoc St., with the entrance to platforms 4/5 on the right, and the cab approach in the centre.

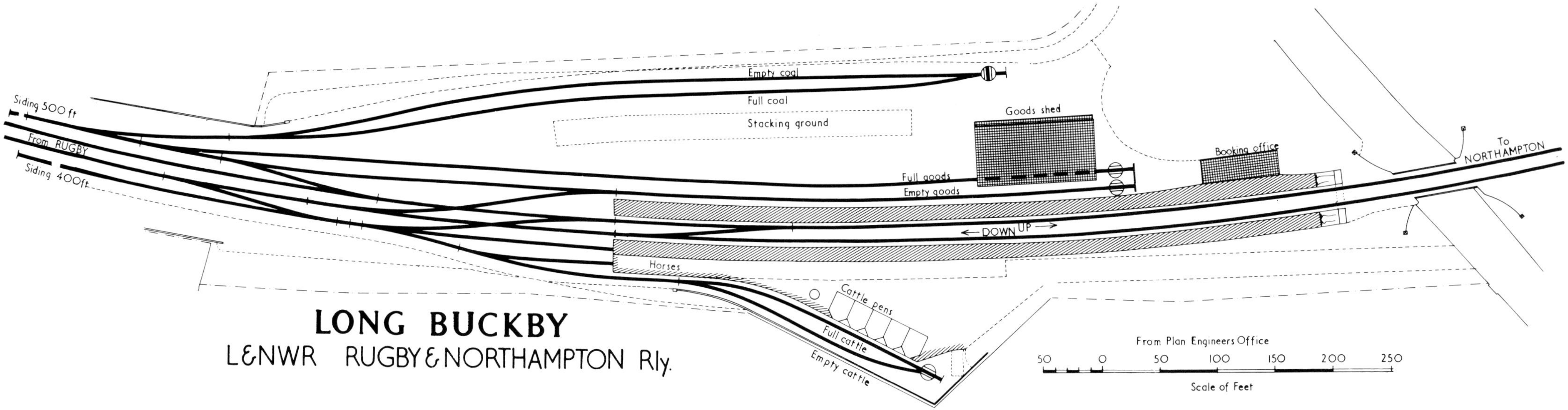

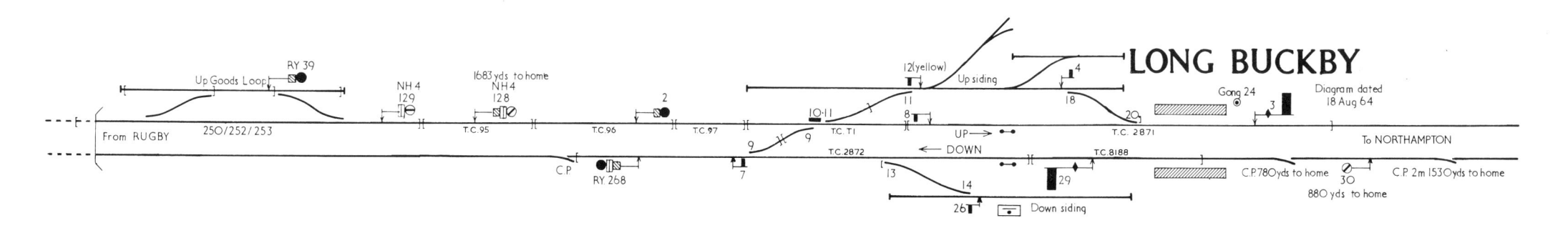

LONG BUCKBY
L&NWR   RUGBY & NORTHAMPTON Rly.

Siding 500 ft

From RUGBY

Siding 400ft

Empty coal

Full coal

Stacking ground

Goods shed

Booking office

To NORTHAMPTON

Full goods

Empty goods

← DOWN UP →

Horses

Cattle pens

Full cattle

Empty cattle

From Plan Engineers Office

50   0   50   100   150   200   250

Scale of Feet

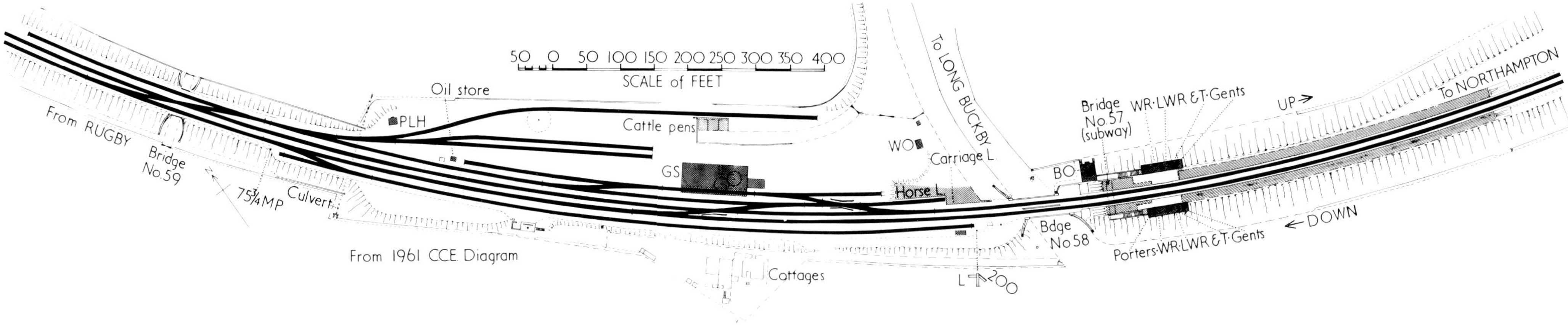

From RUGBY

Bridge No.59

75¾ MP

Culvert

Oil store

PLH

GS

Cattle pens

Horse L.

From 1961 CCE Diagram

Cottages

50   0   50   100   150   200   250   300   350   400

SCALE of FEET

To LONG BUCKBY

WO

Carriage L.

Bridge No.57 (subway)

WR·LWR &T·Gents

UP →

To NORTHAMPTON

BO

Bdge No.58

← DOWN

Porters WR·LWR &T·Gents

L 200

Top & Above: The 1870s and early 1880s were a period of transition, from the time interval era, without proper inter-locking or continuous brakes, to the developed railway system, which survived to the end of the steam era. As civil engineers strove to adapt existing stations or plan new lines, many extraordinary schemes were discussed, and some even built. One of the most peculiar for a minor wayside station was the proposal drawing at the top of this page for Long Buckby. Land boundaries sometimes presented civil engineers with peculiar sites to work on, as with the triangu-lar projection on one side of the line, but the proposed use for this, with cattle pens at an angle to the line, is eclipsed by the use of wagon turntables instead of points at the buffer stop ends of sidings, provision of full and empty roads, and the mass of yard connections. Signalling and interlocking would have been complex and, interestingly, no decision seems to have been made as to where the box should be. A more normal layout prevailed, and the plan was pigeon-holed for a century.

LONG BUCKBY

Up Goods Loop

RY 39

NH 4 129

1683 yds to home NH 4 128

2

10·11

12 (yellow)

11

8

Up siding

4

18

20

Gong 24

Diagram dated 18 Aug 64

3

From RUGBY

250/252/253

T.C.95

T.C.96

T.C.97

T.C.T1

9   9

T.C.2872

UP →

← DOWN

T.C.2871

To NORTHAMPTON

C.P.

RY 268

7

13

14

26

Down siding

29

T.C.8188

C.P.780yds to home

30

C.P. 2m 1530yds to home

880 yds to home

Above: A view looking towards Rugby from the 'down' platform. The goods shed is visible beyond the Buckby road bridge, No. 58. The totem on the right would now be a collector's item.

Right: Except for the removal of the station canopies during electrification work, Long Buckby Station had altered remarkably little from LNWR days when this 1970s' photograph, looking towards Northampton, was taken. The line is on an embankment, and the buildings are carried on deep masonry foundations. The 'up' platform, although of timber construction, is carried, as in LNWR days, on brick pillars. The superelevation of the running lines on this sharp curve is noticeable.

LONG BUCKBY (Map Ref. H5)

Long Buckby Station is on the Rugby & Northampton line of the LNWR. In the 1830s, when the London & Birmingham Railway's main line was being planned, Northampton was bypassed to the west, and the line was taken by way of Kilsby Tunnel. A branch from Blisworth to Northampton and Peterborough was opened in 1845, but Northampton's situation on a minor branch line, coupled with ever increasing traffic on the main line, prompted fresh thoughts in the 1870s. Two possibilities existed. Either the LNWR could quadruple the L&B main line from Blisworth through to Rugby, which would involve boring a second tunnel at Kilsby, or the additional metals could be run via Northampton. The latter course catered for a deep public wish, and whilst the route would not be to the same standards as the L&B, it would be adequate for the slow lines, and would block any potential competitive line.

In 1875, the LNWR obtained powers to construct the Northampton Loop, or 'New Line', as it is still known today. The 'New Line' ran from Rugby, through Long Buckby, to Northampton, where it crossed over the old Blisworth branch on a high bridge, and continued on to a new main line junction at Roade. The Rugby to Northampton section opened to goods on 1st August 1881, and to passengers on 1st December, with four local trains in each direction.

Long Buckby was one of the original intermediate stations. It was sited half a mile south of the village, where the line crossed over the Daventry road by an overbridge. The booking office was at road level, and shelters were provided on both platforms, initially provided with ridge and furrow canopies. The passenger station was on the south side of the road, whilst freight facilities were north of the road bridge.

In 1895, six northbound and five southbound trains called. By 1927, there were nine northbound and seven southbound services, and the trend has continued. The closure of local stations on the main line between Wolverton and Rugby has resulted in the stopping service being routed via Northampton, so that Long Buckby enjoys an hour interval service for much of the day. It is now only a passenger station, freight facilities having ended in April 1968.

LONG BUCKBY

Signalling Plan. Just as the 1880s had been a period of transition, so were the 1960s, this time from mechanical signalling and steam, to power boxes and electric traction. One aspect of the electrification of the West Coast Main Line, which included the Northampton Loop, was replacement of many of the old LNWR boxes by a few power boxes. The Long Buckby signal diagram of 18th August 1964 was prepared for Stage 2 of the Rugby power box commissioning on 20th September 1964. The signal boxes north of Long Buckby were replaced by Rugby PSB, to which Buckby became a temporary fringe box. In the diagram, the Watford Lodge 'up' goods loop is shown as controlled from Rugby, with exit signal RY39. Three new 'up' signals were installed between Watford Lodge and Long Buckby, the third of which, Buckby No. 2 was to become Northampton No. 4 box 127 when Buckby was abolished. The other two auto signals, NH4 128 and 129, although accorded Northampton No. 4 designations, became partially controlled signals to Long Buckby (e.g. a red aspect on Buckby No. 2 would give single yellow to NH4 128 and double yellow to NH4 129). These signals replaced the old 'up' home and 'up' distant signals. In the 'down' direction, the advance starting signal was removed, so that any 'down' train requiring to shunt, had to set into foward section. As no outer home protected the 'down' platform, Buckby was reduced to one running signal and a distant for northbound trains. During 13th/15th February 1965, MAS colour light signalling and train describers, worked from the existing Northampton Nos. 1, 2, 3 and 4 boxes, replaced Long Buckby and various other boxes. Freight traffic was still being handled at Buckby, and the yard connections remained basically as per the diagram of August 1964, but were worked from three open-air ground frames, Long Buckby 'up' line North, South, and Down, electrically released from Northampton No. 4.

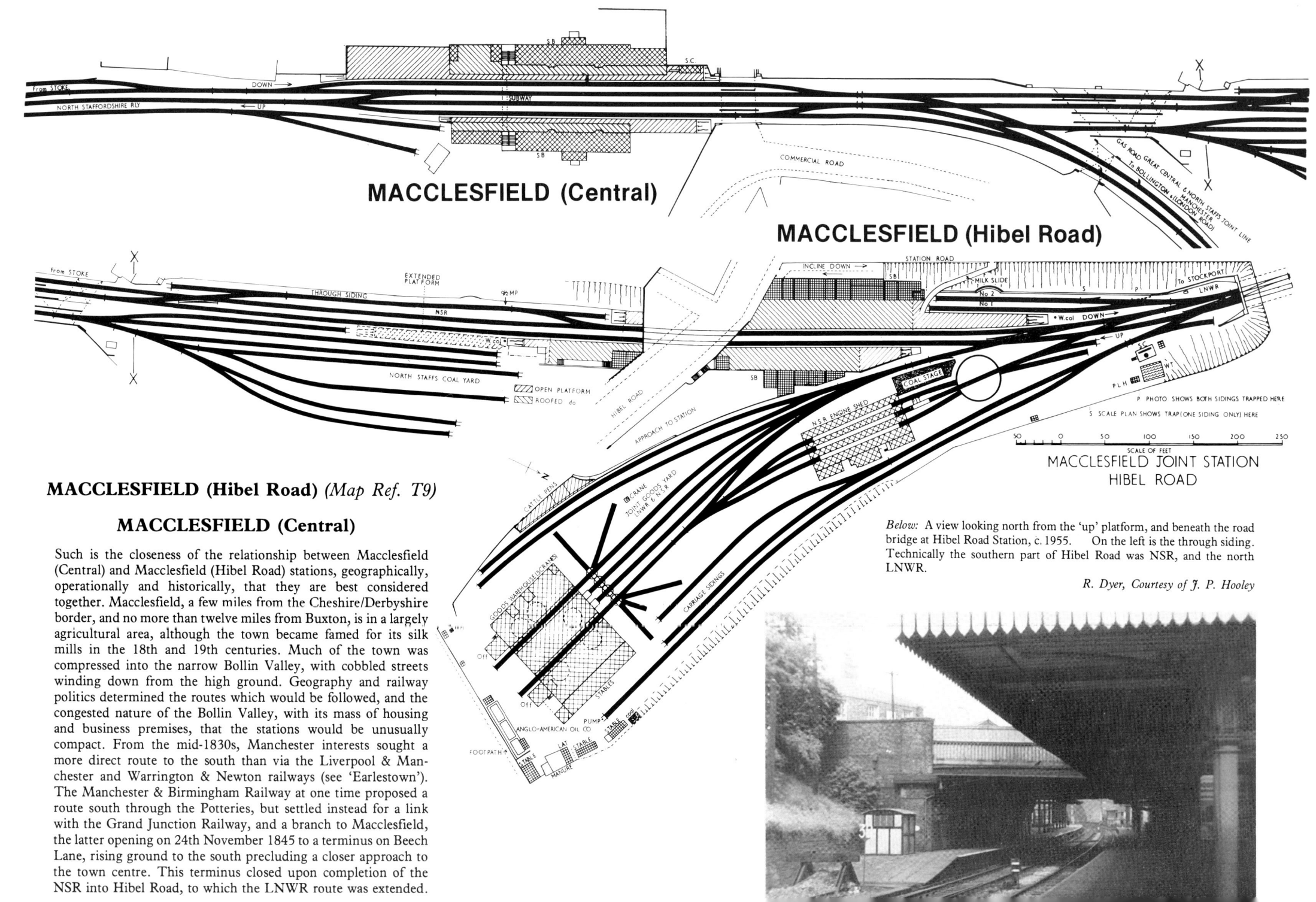

MACCLESFIELD (Central)

From STOKE

DOWN →

← UP

NORTH STAFFORDSHIRE RLY

SB

S.C.

SUBWAY

SB

COMMERCIAL ROAD

GAS ROAD GREAT CENTRAL & NORTH STAFFS JOINT LINE
To BOLLINGTON & (LONDON ROAD) MANCHESTER

MACCLESFIELD (Hibel Road)

From STOKE

THROUGH SIDING

EXTENDED PLATFORM

9½ MP

NSR

W.col

NORTH STAFFS COAL YARD

▨ OPEN PLATFORM
▧ ROOFED do

INCLINE DOWN →

STATION ROAD

SB

MILK SLIDE

No 2

No 1

S P LNWR

● W.col DOWN →

← UP

SC

WT

To STOCKPORT

PLH

HIBEL ROAD

APPROACH TO STATION

SB

COAL STAGE

N.S.R. ENGINE SHED

P PHOTO SHOWS BOTH SIDINGS TRAPPED HERE

S SCALE PLAN SHOWS TRAP (ONE SIDING ONLY) HERE

50   0   50   100   150   200   250
SCALE OF FEET

MACCLESFIELD JOINT STATION
HIBEL ROAD

CATTLE PENS

CRANE
JOINT GOODS YARD
LNWR & NSR

GOODS WAREHOUSE & CRANES

CARRIAGE SIDINGS

STABLES

Off

Off

ANGLO-AMERICAN OIL CO

FOOTPATH

PUMP

STABLE coal

STABLE

TABLE

MANURE

LAT

STABLES

Below: A view looking north from the 'up' platform, and beneath the road bridge at Hibel Road Station, c. 1955.   On the left is the through siding. Technically the southern part of Hibel Road was NSR, and the north LNWR.

R. Dyer, Courtesy of J. P. Hooley

MACCLESFIELD (Hibel Road) *(Map Ref. T9)*

MACCLESFIELD (Central)

Such is the closeness of the relationship between Macclesfield (Central) and Macclesfield (Hibel Road) stations, geographically, operationally and historically, that they are best considered together. Macclesfield, a few miles from the Cheshire/Derbyshire border, and no more than twelve miles from Buxton, is in a largely agricultural area, although the town became famed for its silk mills in the 18th and 19th centuries. Much of the town was compressed into the narrow Bollin Valley, with cobbled streets winding down from the high ground. Geography and railway politics determined the routes which would be followed, and the congested nature of the Bollin Valley, with its mass of housing and business premises, that the stations would be unusually compact. From the mid-1830s, Manchester interests sought a more direct route to the south than via the Liverpool & Manchester and Warrington & Newton railways (see 'Earlestown'). The Manchester & Birmingham Railway at one time proposed a route south through the Potteries, but settled instead for a link with the Grand Junction Railway, and a branch to Macclesfield, the latter opening on 24th November 1845 to a terminus on Beech Lane, rising ground to the south precluding a closer approach to the town centre. This terminus closed upon completion of the NSR into Hibel Road, to which the LNWR route was extended.

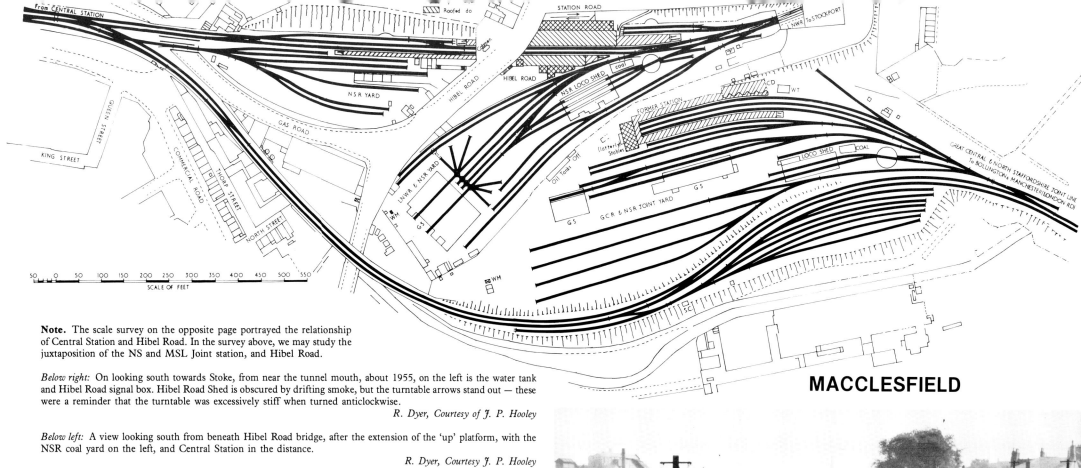

Note. The scale survey on the opposite page portrayed the relationship of Central Station and Hibel Road. In the survey above, we may study the juxtaposition of the NS and MSL Joint station, and Hibel Road.

Below right: On looking south towards Stoke, from near the tunnel mouth, about 1955, on the left is the water tank and Hibel Road signal box. Hibel Road Shed is obscured by drifting smoke, but the turntable arrows stand out — these were a reminder that the turntable was excessively stiff when turned anticlockwise.

R. Dyer, Courtesy of J. P. Hooley

Below left: A view looking south from beneath Hibel Road bridge, after the extension of the 'up' platform, with the NSR coal yard on the left, and Central Station in the distance.

R. Dyer, Courtesy J. P. Hooley

MACCLESFIELD

MACCLESFIELD (Hibel Road)

Above: A view looking across the turntable from the coaling platform towards the tunnel and Stockport in 1955. With a tunnel at one end of the station, a bridge at the far end, high ground on one side, and a small yard and locomotive shed, the station would make a superb prototype for the modeller.

R. Dyer

Below: The scene from the tunnel mouth, looking towards the yard, with the carriage sidings on the left, goods shed in the distance, and NSR shed and coal stage to the right.

R. Dyer

MACCLESFIELD *(Hibel Road) (Map Ref. T9)*

Various proposals were made to build through the Potteries during the early months of the 'Railway Mania' of 1845, leading to three Bills, all passed on 26th June 1846, which created the backbone of the North Staffordshire Railway, which was to serve not only the Potteries and Stoke, but as a through link between Manchester and the south. Lines were to strike north from the GJR at Colwich (see 'Sandon') and Norton Bridge, and up the Churnet Valley from the Midland Railway at Burton. All these connections funnelled into a single route beyond North Rode, which would make an end-on junction with the M&B at Macclesfield, (Hibel Road) 17¼ miles south of Manchester (London Road). The NSR opened into Macclesfield on 18th June 1849, although the new joint LNWR/NSR station was not quite ready. A joint NSR/LNW goods yard was opened to the east of the passenger station, together with a 3-track NSR locomotive shed. As the tracks at the north end of Hibel Road were LNWR property, the NSR reached the joint yard and their own engine shed by running powers! The station was on a cramped site with rising ground to the north and west, and shunting moves necessitated entering the tunnel. As the north end of the station was LNWR property, an 1870s' LNWR hipped-roof signal cabin was erected just south of the tunnel mouth. Most contemporary boxes were replaced by 1914, during station enlargements, but there was precious little room to do anything more at Hibel Road!

Below: Hibel Road, looking south from near the 'down' water column. On the left is the coaling shed, the road to the cattle pens and goods shed, and the high wall between the locomotive yard and 'up' platform. The trap ex the sidings can clearly be seen. From the scale plan and illustrations, it will be seen that three connections led from the yard/locomotive depot into the 'down' line, not one with an adequate headshunt, due to the cramped site.

R. Dyer

Above: Macclesfield (Central) Station, from the 'down' platform, looking south towards Stoke, circa 1955.

H. Bostock, Courtesy of J. P. Hooley

Above: An evocative view of Macclesfield (Central) Station, looking north from the 'down' side towards the junction of the Marple line and Hibel Road. A freight is just coming off the Bollington and Marple line.
R. Dyer, Courtesy of J. P. Hooley

Below: The 'down' buildings and approach to Macclesfield (Central) Station, circa 1900. Note the elevated approach and stock pens in the foreground.
J. P. Hooley Collection

MACCLESFIELD (Central)

MACCLESFIELD (Central) *(Map Ref. T9)*

Had relationships between the NSR and LNWR remained cordial throughout, the story migh have been confined to Hibel Road, but periodic rows brewed up, the 'Knotty' seeking independent outlets to the north and south. One of these disputes, in the vicinity of Market Drayton, prompted the NSR to seek contact with the Manchester, Sheffield & Lincolnshire Railway, 10¾ miles to the north east, at Marple. As well as providing an alternative access to Manchester, this opened up parts of Yorkshire and the east. The Macclesfield, Bollington & Marple Railway was authorised on 14th July 1864, but by the time it was opened, closer working with the LNWR had removed much of its value. The LNWR, which had wrung concessions from both the NSR and MSL for not fighting the proposal in Parliament, would not accept a joint MSL/LNWR/NSR station at Hibel Road, and plans to bring the Marple line into the town, north of Hibel Road were dropped. The Marple line opened to a temporary terminus for passengers on the east side of Hibel Road Station on 2nd August 1869, and to goods on 1st March 1870. The NSR gained no benefit from the branch, as it was isolated from the rest of the 'Knotty', and it was not until 13th February 1871, that the last half mile, on embankment or viaduct, carried the MB&M to a junction with the NSR near Queen St. In May 1871, the MB&M was vested in the NSR and MS&LR, under a joint committee, and on 1st July 1873, a new station, south of the MB&M Junction, Macclesfield (Central) replaced the original MB&M terminus, which became a goods depot, and remained active until 22nd September 1969. The NSR now possessed two passenger stations, both with a joint interest, within a quarter of a mile. Through trains tended to call at one or the other. Hibel Road passenger station was closed on 7th November 1960, and the LNW/NSR goods depot in 1962. Central Station was completely rebuilt, with new buildings and four through platforms, and controlled from a new BR signal box. From 1967, the NSR route through the Potteries became a part of the LMS 25kV electrified network. On 5th January 1970, the MB&M passenger service was withdrawn.

MANCHESTER (Victoria & Exchange) (Map Ref. T9)

In 1825, when the proprietors of the Liverpool & Manchester Railway were seeking their Act from a sceptical Parliament, others were discussing carrying a line across the Pennines from Manchester to Leeds. The L&MR was authorised in 1826, and opened to the Liverpool Road terminus in Manchester on 15th September 1830. The M&LR faltered, and after an abortive attempt to secure powers, languished until 1835 when the company was revived, and a Bill was secured in 1836, to run from Oldham Road in Manchester, to Normanton, where a junction would be made with the North Midland Railway to Leeds. Work began the following year, and the section from Manchester to Littleborough opened in July 1839, the line opening throughout on 1st March 1841. Except for the short gap in Manchester, a continuous line of railway now existed from the Mersey to the Humber. In 1831, the Manchester, Bolton & Bury Canal had secured powers to build a railway — in preference to leaving it to others — and this opened from Salford in May 1838. Discussions took place over a link line from the M&LR at Miles Platting, about a mile east of Oldham Road Station, via the Bolton company's terminus, to the L&MR, to be constructed by the three companies, but the MB&B was dropped, eventually. The Liverpool & Manchester Railway secured powers to build from Ordsall Lane across Salford, and past the MB&B to Hunts Bank. This Act, of 14th June 1839, was closely followed by an M&LR Act providing the link from Hunts Bank on to Miles Platting. The L&MR dragged its feet, and in 1842, the Manchester & Leeds Railway went ahead on their part, the line falling steeply, at 1 in 47/59 for much of the way to Hunts Bank. It was opened on 1st January 1844, the station being named 'Victoria' by Royal permission. Following a threat from the M&LR that they would build a competing line to Liverpool, the L&MR commenced their half of the link in 1843, the line opening on 4th May 1844. As with many early stations, Victoria was single-sided, with a solitary 852ft. long platform, the west end being used by the L&MR, and the east by the M&LR. Three through roads were provided, and a number of through sidings, reached at each end by wagon turntables. A single-storey Roman Doric station building 266ft. long was erected, again shared by the companies. Bolton trains continued to terminate at Salford until 1846, largely as as result of friction between the companies, a factor in inducing the Bolton company to merge into the Manchester & Leeds Railway. However, the majority of trains continued to expire at Salford. Lines to Ashton and Stalybridge, to the east of Victoria, were opened by the M&LR in 1846, the Stalybridge route becoming a link in the LNWR Manchester to Huddersfield service from 1850. A line from Miles Platting to Ardwick also opened, although passenger services were delayed until 1852. The Manchester, Bury & Rossendale Railway was authorised from a junction on the Bolton line in 1844, became the East Lancashire Railway in 1845, and opened in September 1846. The Liverpool & Manchester Railway had become a part of the LNWR in 1846, and the Manchester & Leeds Railway grew into the LYR in 1847. The ELR became a part of the LYR from 1859, by which time other LYR routes fanned out from Victoria. For the LNWR, Victoria was the terminus for services ex the L&MR and the north-west of England, and a vital link in the Huddersfield route. By 1855, the station was hopelessly inadequate. At the east end, the railway crossed over the River Irk and under a major road. At the west end was the River Irwell. To the north was the workhouse, and to the south, Walker's Croft cemetery. Part of the cemetery was acquired for short platforms, intially known as Ducie Bridge (Cheetham Hill Road then being known as Ducie Road, not to be confused with Great Ducie St. to the west).

Despite the take-over of the Bolton and East Lancashire companies, services from the western part of the system, including Liverpool, Wigan, and Blackpool, mostly still terminated alongside the LNWR at New Bailey St., Salford. In 1861, the LYR obtained

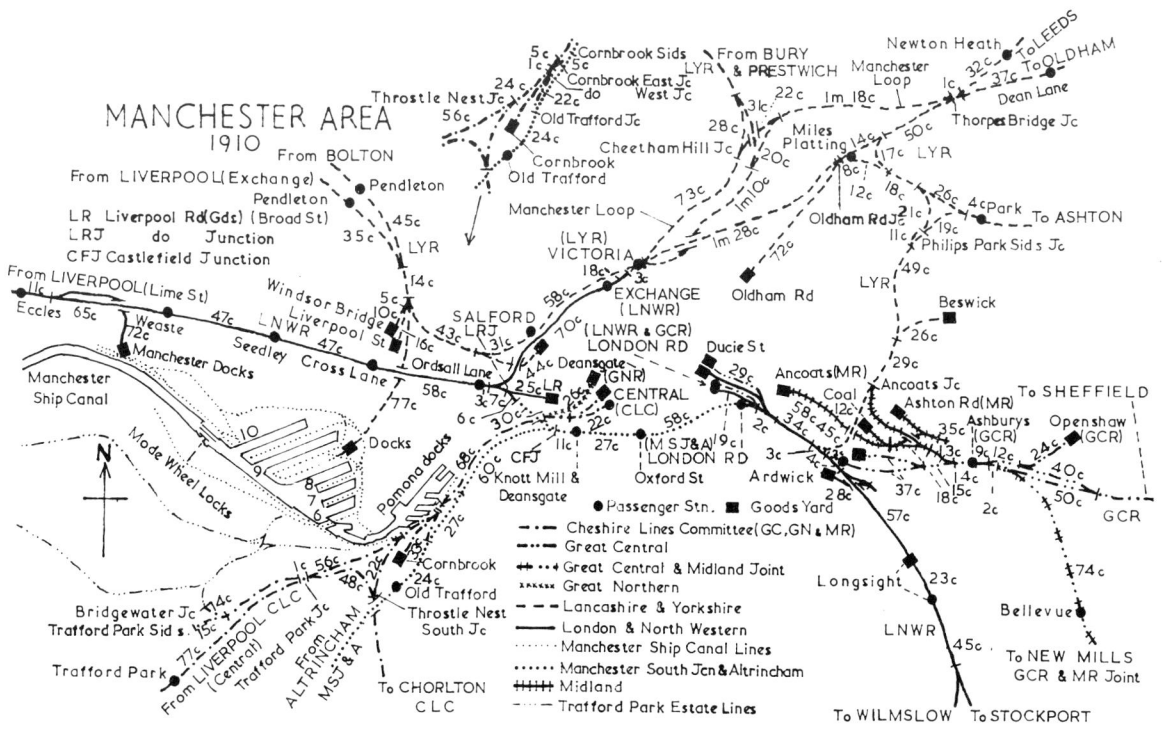

powers for a parallel line into Victoria Station, which was opened on 1st August 1865. Enlargements were made on the north side of the line, and the 1844 train shed was replaced, some of the pillars for the new roof being still in use a century later. Traffic continued to increase, and the Ducie Bridge bays were remodelled in November 1877. In the early 1880s, part of the 1865 extension was swept away, and five new through platforms (latterly Nos. 12-16) were provided, with a substantial train shed. A subway connected the old and new stations, whilst a carriage drive from Great Ducie St. burrowed under the new lines, and surfaced at the west end of what later became the massive island platform (Nos. 12/13). LMS period platform numbers have been used for clarity, but by 1884, when the new section opened, Victoria possessed 13 platforms.

Congestion was so endemic, that the LNWR decided to build its own station on the west bank of the River Irwell, and Manchester Exchange Station, actually in Salford, opened on 30th June 1884, LNWR trains ceasing to use the Victoria platforms, although Huddersfield services still used the through roads between the 1844 and 1884 stations. 'G. P. Neele, LNWR Superintendent of the line, loathed the place, 'A little more friendly conference between the two companies, could have produced — so I have often thought — a far more successful joint station'.

The massive increase in traffic, from new routes, improved long-distance services, and suburban development, placed pressure on the approaches to Victoria. A 4-track avoiding line, the Manchester Loop, to relieve pressure on Miles Platting and the Oldham Road goods junction, was completed on 1st August 1878. This ran from Victoria East Junction, via Cheetham Hill to Thorpes Bridge Junction near Newton Heath. Even this was insufficient, and the old route, via Miles Platting, was quadrupled on 29th September 1896, the new lines, on the south side, coming into the east-side suburban bays.

Concurrently with the Manchester Loop, the LYR was building north from Cheetham Hill, through Crumpsall and Prestwich, to the ELR at Radcliffe, providing an alternative route to Bolton and Bury. Bury passenger services began on 1st September 1879, and the Bolton service on 1st December. Until the extensions to Victoria were completed in 1884, Prestwich trains terminated at a temporary station by what ultimately became Cheetham Hill road bridge.

The LYR route to Liverpool, via Bolton, was forty miles long, compared to just over thirty miles by the LNWR.

Under instruction 17, this was reduced from 440yds. to 30yds., in itself hazardous enough, but with a falling gradient of 1 in 57 into Victoria on the eastern approaches, was a graphic indication of the desperate struggle to keep traffic flowing. A marginal error by a driver in judging his braking distance could spell disaster. Instruction 3 increased the peril, for a signalman could offer a train forward, even though the box in advance had not 'blocked out'. The receiving box 'accepted' this second train, not by repeating the bell code, but by a single beat. The safeguards on a busy passenger line were thus less than those applied under permissive working on a freight line. Trains entering the 1884 platforms from the east, came under Victoria East Junction, and then the 10-lever Platform cabin, 240yds. further on. The East box kept a train register, entered by a booking boy, but no reference was made as to how trains were accepted. The Platform Box, which opened in the 1890s, did not keep a train register. The trap was set.

On 11th September 1899, the 8.05a.m. Whitefield to Manchester and Blackpool, running a few minutes late, was admitted under normal acceptance to No. 10 road (then platform 6 — later platform 12). The 8.12a.m. Radcliffe to Manchester, headed by a brand new Aspinall 'Highflyer' Atlantic, No. 1402, was offered by East box to the platform. The signalmen differed, as to whether one beat or normal acceptance was made, but the 8.12a.m. entered the station expecting to find the line clear to the home signal. The previous train was unusually long, and overhung the signal by 40yds., and two passengers in the first train lost their lives. Lt. Col. Addison slated the interlocking and whole system of working.

Since the opening of the Prestwich line, these services had arrived in the through lines at the north side of the station, rather than cross all running lines to the east-end bays but, in 1895, powers had been secured to build a one mile connection from the Prestwich line, clearing the Cheetham and Miles Platting lines, and entering the east bays. This would overtax the bays, and authority to extend further south, over more of the Walker's Croft cemetery, was gained in 1896, whilst the River Irk had to be diverted or culverted. A new road bridge was provided for Cheetham Hill Road, and the new east bays, increased from 5 to 10, opened on 1st February 1904. New buildings fronting the Victoria Station approach were erected during the period 1904-09. In 1916, the Manchester-Whitefield-Bury-Holcombe Brook service was electrified, using 1,200 volt d.c. third rail. The Bury to Holcombe Brook line had been used as a test bed by Dick, Kerr & Co. for a high tension overhead electrification from 1912-13. Signalling alterations of 1928/9 are covered in detail later; these included the joining of Exchange 3 and Victoria 11 platforms. In 1934, and during the war, parts of the Victoria Station's roof were cut back. With the decline in rail services, platforms 7-10 were taken out of passenger use on 1st May 1967, and later became a car park. The LNWR station, Exchange, closed to passengers on 5th May 1969, but continued to handle parcels. Services were diverted to Victoria, the wheel thus coming full circle.

Below: Looking from platform 11 along the through roads towards Victoria West Junction cabin and Exchange Station. A Class 5 locomotive occupies the standby siding, another is on permanent way duties and two more engines double-head a train in platform 12.

A tiled wall map of the LYR system decorated the northern wall of the 1909 booking hall. Below it was the LYR Roll of Honour, to those who fell in the Great War; seven panels of names flanked by allegorical reliefs.

MANCHESTER

In 1883, a cut-off was authorised, from Pendleton, just outside Salford on the M&B line, to Hindley. This opened to passengers on 1st June 1889. It in turn threw more strain on the Western approaches to Victoria, and powers to widen this section were secured in 1890. The quadrupling from Victoria to Deal St. came into use in June 1896, and out to Windsor Bridge in 1900. The LNWR had also experienced congestion on the approaches to Exchange. From 12th July 1886, a short quadruple section existed between Cross Lane and Ordsall Lane, with a third, 'up' road into Exchange itself. The fourth line reached Exchange in 1890.

In 1896, the Board of Trade noted that the east end of Victoria was the most heavily used line in the country. Station Yard working instructions are common for large stations, but the pressure on Victoria led the LYR into a set of instructions in December 1896 with frightening weaknesses. In normal working, a signalman can only 'block out' when the rear of the train is ¼ mile past his outermost stop signal.

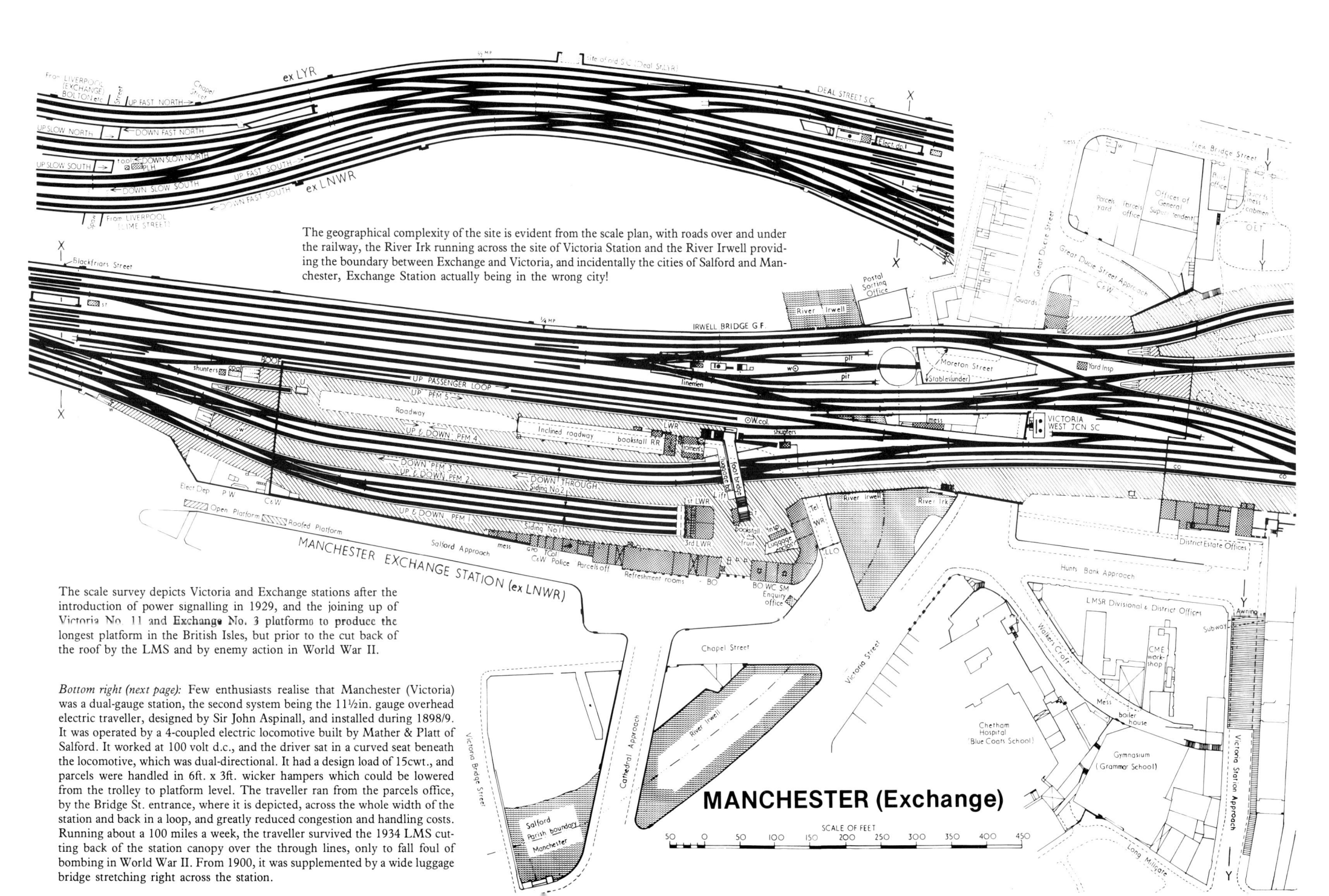

The geographical complexity of the site is evident from the scale plan, with roads over and under the railway, the River Irk running across the site of Victoria Station and the River Irwell providing the boundary between Exchange and Victoria, and incidentally the cities of Salford and Manchester, Exchange Station actually being in the wrong city!

The scale survey depicts Victoria and Exchange stations after the introduction of power signalling in 1929, and the joining up of Victoria No. 11 and Exchange No. 3 platforms to produce the longest platform in the British Isles, but prior to the cut back of the roof by the LMS and by enemy action in World War II.

Bottom right (next page): Few enthusiasts realise that Manchester (Victoria) was a dual-gauge station, the second system being the 11½in. gauge overhead electric traveller, designed by Sir John Aspinall, and installed during 1898/9. It was operated by a 4-coupled electric locomotive built by Mather & Platt of Salford. It worked at 100 volt d.c., and the driver sat in a curved seat beneath the locomotive, which was dual-directional. It had a design load of 15cwt., and parcels were handled in 6ft. x 3ft. wicker hampers which could be lowered from the trolley to platform level. The traveller ran from the parcels office, by the Bridge St. entrance, where it is depicted, across the whole width of the station and back in a loop, and greatly reduced congestion and handling costs. Running about a 100 miles a week, the traveller survived the 1934 LMS cutting back of the station canopy over the through lines, only to fall foul of bombing in World War II. From 1900, it was supplemented by a wide luggage bridge stretching right across the station.

MANCHESTER (Exchange)

SCALE OF FEET
50 0 50 100 150 200 250 300 350 400 450

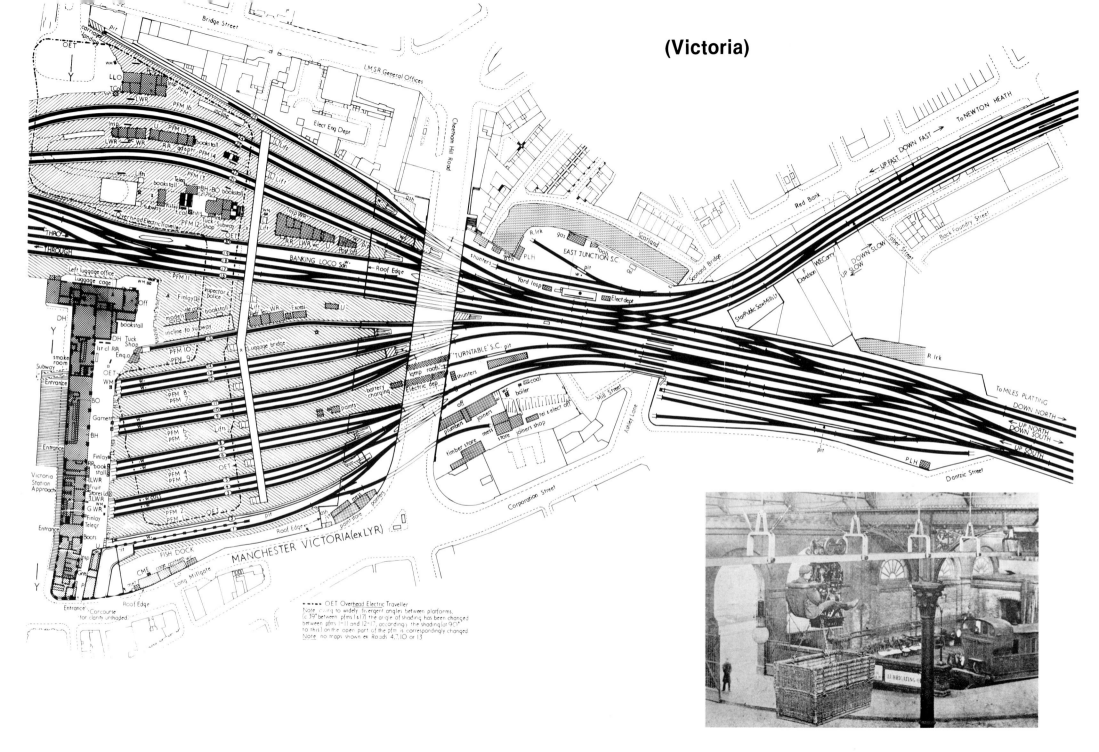

(Victoria)

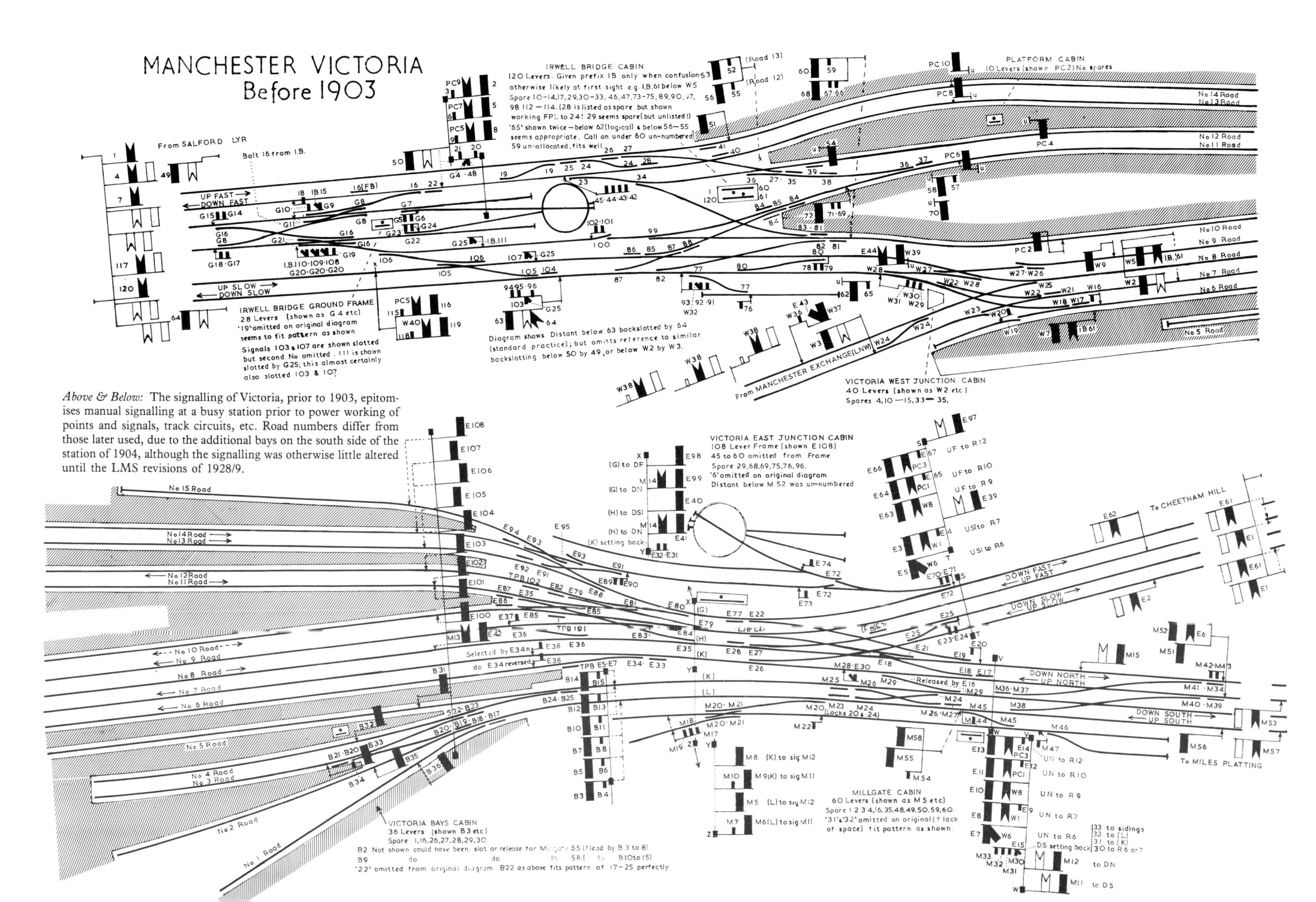

MANCHESTER VICTORIA
Before 1903

Above & Below: The signalling of Victoria, prior to 1903, epitomises manual signalling at a busy station prior to power working of points and signals, track circuits, etc. Road numbers differ from those later used, due to the additional bays on the south side of the station of 1904, although the signalling was otherwise little altered until the LMS revisions of 1928/9.

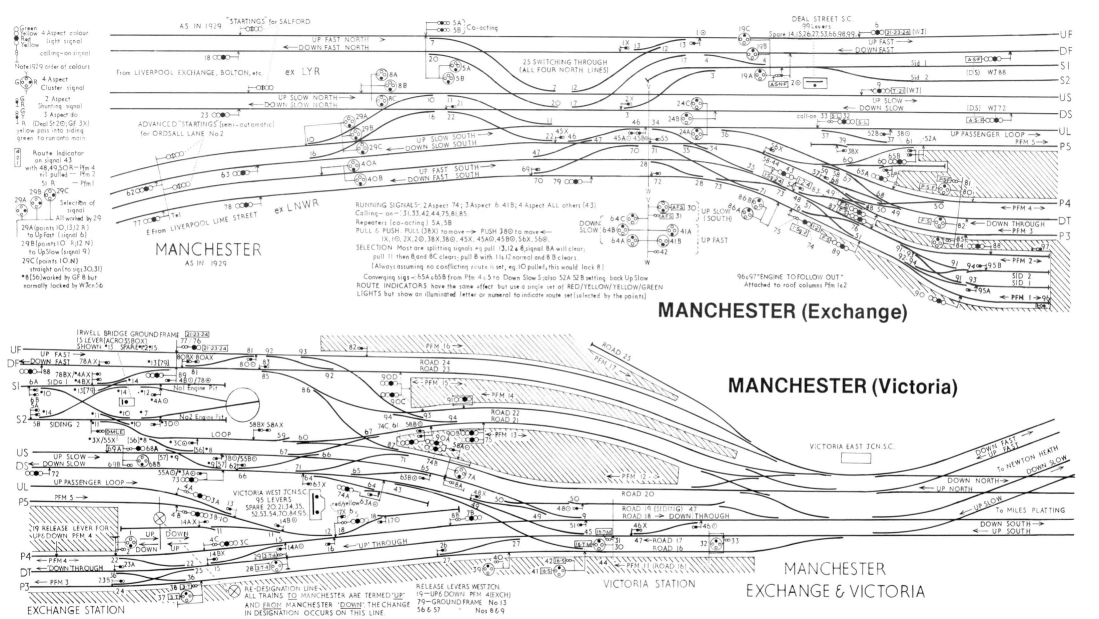

MANCHESTER (Exchange)

MANCHESTER (Victoria)

MANCHESTER EXCHANGE & VICTORIA

The LMS resignalling of 1928/9 marked a complete break with the past, for not only did power working come in, but the signalling of Exchange and Victoria was co-ordinated. Six signal boxes and one ground frame, with a total of 332 levers, were replaced by two power boxes and one power ground frame with 188 working levers. Four LYR cabins were swept away, Deal St., with 43 levers, Irwell Bridge, of 100 levers working (but space for 120) Victoria West Junction, 31 levers and Irwell Bridge ground frame of 29 levers. Three LNWR cabins went, Salford LNWR, an 8-lever viaduct box, Exchange No. 2, of 88 levers, straddling the approach to Exchange, and the 33-lever Exchange No. 1 at the east end of 'up' platform No. 5. Three new cabins, Victoria West Junction (95 levers) Deal St. (99 levers) and

Irwell Bridge Sidings ground frame (15 levers) were provided on the all-electric system of the Westinghouse Brake & Saxby Signal Co. The LYR box at Victoria East Junction survived as did Salford LYR. Points were operated by Westinghouse M2 DC machines, and signals supplied at 110 volts transformed down at each signal to 12/14 volts. A total of 175 track circuits protected 11¾ track miles, and power for the whole system was drawn from two separate 400 volt 3-phase 50-cycle a.c. supplies from Salford, and a contingency 400 volts d.c. supply ex-Manchester Corporation, with motor alternator.

Left: The interior of the new Irwell Bridge Sidings ground frame, prior to commissioning, with the LYR box, still manned, visible through the windows. Levers 8 and 9 are 'FREE' for testing (released by 56/57 in the new West Junction box). West Junction has also released lever 3 in the pull position, although the lever, one of two push-pull levers in the frame, remains in its 'normal' (i.e. vertical) position. Lever 3 works four separate signals regulating westbound movements, and one for eastbound moves, the latter with a 4-way route indicator. The strip of five indicators in the casing comprise, from top to bottom, a green, which clears when lever 3 is pushed, and four reds, designated A, B, C, D for the four separate westbound signals, the appropriate one of which is extinguished, this being determined by the route set. The 'FREE' indicators for push or pull, have to be accommodated above lever 2. The four repeaters above the 'FREE' indicators repeat the route indicator on the eastbound signal ex-Siding 2, and work with the red/green indicators to their right. Note the two LNWR bell/tappers for slow lines (left) and fast lines (right). Lever 4 is also a push-pull, standing vertical.

Right upper: A view looking from Siding No. 1, past Irwell Bridge Sidings ground frame to Victoria Station, during commissioning in 1929. Since the view opposite was taken, the new box has come into use, and the LYR cabin reduced to its brick base. A train on the 'up' fast passes new signals 13/15/16. The road is set from the 'down' fast to Siding 2 – i.e. ground frame 13 (released by West Junction 79) and GF14 are pulled. The plates by the ground signal (GF4) show the degree of route selection. Extra signals, worked by lever 4, for westbound movements are visible in the distance. The old LYR Irwell Bridge cabin is still extant, visible beyond the engine on No. 1 pit road. Also visible is Victoria Station roof, and the train shed screen by Victoria 11/Exchange 3 platform.

Right lower: The same inspection team are at work between the 'up' and 'down' fast roads on Great Ducie St. bridge, checking the mechanism of point 92, the crossover to platform 15. The signal in the foreground, Victoria West Junction 83, is a set back signal from the right-hand, or 'down' fast, road for points 85. An LYR 2-4-2 tank, carrying an express headcode, blows off vigorously in platform 15. The elevated LYR Irwell Bridge cabin, which possessed two parallel lever frames, hence its unusual width, still stands, but is partially obscured by the station yard inspector's hut between platforms 14 and 13. In the background is a part of the once extensive Victoria train shed.

Above: Deal St. frame on 13th November 1928, after installation of the frame castings and levers, but prior to the installation of the 'electrics'. In this ultra-modern cabin, it is amusing to note the traditional stove for heating!

Above: Deal St. box during commissioning. The casing, indicators, block instruments and illuminated track circuit diagram are all in situ, but the Xs, taped over the ex-LNWR South Lines and Exchange Station, suggest that this part of the box was not yet operational, only the ex-LYR side being completed. Push-pull levers, such as 1 and 2, are conspicuous in their vertical 'normal' position. They are further distinguished by two horizontal bands.

Left: A detailed study of levers 16-30 and the block instruments at Deal St., the latter being most unusual. They are mounted in the console, instead of being separate wooden-cased instruments. Instead of needles worked by solenoid, indications are given by lights, green for 'line clear', red for 'train on line', and no light for 'line blocked' (i.e. no train offered or accepted). A conventional bell tapper is provided, with a bell above the console, but a 3-position switch replaces the usual commutator. Finally, the upper lights are for 'trains received', and the lower lights for 'trains sent'; the opposite to normal practice. Point levers are provided with two indications (N — normal and R — reverse). On changing a point, the light is extinguished and the lever held in mid-position, until all blades are shifted home, locked and proved, whereupon the lever stroke can be completed, and an 'N' or 'R' indication shown. The 'N' and 'R' indicators reproduce as pale discs in the plate. Signals may have just two aspects (e.g. 21, a red/green ground signal setting back over crossover 22) or may be complex. Lever 19 works three 4-aspect cluster signals, from the 'down' fast to 'down' slow south (19A), 'down' slow north (19B) and 'down' fast north (19C). When lever 19 is normal, the bottom three lights give red indications for A, B and C signals. As a 4-aspect signal, when 19 is pulled, it can give yellow, double yellow or green aspects, indicated by the top three bulbs, the appropriate red indication being extinguished. Signal 30 shares a 3-display route indicator with subsidiary signal 31. The repeater is mounted centrally above the two levers, with a further tell-tale on No. 30's strip. Levers 26/27, being spare, have no indicators. Lever 25 is a switching-out lever for the four north lines, enabling Deal St. to lock the points and signals for the four north lines in the through position, and then switch out his block instruments.

Upper left: The Victoria/Exchange resignalling came at an early stage in the evolution of multiple aspect colour-light signalling, and included 4-aspect signals mounted vertically (as is modern practice) some with route indicators, and cluster signals, with the 4 aspects grouped together, red to the right, single yellow — bottom; double yellow — top and bottom; and green — left. The evolution of 'feathers' later removed the need for multiple heads, straight or cluster, but as with lever 19 illustrated overleaf, Deal St. 29, signalled a triple cluster, the signal clearing when lever 29 was pulled, being determined by the route set.

Right: The lower floors of the new boxes were given over to the electrical equipment, as with these relay racks at Victoria West Junction. The busbars, terminal blocks and resistances are mounted on the ends of the teak cabinets.

Lower left: The approach to Exchange Station in mechanical signalling days, with a Fowler 4F locomotive waiting at the approach gantry to enter the station from the slow south line. An LNWR 4-6-0 puts out a column of smoke by the 88-lever Exchange No. 2 box; an elevated structure similar to Kensington Middle box (q.v.). The old LYR Deal St. box, further out than the replacement cabin, is just visible to the right of the 4F's tender. The five left-hand 'dolls' on the gantry refer to the 'up' slow south, and the five right-hand posts to the 'up' fast south. The comparison between traditional LNWR signalling and the LYR bracket in one view is of particular interest.

Lower right; A view looking from the Great Ducie St. bridge at Victoria West Junction cabin in 1929. These cabins were completely different from standard cabins, built before or after the Manchester resignalling, and reflect Westinghouse thinking. The 4-aspect vertical signal is West Junction No. 5, with its subsidiary, No. 6, and offset to the left, 17 'pull' into the locomotive standby siding.

Authors' Collection

MANCHESTER   Victoria & Exchange

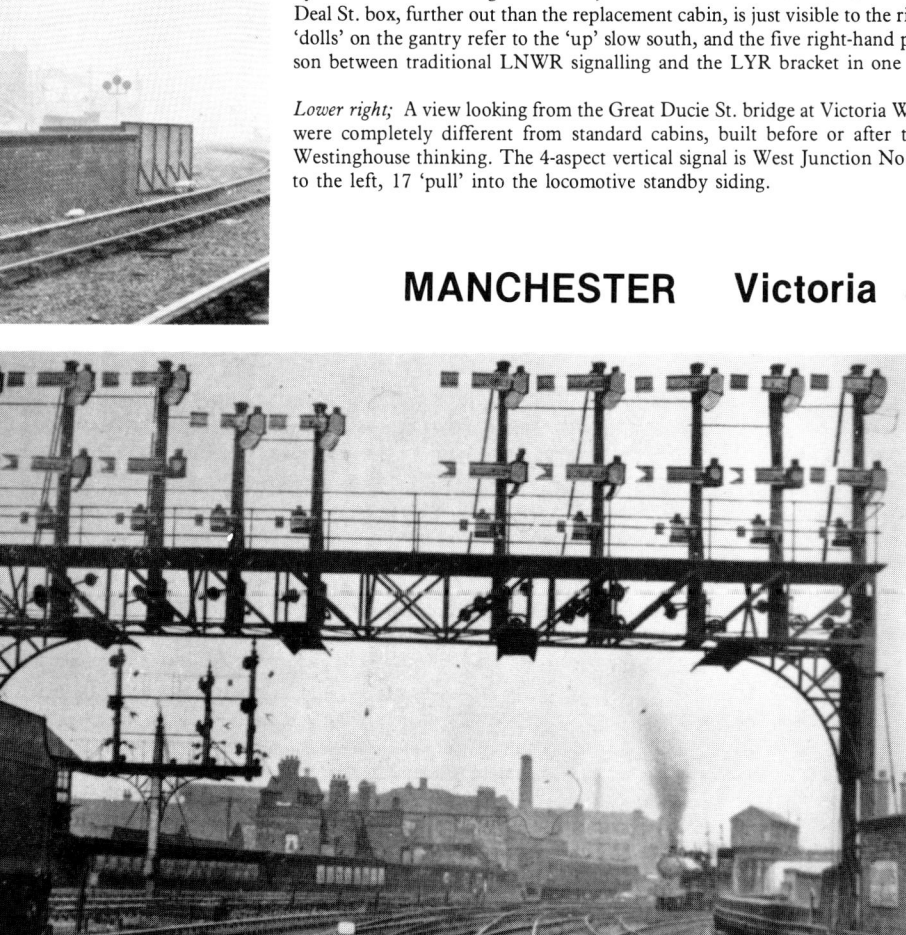

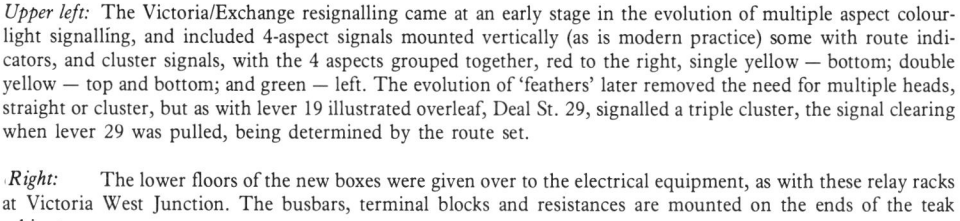

Above left: The frontage of the LNWR's Exchange Station, opened in 1884. *Authors' Collection*

Above right: A view looking south, along the Victoria Station approach, in the 1920s. *Authors' Collection*

Lower right: An 8F, No. 48773, heads an Engineer's Department train through road 17 to the 'down' slow. The abrupt climb towards Miles Platting is visible to the right of the photograph.

Lower left: A Stanier 8F, No. 48504, trundles along the 'down' through line, road 18, with a pick-up goods. A diesel multiple unit stands in platform 11, whilst another locomotive blows off on the Miles Platting bank engine siding. Note the luggage bridge in the distance.

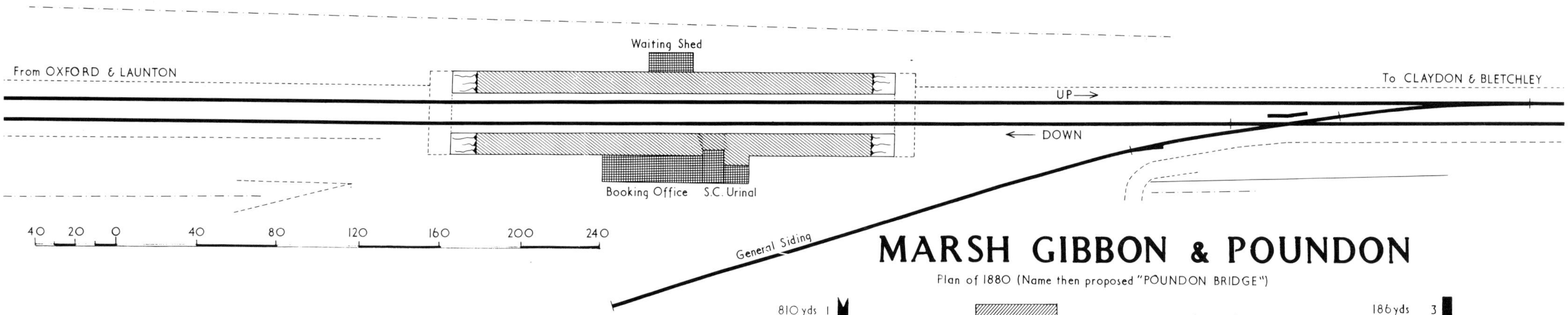

Waiting Shed

From OXFORD & LAUNTON

To CLAYDON & BLETCHLEY

UP→

← DOWN

Booking Office   S.C. Urinal

40 20 0   40   80   120   160   200   240

General Siding

MARSH GIBBON & POUNDON

Plan of 1880 (Name then proposed "POUNDON BRIDGE")

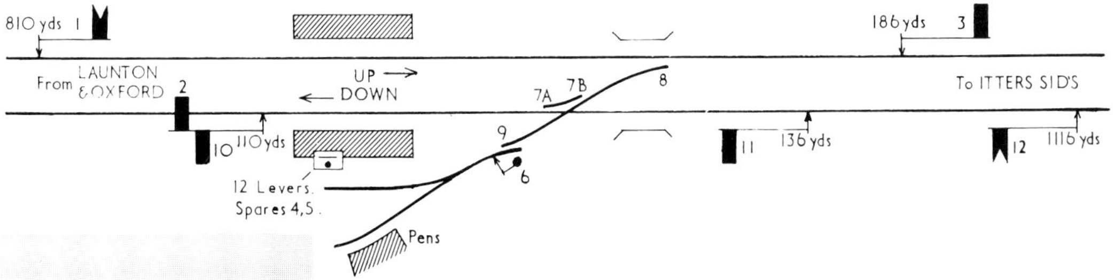

810 yds I

186 yds 3

From LAUNTON & OXFORD   2

UP →
← DOWN

7A 7B   8

To ITTERS SID'S

9
10 110yds   6   11 136yds   12 1116yds

12 Levers.
Spares 4,5.

Pens

Below: The approach to the main buildings on the 'down' platform was via a wide approach drive from the nearby road, linking the two villages. The waiting shed on the 'up' platform is visible through the double gates on the platform.

MARSH GIBBON & POUNDON *(Map Ref. H2)*

Marsh Gibbon & Poundon Station was on the Oxford & Bletchley branch of the LNWR, between Claydon and Launton and, although the line appears to be straight, is in fact on a three mile radius curve. This section, to the west of Verney Junction, where the Banbury branch diverged to the north (see 'Brackley') opened during 1850/1, and passengers had to make do with Launton Station, over two miles away. On 2nd August 1880, a new 2-platform station was opened. This had intially been known as Poundon Bridge, and was so notified to the Board of Trade, whose Inspecting Officer, Major General Hutchinson, arrived to examine the new station on 20th August.

By the 1880s, it was apparent that country stations, especially those set amongst open fields, were not goldmines, and the extravagances of the earlier days were long gone. The buildings at Poundon were plain, almost austere, and lacked awnings. This was understandable, but surprisingly, the low platform height, so much a feature of the original Buckinghamshire branch stations, was perpetuated as late as 1880, and survived an early 1900s proposal to raise the platforms. As a result, small movable flights of steps were required here, as at other stations, right up to closure on 1st January 1968.

Above left: Signalling and goods yard connections were controlled from a signal room in the main buildings. This projected forward beyond the 'building line', to give the signalman a better view. The station clock was positioned at the centre of this bay window, 'visible from the platforms', as the Board of Trade required. The box could be switched in or out, as necessary. Initially, one siding was provided, coming off the 'up' line, but by 1886, a second siding had been added. The yard closed in November 1964.

MARSH GIBBON & POUNDON

Below left: The 'up' shelter, in a view looking towards Claydon and Bletchley in 1966.

Below: 'Small movable flights of steps were required' — suitably inscribed with the station name, region and date of painting. This is a feature one seldom sees modelled, and would add character to a small country station.

MELTON MOWBRAY

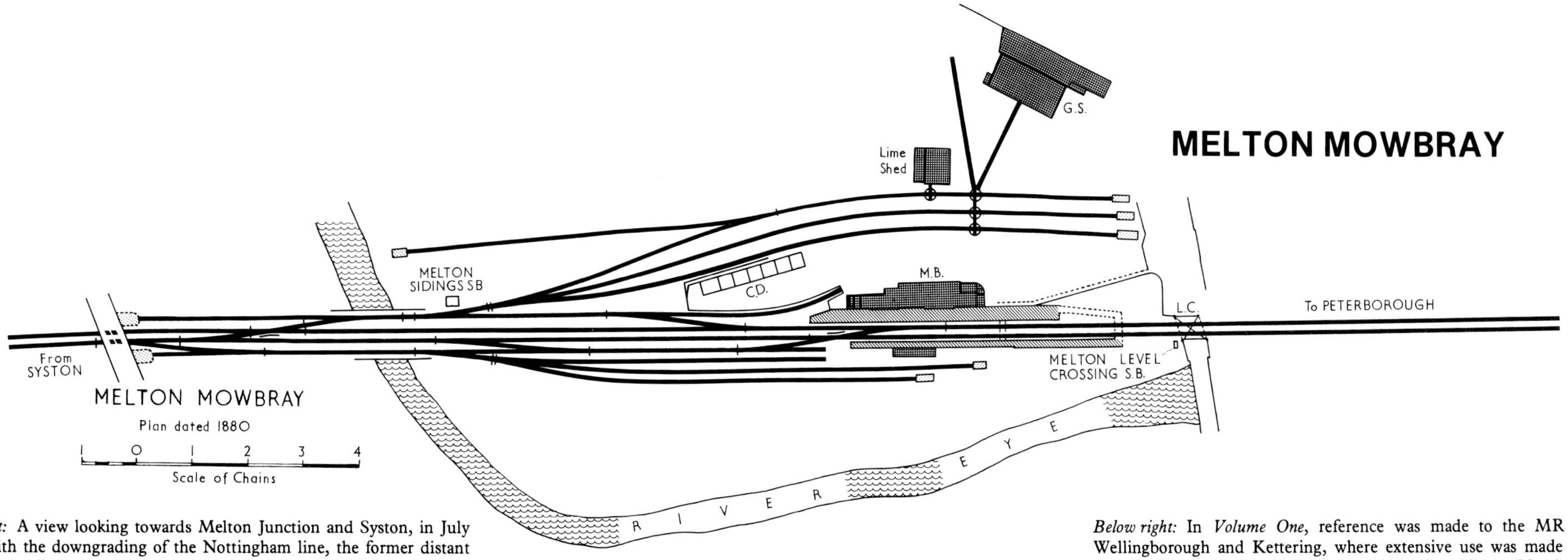

G.S.

Lime
Shed

MELTON
SIDINGS SB

C.D.

M.B.

L.C.

To PETERBOROUGH

From
SYSTON

MELTON LEVEL
CROSSING S.B.

MELTON MOWBRAY

Plan dated 1880

Scale of Chains

0 1 2 3 4

RIVER EYE

Below left: A view looking towards Melton Junction and Syston, in July 1971. With the downgrading of the Nottingham line, the former distant for the Syston/Leicester line has been removed from the left-hand post on the bracket signal, and the ex-Nottingham distant redesignated as the Syston line distant. Shunt signals 17/35 (middle distance) are so close as to obstruct clear visibility *(see signal diagram).*

Above: Melton Mowbray in 1880, prior to the construction of the overbridge or loops out to Brentingby. Otherwise the station had altered little by 1971.

Below right: In *Volume One*, reference was made to the MR stations at Wellingborough and Kettering, where extensive use was made of awnings supported by cast-iron spandrels. By 1871, when Melton Mowbray received elegant ridge and furrow canopies, MR thinking had progressed towards lattice girders, and a carefully-balanced construction to minimise the size of brackets. Note the milk churns still in use in 1971.

MELTON MOWBRAY (Map Ref. V8)

Melton Mowbray is a picturesque market town (population 23,000) and is best-known for pork pies, Stilton cheese and hunting. It lies on the Syston and Peterborough branch of the Midland Railway. This was authorised in 1845 and the first section, from Syston, just north of Leicester, to Melton, came into use on 1st September 1846. The Stamford to Peterborough portion followed during that October, but it was not until 1st May 1848 that the line was completed as a through route, largely due to the opposition of Lord Harborough, to the course of the line near Saxby. Located in the heart of hunting country, Melton was frequented by the gentry, and the station was both elegant and spacious, and in the century from the completion of the station awnings in 1871, altered remarkably little, as a comparison of the 1881 and 1965 plans will reveal. The earlier plan shows the layout prior to replacement of the station level crossing which was a source of fury to local people, and led to angry scenes in Parliament. The layout at the eastern end of the station was

eventually modified to include 'up' and 'down' goods running loops from just beyond the platforms as far as Brentingby Junction, a distance of 1 mile 397yds. The 'junction' referred not to a divergence of routes, but to the junction of the main and goods lines!

For many years, the station was worked by two cabins, one near the level crossing, and the other in the yard. Eventually, an LMS partially-overhung cabin was erected 80yds. nearer the station than the old sidings box, replacing both earlier structures. One of the problems with any complex railway system, such as the Midland, is designation of 'up' and 'down' directions, and many lines have changed 'direction' over the decades. A train from Syston to Peterborough, the original line, was a 'down' train leaving Syston; at Melton Junction (q.v.) it became an 'up' train; and at Manton, it became 'down' once more. This particular eccentricity was due to the construction of the Nottingham direct line of the MR, of which the S&PR formed the central section.

Left: The position map locates Melton astride the S&PR and Nottingham direct routes, and shows the direction of the 'up' lines on this complex MR spider's web. A train from Loughborough to Peterborough would be an 'up'/'down'/'up'/'down' train!

MELTON MOWBRAY

MELTON MOWBRAY TOWN
1965 Plan

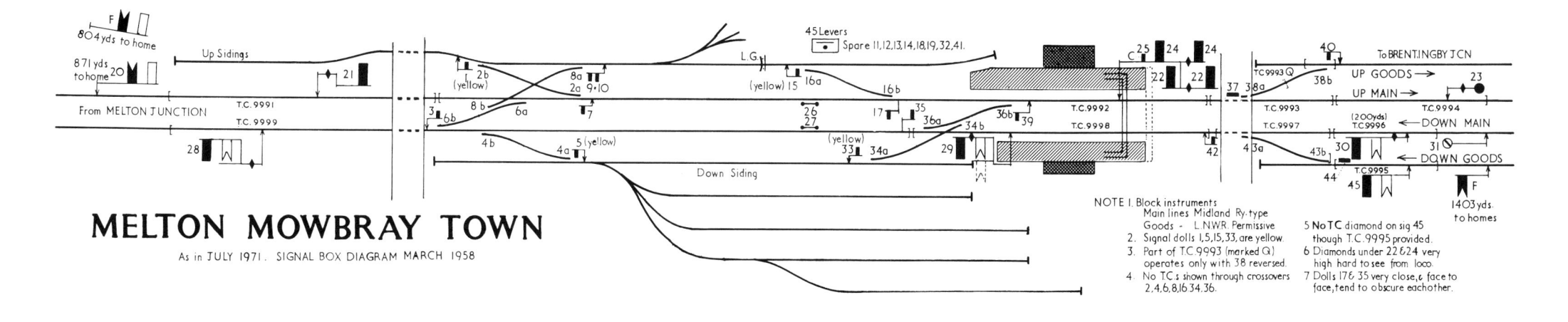

MELTON MOWBRAY TOWN

As in JULY 1971. SIGNAL BOX DIAGRAM MARCH 1958

804 yds to home F

871 yds to home 20

Up Sidings

From MELTON JUNCTION

T.C.9991
T.C.9999

45 Levers
Spare 11,12,13,14,18,19,32,41.

L.G.

To BRENT.INGBY JCN
UP GOODS
UP MAIN →

DOWN MAIN
DOWN GOODS

Down Siding

1403 yds. to homes

NOTE 1. Block instruments
Main lines Midland Ry-type
Goods - L.N.W.R. Permissive
2. Signal dolls 1,5,15,33, are yellow
3. Part of T.C.9993 (marked Q)
operates only with 38 reversed.
4. No TC's shown through crossovers
2,4,6,8,16,34,36.

5 No TC diamond on sig 45
though T.C.9995 provided.
6 Diamonds under 22&24 very
high hard to see from loco.
7 Dolls 17& 35 very close,& face to
face,tend to obscure each other.

Below left: A signalman's view, looking towards Melton and Syston in 1971, as a Class 25 diesel shunts in the 'down' sidings. The basic passenger service included through trains between Leicester or Nottingham, to Peterborough, or Corby and London. These were supplemented by through East Anglian expresses for the Midland & Great Northern Joint Railway, a largely seasonal service, intensive in summer but infrequent in winter — as for example in December 1905, with but two through trains each way. Certain local trains ex-Nottingham terminated at Melton, whilst some local trains ex the M&GN expired at the next station to the east, Saxby. With a little foresight, this 4-mile gap in through connections could have been avoided to the benefit of all.

Below right: A signalman's view, looking east, towards Peterborough and the Manton line. A wagon repair depot existed on the 'down' side, sandwiched between the 'down' platform and River Eye. Such repair yards were once commonplace, when private owner wagons abounded, and timber was the usual structural material, but succumbed under the assault of steel bodywork, which required capital equipment, and nationalisation. The survival of such a yard at Melton in 1971 is remarkable. Note how very short the 'down' platform is, some 290ft. or barely six coaches. The quaint positioning of shunt signals Nos. 17/35, is apparent, only the height of the box enabling us to see No. 35. The bridge carrying the road over the railway and the river is visible beyond the platform awnings, and between the trees by the wagon yard.

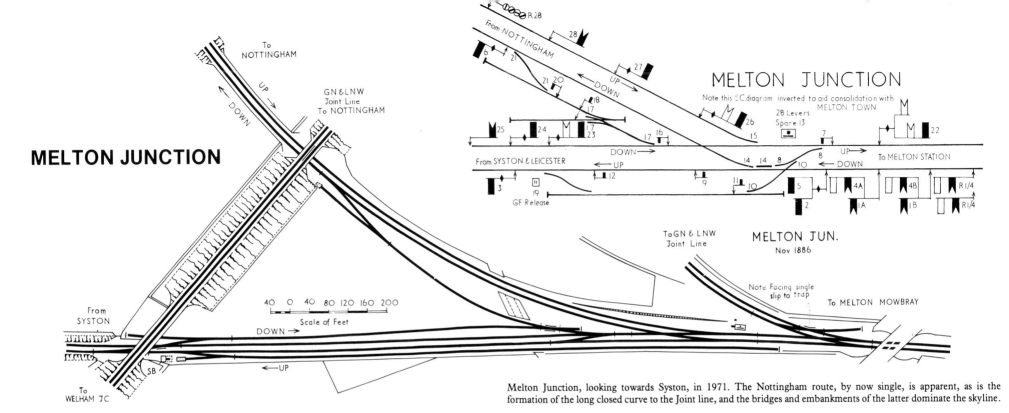

MELTON JUNCTION

To NOTTINGHAM

UP

DOWN

GN & LNW Joint Line To NOTTINGHAM

From SYSTON

40 0 40 80 120 160 200
Scale of Feet

DOWN→

←UP

SB

To WELHAM JC

MELTON JUNCTION

From NOTTINGHAM

R 28

28

6 21

21 20

UP

DOWN→

18

17

17 16

27

26

Note this S.C.diagram inverted to aid consolidation with MELTON TOWN

28 Levers
Spare 13

7

15

25

24

M

23

From SYSTON & LEICESTER

←UP

DOWN→

14 14 8

UP→

←DOWN

To MELTON STATION

3

19

GF Release

12

9

11 10

5

10

8

4A

4B

R1/4

2

1A

1B

R1/4

22

M M

MELTON JUN.

To GN & LNW Joint Line

Nov 1886

Note Facing single slip to trap

To MELTON MOWBRAY

Melton Junction, looking towards Syston, in 1971. The Nottingham route, by now single, is apparent, as is the formation of the long closed curve to the Joint line, and the bridges and embankments of the latter dominate the skyline.

MELTON JUNCTION *(Map Ref. V8)*

Melton Junction is 1,150yds. west of Melton Mowbray Town Station, and was formerly the junction of the Syston & Peterborough line with the MR Nottingham direct route. The latter was authorised in 1872, opened to goods on 1st November 1879, and to passengers on 2nd February 1880. For most of its life, Melton Junction controlled this divergence and some exchange sidings, but in the early days the picture was more complex. As the MR were building their Nottingham route, the GNR and LNWR were constructing a joint line southwards from Bottesford to Welham Junction, near Market Harborough. This line, which opened in 1879, crossed the Nottingham and Syston lines just west of Melton Junction, and a sharply-curved chord was laid in. The scale plan of 1886 shows the Midland end of this connection, which was built for ironstone traffic from Waltham-on-the-Wolds (GN/LNW Jt.) to Holwell Ironworks (MR). It fell out of use when an MR branch reached Waltham, but this did not stop the MR claiming £2 per annum from the GN&LNW Jt. Committee, on the grounds that their cabin was larger than necessary for their purposes! The MR Nottingham line closed in 1967, having been predeceased by the GN&LNW line. The section from Melton to Edwalton was retained for use by the BR advanced projects section. Prior to closure, the Nottingham line was the more important route, and the Nottingham splitting signal at the junction was mounted higher on its 'doll' than the Syston arm. This ought to have been reflected in the positioning of the junction distant arms, but a study of the junction and station signal diagrams show that these did not agree with one another, or with the signals actually provided! This is one of the problems in studying signalling and station evolution.

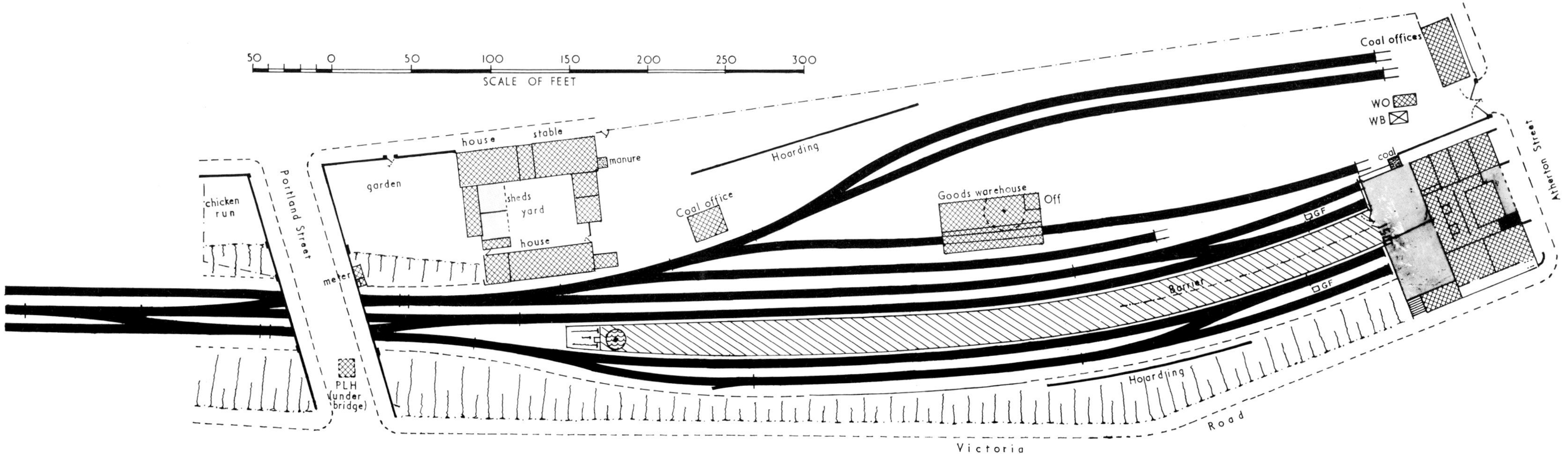

The plan at the top of the page shows the track layout with a scale of feet (50, 0, 50, 100, 150, 200, 250, 300), labelled with features including chicken run, Portland Street, garden, house, stable, sheds yard, manure, house, meter, PLH (under bridge), Coal office, Hoarding, Goods warehouse, Off, Barrier, GF, GF, coal, Coal offices, WO, WB, Atherton Street, Hoarding, Road, Victoria.

NEW BRIGHTON

Left: A view looking towards the buffer stops from the solitary island platform in 1965. To the left is the goods shed and coal-stacking area. Adjoining the goods shed is a carriage siding, which regularly proved its worth in peak periods, and the two platform faces, each with their own runrounds. In both Wirral Railway and early LMS days, these were used for the intensive service from Liverpool, via the Mersey Railway Tunnel but, after electrification, this need disappeared. Freight services continued to be steam-worked, so that some run-round facilities were essential, but another important reason was to cope with steam-hauled specials ex the Birkenhead Joint or former MS&L route through the centre of the Wirral to Bidston. Interestingly, a regular service was provided by the MSLR, GCR. LNER and BR over the central Wirral line to Bidston, and by running powers to Seacombe terminus. A dozen trains still traversed this route in the 1950s, but with the closure of Seacombe in 1960, the old GCR service switched to New Brighton, with as many as twenty workings a day by 1962. This photograph, in fact, shows a dieset multiple unit on the central Wirral service on the left, and ex-LMSR electric stock on the right. Timetable revisions later resulted in the DMUs normally running into Birkenhead North, with cross-platform connection to electric services, except on Sundays! In 1972, for example, there were four through Sunday DMU workings between Wrexham and New Brighton. A very short canopy, of traditional style, was provided in Wirral Railway days, but for the 1938 electrification, the LMS produced a much longer reinforced-concrete canopy, here depicted, supported by longitudinal beams from above, and T-shaped columns from beneath.

Right: Portland St. was carried over the railway at the station throat, and New Brighton Station cabin stood at the far side of the bridge, adjacent to the goods yard headshunt; the most northerly of the three tracks to go through the bridge. This study shows how extraordinarily uneven is the sleeper spacing on the headshunt. The headshunt was not electrified, but electric stock could be stabled in the run-round loop or carriage siding reached off the facing lead from the running lines.

NEW BRIGHTON

Below: At a terminus of any size, run-round connections are invariably out of the permitted range of manual operation from the signal box, and small ground frames are called for. This is a feature seldom seen on model railway termini, and we have therefore chosen to illustrate the northernmost ground frame at New Brighton. The signalman has an electric release lever to each ground frame. Upon pulling this, conflicting movements within his own frame are prevented by his interlocking, and the ground frame is free. The rectangular box, with 'LMS' cast on the lid, is the electric release. The shunter pulls the release lever, so locking the ground frame release in the signal box, so that the signalman cannot forget and throw the release during shunting. A lug, bolted to the ground frame lever, No. 1, prevents the point lever being moved, or the release being put back!

NEW BRIGHTON *(Map Ref. A1)*

The Hoylake Railway (see under 'Bidston') was authorised in 1863 between Hoylake and Birkenhead/Seacombe. A 4¾ mile branch to New Brighton was authorised in 1865, but the early collapse of the Hoylake Railway eliminated this venture. In 1872, the Hoylake Railway was reopened under fresh auspices, and the new company became the Seacombe, Hoylake & Deeside Railway in 1881. On 12th July 1882, the SH&DR was authorised to extend from Bidston to Warren Drive, on the outskirts of New Brighton. On 25th September 1886, the SH&DR was authorised to extend the line into New Brighton itself, and to extend the 5 year completion date on the original section. The line, double track and worked on the absolute block system, opened from Bidston to Wallasey on 2nd January 1888, and to New Brighton on 30th March 1888. In 1891, the SH&DR was amalgamated into the Wirral Railway. By the close of the 1890s, 25-30 trains were operating over the branch daily, and the Mersey and Wirral Railways were in hot competition with the Pier Head to New Brighton ferry service of Wallasey Corporation, of which New Brighton is a part. From 1906 to 1911, the *Dodger*, some lightweight coaches and a 2-4-0 tank too small for modern services, provided a high frequency shuttle service between New Brighton and Seacombe, via the north curve at Seacombe Junction, but this was not a success. In 1923, the LMS introduced a through coach service between New Brighton and Euston, running via the Birkenhead Joint. In 1934, towards the end of steam working on the Birkenhead services, a favourable/unfavourable weather service was instituted, with ten or twenty minute afternoon services on summer weekends. The New Brighton branch was electrified on 13th March 1938, and is a part of the Merseyside electrified service. Freight services ceased on 30th October 1965.

NEWTON-LE-WILLOWS

PLAN DATE 1916

CHANGES BETWEEN 1916 and 1960

A. Only 2 (cf 3) lines over Bridge No 98
B. Bridge No 80 seperated from No 98
C. Three sidings along the North removed
D. Loop through Goods Shed removed
E. New Crossover added beteen sidings near up platform
F. Slip crossing from up/down crossover to up sid's removed
G. Up/down crossover moved c. 60 ft to East
H. Double slip/crossover down sidings to down main replaced by Trap/Point c. 170 ft to East

Private Siding GARTON & Co

From LIVERPOOL

UP →
← DOWN

Private Siding R.T. STONES

To MANCHESTER

NEWTON-LE-WILLOWS (Map Ref. O1)

Newton-le-Willows Station lies on the Liverpool & Manchester Railway, just to the east of Earlestown (q.v.) and at about the mid-point of the L&MR. The Liverpool & Manchester Railway was authorised on 5th May 1826, and formally opened on 15th September 1830. At this early stage in railway development, many matters were still on an experimental basis. Passengers had to be dissuaded from occupying the roofs of carriages, as in stage-coach days, or in jumping off trains when nearing their destinations. Wayside stations initially comprised little more than an area of level ground by the lineside, one such stopping place being just east of Newton Viaduct, a four arch masonry structure carrying the line over a mill stream and adjacent turnpike. In coaching days, innkeepers had done a thriving business selling refreshments to weary travellers and, by 1832, the proprietor of the Legh Arms Hotel, less than a hundred yards from the lineside, was so successfully intoxicating passengers, that he was warned that his staff, who hung about the station, would be fined if they persisted in selling drink! By 1839, small cottage-like buildings, with a booking office and waiting-room, had been erected on each side of the line. A small carriage shed, holding two vehicles, and substantial urinals, completed the facilities. Thus equipped, the station was markedly superior to the majority of other wayside L&MR stopping places, although the

company had yet to go to the expense of platforms. By the mid-1840s, railways had emerged from the experimental phase, and with quite minor wayside stations on new lines accorded impressive buildings, continuous upgrading was called for. New buildings were erected at Newton in 1845, and the station was periodically enlarged thereafter.

Until 1868, the station had been known as Newton, but its proximity to the viaduct, and confusion with nearby Earlestown, originally known as Newton Junction, resulted in the regularisation of a colloquial name, Newton Bridge. In June 1888, the station became Newton-le-Willows. Those familiar with LNWR timetables will know the line 'McCorquodale and Co. Limited, Printers to the Company' which graced such documents for decades. One of McCorquodale's principal works was located adjacent to the goods yard on the north side of the line, and much of the freight flowing through the small yard was to or from the printing works.

The small goods yard closed to general traffic on 3rd August 1953, but became busier than ever, with the establishment of a Motorail terminal for the north-west, the car loading dock adjoining the 'up' platform. Regrettably this facility, along with Sutton Coldfield in the West Midlands, was closed in 1972, when services were moved to Crewe. The station remains open for passenger traffic, the road entrance being shared with the Legh Arms Hotel.

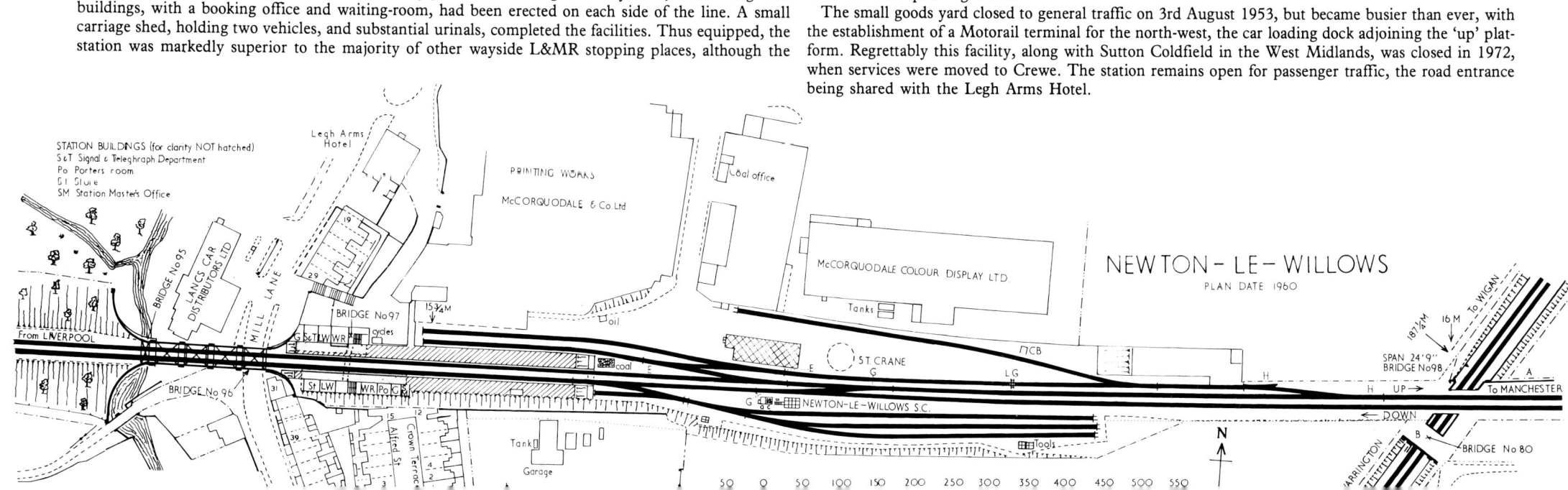

Above left: A view looking along the 'up' platform towards Newton Viaduct and Liverpool. With the introduction of power box working, a facing emergency crossover, controlled by a local ground frame released by the power box, has been provided. At one time, the Board of Trade would have resolutely opposed the idea of such a facing connection!

Above right: The main buildings on the 'up' platform, in a view looking towards Manchester. The buildings continue virtually to the commencement of the viaduct itself.

NEWTON-LE-WILLOWS

Below left: The scene looking across the station forecourt from the approach road to the 'ground floor' of the station buildings, and subway to the 'down' platform.

Below right: On the scale plans, a small shelter is depicted near the Manchester end of the 'down' platform. Humble structures like this seldom receive a mention, hence this illustration.

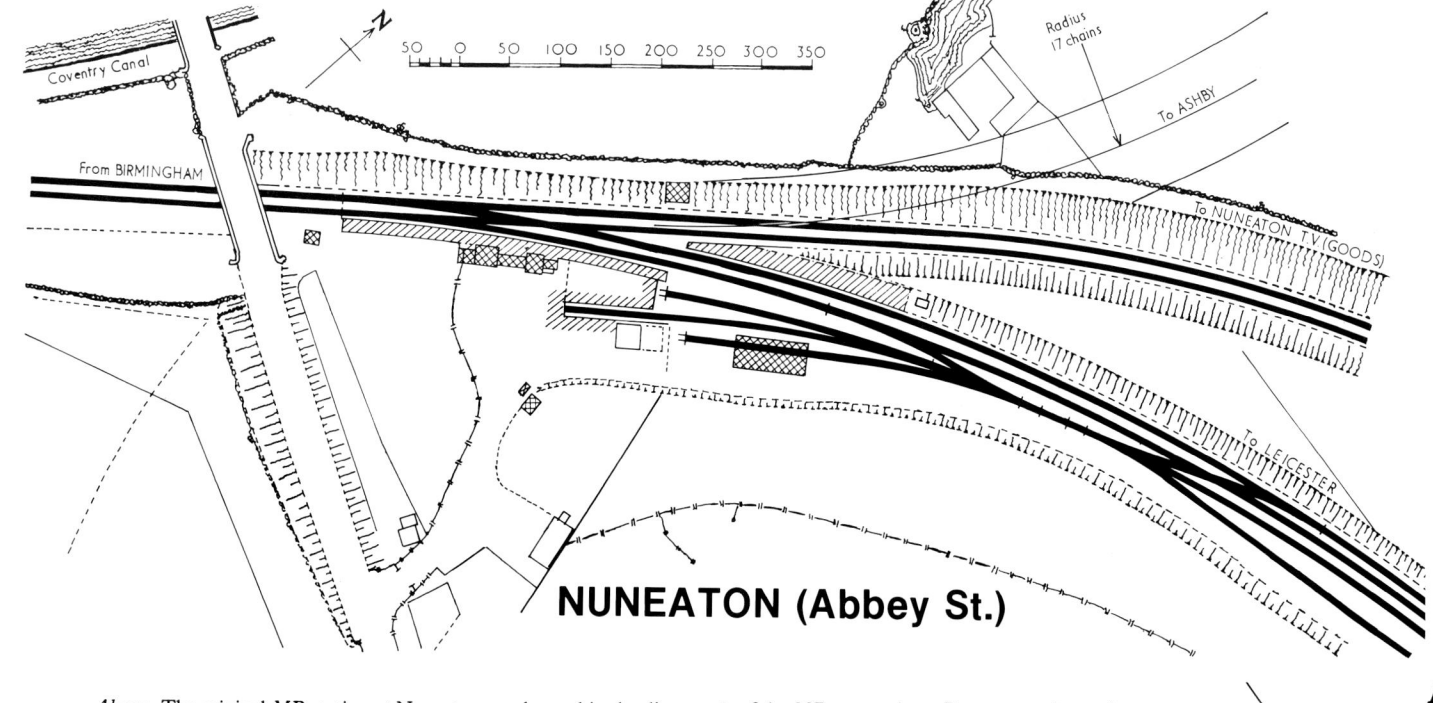

NUNEATON (Abbey St.)

NUNEATON (Abbey St.) *(Map Ref. F7)*

Nuneaton, two miles south of the Watling St., and the Warwickshire/Leicestershire border, is an interesting example of LNWR/Midland rivalry and co-operation. The first line through the town was the Trent Valley route of the LNWR of 1847. This was followed by the LNWR's Coventry & Nuneaton line in 1850, whilst an LNWR associate, the South Leicestershire Railway, opened east from Nuneaton to Hinckley in 1862, and to a connection with the MR south of Leicester in 1864. By this time, the Warwickshire and Leicester Coalfields were of increasing importance and, in 1860, the MR and LNWR agreed a package of measures, which permitted the LNWR to run over the MR's Rugby to Leicester branch, and gave the MR running powers over the South Leicester line, and for freight traffic only over the Coventry & Nuneaton line. As a sequel, the MR took powers, on 7th June 1861, for a branch from the Birmingham & Derby Junction line at Whitacre, to Nuneaton, with a station of their own in Nuneaton, and connections to the LNWR's Trent Valley line and, via a flyover, to the South Leicester branch. This opened to passengers on 1st November 1864, and to goods a month later.

Above: The original MR station at Nuneaton was located in the divergence of the MR connections. Passenger trains took the more southerly route, which was carried over the Trent Valley line north of the LNWR station. Freight trains took the other connection (which had no passenger platforms) to facilitate interchange with the LNWR. The survey shows the projected route of the Ashby & Nuneaton line, which led to the original station being replaced in 1873.

Below: To cater for the Ashby & Nuneaton services, a new station was opened on the west side of the Midland Road overbridge on 1st September 1873. This is seen, looking from the Station forecourt towards Ashby.

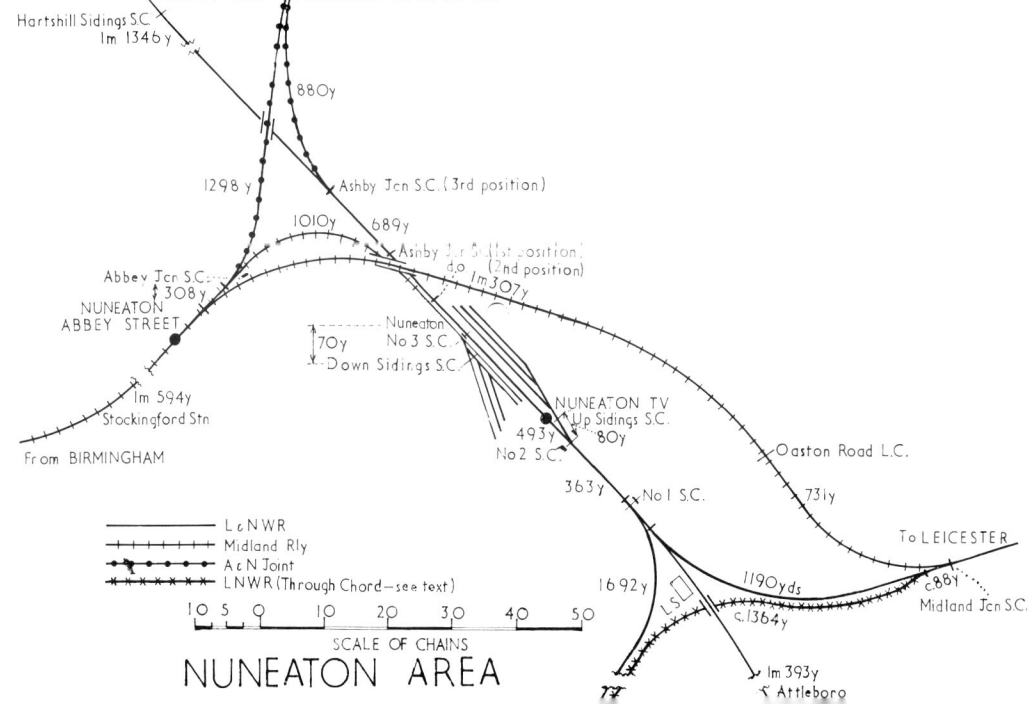

Above: The view looking from the site of the 1864 (westbound) platform towards Ashby and Leicester. The nearest double junction to the right is the old MR passenger line to the South Leicester branch, which crossed the Trent Valley line by a flyover. The next pair of running lines is the MR freight connection to the LNWR, whilst the MR/LNWR Ashby & Nuneaton line curves to the left, beyond Abbey Junction Signal cabin.

Above: Abbey Junction signal cabin, looking towards Ashby on 30th September 1971. The Leicester line is in the foreground, and the Ashby and Trent Valley lines are behind the box, which is of typical Midland design. A wharf on the Ashby Curve beyond the box served Judkin's stone siding, which boasted its own narrow gauge system from the wharf to the quarry, just to the north.

NUNEATON (Abbey St.)

Below: Severe gradients necessitated much double-heading or banking. Nos. 49120, and 48927 bring a coal train in from Ashby. Connor's Shed is in the background.

E. M. Bray

Below: A ballast train sets back 'wrong road' into the station under Midland Road bridge.

E. M. Bray

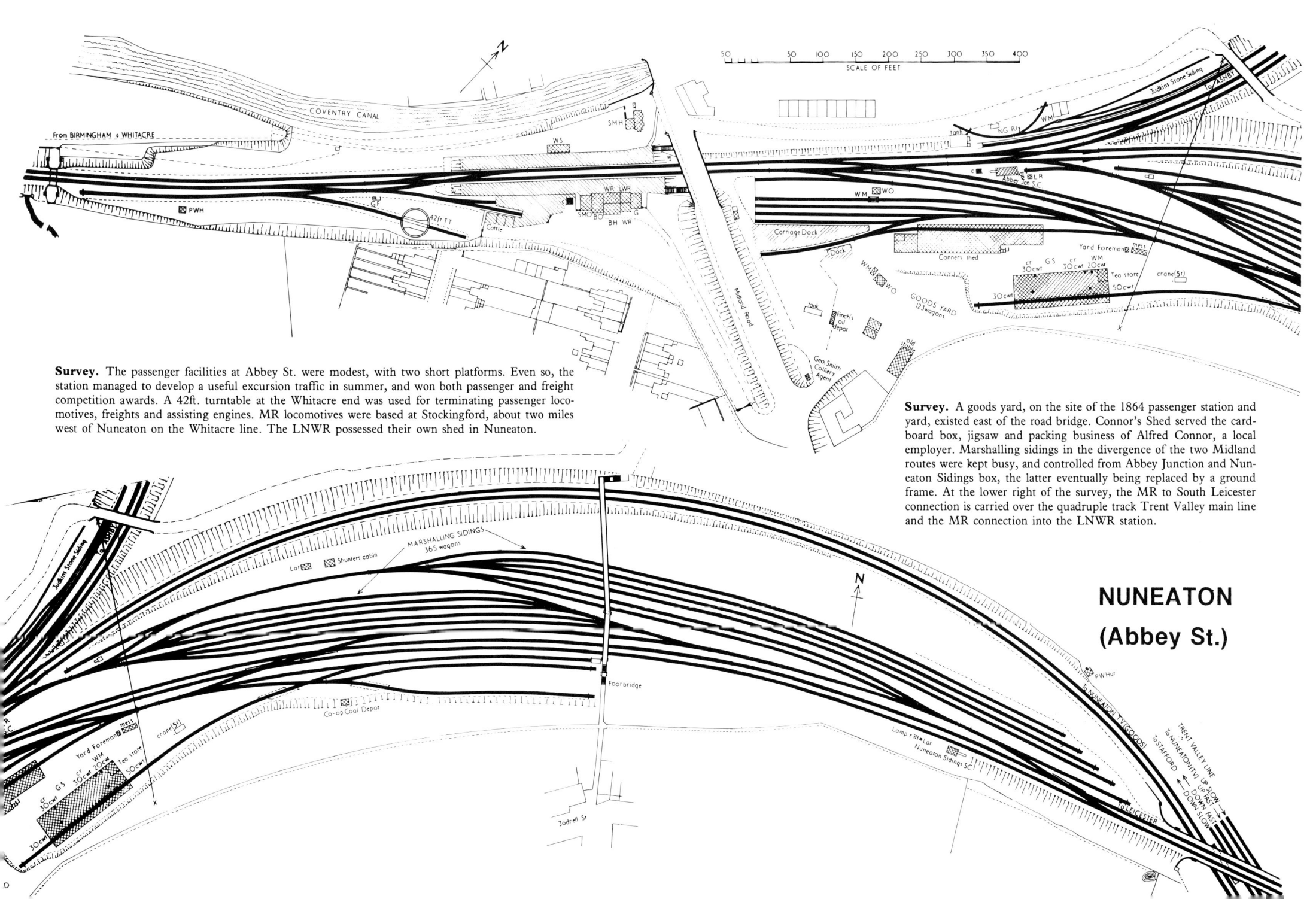

Survey. The passenger facilities at Abbey St. were modest, with two short platforms. Even so, the station managed to develop a useful excursion traffic in summer, and won both passenger and freight competition awards. A 42ft. turntable at the Whitacre end was used for terminating passenger locomotives, freights and assisting engines. MR locomotives were based at Stockingford, about two miles west of Nuneaton on the Whitacre line. The LNWR possessed their own shed in Nuneaton.

Survey. A goods yard, on the site of the 1864 passenger station and yard, existed east of the road bridge. Connor's Shed served the cardboard box, jigsaw and packing business of Alfred Connor, a local employer. Marshalling sidings in the divergence of the two Midland routes were kept busy, and controlled from Abbey Junction and Nuneaton Sidings box, the latter eventually being replaced by a ground frame. At the lower right of the survey, the MR to South Leicester connection is carried over the quadruple track Trent Valley main line and the MR connection into the LNWR station.

NUNEATON

(Abbey St.)

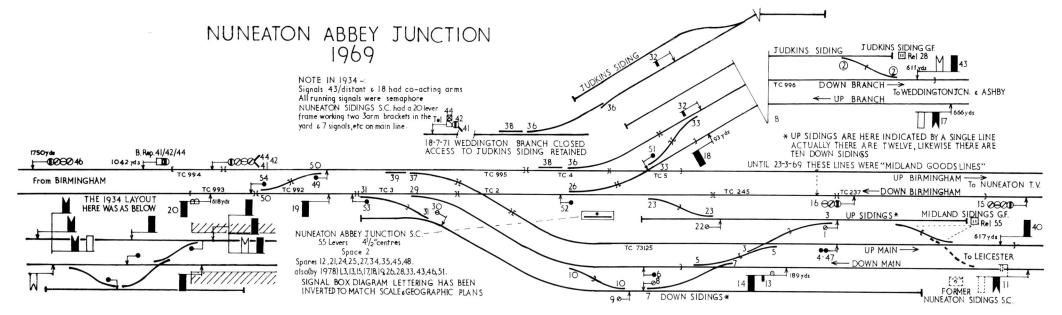

NUNEATON (Abbey St.)

Parts of the Leicestershire Coalfield had been worked for generations, but the coming of the canals, and then the railways, permitted a massive expansion, with many new pits. One of the most historic sections of the MR, the Leicester & Swannington line, struck north-west from Leicester, through Desford and Coalville, and with other lines round Moira and Burton, this was Midland territory, so much so that the MR had not felt it necessary to exercise powers of 1846 for a line protecting them from assault from the Nuneaton direction. In the 1860s, an LNWR-orientated scheme projected a line from Nuneaton to Market Bosworth and Ashby. Predictably, the Midland retaliated with a rehash of their 1846 ideas. A head-on clash was avoided by eventual agreement to construct a joint line, the Ashby & Nuneaton, with Acts of 1866, 1867 and 1868. The A&N ran north-east from Nuneaton, where it made connection with the MR at Abbey Junction, on the site of the 1864 passenger station, and from the LNWR at Ashby Junction, north of the Trent Valley line station. The original Ashby Junction was just north of the Midland flyover, the joint metals paralleling the then double track Trent Valley line. The junction was later moved south of the flyover, and when the Trent Valley line was quadrupled, north of Nuneaton, the junction became the point of physical divergence of the two routes. A connection from Hinckley, on the South Leicester branch, joined the Nuneaton line near Stoke Golding, but was lifted within a few years. The A&N ran north, past the site of Bosworth Field, to Shackerstone, where one limb continued north west to Moira and the MR, and the other to Coalville. The A&N Joint opened to coal on 1st August 1873, to freight on 18th August, and to passengers on 1st September. An LNWR-backed line, the Charnwood Forest Railway, ran east from Coalville to Loughborough. This was authorised in 1874 and opened in 1883.

By the turn of the century, ten trains, including some semi-fasts and short workings served Abbey St. in each direction on the Birmingham-Nuneaton-Leicester route. Although the LNWR offered five or six

trains daily from the Trent Valley station over the A&N, the MR was less lavish, with but two trains ex-Abbey St., for the line had been built for coal, and passengers were few. Until the Grouping, the station was known as Nuneaton (Midland) or, sometimes, Nuneaton Abbey. The Abbey St. suffix was formally adopted on 2nd June 1924. Under the LMS, Abbey St. came under control area No. 48, 'Saltley', the A&N, from the junction of the Abbey St. and Trent Valley spurs, becoming area No. 47, 'Coalville'. With mounting deficits, all passenger services over the A&N and Charnwood Forest lines were withdrawn on 13th April 1931. Leicester services continued to call at Abbey St. until 4th March 1968, when the station was closed, passenger workings henceforth only calling at the Trent Valley station. This marked the conclusion of a trend which had begun in Midland days, with a number of passenger services running via the goods lines, which were upgraded, to the LNWR station, providing convenient connections between LNWR and MR routes.

General freight ceased over the A&N by 1968, with colliery traffic surviving a little longer. Today, the A&N is lifted, except for the Shackerstone to Market Bosworth section, in preservation auspices. At Abbey Junction, the stump of the A&N survived to provide access to Judkin's Sidings. One curious result of the switch of passenger services to the ex-LNWR station was that whilst the original freight connection became the passenger line, the old passenger line, from Abbey St. to the South Leicester branch, became freight only! Although not directly linked to Abbey St., reference should be made to the chord from the Coventry branch at Chilvers Coton to the SLR at Midland Junction. This was installed as a part of the 1860s deal to permit through running by MR trains between Coventry and Leicester, but saw little, if any, use. Parts were lifted, and its main function from World War II was to provide an additional access to the LNWR shed, which it adjoined.

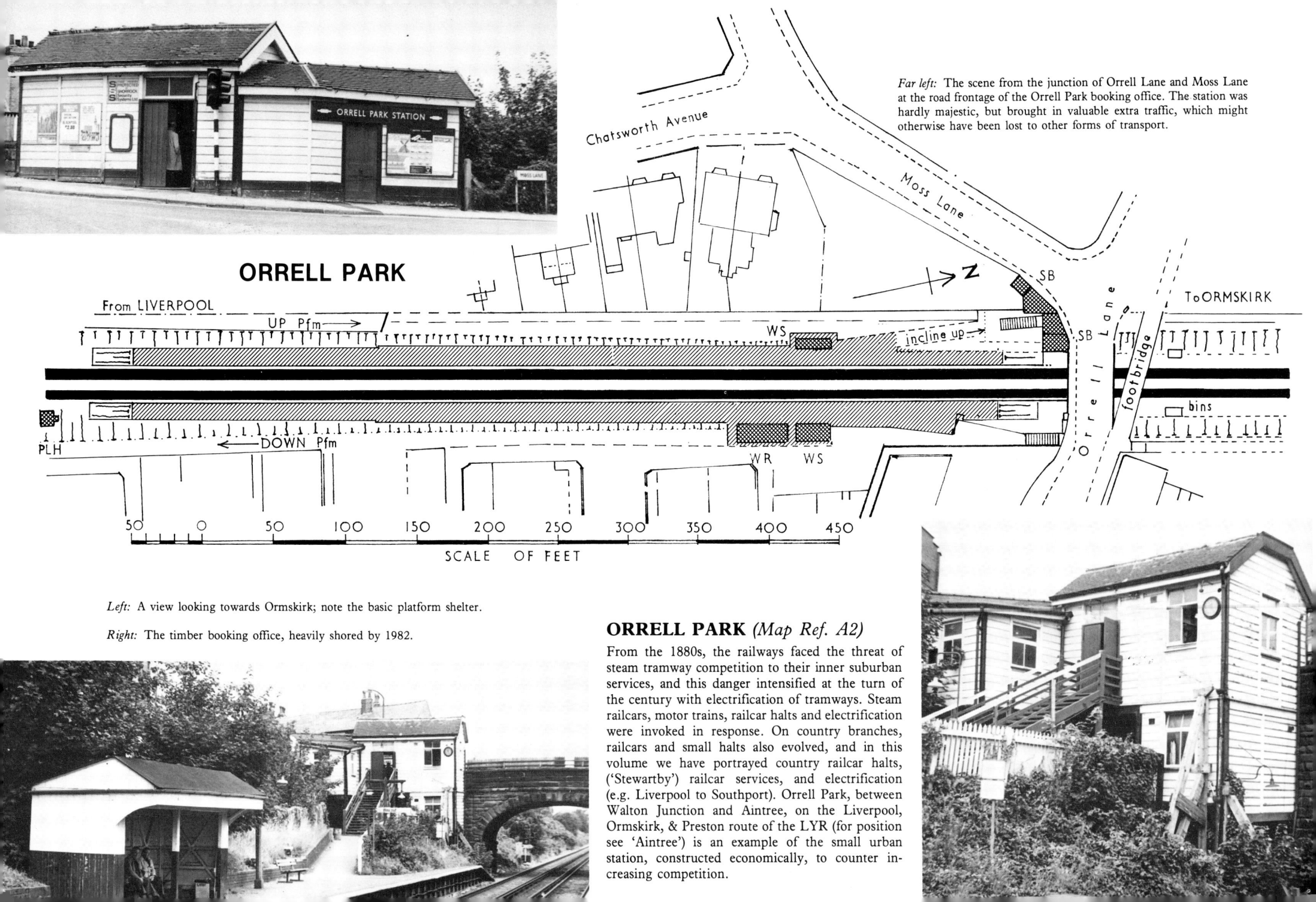

Far left: The scene from the junction of Orrell Lane and Moss Lane at the road frontage of the Orrell Park booking office. The station was hardly majestic, but brought in valuable extra traffic, which might otherwise have been lost to other forms of transport.

ORRELL PARK

From LIVERPOOL

UP Pfm →

← DOWN Pfm

PLH

WS

incline up →

WR   WS

To ORMSKIRK

footbridge

Orrell Lane

SB

SB

bins

Chatsworth Avenue

Moss Lane

SCALE OF FEET

50 0 50 100 150 200 250 300 350 400 450

Left: A view looking towards Ormskirk; note the basic platform shelter.

Right: The timber booking office, heavily shored by 1982.

ORRELL PARK *(Map Ref. A2)*

From the 1880s, the railways faced the threat of steam tramway competition to their inner suburban services, and this danger intensified at the turn of the century with electrification of tramways. Steam railcars, motor trains, railcar halts and electrification were invoked in response. On country branches, railcars and small halts also evolved, and in this volume we have portrayed country railcar halts, ('Stewartby') railcar services, and electrification (e.g. Liverpool to Southport). Orrell Park, between Walton Junction and Aintree, on the Liverpool, Ormskirk, & Preston route of the LYR (for position see 'Aintree') is an example of the small urban station, constructed economically, to counter increasing competition.

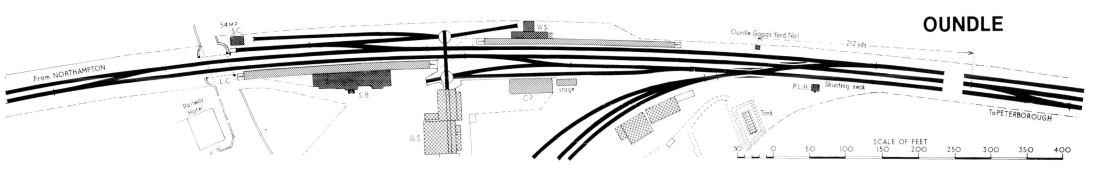

OUNDLE *(Map Ref. L7)*

Oundle is a small market town, with a population of less than 4,000, lying on the River Nene about twelve miles south-west of Peterborough. The period charm of its ancient main street is enhanced by the soft grey limestone of so many of the buildings. Having elected to bypass Northampton on its main line in the 1830s, the London & Birmingham Railway decided to put the town on the railway map, by means of a long branch from Blisworth to Peterborough. This was opened on 2nd June 1845. Wayside stations on some of the earliest main lines had been very simple, but by the 1840s the country was caught up in a euphoric mood, and in common with contemporary lines elsewhere, no expense was spared in creating magnificent wayside stations, wholly out of keeping with any prospects of traffic. The stations on the Northampton & Peterborough line were some of the most magnificent ever built. Designed by J. W. Livock, in the Jacobean style, they were constructed from local stone, Oundle being of the grey limestone which dominates the town. In contrast to Wansford Station *(see Volume One)* three straight-edged gables dominated the front elevation of the building. The line was completed as a single track, but had been doubled by September 1846, and in common with other N&P stations, the second platform boasted minimal facilities. At this time, wagon turntables predominated in goods yards, and at Oundle the goods shed was at right-angles to the running lines, and reached off wagon turntables, as per the LNWR scale plan.

Below left: A view looking from the goods yard connections towards Northampton. Although closed to passenger traffic, other than the occasional school special, and with tracks lifted south of the station, Oundle still handled a heavy mineral traffic into the 1970s.

The initial train service was three trains each way daily, but by 1883 this had increased to six workings. Oundle Station lay just outside the town, and an omnibus, Fly's, or post-horses, could be secured on application to the Talbot Hotel. Oundle School, with an endowment from a former Lord Mayor of London, provided regular traffic at the beginning and end of each term and, even after passenger services ceased over the N&P branch, on 4th May 1964, school specials continued to operate, whilst Oundle also handled freight traffic. The BR retreat from such old style branches meant that a part of the N&P (between Yarwell Junction, north-east of Oundle, and Orton Longueville outside Peterborough) was taken over from 1974 by the Nene Valley Railway. Sadly, this did not include Oundle with its magnificent station, and the rails were lifted in the 1970s.

Below right: One wonders how many generations of boarders en route to and from Oundle School have memories of the low platforms, towering gables and chimney stacks, and mullioned windows of this most picturesque of stations. The doorway in the foreground, at the Northampton end of the building, was blocked up even in LNWR times. What schoolboy legends may have been woven around the blocked-off door?

OXFORD (Rewley Road) *(Map Ref. G1 & V5)*

Oxford was at the western extremity of the long cross-country branch of the LNWR which tapped the West Coast Main Line at Bletchley, and then continued eastwards to Bedford and Cambridge. The Oxford to Bletchley section was built under the aegis of the Buckinghamshire Railway, an LNWR offshoot, leased from opening, and later taken over by Euston. The line was authorised in 1846 as the Oxford and Bletchley Junction Railway, merged with the closely-associated Buckingham & Brackley Junction Railway, as the Buckinghamshire Railway in 1847, and opened from the east, as far as Islip (q.v.) on 1st October 1850. The line was extended to Oxford Road, 3½ miles short of Oxford, on 2nd December. The approach into Oxford was bedevilled by the railway politics which had so dominated the history of the branch. A proposal to use the GWR station at Oxford was dropped due to the broad gauge, and railway relations, and, in the end, a separate terminus, Rewley Road, only yards from the GWR station, but without any running connection, opened on 20th May 1851. At Oxford Road, the temporary terminus, a second line curved to the west to join the Oxford, Worcester & Wolverhampton Railway, opening on 1st April 1854. A further chord provided direct access from the Buckinghamshire Railway station in Oxford to the OW&W, but this fared even worse than the curve to Bletchley. When the GWR gained control of the 'Old Worse & Worse' in 1861, it had already lain idle for some time.

In Oxford, the LNWR station was on a restricted site between the River Isis, to the east, and the GWR, to the west, with the Sheepwash Channel, connecting the Thames and Isis, cutting through the formation, and Rewley Road/Parkend St. at the south. Freight facilities had to be separated to opposite sides of the line, with a wagon repair depot, reached off the engine head headshunt, on a third site largely surrounded by water. All freight shunting had to block not only the running lines, but the swing bridge over the Sheepwash Channel, as the latter, unfortunately, was a navigable waterway. Owing to the style of train shed adopted, it was not possible to run-round a passenger train in the station, and either a pilot engine had to be called in, or the train propelled out, and run-round, blocking the arrival and departure lines and, inevitably, the swing bridge. There was also a pedestrian crossing across the line at the north end of the bridge.

Right: Looking from Rewley Road at the station frontage, in 1951. In LNWR and LMS days, prominent boards, proclaiming the station's owners, hid the cross or circle ironwork of the forecourt canopy. As we shall see later, the lattice pattern was widely used in the structure, but the less robust ring pattern seems to have been confined to the forecourt. The lattice section is a replacement. Careful study reveals that the ring pattern tops the wooden frontage of the building, and that curved spandrels grace three of the four sides of the structure, but not the repaired section.

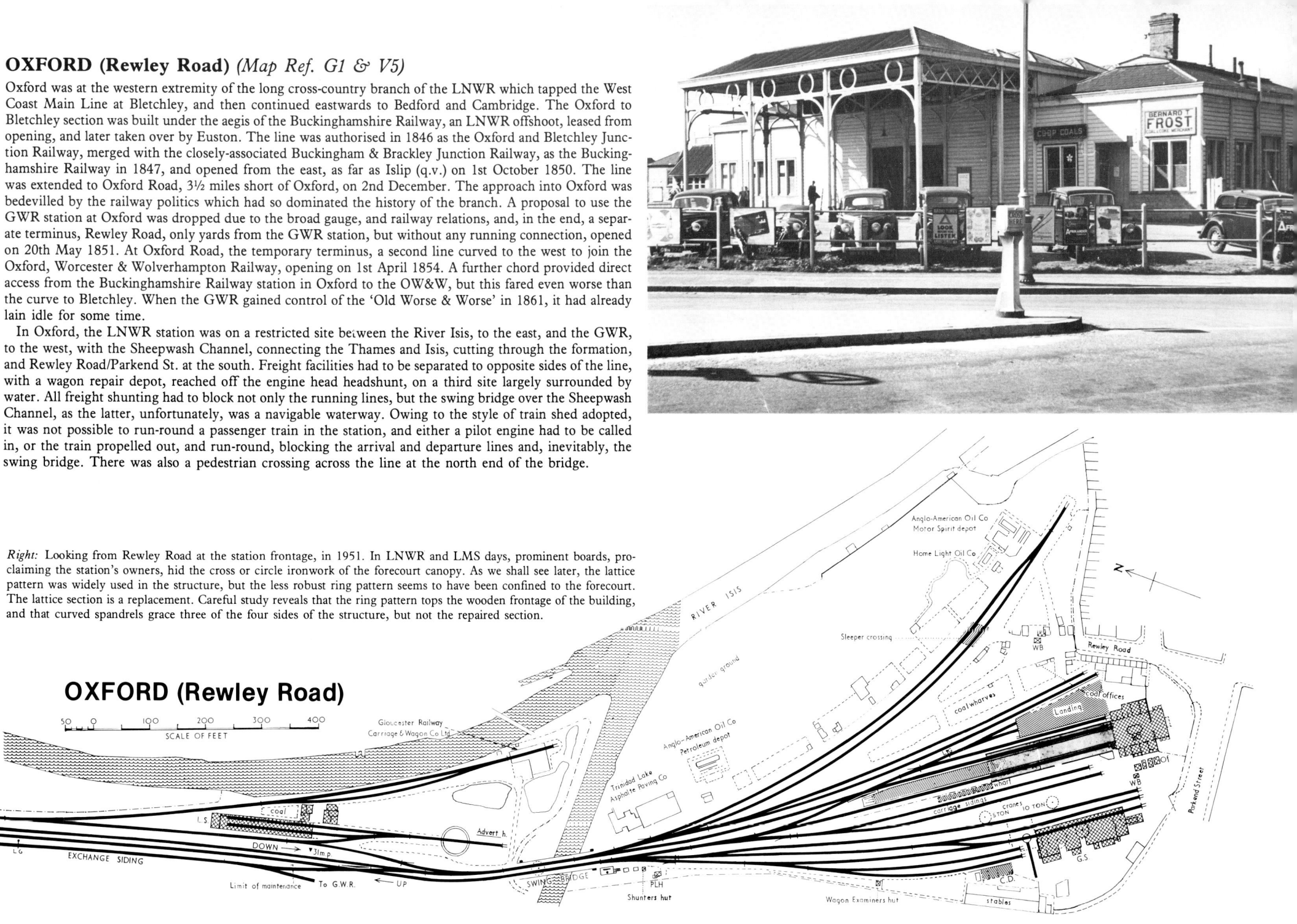

OXFORD (Rewley Road)

In pre-grouping days, there was intense rivalry between the GWR and LNWR stations, and the exchange siding does not appear to have been laid in until the 1860s. In 1883, there were seven passenger arrivals and departures. From 1905, the Oxford to Bicester service was augmented by LNWR steam railcar workings. By 1915, there were nine through trains, some running as far as Cambridge, and six railcars. From 1934, Oxford's LMS station was placed under the GWR stationmaster, and under the impetus of war, a running connection was provided, permitting through running from the Bletchley direction into the GWR station. The 1940 connection permitted British Railways to transfer passenger services to the GWR station from 1st October 1951, Rewley Road becoming freight only. From 1935, the GWR had owned the LMS swing bridge and, in 1959, the Western Region replaced the old LNWR signal box with a ground frame by the bridge, although the box survived out of use for several years.

Rewley Road's greatest claim to fame, however, was its train shed, fashioned after the celebrated 'Crystal Palace', which housed the Great Exhibition of 1851. Legend has it that the train shed was designed by Sir Joseph Paxton, creator of the exhibition building or, that as the contractors of the Great Exhibition building won the contract for Oxford, they simply adapted the design, with a cheap run-on of parts, for which jigs and moulds were to hand. As the 'Crystal Palace', which was intended to be moved, was a kind of giant 'Meccano' set, this is quite feasible. When completed, Rewley Road boasted a longitudinal ridge and furrow roof over the structural steelwork. In 1888, the roof cladding was replaced by a hipped style, with transverse ridge and furrow. It is often suggested that the 'Crystal Palace' structure was replaced or substantially altered, which, given the magnitude of the change, is logical. Pre and post-reconstruction illustrations show that although the roof cladding was drastically altered, the structural steelwork was little changed, and that both types of upright predated the change, namely combined columns and water downpipes, and twin steel members bolted in a tall 'A' form.

OXFORD (Rewley Road)

Above: The oval booking kiosk in the concourse, in a view looking towards the forecourt. The kiosk was reputed to come from the Great Exhibition, largely on account of the 'coronet' valance, which was identical to that used for the 'Crystal Palace', and also at first decorated the canopy at Rewley Road.

Below: Under the canopy at Rewley Road. Note the columns and 'A' members, longitudinal lattice girders and lightly-braced cross-girders, all of which predated the 1880s rebuilding. An LMS motor 'push-pull' coach is seen in the yard to the left.

Below: Looking from the foot of the platform towards Bletchley, the LNWR cabin is visible to the left of the locomotive, and partially obscures the GWR's Oxford Station North box. Oxford GWR shed is visible to the left of these boxes, and the LNWR shed is left of the far (dark-liveried) row of petrol tankers.

Above: Looking towards the stops in 1951, before closure to passengers. Note that even at this date, much of the glazing had been stripped off, as had the timber cladding from the side walls. It does, however, give us a better opportunity to study this strange creation, and ponder. Was it Paxton or Fox Henderson who was the moving force? Why was the original roof cladding removed, and replaced by one so different? A possible answer may be inadequacy of water run-off, and corrosion.

Left & Below: In its passenger days, Rewley Road required full signalling. After closure to passengers, the LNW facilities were excessive, and the North Western box *(diagram below)* was replaced by a GWR ground frame, controlling just the swing bridge, wickets, approach and departure signals, and a crossover.

Above centre & Above right: A 9-lever 'Reading' frame was installed by the Western Region in 1959, partly as rationalisation, partly as 'Westernisation'. This worked to the GWR Oxford North Junction box, and controlled four ground shunt discs, each mounted on the top of a tall pole, one being so near the disused LNWR box, that the signalman, had there been one, could have reached out of his window to work it! The ground frame was located just north of the bridge on the east side of the line, and *(above centre)* we see this typically GWR frame, and *(above right)* we look across the Sheepwash Channel towards Rewley Road in 1964, as a 61XX prairie tank drifts along the arrival road. The ground frame is on the left, whilst the wickets and timbered pedestrian crossing add interest. The roof of the LNWR box pokes up above the bushes on the right-hand side, beyond the swing bridge.

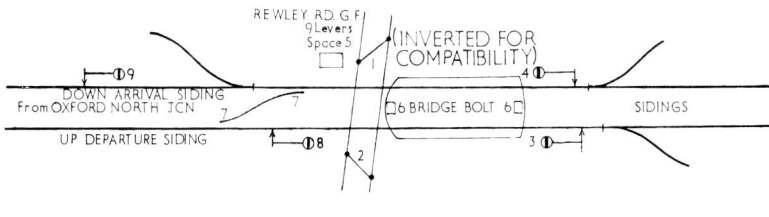

OXFORD (Rewley Road)

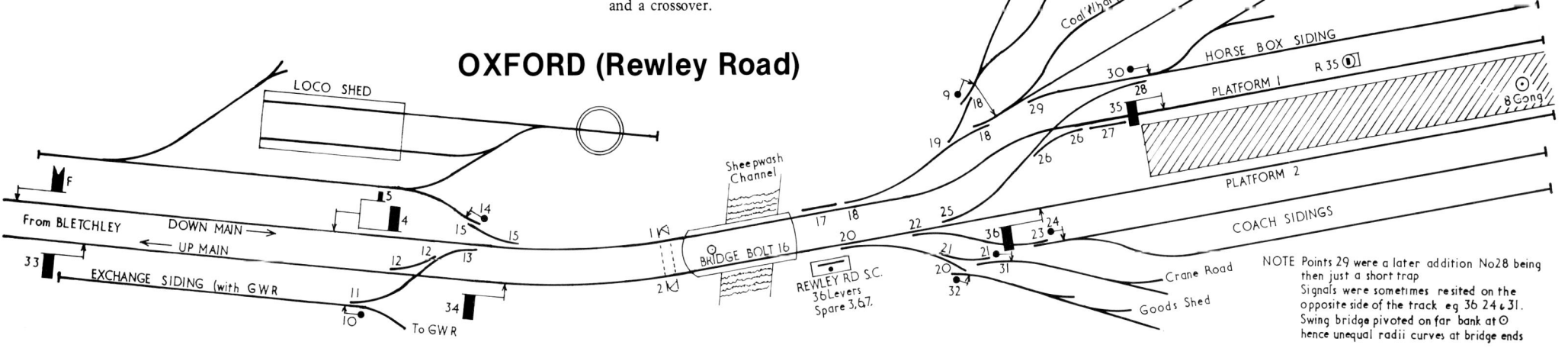

NOTE Points 29 were a later addition No28 being then just a short trap
Signals were sometimes resited on the opposite side of the track eg 36 24 &31.
Swing bridge pivoted on far bank at ⊙ hence unequal radii curves at bridge ends

ROCK FERRY (*Map Ref. A0*)

Rock Ferry Station is located towards the northern end of the Chester & Birkenhead Railway, where connection was made with the independent Mersey Railway into Liverpool. The Chester & Birkenhead Railway was authorised in July 1837, and opened in September 1840. A branch, one mile north of what later became Rock Ferry, gave access to one of the cross-river services at Monk's Ferry. Had the GWR not embarked upon its drive through the West Midlands, partly as as result of the activities of the London & Birmingham Railway, the C&BR would almost certainly have fallen into the LNWR orbit quite quickly. The Great Western spearhead to Chester created a complex pattern, with pro-Euston and pro-Paddington factions. Meanwhile, the C&BR amalgamated with the Birkenhead, Lancashire & Cheshire Junction Railway from 1847, although the latter did not open until 1850. On 1st August 1859, the company curtailed its title to the Birkenhead Railway and, after years of intrigue, it was agreed that operation would be passed to the LNWR and GWR jointly, from 1st January 1860. Legal problems delayed the actual hand-over until 18th November 1860. On 1st November 1862, the new joint committee replaced the original passenger station at Rock Lane (*see scale plan*) with a new station, Rock Ferry, ¼ mile to the north.

In 1866, the Mersey Railway, at first to be an atmospheric line, was authorised, but construction did not commence until the 1880s, and the line opened with steam traction, from Birkenhead to an isolated underground station in Liverpool, in 1886.

On 25th September 1886, powers were obtained to build south from Birkenhead (Green Lane) to a junction with the Birkenhead Railway at Rock Ferry, this connection opening on 15th June 1891. The Mersey Railway provided the northern part of this link, and the Joint Committee the southern section, the Mersey Railway paying a passenger toll and contributing to working expenses at the enlarged station, where the Mersey Railway trains terminated in two bay platforms. As a steam-worked dead-end system operating high-intensity services through stygian tunnels, through services were hardly to be expected, although a double junction was laid in from the south. The GWR did provide an annual through train from Paddington to Liverpool Central (Low Level) for the 'Grand National' and, for 1899, a through coach ran between Central (Low Level) and Folkestone, with connections to Paris!

In July 1893, the LNWR and GWR obtained powers to quadruple the Birkenhead Joint Railway, our second scale plan showing the station after quadrupling. By this time, conditions in the Mersey tunnels had driven most passengers back to the ferries and, in desperation, the Mersey switched to electric traction, from 3rd May 1903, with immediate success. The Mersey Railway remained independent in 1923, but fell into the British Railways net in 1948.

Left: A view looking from the former 'down' slow platform towards Bedford St. bridge and Chester. By this time the former 'down' fast lines on the left had been reduced to freight only.

Right: Platforms 3/4 and the centre siding, originally installed in the 1890s as as run-round siding for Mersey Railway's steam locomotives, and retained for stock stabling after electrification in 1903. These platforms, although only used by the Mersey Railway, remained LNW&GW Joint Committee property!

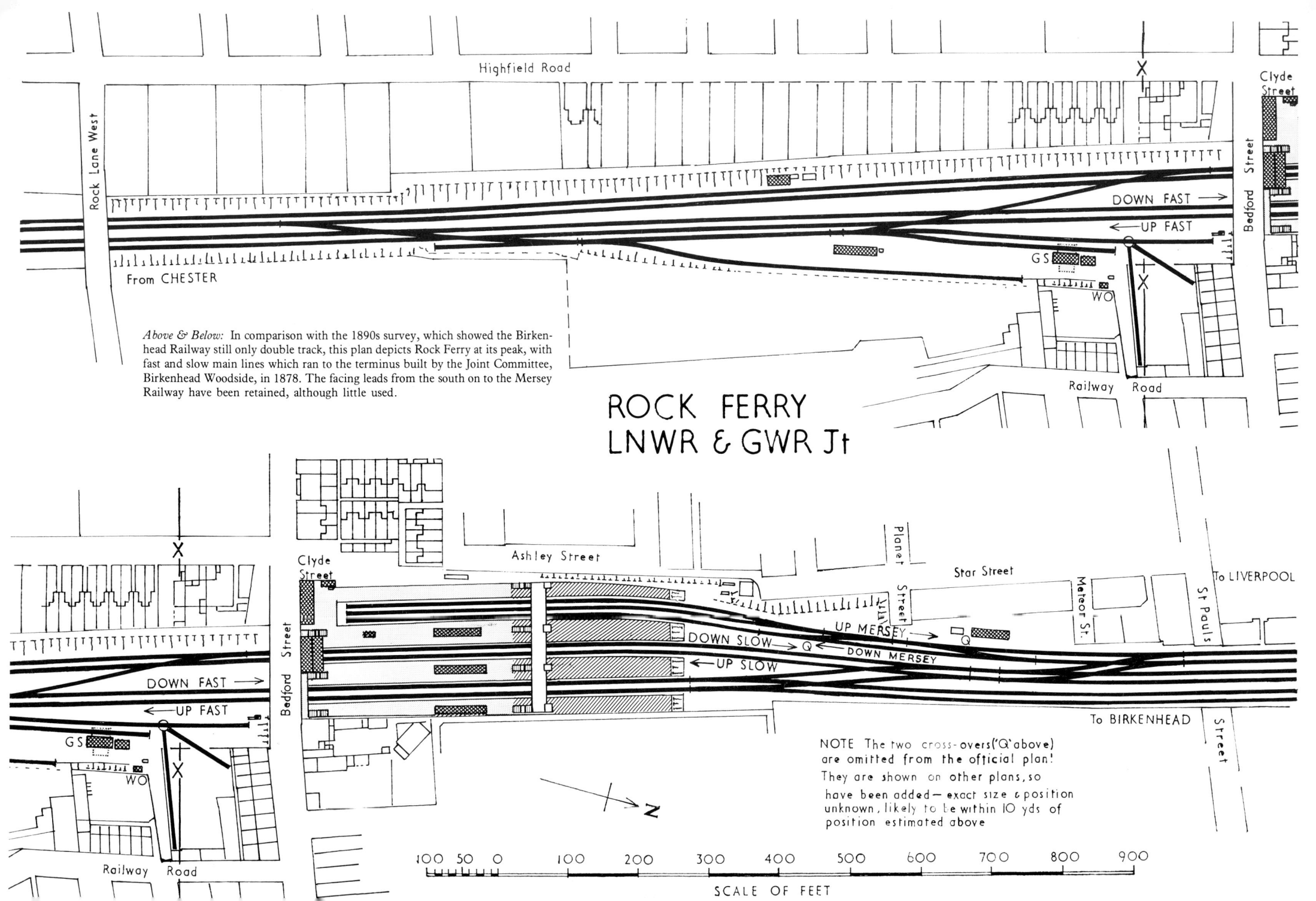

Highfield Road

Rock Lane West

Clyde Street

Bedford Street

DOWN FAST →

← UP FAST

From CHESTER

GS

WO

Above & Below: In comparison with the 1890s survey, which showed the Birkenhead Railway still only double track, this plan depicts Rock Ferry at its peak, with fast and slow main lines which ran to the terminus built by the Joint Committee, Birkenhead Woodside, in 1878. The facing leads from the south on to the Mersey Railway have been retained, although little used.

Railway Road

ROCK FERRY
LNWR & GWR Jt

Ashley Street

Clyde Street

Bedford Street

Planet Street

Star Street

Meteor St.

St Pauls Street

To LIVERPOOL

UP MERSEY →

DOWN SLOW → Q ← DOWN MERSEY

DOWN FAST →

← UP FAST

← UP SLOW

GS

WO

Railway Road

To BIRKENHEAD

Z

NOTE The two cross-overs ('Q' above) are omitted from the official plan! They are shown on other plans, so have been added — exact size & position unknown, likely to be within 10 yds of position estimated above

100 50 0   100   200   300   400   500   600   700   800   900

SCALE OF FEET

ROCK FERRY

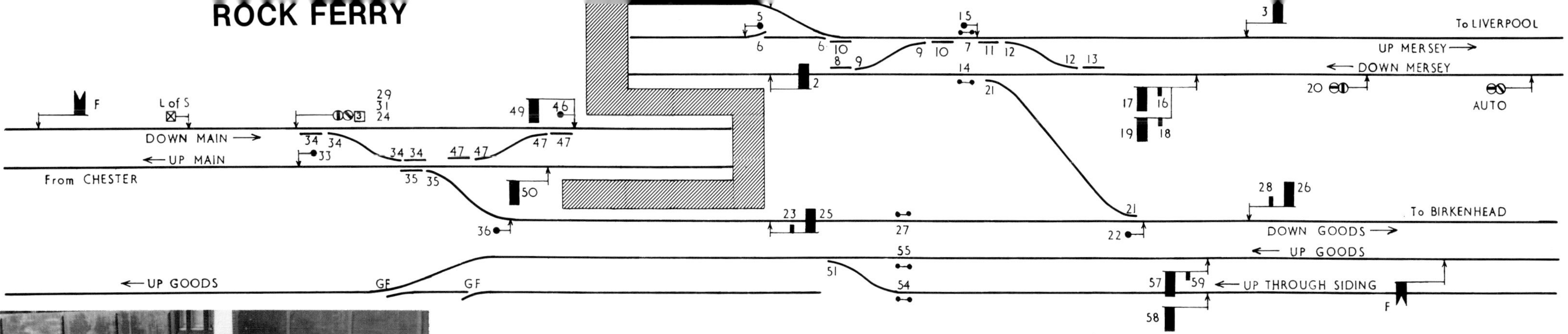
To LIVERPOOL
UP MERSEY
DOWN MERSEY
AUTO
L of S
DOWN MAIN
UP MAIN
From CHESTER
To BIRKENHEAD
DOWN GOODS
UP GOODS
UP GOODS
UP THROUGH SIDING
GF
GF
F
F

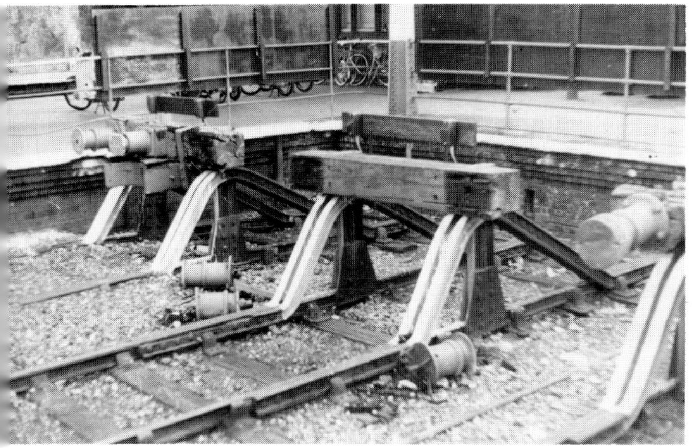

Birkenhead Woodside closed to passengers on 5th November 1967; the prelude to a truly weird 'rationalisation'. Diesel multiple unit services operated from Chester to Rock Ferry, where passengers made a cross-platform interchange to the electric Mersey Railway line trains, to continue into Birkenhead or Liverpool. As a consequence, the old slow lines became the main lines, and were truncated at the north end of the platforms, and a level access to the platforms was built across the former 'four foot', permitting the removal of the footbridge, albeit at the expense of a longer walk for passengers. The 'down' fast line was lifted, and the 'up' fast became an 'up' goods. 'Down' freights reached Birkenhead via the 'down' main, and a connection just south of the station. North of Rock Ferry, the joint lines were freight only, serving the Birkenhead Docks complex; one of the few docks to remain rail connected into the 1980s. Electric services are to be extended south to Hooton in 1985.

Left: The buffer stops for platforms 3/4 and the siding bore a striking resemblance to the old Hornby 'O' gauge buffers!

Below left: Buffer stops at the northern end of the slow lines are an eloquent reminder that this 4-track main line, which once carried through expresses from Paddington to Birkenhead, and a mass of LNWR traffic too, carries but a local passenger service.

Below right: A London Midland Region-built local set of 1956/7, but based upon pre-war stock for the Wirral section, departs for Liverpool. Since 1977, the Mersey Railway has not terminated at Liverpool Central (Low Level) but has operated round a new underground loop line.

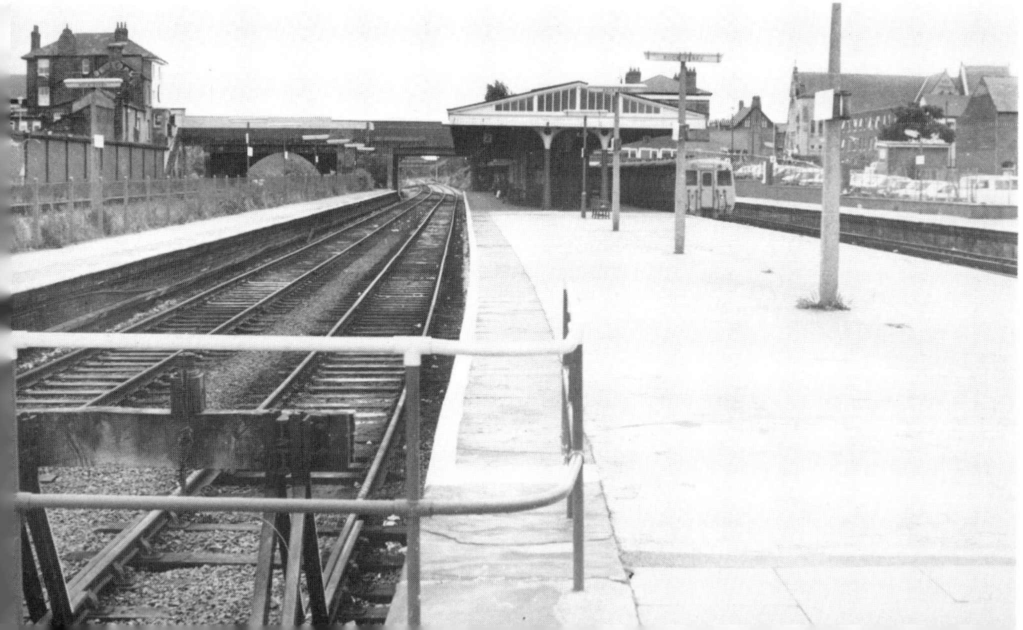

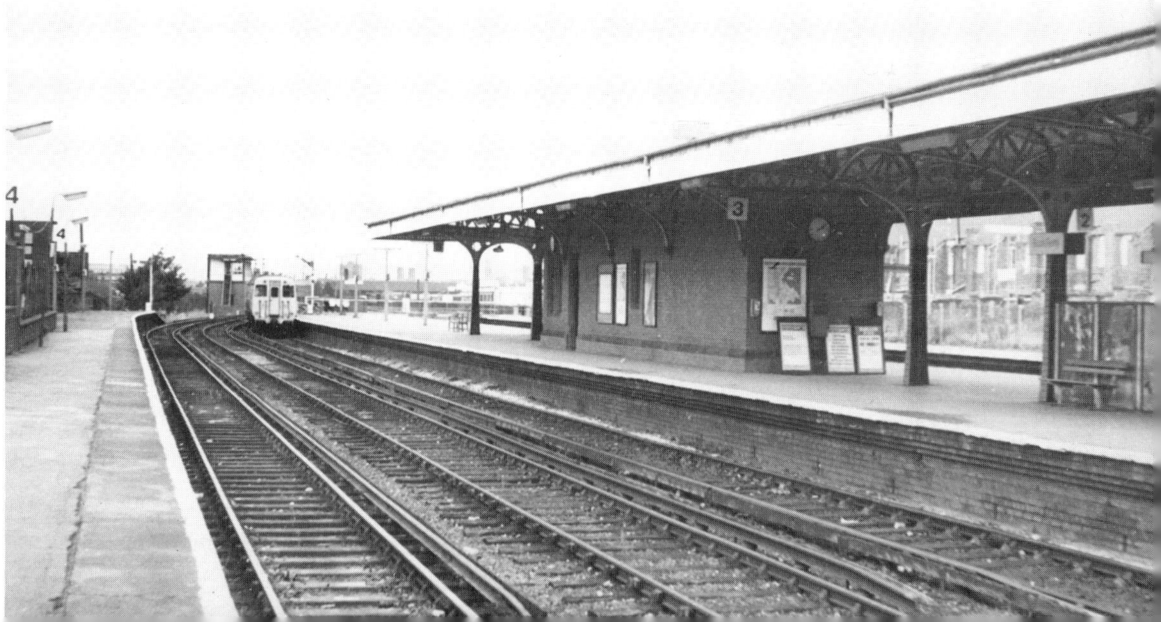
4
4
3
2

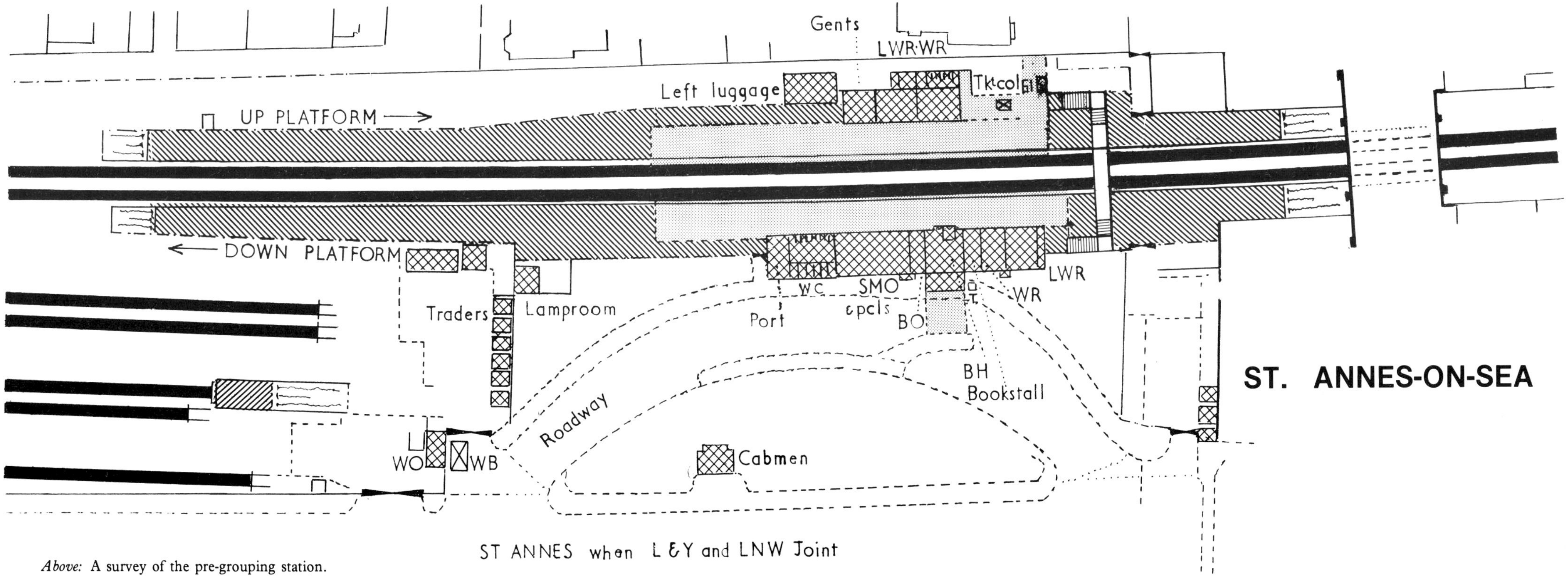

Gents

LWR WR

Tk col

Left luggage

UP PLATFORM →

← DOWN PLATFORM

Traders   Lamproom

WC   SMO & pcls

Port   BO

LWR

WR

ST. ANNES-ON-SEA

BH

Bookstall

Roadway

WO   WB

Cabmen

ST ANNES when L&Y and LNW Joint

Above: A survey of the pre-grouping station.

Below: Looking across the approach road at the frontage of the 1924 station, these attractive buildings being erected on the roadside of the old P&WR structure, which was, of course, demolished.

Below: In the booking hall, looking towards Blackpool. The booking office is on the left. Concertina lattice gates were found at a number of 'early LMS period' stations. The style, as one would expect, is a mixture of LYR, LNWR and LMS ideas.

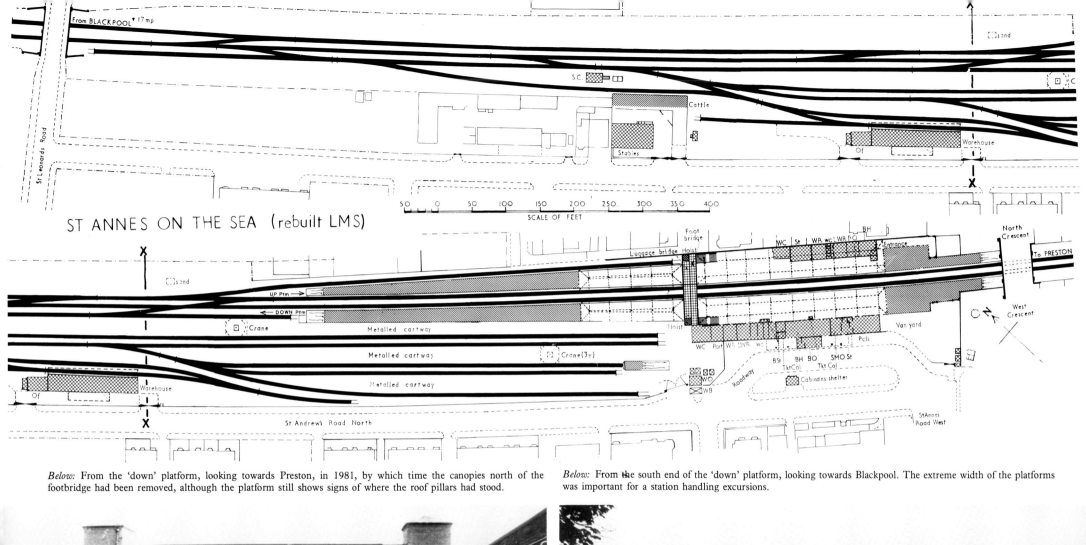

From BLACKPOOL ▼ 17 mp

St Leonards Road

S.C.

Cattle

Stables

Of

Warehouse

sand

SCALE OF FEET
50   0   50   100   150   200   250   300   350   400

ST ANNES ON THE SEA (rebuilt LMS)

sand

Foot bridge

Luggage bridge Hoist

North Crescent

To PRESTON

WC St WR wc WR P.O. BH

Entrance

UP Ptm

DOWN Ptm

Crane

Metalled cartway

Metalled cartway

Metalled cartway

Crane (3T)

Hoist

WC Port WR LWR wc

Pcls

West Crescent

Van yard

WO

WB

BSt   BH BO   SMO St
TktCol   TktCol

Cabmans shelter

Roadway

Of   Warehouse

St Andrew's Road North

St Annes Road West

Below: From the 'down' platform, looking towards Preston, in 1981, by which time the canopies north of the footbridge had been removed, although the platform still shows signs of where the roof pillars had stood.

Below: From the south end of the 'down' platform, looking towards Blackpool. The extreme width of the platforms was important for a station handling excursions.

Above left: The view from the 'up' platform, looking towards Preston, with the steps on the left-hand side.

Above right: Under the 'down' canopy, looking towards Preston; note the lattice gates.

ST. ANNES-ON-SEA

Below: Looking from near the luggage bridge, towards Preston.

ST. ANNE'S-ON-SEA *(Map Ref. S10)*

The Fylde Coast owes its development as a seaside resort and residential area to the drive of Sir Peter Hesketh Fleetwood, whose determination created the port of Fleetwood, and turned the desolate Fylde Coast into a string of resorts, in less than seventy years. The first railway into the Fylde was the Preston & Wyre Railway, which opened to Fleetwood in 1840. In 1846, branches were opened to Blackpool and Lytham, but the coast in between remained undeveloped. From 1849, the P&WR was taken over jointly by the LYR and LNWR. On 17th May 1861, an independent company, the Blackpool & Lytham Railway, was incorporated to build a 7½ mile branch along the Fylde Coast. This opened as a single track route, isolated from other railways, on 6th April 1863. The resort of St. Anne's, part-way between Blackpool and Lytham, did not then exist. In the LYR & LNWR Act of 29th June 1871, the little B&LR was taken over by these two giants, and extensions to create a through route authorised at Lytham. In November 1873 a station was opened at Cross Slack, renamed St. Anne's in January 1875. The B&LR was doubled the following year.

As the Fylde resorts developed, traffic mushroomed, and by 1920, St. Anne's Station was utterly inadequate. Major improvements were planned, with the platforms being lengthened by 50 per cent, a much enlarged building on the 'down' side, and a combined covered footbridge and luggage bridge to replace the original structure. Work began under LMS auspices in 1923, with the station well advanced for the 1924 season, an LMS estimate of £38,686 covering work for the year. Further minor expenditure was made during 1925/6, to create a spacious station well-suited to peak crowds. Freight facilities ceased on 25th November 1968, but the station was otherwise little changed prior to singling in 1985.

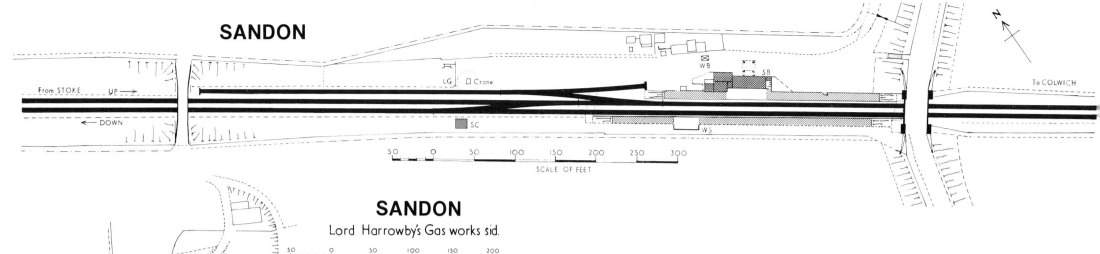

SANDON

From STOKE   UP →

← DOWN

LG   □ Crane

SC

WB

SB

WS

To COLWICH

N

50   0   50   100   150   200   250   300
SCALE OF FEET

SANDON

Lord Harrowby's Gas works sid.

50   0   50   100   150   200
SCALE OF FEET

From STOKE &
SANDON

Capacity 8 wagons

To COLWICH

UP →

← DOWN

Below: A view looking from the overbridge towards Stone and Stoke, in July 1928. One can see why the LMS was not impressed with the traffic potential of this station in the open fields.

SANDON *(Map Ref. U8)*

Sandon Station was located on the Stone to Colwich line of the North Staffordshire Railway, one of the two principal 'Knotty' routes to the Trent Valley line and the south. Both of these alternative routes were authorised on 26th June 1846, the Norton Bridge route, which joins the LNWR north of Stafford, opening in 1848, and the Stone to Colwich section, to its junction with the LNWR at Colwich, roughly midway between Stafford and Rugeley, on 1st May 1849. The 'Knotty' came into being at a time when the Gothic revival was in full spate, and Tudor or Jacobean stations were the craze. Although Sandon Station, set amid the fields, away from a modest community, could hardly offer a lucrative traffic, it received the full Jacobean treatment, with the upper storey of the building carried out over an arched carriage entrance. A single-siding goods yard, and a small timber shelter on the opposite platform, completed the facilities.

To simplify shunting, particularly with 'down' trains, tow-roping was authorised to move wagons from the 'up' line into the siding, the tow rope being kept under the signal box. The signalman was also responsible for the Earl of Harrowby's gasworks siding, a private connection between Sandon and the next station to the south, Weston, the padlock to the ground frame being kept in the box.

Although the route carried substantial through traffic, stopping services were infrequent; two trains on weekdays and four on Saturdays, by 1938. The station closed to passengers on 6th January 1947 and to goods on 5th September 1955. Although regularly under threat, the Stone to Colwich route survives as part of the inter-city network.

Below: The Sandon 'up' starting signal, a tall co-acting NSR signal, dominates the view from the overbridge looking towards Colwich, in 1928. The isolation of the station is highlighted.

SEATON
18 June 1879

From WANSFORD

UP →

← DOWN

UP →

From STAMFORD ← DOWN

50 0 50 100 150 200 250
Scale of Feet

Contractor's Siding · CD · Carriage Landing · G.S. · W.B. · B.O. · L.C.

To MARKET HARBOROUGH

W.S. · G.F.

SEATON *(Map Ref. K7)*

Seaton Station was in Rutland, about nineteen miles west of Peterborough, and on the fifty mile long Rugby to Peterborough cross-country branch of the LNWR. The line, from Rugby to a junction with the Midland Railway's Syston & Peterborough line, was sanctioned by the proprietors of the London & Birmingham Railway in February 1846, and Parliamentary approval was secured in June of that year. It was opened to Market Harborough on 27th April 1850, to the small village of Rockingham on 1st June 1850, and through Seaton to the MR at Luffenham on 2nd June 1851. LNWR trains reached Peterborough over Midland metals.

Until 1879, Seaton was a simple wayside station. The detour via the Midland Railway, the desire for independence, and the expectation of traffic arising from the construction of the GN&LNWR Joint line, from Drayton Junction (east of Market Harborough) to Bottesford, on the GNR near Nottingham, prompted the LNWR to build a cut-off. This ran from Seaton, on the Rugby to Stamford line, to Yarwell, south of Wansford, on the company's Northampton to Peterborough branch. The new line, which opened to goods on 21st July 1879, and to passengers on 1st November, was 11½ miles in length, and left the double-track Market Harborough to Luffenham line just east of Seaton Station. It was also double track, and the junction was controlled from a cabin at the Peterborough end of the station. The level crossing, at the east end, was controlled from a platform ground frame.

The new line was inspected by Major Marindin of the Board of Trade and, as well as noticing that

the booking office was just 5ft. from the platform edge, rather than the regulation 6ft., he instructed the company to provide a turntable, 'as Seaton Junction will become a terminal station for passenger trains from Stamford'. The turntable was provided in the summer of 1880 in the angle between the Stamford and Wansford lines. It has been stated that the Seaton to Luffenham section was singled at this time, but this was not so. In the Board of Trade 'Signal Arrangements and Systems of Working Returns' in the 1880s, the Seaton to Luffenham section is recorded as double track, 3 miles 60 chains in length. LNWR plans of 1894 and 1898 confirm this, and the branch was in fact not singled until 1907. Improbably, an MR single line train tablet system was in use before the Grouping.

In the LNWR Act of 1890, a single track branch, 3¾ miles in length, was authorised between Seaton and Uppingham. This was inspected by Major Yorke on 23rd August 1894. A new crossover had been laid in between the 'up' and 'down' platforms to simplify shunting. This was worked from the level crossing ground frame, which contained seven working and one gong lever. The station cabin contained a 48-lever frame, (42 working). At this time, the Luffenham line was still double, and Uppingham trains diverged from the double-track formation a short distance outside the station. A 27-lever junction box controlled the divergence. This was made superfluous when the Luffenham route was singled, utilising the 'up' formation, freeing the 'down' formation for Uppingham trains, both branch divergences being controlled from the station cabin.

SEATON

Below: A view looking from the 'up' platform towards the junction and Luffenham on the last day of services, 4th June 1966. The weeds were coming along nicely.

Below: Looking from the 'up' platform towards Market Harborough with the Stamford DMU in the 'down' bay. Note the red/white harlequin 'Limited Clearance' sign on the goods shed.

On 1st October 1894 the Uppingham branch opened to passengers and, although not heavily used, carried regular passenger services until 13th June 1960. The Luffenham and Peterborough lines closed on 6th June 1966. The two branches became the haunt of push-pull or motor trains, the Luffenham branch being dieselised shortly before closure. In 1895, eight trains arrived at Seaton from the Peterborough line. Three of these were GNR trains for Leicester; the others carried on over the LNWR to Rugby, or further afield. The Stamford and Uppingham branches each contributed five trains. As there was no turntable at Uppingham, an undertaking was given to the Board of Trade that only tank engines would be used on that branch, and LNWR working timetables were so headed.

The busiest period in the life of the Uppingham branch was from 1912 to 1926, whilst the James Pain ironstone quarries were in use. In the immediate pre-grouping period, four passenger trains, four mineral trains and one light engine arrived from Uppingham, whilst departures to the branch were six passenger/mixed trains, two light engines and an empty wagon train.

SEATON

Above: The waiting shelter on the 'down' platform and the Stamford diesel multiple unit.

When the Wansford line was built, it was laid into the old main line to Luffenham. With the declining importance of that route, the junction was eventually slewed to give a better alignment for the direct Wansford line, at the expense of an awkward reverse curve on to the old lines, as is evident from the illustrations.

A small locomotive shed was provided off the turntable siding and, after the shed was demolished, the remnants of this line were used as a trap to protect the branch.

Left: A detailed study of the platform frame which controlled the adjoining crossover and gates. This is a standard Webb frame, similar to those in signal boxes, rather than the simplified type used for many smaller ground frames. Signal repeaters adorn the waiting-room wall.

SEATON

Above: No. 69287, an MSLR Parker N5 class 0-6-2T, provides unusual motive power for the Uppingham train in 1950. Motor working was not in force on that day, and the driving end of the coach is next to the locomotive's chimney. A Midland Railway Johnson 0-4-4T, with the Stamford push-pull train, shares the platform.

Left: A sad scene, as a 6-car diesel multiple unit pulls into Seaton on the last day of service, 4th June 1966. The earthworks of the Midland Railway's Nottingham Direct line, via Manton, now closed to passengers, sweep across the horizon, with masonry arches across the LNWR routes.

SHILTON

SHILTON *(Map Ref. F6)*

Shilton Station was on the Trent Valley route of the LNWR, six miles south-east of Nuneaton. The line opened on a limited basis on 15th September 1847, although Shilton did not come into use until 1st December. The station served a small community and had a very limited service. It closed to passengers on 16th September 1957, and to goods in 1965.

Initially, there were just two running lines but, in 1871, the 'up' third line between Bulkington and Rugby came into use. This was regraded as a passenger line in June 1876. At this time, the only siding accommodation at Shilton was a 'down' refuge siding just north of the station, and there was no ordinary goods accommodation of any sort. This deficiency was rectified in 1880 when a single siding was laid in to the 'up' third line. From the preparation of drawings to approval by all chief officers, including the traffic, locomotive, signal and superintendent's departments, and sanction by the General Manager and Chairman, took barely a month! One wonders if such a procedure could be completed within a year nowadays! The new siding, which was controlled from a small cabin on the 'down' platform, was about 350ft. in length. It was stated as being capable of holding twenty two wagons, although later LMS surveys gave the capacity as fourteen.

Left: The road elevation of Shilton Station in 1956. The front and side walls were of brick, and the rest of the structure was of timber. The name was carved on to tablets above the windows facing the road.

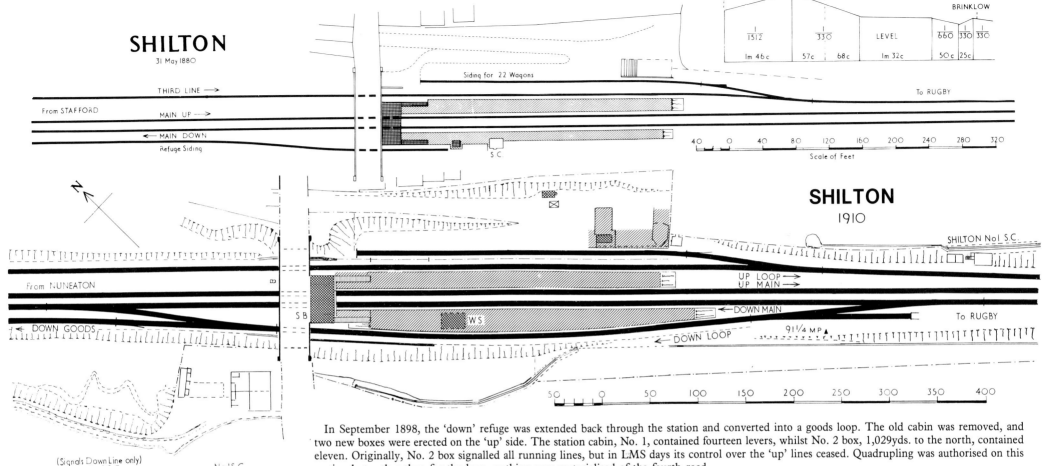

SHILTON
31 May 1880

BULKINGTON ... BRINKLOW

| | 1512 | 330 | LEVEL | 660 | 330 | 330 |
| | Im 46c | 57c | 68c | Im 32c | 50c | 25c |

THIRD LINE →

From STAFFORD

MAIN UP →

← MAIN DOWN

Refuge Siding

Siding for 22 Wagons

To RUGBY

S.C.

40 0 40 80 120 160 200 240 280 320

Scale of Feet

SHILTON
1910

N

From NUNEATON

S B

UP LOOP →
UP MAIN →

← DOWN MAIN

W S

SHILTON No1 S.C.

DOWN GOODS

← DOWN LOOP

91¼ MP ▲

To RUGBY

50 0 50 100 150 200 250 300 350 400

(Signals Down Line only)

No 2 S.C.   No 1 S.C.

← 1029 yds →
UP LOOP → 14 wags

UP MAIN →

← DOWN MAIN ← ←

← DOWN GOODS DOWN
(Permissive) LOOP

In September 1898, the 'down' refuge was extended back through the station and converted into a goods loop. The old cabin was removed, and two new boxes were erected on the 'up' side. The station cabin, No. 1, contained fourteen levers, whilst No. 2 box, 1,029yds. to the north, contained eleven. Originally, No. 2 box signalled all running lines, but in LMS days its control over the 'up' lines ceased. Quadrupling was authorised on this section but, other than for the loop, nothing ever materialised of the fourth road.

Shilton No. 2 box closed in the early 1950s, and the loop platform to 'down' main crossover was removed, the whole 'down' goods loop being worked by former No. 1 box.

Right: A detailed study of the station buildings at Shilton. Even in their heyday, they could hardly have been called elegant, but with peeling paintwork, decaying timbers, and crude patching, with what resembles a second-hand tea chest, plus a liberal coating of engine grime, the station would hardly win many prizes. The corrugated-iron covering to the stairways is a poor substitute for the neat timber roofing commonly provided. One has to admit that, in this instance, the LNWR civil engineers created a structure as devoid of merit as anything that modern architects can produce.

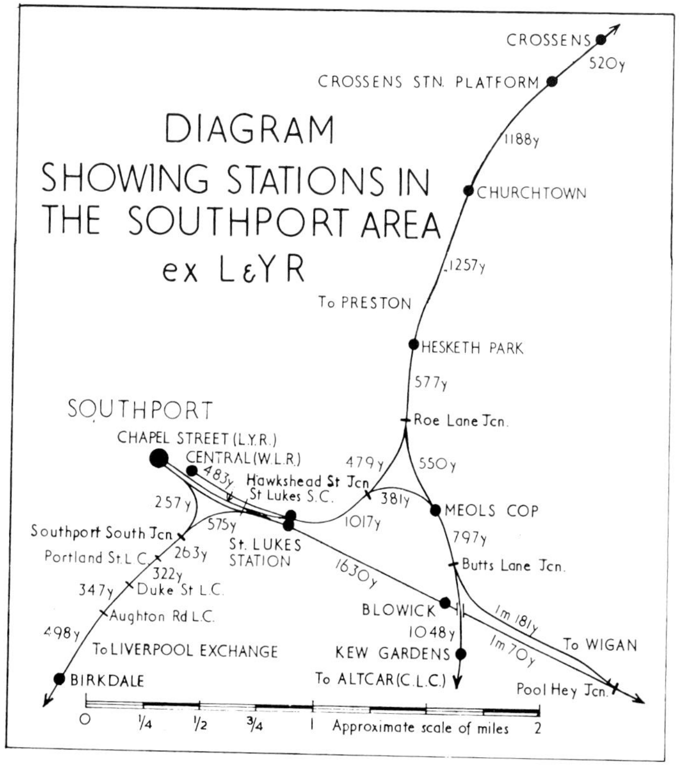

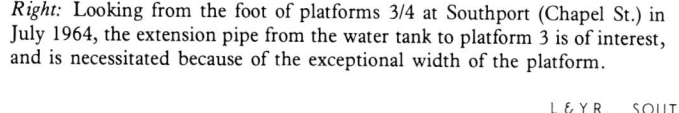

DIAGRAM
SHOWING STATIONS IN
THE SOUTHPORT AREA
ex L&YR

CROSSENS
520y
CROSSENS STN. PLATFORM
1188y
CHURCHTOWN
1257y
To PRESTON
HESKETH PARK
577y
Roe Lane Jcn.
550y
SOUTHPORT
CHAPEL STREET (L.Y.R.)
CENTRAL (W.L.R.)
479y
483y   Hawkshead St Jcn.
St Lukes S.C.
257y   381y
MEOLS COP
575y   1017y   797y
Southport South Jcn.
263y   St. LUKES
Portland St L C.   STATION   Butts Lane Jcn.
322y
347y   Duke St L.C.   1630y
Aughton Rd L.C.   BLOWICK   1m 181y
498y   1048y   To WIGAN
To LIVERPOOL EXCHANGE   KEW GARDENS   1m 70y
BIRKDALE   To ALTCAR (C.L.C.)   Pool Hey Jcn.

0   ¼   ½   ¾   1 Approximate scale of miles   2

Right: Looking from the foot of platforms 3/4 at Southport (Chapel St.) in
July 1964, the extension pipe from the water tank to platform 3 is of interest,
and is necessitated because of the exceptional width of the platform.

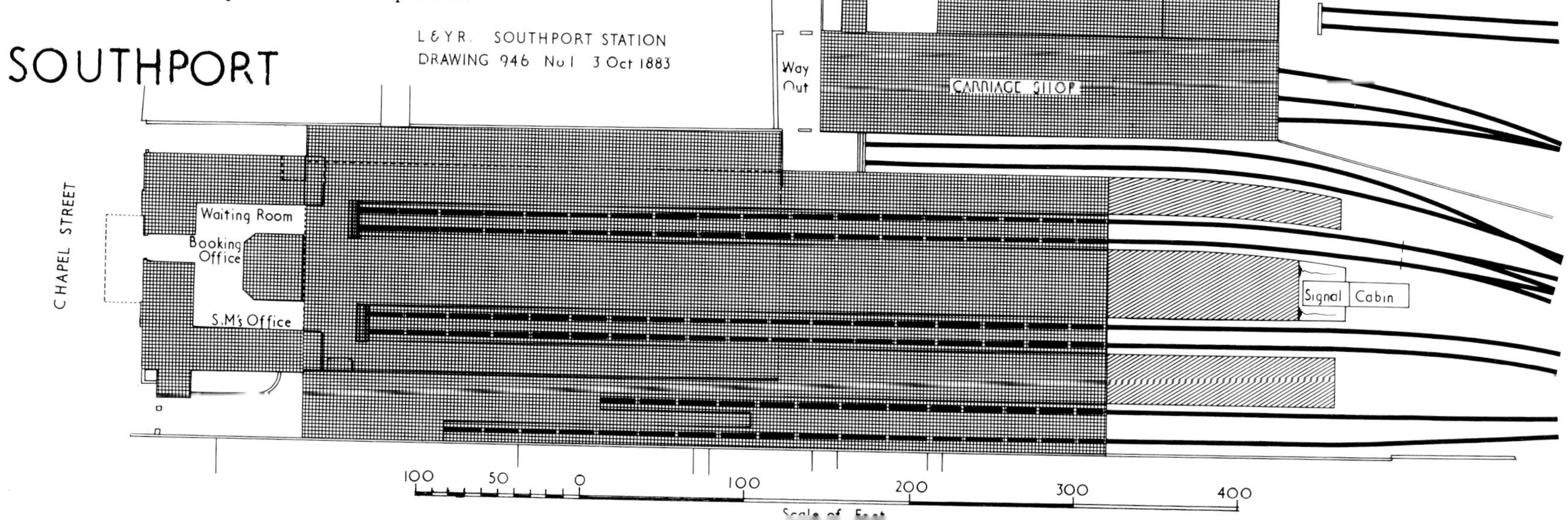

SOUTHPORT

L&Y.R. SOUTHPORT STATION
DRAWING 946 No 1 3 Oct 1883

Way
Out

CARRIAGE SHOP

CHAPEL STREET

Waiting Room
Booking
Office

S.M's Office

Signal Cabin

100   50   0   100   200   300   400

Scale of Feet

SOUTHPORT *(Map Ref. A6)*

Today, Southport is one of the leading resorts and residential towns on the Lancashire Coast, yet in 1837, when Queen Victoria came to the throne, it was an unimportant village. Its spectacular growth, from the 1840s, was a direct result of the 'Railway Age'. In its heyday, five routes converged upon the town. Four were part of the LYR, and ran into Chapel St. Station, whilst the fifth belonged to the Cheshire Lines Committee, and terminated at Lord St. The oldest of the LYR routes was the Liverpool, Crosby & Southport Railway, authorised on 2nd July 1847. It was to run from Tithebarn St., Liverpool (later Exchange Station) to the bathing village of Southport, which was seen as possessing a residential and holiday potential. The line opened between Waterloo and Southport on 24th July 1848, the Southport terminus being at Eastbank St. The line was extended to join the LYR just outside Tithebarn St., Liverpool in 1850, and to a new station in the centre of Southport, fronting on to Chapel St., on 22nd August 1851. Doubling of the LC&SR was completed in 1852. Southport became a fashionable residential area for the wealthy Liverpool merchants and professional men.

SOUTHPORT (Chapel St.)

Left: A view looking from platforms 2/3 towards Chapel St. box and Wigan. The fouling bars at the ends of the platforms are common, as track circuits may become unreliable due to infrequent use, and fouling from locomotives. The 7th and 8th pillars from the end of platforms 1/2 are closer than the normal spacing, as per plan.

Mancunians were equally keen to utilise this new-found mobility, and the Manchester & Southport Railway was authorised in 1847, but did not reach Southport until 9th April 1855, by which time it was a part of the LYR. The last seven miles, from Burscough Bridge into Chapel St., were built jointly with the East Lancashire Railway, which established its own passenger terminal on London St., adjacent to Chapel St. This station was forced upon the ELR, which now had an (albeit) roundabout route between Liverpool and Southport, by the Liverpool, Crosby & Southport Railway, which would not allow the ELR into Chapel St.! The LC&SR was taken over by the LYR later in 1855, and the ELR in 1859. The ELR station became a goods depot as trains were switched to Chapel St. from 1st April 1857. A few months later, a chord was laid in — without Parliamentary authority — from the Wigan and Manchester line at St. Luke's, to the Liverpool route at South Junction.

The West Lancashire Railway was authorised in 1871 between Southport and Preston. Part of the route, at the Southport end, commencing from a temporary terminus, was opened in 1878. On 4th September 1882, the WLR extended to Southport (Central) Station, which was to the north and east of Chapel St., providing no fewer than three stations en echelon, reached by parallel metals! In 1883, the LYR decided to extend the train shed of the old LC&SR station, the work being shown on the October 1883 scale survey.

Right: St. Luke's signal box, looking across the east lines, circa 1919.

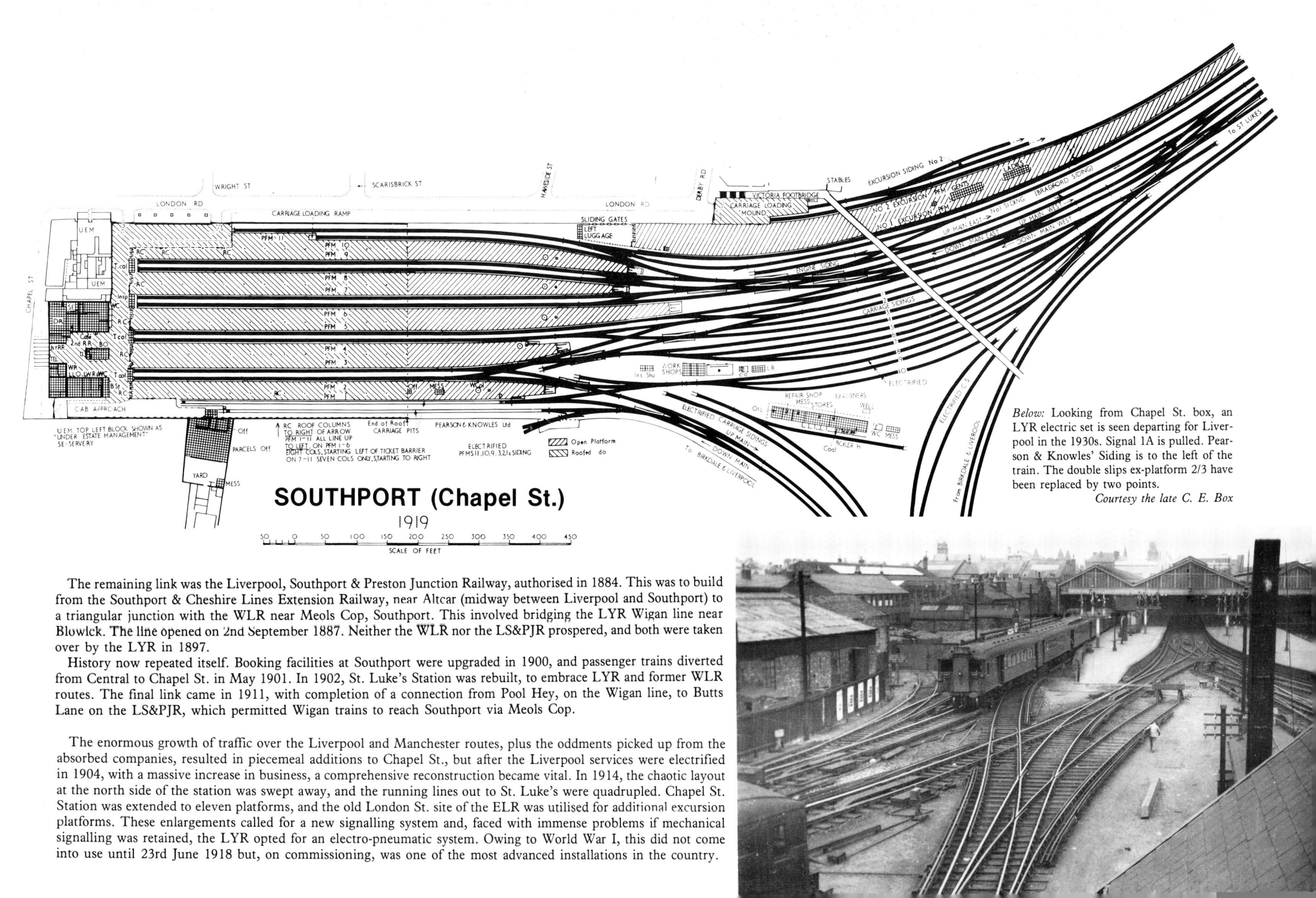

SOUTHPORT (Chapel St.)

1919

SCALE OF FEET
50 0 50 100 150 200 250 300 350 400 450

Below: Looking from Chapel St. box, an LYR electric set is seen departing for Liverpool in the 1930s. Signal 1A is pulled. Pearson & Knowles' Siding is to the left of the train. The double slips ex-platform 2/3 have been replaced by two points.
Courtesy the late C. E. Box

The remaining link was the Liverpool, Southport & Preston Junction Railway, authorised in 1884. This was to build from the Southport & Cheshire Lines Extension Railway, near Altcar (midway between Liverpool and Southport) to a triangular junction with the WLR near Meols Cop, Southport. This involved bridging the LYR Wigan line near Blowick. The line opened on 2nd September 1887. Neither the WLR nor the LS&PJR prospered, and both were taken over by the LYR in 1897.

History now repeated itself. Booking facilities at Southport were upgraded in 1900, and passenger trains diverted from Central to Chapel St. in May 1901. In 1902, St. Luke's Station was rebuilt, to embrace LYR and former WLR routes. The final link came in 1911, with completion of a connection from Pool Hey, on the Wigan line, to Butts Lane on the LS&PJR, which permitted Wigan trains to reach Southport via Meols Cop.

The enormous growth of traffic over the Liverpool and Manchester routes, plus the oddments picked up from the absorbed companies, resulted in piecemeal additions to Chapel St., but after the Liverpool services were electrified in 1904, with a massive increase in business, a comprehensive reconstruction became vital. In 1914, the chaotic layout at the north side of the station was swept away, and the running lines out to St. Luke's were quadrupled. Chapel St. Station was extended to eleven platforms, and the old London St. site of the ELR was utilised for additional excursion platforms. These enlargements called for a new signalling system and, faced with immense problems if mechanical signalling was retained, the LYR opted for an electro-pneumatic system. Owing to World War I, this did not come into use until 23rd June 1918 but, on commissioning, was one of the most advanced installations in the country.

Above: From the Victoria footbridge, looking towards the stops, in July 1964, the 3-storey Chapel St. box is seen to the left. The first, third and sixth roof spans are slightly smaller than the other three. The London St. excursion platforms and ticket collectors' booths are visible to the right.

Above: A view looking towards Wigan from the Victoria footbridge in July 1964. To the left are the coach sidings beyond the London St. platforms (the excursion platforms) locomotive water tank, Wigan lines, and stock in the sidings within the triangle. St. Luke's cabin, supported on girders, is visible in the distance, whilst an LMS electric set occupies the foreground. To the right is the Wigan to Liverpool curve.

SOUTHPORT (Chapel St.)

Below: A 1977 view, looking from platform 2 towards Wigan. It is still possible to run from platform 2 or 3 to Liverpool, to the right, but the connection from platform 2 to Wigan has gone. The siding access is also reduced.

Below: Looking from Chapel St. box towards South Junction, in 1977, on the extreme left is seen part of sidings 9/10. Next comes the repair shop/boiler house, the stock sidings, and the Liverpool line curving towards the former South Junction. The formation of the Wigan to Liverpool curve is visible just short of the boundary fence. The siding near the repair shop is for stores.

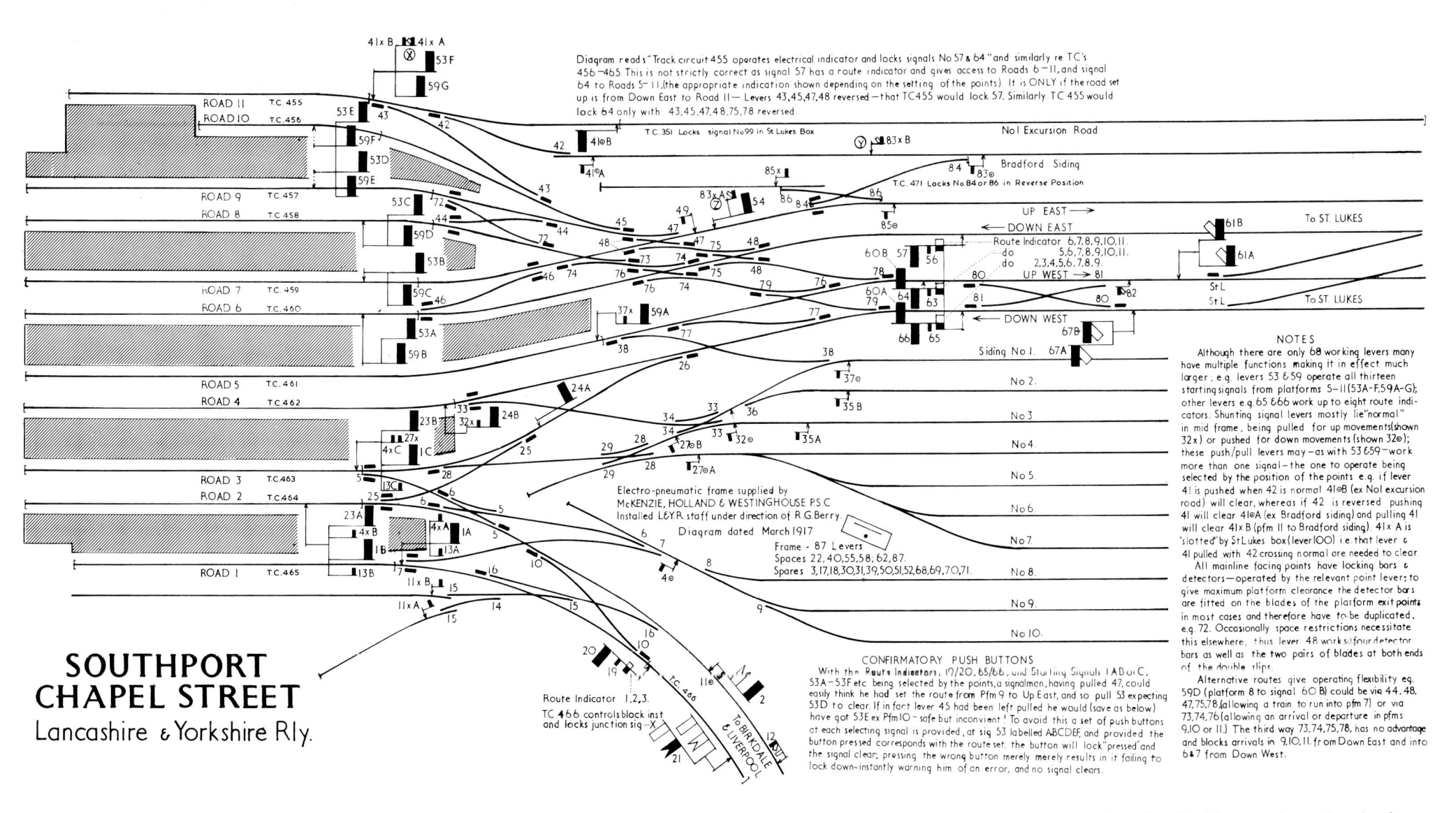

Diagram reads "Track circuit 455 operates electrical indicator and locks signals No 57 & 64" and similarly re TC's 456 −465 This is not strictly correct as signal 57 has a route indicator and gives access to Roads 6 −11, and signal 64 to Roads 5 − 11, (the appropriate indication shown depending on the setting of the points). It is ONLY if the road set up is from Down East to Road 11 − Levers 43,45,47,48 reversed −that TC455 would lock 57. Similarly TC 455 would lock 64 only with - 43,45,47,48,75,78 reversed.

NOTES

Although there are only 68 working levers many have multiple functions making it in effect much larger, e.g. levers 53 &59 operate all thirteen starting signals from platforms 5−11(53A−F,59A−G); other levers e.g. 65 &66 work up to eight route indicators. Shunting signal levers mostly "lie" normal", being pulled in mid frame, being pulled for up movements(shown 32x) or pushed for down movements (shown 32●); these push/pull levers may −as with 53 &59 −work more than one signal −the one to operate being selected by the position of the points e.g. if lever 41 is pushed when 42 is normal 41●B (ex No1 excursion road) will clear, whereas if 42 is reversed pushing 41 will clear 41●A (ex Bradford siding) and pulling 41 will clear 41x B (pfm 11 to Bradford siding). 41x A is "slotted" by St Lukes box (lever 100) i.e. that lever & 41 pulled with 42 crossing normal are needed to clear.

All mainline facing points have locking bars & detectors −operated by the relevant point lever; to give maximum platform clearance the detector bars are fitted on the blades of the platform exit points in most cases and therefore have to be duplicated, e.g. 72. Occasionally space restrictions necessitate this elsewhere, thus lever 48 works four detector bars as well as the two pairs of blades at both ends of the double slips.

Alternative routes give operating flexibility eg. 59D (platform 8 to signal 60 B) could be via 44,48, 47,75,78,(allowing a train to run into pfm 7) or via 73,74,76 (allowing an arrival or departure in pfms 9,10 or 11). The third way 73,74,75,78, has no advantage and blocks arrivals in 9,10,11. from Down East and into 6 & 7 from Down West.

SOUTHPORT
CHAPEL STREET
Lancashire & Yorkshire Rly.

Route Indicator 1,2,3.
TC 466 controls block inst and locks junction sig −X

CONFIRMATORY PUSH BUTTONS

With the Route Indicators, 19/20, 65/66, and Starting Signals 1 AD or C, 53A −53F etc being selected by the points, a signalman, having pulled 47, could easily think he had set the route from Pfm 9 to Up East, and so pull 53 expecting 53D to clear. If in fact lever 45 had been left pulled he would (save as below) have got 53E ex Pfm 10 − safe but inconvient ! To avoid this a set of push buttons at each selecting signal is provided, at sig 53 labelled ABCDEF, and provided the button pressed corresponds with the route set, the button will lock "pressed" and the signal clear; pressing the wrong button merely merely results in it failing to lock down-instantly warning him of an error, and no signal clears.

Electro-pneumatic frame supplied by McKENZIE, HOLLAND & WESTINGHOUSE P.S.C Installed L&Y.R. staff under direction of R.G.Berry. Diagram dated March 1917
Frame - 87 Levers
Spaces 22,40,55,58, 62,87.
Spares 3,17,18,30,31,39,50,51,52,68,69,70,71.

Two electro-pneumatic frames were provided by McKenzie, Holland & Westinghouse, and installed by LYR staff during 1917/18, permitting a great saving in levers and boxes. Chapel St. frame, of 87 levers, was on the top floor of a brick cabin, the middle floor housing the relays, and the ground floor the compressors and standby equipment. Two 'Sentinel' compressors, powered off the traction supply of 600 volts d.c., worked to 130p.s.i., reduced to 70p.s.i. for operation. Should the traction current fail, the Southport town supply at 250 volts a.c. would cut in automatically via Brush equipment, whilst storage batteries gave 930 amp-hours as a last resort. St. Luke's box, about ½ mile out, was carried on girders, about 20ft. above track level, and possessed a 103-lever frame (91 working), and it was estimated that mechanical boxes with 340 levers would have been needed, in comparison. There were several reasons. With power working, one lever controlled points, facing point locks and detectors; indeed up to four pairs

of blades in some cases. Selection of signals was prevalent, thus the thirteen main starting signals ex-platforms 5-11 were worked by two levers, 53 and 59, the setting of the points determining which signal was cleared. Route indicators were provided for incoming trains, four signals doing the work of twenty four. Some levers were 'push-pull', being pushed from mid-point for a movement one way, and pulled for the reverse direction. The old working distances which resulted in a multitude of frequently small boxes in a station did not apply, so that one box could control a larger area, reducing the number of individual signals, and slotting, whereby one signal is worked from two or more boxes. Continuous track circuiting, then a novelty, check locks on levers to confirm that point blades had moved fully, before the lever movement could be completed, constant detection of points and push buttons, to confirm that the route set up was that intended, all added to safety.

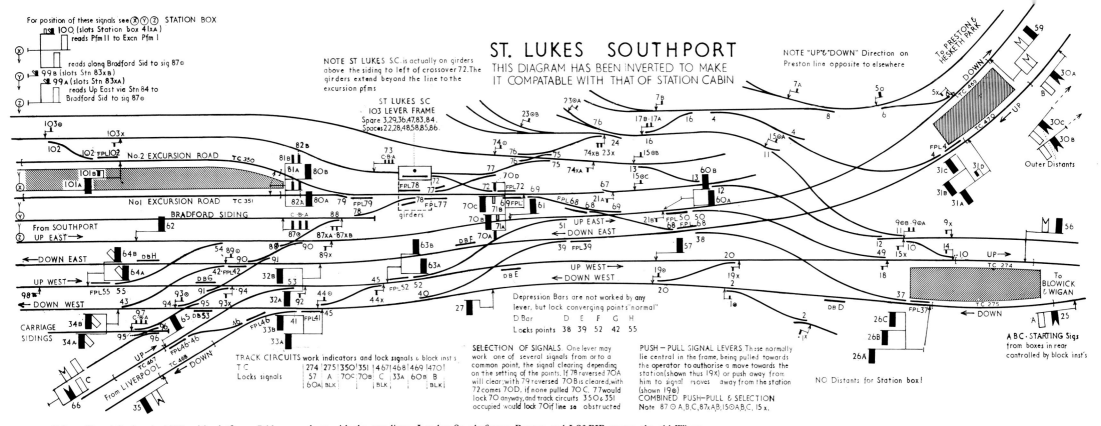

ST. LUKES SOUTHPORT
THIS DIAGRAM HAS BEEN INVERTED TO MAKE IT COMPATABLE WITH THAT OF STATION CABIN

Below: Chapel St. box in 1977, with platforms 7-11 gone, along with the east lines, London St. platforms, Preston and LS&PJR routes, the old Wigan formation through Blowick, and the Wigan to Liverpool curve. Chapel St. has acquired the remains of St. Luke's Station, the goods and coal yard connections (most awkward!) and the Liverpool line almost to Birkdale, with two subsidiary frames, Portland St. and Duke St. for level crossings. Points 14 control the sidings which were once within the triangle worked by South Junction.

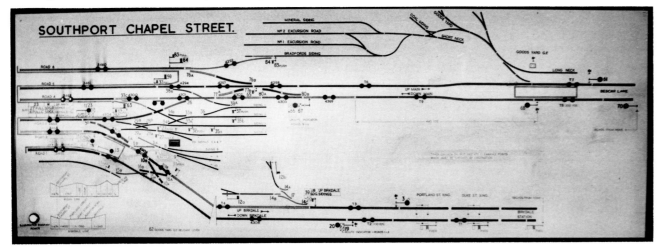

In 1919, Southport was a busy terminal, with 146 arrivals daily in summer, rising to 200 on peak Saturdays. Electric sets shuttled to and from Liverpool, and to Crossens on the Preston line. Steam railcars scurried back and forth, and the graceful Aspinall 'Highflyers' rolled in on express after express. Retrenchment began in the 1930s, the LS&PJR losing its passenger service in 1938, and goods services in 1952, although a short section remained until 1964 for stabling excursion stock. The Preston line closed on 7th September 1964, and the Pool Hey to St. Luke's section in June 1965, Manchester trains running via Meols Cop, and so avoiding a busy level crossing at Blowick. The simplification of the layout at St. Luke's, closure of the steam shed, and reduction in the number of platforms at Chapel St. from 11 to 6, enabled British Railways to dispense with St. Luke's box, and control the remaining lines from the old LYR frame at Chapel St. Freight traffic was handled at Southport (Central) and London Road. This continued after extension of Chapel St. box to control the various connections at St. Luke's.

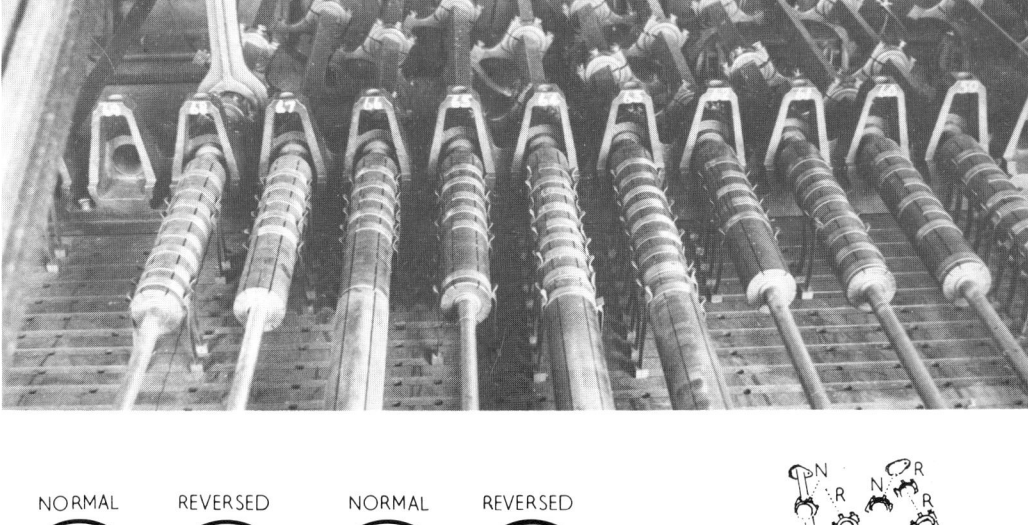

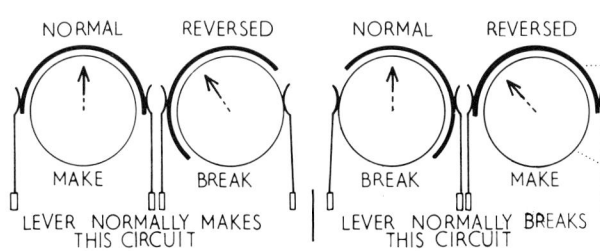

Above: Chapel St. lever frame in 1977. Note the 'pull-push' levers, with their two white bands, which usually stand in mid-position.

SOUTHPORT (Chapel St.)

Below: A study of levers 56-69. Spares are painted white, and the catch handles have been removed.

Above: A rear view of the locking and contacts, with an explanatory diagram. The lever numbers are painted on the middle bearing (e.g. No. 69 has no contact drum, as lever 69 is spare — *(see adjacent illustration)*. Beyond these bearings are the square pivot rods, with their cranks at the far end, from which a linkage goes to the lever. All cranks, except 61/63, point down, the levers being normal in the frame. Mechanical linkages, in up to four positions, can be bolted to the square pivot rods, between the lever links and numbered bearings. Levers 59, 61 and 63 each have two linkages. Even numbers, seemingly, could have linkages in the second and fourth positions, and odd number levers in the first and third positions. On Nos. 61 and 63, the lever cranks and linkages stand in the opposite direction to the rest of the frame, indicating that these levers are pulled. In fact, they are the starter ex-platform 4 and advance starter. On the near side of the numbered bearing are the rotating electric contacts, which are mounted upon an insulated sleeve, of approximately 1 inch diameter. The drums are of varying lengths, depending upon the number of contacts, which vary from 5 to 9, although marks, where further contacts have been, can be seen on some drums. These make or break contact with the sprung arms — on lever 64 for example, the fifth, seventh and ninth contacts from the near side on the left are open. Lever 63 is pulled, and 1, 2, 3, 6 and 8 do not make contact, (on the right) whilst 4, 5, 7 and 9 complete circuits. Lever 66, with only five contacts left, has a long insulating sleeve, from the time when it was the inner home, with eight route indicators. The diagrams explain the method by which these contacts work, and the effect of mounting the rotating segment in differing positions for contacts normally made pulled, or broken in the pulled position.

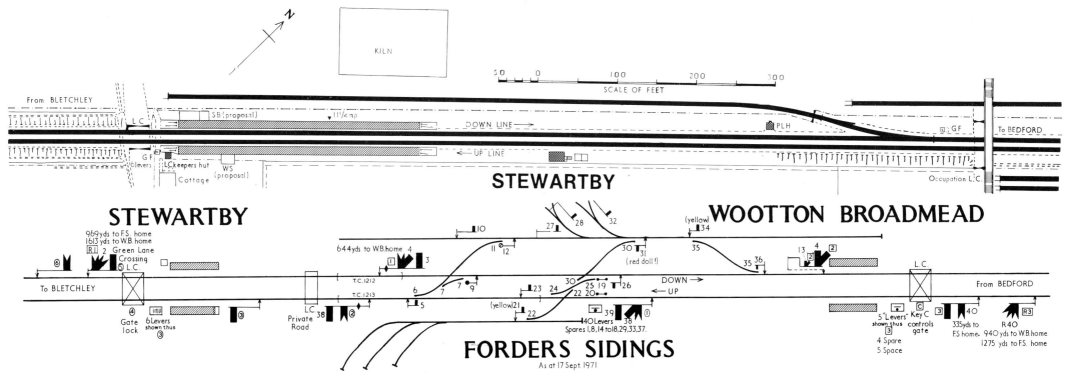

STEWARTBY

STEWARTBY   WOOTTON BROADMEAD

FORDERS SIDINGS

As at 17 Sept. 1971

STEWARTBY (Map Ref. L3)

Stewartby, as it is known today, is a small halt on the Bletchley to Bedford branch of the erstwhile LNWR. This was authorised as the Bedford Railway in 1845, and formally opened on 17th November 1846, regular services commencing the next day. Just short of Bedford was a group of small villages, the Woottons, including Wootton Pillinge and Wootton Broadmead; Wootton Green was close-by. However, they were not judged worthy of a station, and LNWR trains rolled imperiously over the level crossings for the next sixty years. It was due to the introduction of the LNWR steam railcars, of which there were but half a dozen for the whole system, that the Woottons burst upon the railway scene. Steam railcar working was instituted on the Bletchley to Bedford section on 30th October 1905, and a string of new halts was provided, two of them being just 1,600yds. apart, Wootton Pillinge and Wootton Broadmead (an older spelling rendered the name Wotton Pullinge, but this was never used on the railway). Due to World War I staff shortages, both halts were closed as an economy measure on 1st January 1917, and reopened on 5th May 1919, at which time, Wootton Pillinge (which was also referred to as Green Lane Crossing) was renamed Stewartby, to reduce confusion — or make it absolute!

Right: The Wootton Broadmead signal diagram.

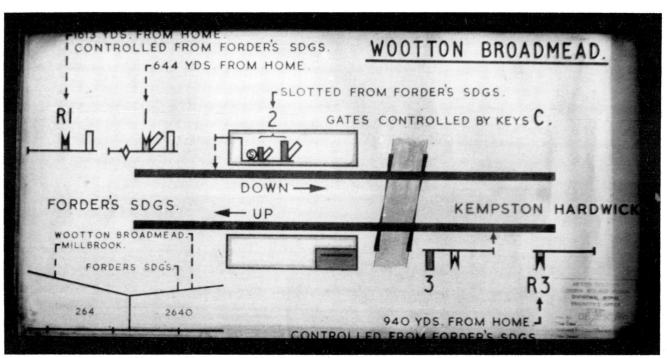

Below left: The level crossing keeper's hut and outdoor ground frame at Stewartby.

STEWARTBY

Brick-making developed rapidly in the Bedford area between the wars, a trend encouraged by the demise of many local brickworks unable to cope with the giants. An LMS standard all-timber signal box, of the type first introduced in 1928, was installed, for although Forder & Son's Sidings had been in existence prior to World War I, the greater volume of traffic required extended facilities. In 1941, Wootton Broadmead was closed once more as a temporary measure, only this time the closure was later made permanent (in 1949). Despite this closure, and indeed physical removal of the platforms, the diagram in the crossing keeper's cabin still stubbornly proclaimed platforms in the early 1970s. As one passenger train continued to call each week, to deliver the keeper's wages, there was perhaps method in the madness! The provision of two halts less than a mile apart, both at level crossings, but neither being a block post, separated by a large works and box, with facilities on both sides of the lines, and its own occupation over the railway, is unusual. With Forder's Sidings box controlling what was to become the London Brick Company's connections, complex slotting of signals was necessary. Arrangements of this sort were common in large town stations, but rare at small country halts! They merit recording.

Above right: The 'up' platform at Stewartby, looking towards Bedford, with more of the brickworks in evidence.

Above left: The 'down' platform at Stewartby, looking towards Forder's Sidings and Bedford, with a plethora of brickworks' chimneys in the background.

Above: Forder's Sidings signal box, an LMS all-timber cabin of the type first introduced in 1928, and which replaced a smaller LNWR box nearer Stewartby.

Below right: A view looking towards Bedford, with Wootton Broadmead crossing keeper's cabin (right centre). On the left is the Forder's Sidings 'down' starter, No. 4, and shunt ahead signal, No. 13, both of which are slotted by Broadmead lever 2. The Broadmead 'up' home, No. 3, and Forder's inner distant, No. 40, are just beyond the gates, the latter being unlocked by Annett's Key.

FORDER'S SIDINGS

Below: Looking towards Broadmead from Forder's Sidings, the 3-way point leads (left) to the brickworks, and is hand-worked. In the centre is the shunting road, and to the right, crossover 30 to the running lines. Signals 31 and 26 are also visible.

Above: Vintage lighting often survived at wayside stations, as in this example at Stewartby, on the 'up' platform.

STEWARTBY

Above: At Wootton Broadmead, the crossing keeper was more favoured than at Stewartby, as the levers were housed in a mini cabin of a decidedly unusual pattern.

WOOTTON BROADMEAD

In the LNWR days, the Woottons were simply railcar halts, and the ordinary passenger services sped by. In 1915, four return railcar trips, calling at the various halts, were provided daily between Bletchley and Bedford. These were, of course, one class only. By 1938, eight or nine trains called at Stewartby, most of which also called at Wootton Broadmead. By May 1946, the service at Stewartby was down to five trains in each direction, still one class only, and Cambridge workings ran through. Wootton Broadmead, although temporarily closed, still appeared in the timetables, but with no scheduled workings! Today, the service is by BR diesel multiple unit.

Although not of course open to public traffic, Forder's Sidings handled a heavy goods traffic, with trains terminating or originating at the works. Three connections were provided to sidings on the 'down' side, and one to the 'up' side. The sidings were comprehensively signalled, three of the shunt signals being yellow. A 'yellow' shunt signal, for example No. 34, refers to one route only. Thus it may be 'passed at danger' by an engine running along the headshunt towards Broadmead platform, but must be pulled before a movement over No. 35 crossover. The slotting is also of interest. Broadmead No. 2 lever slots Forder's 'down' starter (4) and shunt ahead signal (13). Broadmead's 'down' inner distant (1) will only clear if Broadmead's 'down' signal (2) is off, if Forder' slot (4) is off, and finally if Forder's home, (3) above the distant arm, is also off. As this distant is only 644yds. to the home, there is an outer distant, which additionally requires Forder's distant (2) and Stewartby's home (5).

TILE HILL

LM & SR Plan (undated)

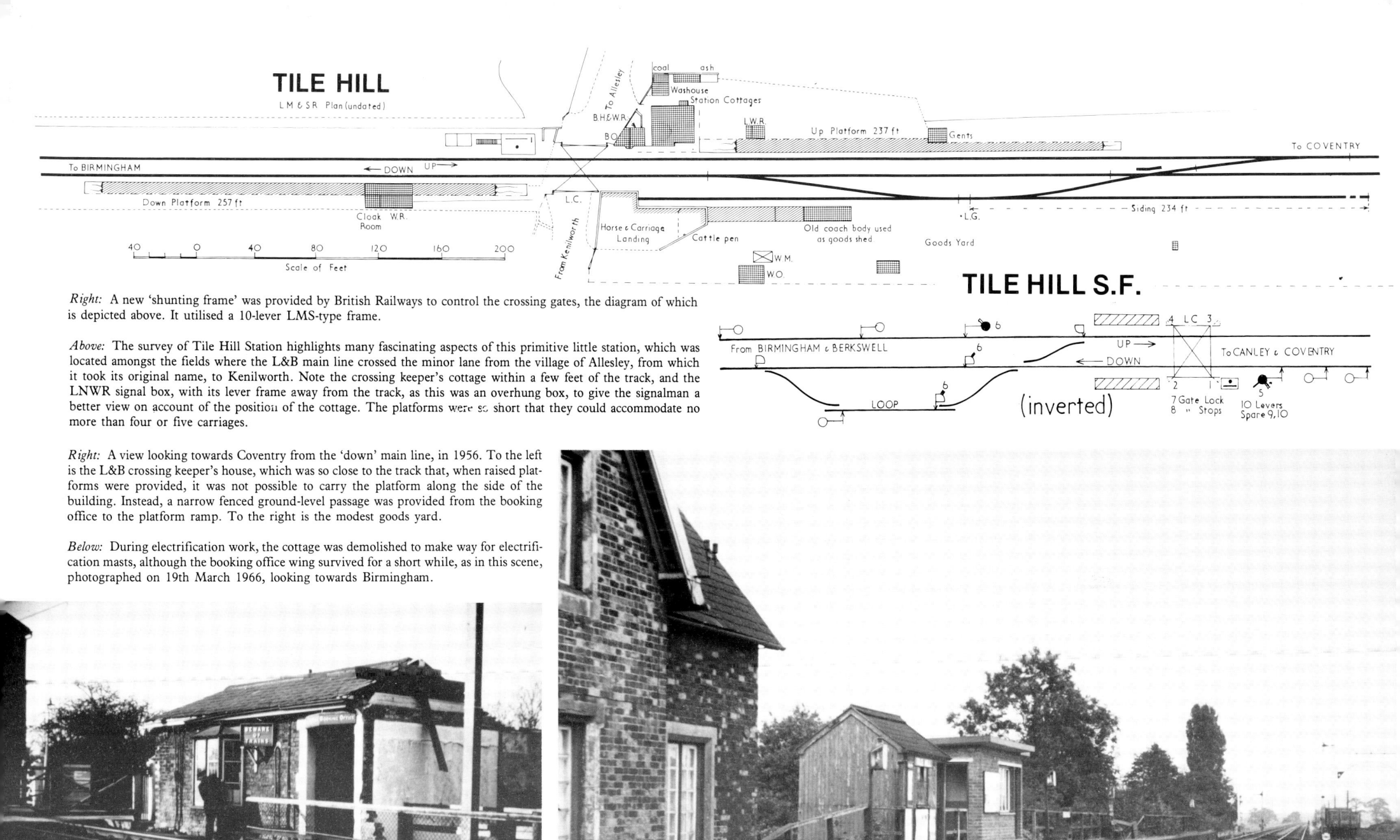

To Allesley

coal   ash

Washouse

Station Cottages

B.H.&W.R.

B.O.

L.W.R.

Up Platform 237 ft

Gents

To COVENTRY

To BIRMINGHAM

← DOWN   UP →

Down Platform 257 ft

L.C.

Cloak W.R. Room

From Kenilworth

Horse & Carriage Landing

Cattle pen

Old coach body used as goods shed

Goods Yard

·L.G.

Siding 234 ft

W.M.

W.O.

40   40   80   120   160   200

Scale of Feet

Right: A new 'shunting frame' was provided by British Railways to control the crossing gates, the diagram of which is depicted above. It utilised a 10-lever LMS-type frame.

Above: The survey of Tile Hill Station highlights many fascinating aspects of this primitive little station, which was located amongst the fields where the L&B main line crossed the minor lane from the village of Allesley, from which it took its original name, to Kenilworth. Note the crossing keeper's cottage within a few feet of the track, and the LNWR signal box, with its lever frame away from the track, as this was an overhung box, to give the signalman a better view on account of the position of the cottage. The platforms were so short that they could accommodate no more than four or five carriages.

TILE HILL S.F.

From BIRMINGHAM & BERKSWELL

UP →

← DOWN

To CANLEY & COVENTRY

LOOP

(inverted)

4   LC   3

2   1

7 Gate Lock
8 " Stops

10 Levers
Spare 9,10

5

Right: A view looking towards Coventry from the 'down' main line, in 1956. To the left is the L&B crossing keeper's house, which was so close to the track that, when raised platforms were provided, it was not possible to carry the platform along the side of the building. Instead, a narrow fenced ground-level passage was provided from the booking office to the platform ramp. To the right is the modest goods yard.

Below: During electrification work, the cottage was demolished to make way for electrification masts, although the booking office wing survived for a short while, as in this scene, photographed on 19th March 1966, looking towards Birmingham.

TILE HILL *(Map Ref. E6)*

The London & Birmingham Railway was authorised on 6th May 1833, and opened between Birmingham and Rugby on 9th April 1838. Work on the daunting Kilsby Tunnel delayed completion as a through route until September 1838. To the traveller of today, whisked through a succession of suburban stations between Coventry and Birmingham, it is hard to believe that when the L&BR opened, there was but one intermediate station between Coventry and Birmingham, at Hampton (ironically long-closed). To the proprietors of the L&BR, it was not so surprising, for there were no communities of any size en route. Coventry itself was in the 'Hundred of Coventry', but the great 'Hundred' of Knightlow' swept up to the west (almost meeting a pincer of the same 'Hundred' from the east). In that spur, was the village of Allesley. In 1844, the L&BR agreed that local trains might call at what later became Berkswell, Marston Green and Stechford. Two years later, the L&BR became a part of the LNWR and, on 19th May 1847, the traffic sub-committee agreed to a few local trains calling at Allesley Gate, where a crossing keeper was already stationed to man the gates. Facilities were scant and, in January 1848, the stations committee noted that a new station was required to meet the wishes of the inhabitants. In October 1850, the LNWR was in less generous mood, rejecting the idea of a new booking office. On 1st September 1863, Allesley Gate was renamed Allesley Lane, although the new name was not destined for a long life, being revised to Tile Hill from 1st April 1864, the name it still retains. A small freight yard, closed on 4th February 1963, was provided on the 'down' side, and private siding traffic was also handled nearby.

TILE HILL

Left: Looking towards Coventry from the down platform, in 1956. The L&B cottage is clearly visible to the left of the track beyond the crossing gates, and to this side of it, is the west wing which housed a diminutive booking office. The overhung LNWR signal cabin is also apparent, the overhang permitting the signalman to see past the cottage. Such boxes, although suited to cramped urban locations or in deep rock cuttings, etc., were most unusual in the middle of level open countryside. The platforms were staggered, and a simple shelter ws provided on the 'down' platform. This was of the rusticated board type beloved of the LNWR, but with its elementary wooden struts supporting the awning, rather than the more elegant cast spandrels, it is thought to be an early example. The platform was very low. During modernisation in 1966, prior to electrification, the 'down' platform was raised and a new BR building provided, and a new 'up' platform was provided on the west side of the level crossing, the old box being swept away.

Below: A new BR timber-built cabin was provided, with slots to control the signals, which were transferred to Birmingham (New St.) power box. This box is depicted, in a view looking towards Coventry, on 19th March 1966, prior to commissioning. Little survives of this station which witnessed the passage of McConnell 'Bloomers' and Webb Compounds, and whose successor now sees the 25kV electric locomotives of Britsh Rail hurtle past.

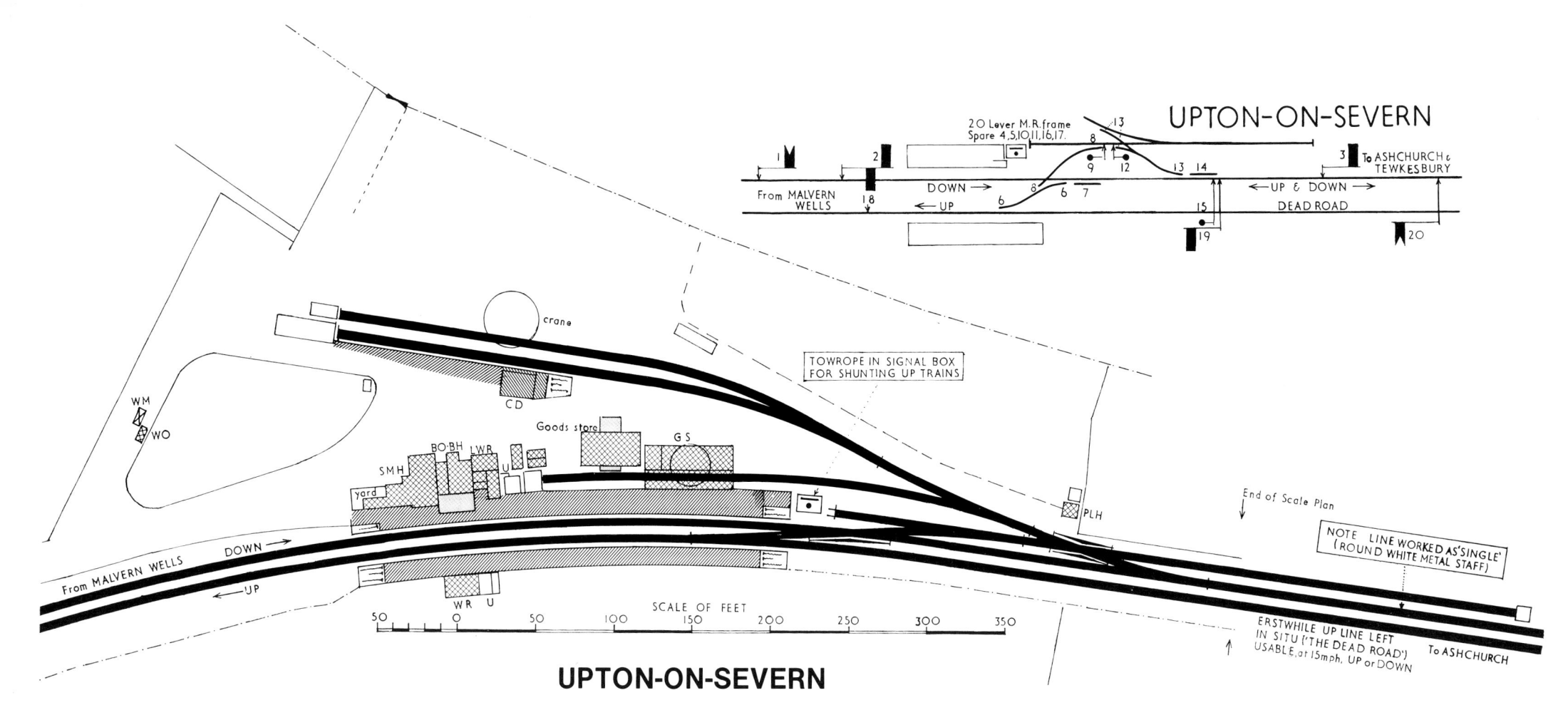

UPTON-ON-SEVERN

20 Lever M.R. frame
Spare 4,5,10,11,16,17.

From MALVERN WELLS

DOWN →
← UP

TOWROPE IN SIGNAL BOX
FOR SHUNTING UP TRAINS

crane

CD

Goods store

GS

BO·BH LWR

SMH

yard

WR U

WM
WO

SCALE OF FEET

50   50   100   150   200   250   300   350

PLH

End of Scale Plan

NOTE   LINE WORKED AS 'SINGLE'
(ROUND WHITE METAL STAFF)

From MALVERN WELLS

DOWN →
← UP

To ASHCHURCH &
TEWKESBURY

← UP & DOWN →
DEAD ROAD

ERSTWHILE UP LINE LEFT
IN SITU ('THE DEAD ROAD')
USABLE, at 15mph, UP or DOWN

To ASHCHURCH

UPTON-ON-SEVERN

UPTON-ON-SEVERN *(Map Ref. B3)*

Upton-on-Severn is a pretty little village about ten miles south of Worcester, and is in the area between the West Midlands and the Bristol Channel, which was fought over so bitterly by the Great Western and the Midland railways. Indeed, Gloucester, one of the most celebrated battlegrounds of the broad gauge/narrow gauge is less than twenty miles away. With the exception of a few sizeable communities on the trunk routes, even today it is an area of tranquility and great natural beauty. The story opens in 1836, with the authorisation of the Birmingham & Gloucester Railway, which opened in sections, north from Cheltenham, during 1840. It had been expected that funds would be tight, and the B&GR avoided the main towns, which could be served by branch lines at a later date. Such a branch, 1¾ miles long, was authorised from Ashchurch, on the B&GR, to Tewkesbury, in 1837, and opened in 1840. In 1846, the Midland captured the B&GR from under the nose of the GWR. In the 1850s, a bitter struggle erupted between the GWR and LNWR to link Worcester and Hereford, a task accomplished in 1860 by the Worcester & Hereford Railway, merged that year with the Oxford, Worcester & Wolverhampton Railway into the West Midland Railway, and in 1863 into the GWR. These lines were GWR, and out of this tangled web, the Midland Railway obtained running powers through Worcester, finally putting the city on the route of Midland Railway's Bristol expresses.

Upton-on-Severn had remained unaffected by all these developments but, in May 1860, concurrently with the opening of the Worcester to Hereford line, the Tewkesbury & Malvern Railway was authorised to run from a junction with the Midland Railway's Tewkesbury branch to the W&HR, just south of Great Malvern. A short section was opened in Malvern in 1862, and the line, worked by the MR, was completed on 16th May 1864. It was vested in the MR from 1st July 1877.

The line opened on the 'Time Interval' system and, as traffic was hardly encouraging, was low on the list for upgrading. At the time of the terrible Armagh accident in Ulster, which led to the 1889 Railways Act, with its requirements for continuous brakes and block working, the Ashchurch to Malvern Junction line, 13 miles 11 chains, was still on 'time interval', but was converted during 1890. With but four or five trains each way, one can understand the Midland Railway's reluctance. A similar service was still running by the late 1930s, but traffic was very sparse north of Upton-on-Severn, and all services were withdrawn between Upton and Malvern on 1st December 1952. The Upton to Ashchurch passenger service succumbed during the Beeching era, on 14th August 1961, freight facilities ending beyond Tewkesbury in July 1963.

Above & Top of facing page: Reference has been made, opposite, to the survival of 'time interval' working on the Ashchurch to Malvern branch until 1890. When absolute block working was instituted, Upton-on-Severn became a block post in the double track section between Tewkesbury and Malvern Wells. With no more than half a dozen passenger workings each way, plus the occasional freight, the route could easily have been singled, as was done, on occasion, elsewhere. However, a quite extraordinary form of working was instituted in pre-war days, which persisted through to closure as a through route. The former 'up' line, or northbound track, between Tewkesbury and Upton-on-Severn was taken out of use, and single line working was instituted on the 'down' line. This caused considerable problems with the interlocking at Upton, which had to be adjusted to a quite improbable layout, with the yard entered off a facing lead from Ashchurch! To add to the peculiarities, the old 'up' road was left in situ, renamed the 'dead road', and was usable at 15m.p.h. 'up' or 'down'. As the former 'up' line home signal, 19, had been filched for the 'up and down' single line, no signal was available to control movements off the dead road. Even prior to these changes, shunting of an 'up' freight was virtually impossible, and tow-roping was authorised, adding a further rarity.

UPTON-ON-SEVERN

Above: A view looking from the 'down' platform towards Tewkesbury and Ashchurch, in 1953. At first sight, this would appear to be a quite normal double-track station, with trailing connections off the 'up' and 'down' lines into the yard, and the usual signals. The first hint that all is not normal comes from the rusted metals of the apparent 'up' line, and the obvious use of the crossover in the foreground. Further study reveals a facing point lock/bar at the far end of No. 6 crossover, which would normally be trailed. A similar bar can be seen by point No. 13. The shunt signal, 15, at the foot of the 'up' home, is another clue. With a normal layout, it would be by the 'down' road, authorising a setting-back move. It does indeed authorise setting-back, but as the former 'up' line signal now refers to the single line, and it would be easier and cheaper to move the shunt signal, they have been brought together one track distant from the road to which they refer.

Left: A Johnson 3F 0-6-0, with a one coach local train, waits to depart for Ashchurch in 1953. The well-tended lawns and flower beds recall a vanished era of pride.

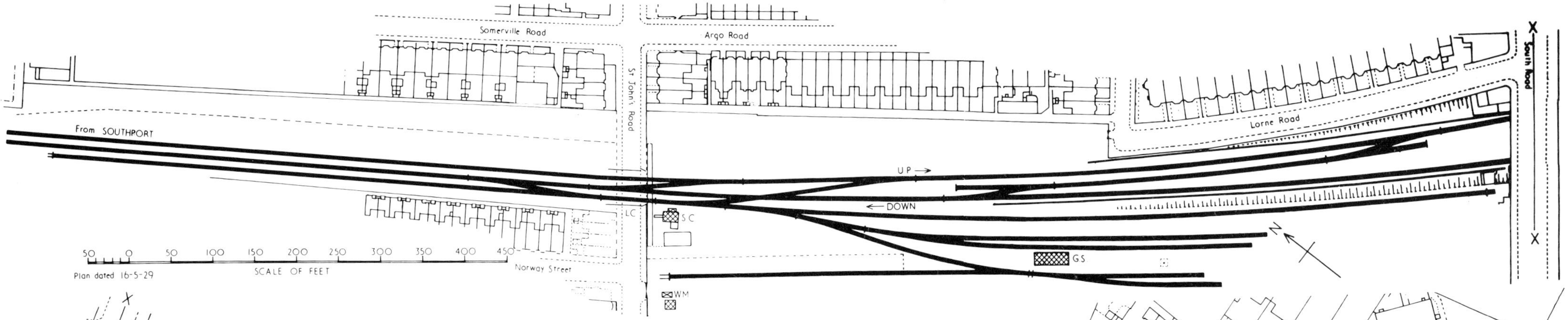

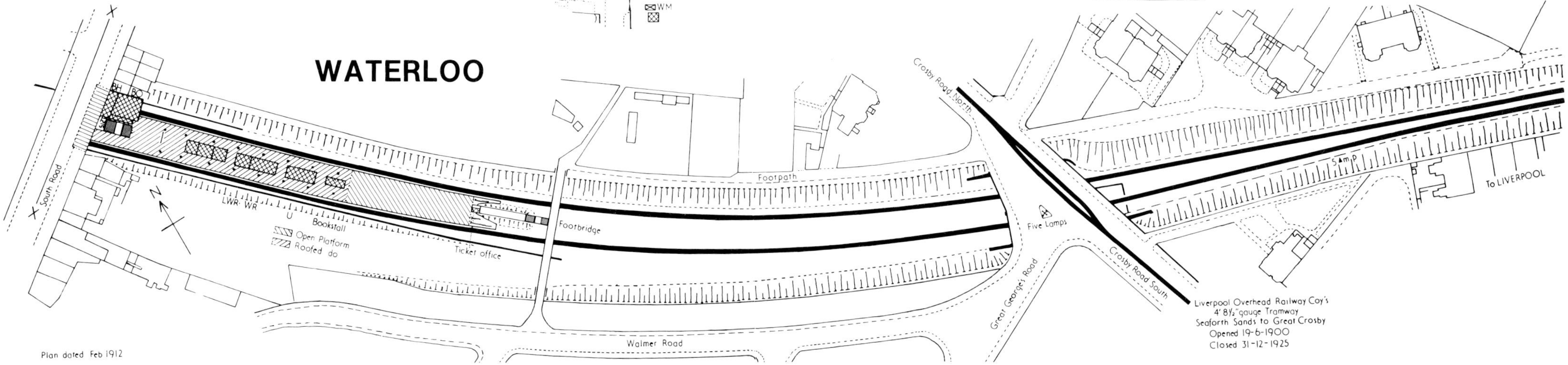

Map and track plan labels:

Somerville Road

Argo Road

St John's Road

South Road

Lorne Road

From SOUTHPORT

UP →

← DOWN

LC

SC

GS

Norway Street

WM

50   0   50   100   150   200   250   300   350   400   450
Plan dated 16-5-29   SCALE OF FEET

WATERLOO

Crosby Road North

Footpath

South Road

N

LWR   WR   U   Bookstall

Open Platform
Roofed do

Ticket office

Footbridge

Five Lamps

Great George's Road

Crosby Road South

Walmer Road

S M P

To LIVERPOOL

Liverpool Overhead Railway Coy's
4' 8½" gauge Tramway
Seaforth Sands to Great Crosby
Opened 19-6-1900
Closed 31-12-1925

Plan dated Feb 1912

Waterloo

RO

WATERLOO (Map Ref. A2)

The Lancashire & Yorkshire version of 'Waterloo', somewhat less renowned than its LSWR name-sake, is on the Liverpool, Crosby & Southport line of the LYR, on the northern outskirts of Liverpool (see LYR Liverpool area map under 'Aintree'). The LC&SR was authorised in 1847, and opened from Southport to a temporary terminus at Waterloo on 24th July 1848, passengers continuing into Liverpool by coach. South of Waterloo, as there were numerous roads to bridge, construction was difficult and costly, and the line was not opened as a through route to the LYR/East Lancashire Railway at Sandhills until 1st October 1850, passenger trains henceforth terminating at Tithebarn St. Station, later to become Liverpool (Exchange). The LC&SR was doubled during 1852. In the LYR Act of 1878, powers were obtained to replace the original station and a level crossing, and a new station was completed during 1881. The stations from Waterloo northwards became the focal points of affluent and thriving residential suburbs to Liverpool and, to cope with rising traffic, the LYR electrified this route in 1904.

Left: A view looking across South Road to the station frontage, with its ridge and furrow awning, in 1977. One of the authors was born within ¼ mile of the station, and has vivid memories of journeys to and from school from 1919-25. Wide steps led up from the island platform, with as many as four ticket collectors on duty at peak periods.

Above: Looking from the 'down' platform towards Liverpool, an LMS-built electric set enters the station. At the south end of the station, a footbridge, latterly disused, provided convenient access to housing in the vicinity of Walmer Road and Crosby Road and, on the scale plan, the Liverpool Overhead Railway's tramway is shown on Crosby Road, a competitor for the Liverpool commuter until 1925. The 'Five Lamps' which gave their name to the bridge, consisted of a five-headed street lamp.

Above: The scene looking north, towards Southport, in 1977, with the station a mixture of ancient and modern structures. On the scale plan, a turn-back siding is shown bewteen the running lines north of the road bridge. This usually stabled a 5-coach set outside peak periods but, if necessary, could accept a 7-coach formation, which necessitated using first one, and then the other short 'headshunts', to bring the set in clear of the north end arrival points, and then set back to clear the south end departure points. In 1929, plans were drafted to replace the St. John's Road level crossing by lowering the railway by some 9ft. in stages, and raising the road level by 7ft., with a 1 in 18 approach slope, but this was never carried out.

WATERLOO

Right: A nostalgic look at Waterloo Station, and an LYR electric set in the 'up' platform in the 1920s. The car, LMS No. 14554, was one of eight elliptical-roofed double-ended driving motor cars, with luggage compartment, of 1912/13. These heavy multiple unit cars were normally used on the Ormskirk service, and the older clerestory roof stock predominated on the Southport line. The 'Stopping Train Southport' destination is nonsense, as the set is bound for Liverpool! With the generous loading gauge on the Southport line, these cars were amongst the largest passenger vehicles ever built, 63ft. 7in. x 10ft. Their ability to shift crowds was prodigious, and the multiple ticket collectors at stations a necessity. As well as an exceptionally broad passenger stairway, Waterloo also boasted a sizeable luggage lift, often used for prams. The Liverpool to Southport line provided an impressive example of suburban high-intensity passenger operation, predating the more celebrated Southern Railway's electrification by many years.

Left: Waterloo signal cabin in 1977, with St. John's Road level crossing in the background.

WELLINGTON *(Map Ref. T7)*

When the 'railway mania' dawned, in 1845, Wellington was a tranquil market town, but in little more than twenty years, lines radiated in five directions, largely the result of LNWR/GWR rivalry. During 1845/6, Shrewsbury was the target of two schemes. The Shrewbury & Birmingham Railway, with GWR backing, was authorised to build 29½ miles from Wolverhampton through Wellington to Shrewsbury, the last 10 miles from Wellington being joint with the Shropshire Union Railways & Canal Co. The SUR, with Grand Junction Railway backing, was to build from Stafford to Wellington, sharing the remaining miles to Shrewsbury with the S&BR. Coincidentally, it too was 29 miles in length, and both schemes were authorised on 3rd August 1846. The S&BR was opened from Shrewsbury to Oakengates, just east of Wellington, on 1st June 1849, the SUR line to Stafford opening on the same day. The eastern half of the S&BR, to Wolverhampton, was opened on 12th November 1849. The SUR&CC had been leased by the LNWR in 1847, whilst the S&BR was vested in the GWR in 1854. The same year, an S&B branch was completed from Madeley Junction, east of Wellington, to Lightmoor, where connection was made with industrial lines to Coalbrookdale, the cradle of the industrial revolution. In 1853, an independent company, the Wellington & Severn Junction Railway, was formed. This opened from Ketley Junction, facing towards Wellington, to Horsehay, in 1857, and to Lightmoor in 1858. This came into GWR control. The northern (now closed) portion of the Severn Valley Railway, from Bridgnorth, via Ironbridge to Shrewsbury, ran south of Wellington, and in 1864 a link was completed from the SVR, via Coalbrookdale to Lightmoor, all of which was in GWR hands, passenger and freight services working to and from Wellington Joint Station.

Above: Looking from the 'up' platform, towards Shrewsbury, in the early 1950s, as a 'Castle', No. 7017 *G. J. Churchward*, pauses with a Birmingham express. A prairie tank has attached a milk tank to the rear of the train, and three other engines are occupied in the vicinity of the shed, a graphic indication of how busy Wellington was in its heyday. A carriage stands in the back platform line, whilst two passenger bays existed on the 'down' side at the east end of the station. As well as Wolverhampton and Coalbrookdale/Buildwas trains of the GWR, these subsidiary platforms had to cater for the LNWR Coalport branch services. This line ran south from Hadley Junction on the SUR to a terminus at Coalport, and was opened, in part on former canal formations, in 1861. It was single track, with four or five trains daily.

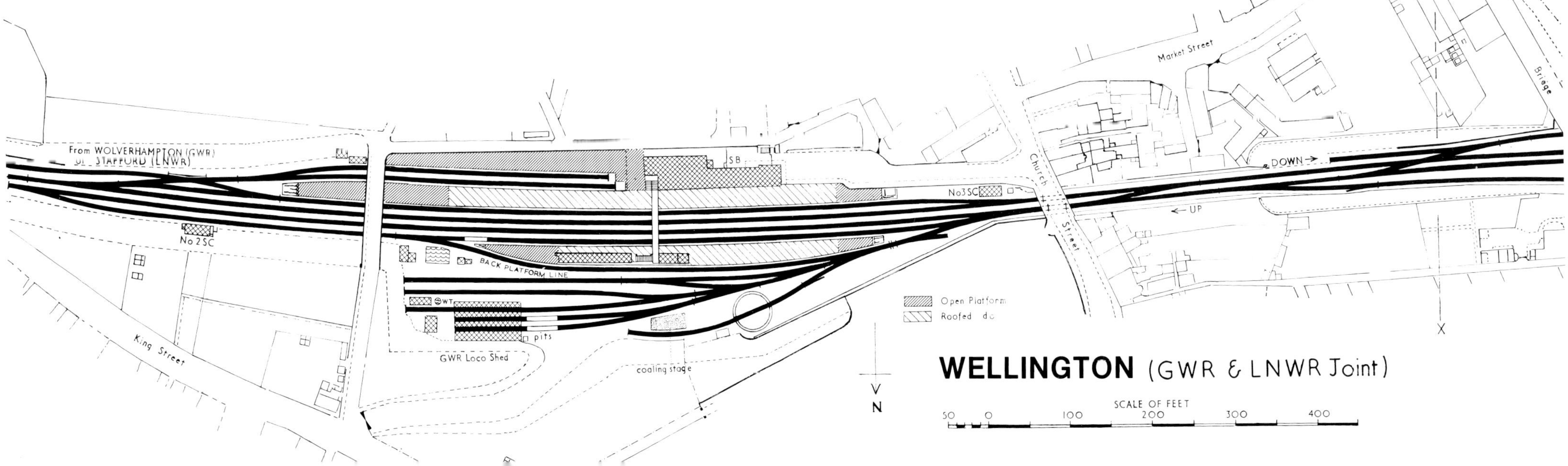

WELLINGTON (GWR & LNWR Joint)

SCALE OF FEET

50   0   100   200   300   400

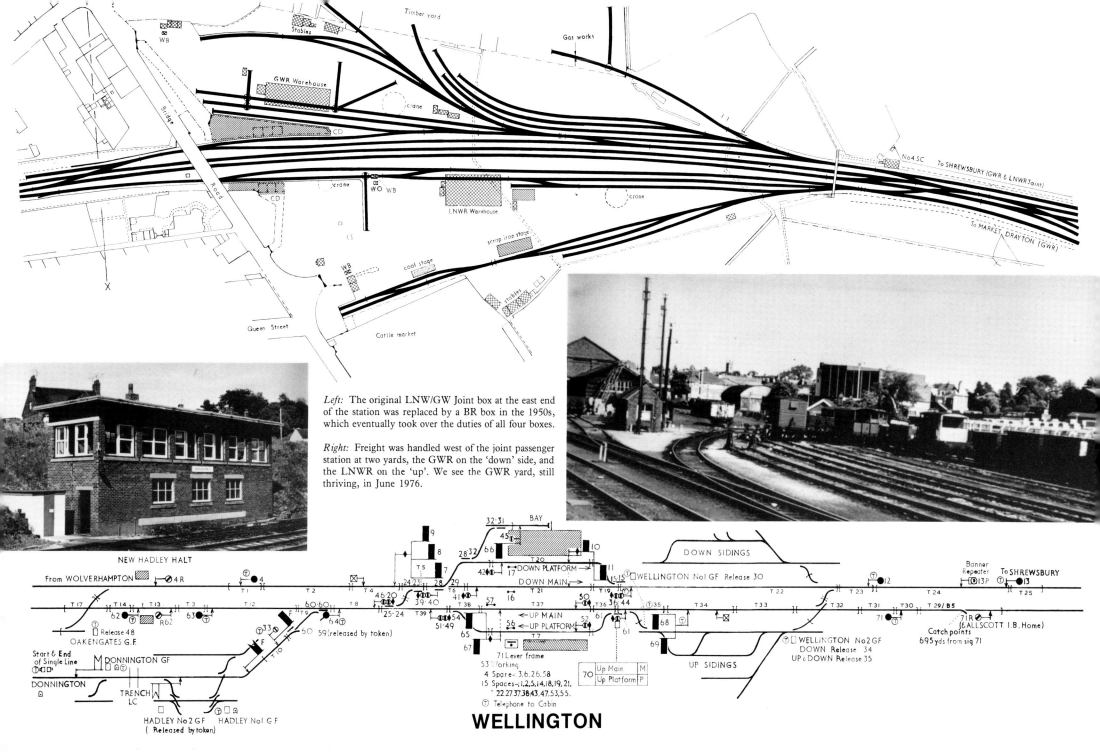

Left: The original LNW/GW Joint box at the east end of the station was replaced by a BR box in the 1950s, which eventually took over the duties of all four boxes.

Right: Freight was handled west of the joint passenger station at two yards, the GWR on the 'down' side, and the LNWR on the 'up'. We see the GWR yard, still thriving, in June 1976.

Timber yard

Stables

WB

GWR Warehouse

CD

crane

crane

WO WB

CD

LNWR Warehouse

WB

scrap iron stage

coal stage

stables

Queen Street

Cattle market

Gas works

No4 SC

To SHREWSBURY (GWR & LNWR Joint)

To MARKET DRAYTON (GWR)

Bridge

Road

NEW HADLEY HALT

From WOLVERHAMPTON 4 R

Release 48

OAKENGATES G.F.

Start & End of Single Line

DONNINGTON

M DONNINGTON GF

TRENCH LC

HADLEY No2 GF   HADLEY No1 GF
(Released by token)

32·31   BAY

45

9

8

28·32   66

T20

DOWN SIDINGS

10

T5   7

42

17   DOWN PLATFORM

11

DOWN MAIN

15·15

WELLINGTON No1 GF Release 30

Banner Repeater

To SHREWSBURY

13 P

12

13

24·23   28   29   41   57   16

46·20   39·40   T36   50   T36 36 44   35   68

T17   62   T14 T13   T3   R62   63   64   25·24   51·49   65   56   UP PLATFORM   52   61   69

60·60   59 (released by token)   67   71 Lever frame   53 Working   4 Spare- 3,6,26,58   15 Spaces-1,2,5,14,18,19,21,   22,27,37,38,43,47,53,55.   Telephone to Cabin

70   Up Main   M
Up Platform   P

UP MAIN

UP SIDINGS

WELLINGTON No2 GF
DOWN Release 34
UP & DOWN Release 35

71 R
(& ALLSCOTT I.B. Home)
Catch points
695 yds from sig 71

T2   T4   T8   T37   T34   T33   T22   T23   T32   T31   T30   T29/B5   T25

Telephone to Cabin

WELLINGTON

Above: A view looking from No. 2 box towards Wolverhampton, in 1976. Signals 67 and 65 boast individual track circuit diamonds.

Below: Looking from the 'down' platform, towards Shrewsbury. The near clock, replete with subsidiary 24-hour numbers, would not appear to be in the same time zone as the further clock, which happened to be correct! The station official box, used between district offices and stations, graces the platform. Cash, and document boxes, bags, or pouches of this sort, were once a vital part of the administrative process.

Above: The station box itself — a largely ignored aspect of railways. This is No. 26 box, used between Wellington and Wolverhampton.

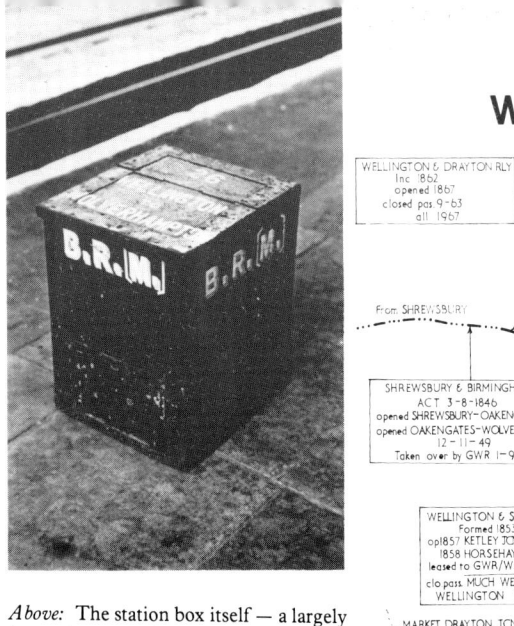

WELLINGTON

WELLINGTON

Although the GWR and LNWR were rivals, both shared a common goal, to strike north from Wellington to Market Drayton, and the exposed flanks of the North Staffordshire Railway. Two lines, the Nantwich & Market Drayton (opened 1863) and the Wellington & Drayton, opened in 1867, provided the GWR with a route into Crewe, but did not break into 'Knotty' territory. A short GWR freight branch, from Hollinswood to Stirchley, completed the lines around Wellington. The Madeley Junction to Lightmoor passenger service closed in 1915. The LNWR Coalport passenger service ceased on 2nd June 1952, and the GWR Stirchley freight branch in 1959. The LNWR Coalport branch closed to freight south of Stirchley in 1960, and was later cut back to colliery sidings near Hadley. The Wellington-Ketley-Buildwas-Much Wenlock service ceased in 1962. The Horsehay to Ketley Junction line was later lifted, with freight access being retained from Madeley Junction to a power-station at Ironbridge, and to sidings at Horsehay. The Stafford to Wellington line closed to passengers on 7th September 1964, freight workings continuing ex-Wellington as far as Newport until 1969, after which they were cut back to Donnington. The Market Drayton passenger service ceased in 1963. Despite this series of closures, Wellington Yard remained busy, and although the old LNWR service via Stafford has gone, with the dismembering of the GWR Birmingham main line, Wolverhampton to Shrewsbury services now work to and from the ex-LNWR Wolverhampton (High Level) station!

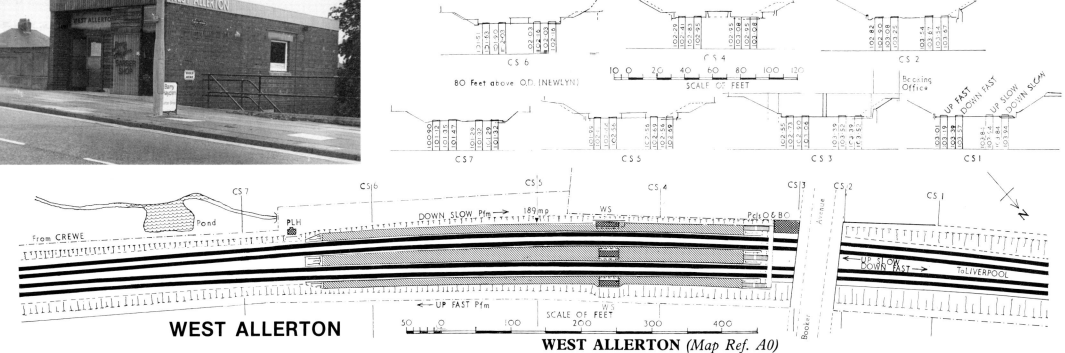

CS 6   C S 4   CS 2

80 Feet above O.D. (NEWLYN)

10 0   20   40   60   80   100   120

SCALE OF FEET

Booking Office

UP FAST   DOWN FAST   UP SLOW   DOWN SLOW

CS 7   CS 5   CS 3   CS 1

WEST ALLERTON

From CREWE   Pond   PLH   DOWN SLOW Pfm   189 mp   WS   Pcls O & BO   Avenue   N

UP SLOW   DOWN FAST   To LIVERPOOL

UP FAST Pfm

WS

SCALE OF FEET

50   0   100   200   300   400

Booker

Above left: By 1982, the stone facing of the LMS booking office had been stripped away to enable part of the building to be leased off, and the building sported a BR totem, but has otherwise little altered.

Below left: The 'down' slow waiting shelter in September 1982. The station opened on Monday, 2nd January 1939, and the excellent condition of the building is a surprising tribute to the lasting qualities of hardboard! The buildings, which bear maker's plates by the Patent Shaft & Axletree Co., hardly differ from the day they were built. The brick structure, a gents' WC and urinal, dates from the opening.

Below right: A scene looking towards Liverpool from the 'down' fast face of the centre platform. From the scale plan and views it will be noted that only passengers on the 'down' slow platform were judged to need a gents' WC. There is a kind of logic here, as this would be the principal platform for services into Liverpool, and most pre-war commuters would be men!

WEST ALLERTON *(Map Ref. A0)*

When the LNWR was formed, in 1846, the route from the south into Liverpool lay over the metals of the Grand Junction, Warrington & Newton and Liverpool & Manchester railways, via Earlestown (q.v.). The present route, diverging from the West Coast Main Line at Weaver Junction, and running via Runcorn and Ditton, to the L&MR at Edge Hill, was built piecemeal in the 1850s and 1860s, the section from Speke Junction to Edge Hill dating from 1864. At that time, cities were much more compact, and Liverpool's outer suburb still in its infancy. North of Speke, the line ran through open fields. A suburban service began to evolve, but it was not for another seventy years that a station was planned for West Allerton, between Allerton and Mossley Hill. A new station was designed in 1937, but unlike other new or rebuilt stations, such as Lea Hall *(Volume One)* or Hoylake and Leasowe in the Wirral, instead of reinforced-concrete and brick, the platform buildings were of hardboard with timber framing! The booking office was of brick with a stone slab facing on to Booker Avenue. No freight facilities were provided.

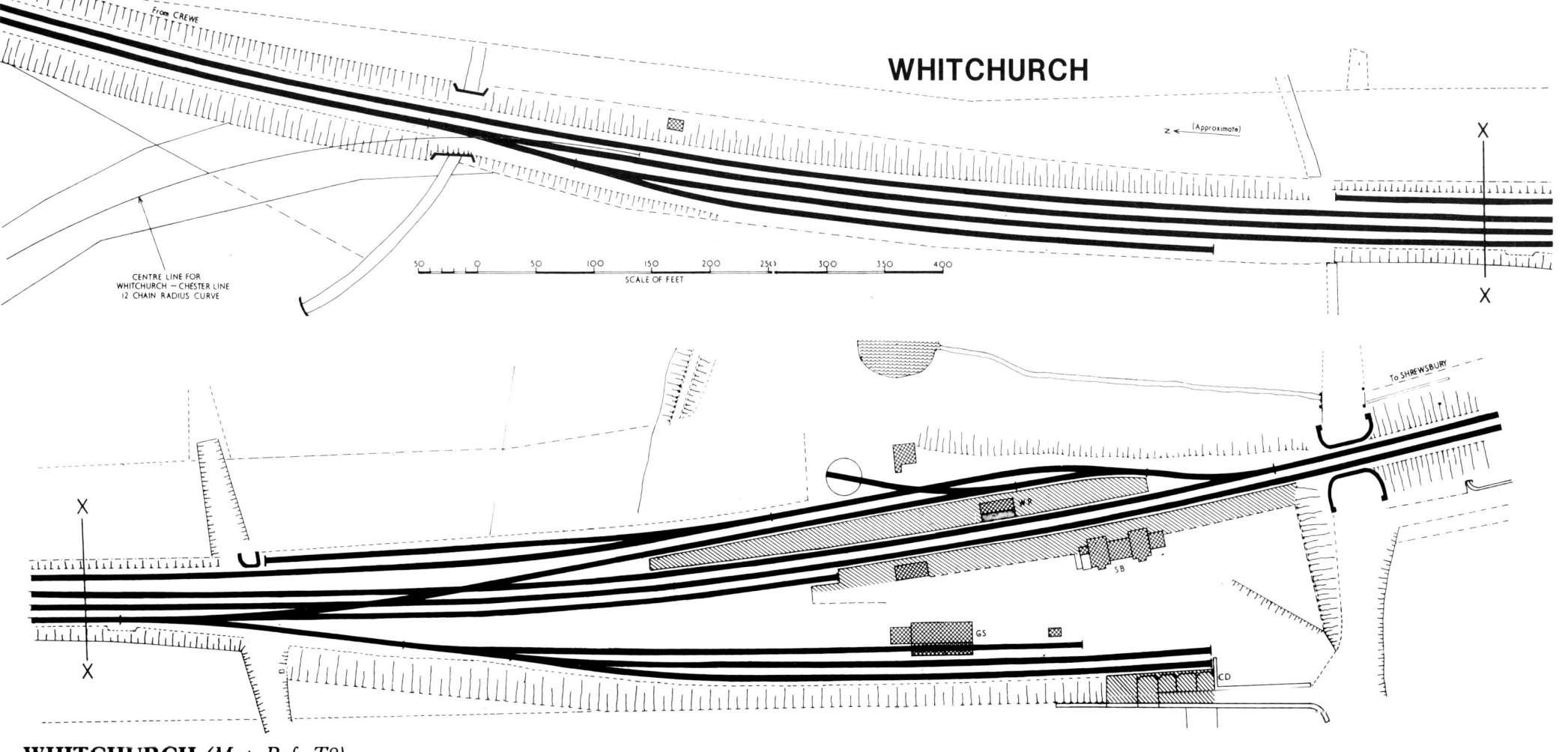

WHITCHURCH

WHITCHURCH *(Map Ref. T8)*

Whitchurch is a pleasant market town in the Shropshire plain, near the Cheshire border, and rather more than half-way between Shrewsbury and Crewe. The West Coast Main Line passes some ten miles to the east, and the GWR Shrewsbury & Chester Railway about fifteen miles to the west. Whitchurch lay in a lightly-populated border zone between the LNWR and GWR territories. In the 1850s, the LNWR sought to develop a through route between Lancashire and South Wales, an important part being the Shrewsbury & Crewe line, which was authorised on 20th August 1853, and opened on 1st September 1858. Although the LNWR had access to North Wales, via the Chester & Crewe and Chester & Holyhead lines, Euston was favourably inclined to Welsh interests, seeking a route through Central Wales to Aberystwyth. A whole string of companies was involved, the most easterly being the Oswestry, Ellesmere & Whitchurch Railway, incorporated on 1st August 1861, and favoured by the LNWR, and opposed, predictably, by the GWR. The OE&WR opened to goods on 20th April 1863, and to passengers on 4th May. The Oswestry line joined the LNWR on an embankment just south of Whitchurch Station, at which a third platform was provided on the 'up' side for Oswestry trains to stand at. A short turntable, reached off a connection from the middle of the platform, served the OE&WR. The scale plan shows the station in the late 1860s and, if the layout was exactly as shown, Whitchurch must have been almost unworkable. Sometimes, even railway draftsmen erred in not showing slips, and the inclusion of 'up' and 'down' trailing slips would make all the difference.

In the 1860s, the LNWR decided to challenge the GWR's monopoly between Shrewsbury and Chester, with a 15-mile double-track line running north-west from Whitchurch to Tattenhall Junction, on the Chester & Crewe line. This opened on 1st October 1872, the proposed junction being depicted on the scale survey. The station was enlarged, and eventually signalled from three boxes, Chester Junction, Goods Yard (which could more accurately be described as 'Station Cabin') and Cambrian Junction. Through traffic never materialised for the Chester line, and with two minor local stations, the seven or eight workings of the 1880s were ample. Six trains ran in 1946, and passenger services ceased on 16th September 1957, although the route remained intact for freight and diversion working until 1963. In pre-grouping days, Whitchurch provided a useful access on to the Cambrian Railways, into which the OE&WR was merged in 1864, but after the Grouping, the GWR naturally preferred their own access to the Cambrian section via Birmingham (Snow Hill) and Shrewsbury.

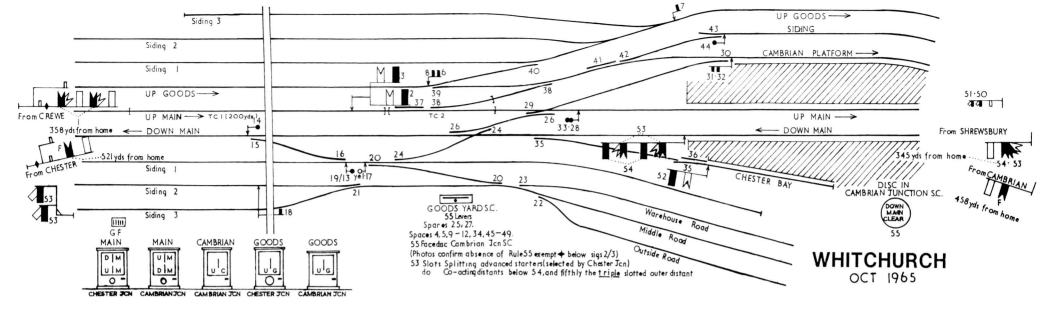

WHITCHURCH

OCT 1965

GOODS YARD S.C.
55 Levers
Spares 2,5,27.
Spaces 4,5,9 – 12,34,45 – 49.
55 Facedisc Cambrian Jcn SC
(Photos confirm absence of Rule 55 exempt + below sigs 2/3)
53 Slots Splitting advanced starters (selected by Chester Jcn)
do Co-acting distants below 54, and fifthly the <u>triple</u> slotted outer distant

In contrast to the Midland Railway, which gave geographical names to its boxes, (e.g. West Junction or Station North) the LNWR believed in numbers, for example, Llandudno Nos. 1 and 2 (or even Edge Hill No. 17). Whitchurch was most unusual for the LNWR, therefore, and the name bestowed upon 'Goods Yard' cabin was utterly misleading. The signal diagram *(above)* additionally shows the block shelf, with standard 'up'/'down' combined instruments to Chester Junction and Cambrian Junction, a 'sending' instrument, via the Cambrian Platform, to Cambrian Junction, and a permissive block 'receiving' instrument ex-Chester Junction for the 'up' goods, and a 'sending' instrument to Cambrian Junction.

Below left: This elevated LNWR ground frame was located by 'down' siding No. 3, between Whitchurch Goods Yard and Chester Junction boxes, and controlled 'down' sidings connections only.

Below right: Whitchurch Cambrian Junction box was a typical LNWR all-timber 'embankment' cabin, and was provided with a porch WC, and a single-line token catcher for the Cambrian section. The Ellesmere line, used by one of the authors when at Ellesmere School (1928-31) closed to passengers on 18th January 1965, and to goods on 29th March 1965. It is depicted in that year.

Left: Looking north from the 'down' main platform to Crewe, in 1965, the island platform is in the centre of the view, with 'up' main and Cambrian faces. The locomotive water tank, and turntable, are beyond the splitting bracket signal ex the Cambrian platform. This accords equal priority to the Shrewsbury and Ellesmere routes, in contrast to the 'up' main signal which provides co-acting arms for the 'up' Shrewsbury line, and a single arm, lower than the lower of the two Shrewsbury arms, for the Cambrian route. In 1883, nine trains arrived ex-Crewe, seven ex-Chester, and there were seven departures for the Cambrian and ten for Shrewsbury.

WHITCHURCH

Below: Goods Yard signal cabin, in a view looking towards Crewe. This box had an internal stairway, and the provision of a porch WC, without the usual external stairway, was most unusual. The signalling in the 'down' direction was also unusual, with distant and stop signals worked off the same lever. In part, this was due to the short distance between signals, but may also have arisen through the LNWR penchant for using the Shrewsbury & Crewe line, so close to Crewe, for trials.

Below: A view looking north from the 'down' platform, with Goods Yard box in the left distance, the 'down' sidings and footbridge beyond, the 'up' sidings and 'up' main platform, No. 3, and Cambrian platform No. 4. Platform 1 was the Chester Bay, and is just visible on the extreme left.

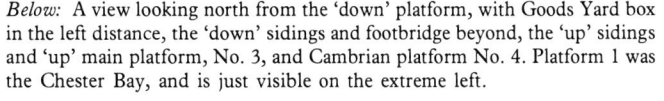

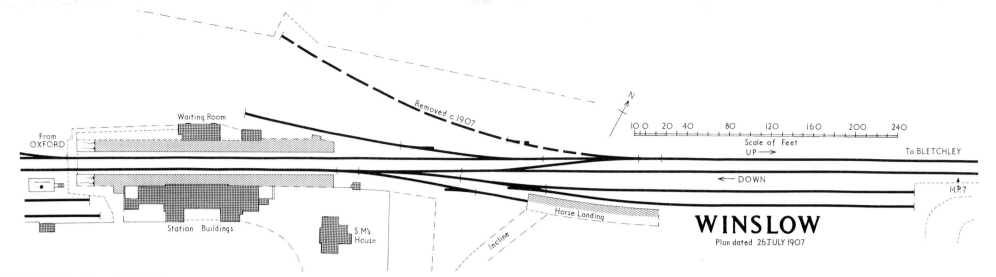

WINSLOW *(Map Ref. J3)*

Winslow Station was on the LNWR's Bletchley to Oxford branch, 2¼ miles east of Verney Junction. When the Banbury and Oxford routes opened during 1850/51, both were single track, and although the actual divergence was at Verney, the two routes ran as parallel single lines to Winslow, where trains were combined or split. It was not until 1868 that Verney Junction became the actual junction, consequent upon the doubling of the Oxford line. Even then, workings were not entirely normal, as Winslow continued to be used for certain shunting movements and, reputedly, for single line staff working.

The goods accommodation at Winslow was generous, with five separate sets of sidings. The main yard was on the 'down' side, near the cabin, with two sidings, later reduced to one, on the far side of the line. A milk dock existed at the back of the 'up' platform, whilst opposite these points, and reached off the 'down' line via a three way point, were two coal sidings and a separate side and end loading dock. When the station served as the junction for the Banbury branch, one of the 'up' sidings at the Banbury end boasted a locomotive turntable. The connection shown dotted on the scale plan, and lifted circa 1907, was to a brickworks.

Below left: Although Winslow had a population of well under 2,000, its original significance as a junction for the Banbury and Oxford lines meant that substantial passenger facilities were provided on both platforms. The waiting-room on the 'up' platform was therefore much larger than those to be found elsewhere. In the middle-distance can be seen the water supply tank in close proximity to the station (another much larger tank existed a quarter of a mile away). Beyond that, and to the left of the platform starter, is one of the two Edward Bury cast-iron water columns which dated from the dawn of the steam age — indeed they may well have been older than the station itself, and arrived ex-store.

WINSLOW

Below right: A view looking towards Bletchley in 1967. The station buildings on the 'down' side were to the customary 'Buckinghamshire' style, with an open circulating area where the booking hall might reasonably have been. Unlike other examples, which used local stone, these were in a very sombre brick (perhaps they too were a local product, from the adjoining brickworks). The station closed to passengers on 1st January 1968. At the foot of the 'down' platform is the second Edward Bury water column, still in situ in 1967. The fire devil is more modern, and too large, and its chimney will heat the atmosphere rather than the water column!

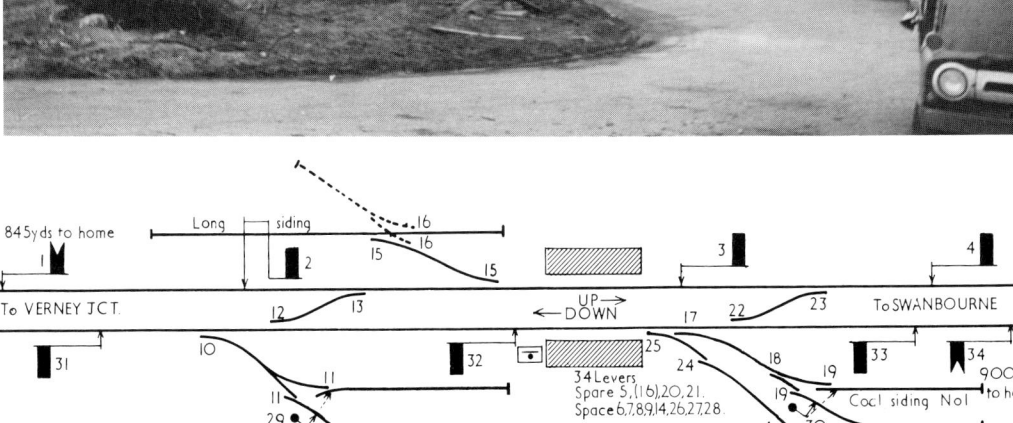

WINSLOW

845 yds to home
Long siding
To VERNEY JCT.
UP
DOWN
To SWANBOURNE
900 yds to home
34 Levers
Spare 5, (11,6), 20, 21.
Space 6, 7, 8, 9, 14, 26, 27, 28.
Train on Line indicators work with crossovers
12/13 & 22/23 controling signals 2 & 33.
Coal siding No 1
Coal siding No 2

Above left: A detail study of the Edward Bury water column on the 'up' platform. Edward Bury was, of course, closely associated with the London & Birmingham Railway, and as a follow-on, the dawn of the LNWR, but the Bury influence spread to many railways, and modellers of the vintage scene might well find this delightful water column, with its fluted form, a perfect match. The timber ramp at the end of a brick-built platform is most unusual.

Above centre: The station approach — an attractive touch was the green in the centre, with its two splendid trees, the effect resembling the divided drive to many fine country houses.

WINSLOW

Left: The water tank by the 'up' platform was carried upon four ornate columns, topped by transverse and longitudinal beams. Its construction suggests a fairly early piece of equipment.

Above: As a consequence of the terrible Quintinshill collision in 1915, the LNWR devised 'Train on line' indicators to install at boxes where there were no refuge sidings, but trains sometimes had to be shunted for others to pass. The indicator was coupled to the interlocking, and moved to 'Blocked' when the points were pulled, and stayed blocked, locking the relevant signals when the point was returned, and had to be reset manually to free the signals. Indicators were provided at each end of the box, one for the 'up' line, and one for the 'down' line. Latterly superseded by track circuits, which could be arranged to lock signals if desired, they became increasingly rare, but survived at Winslow to the end of passenger working. Their main drawbacks were that the signalman could reset them, as was essential, and that they worked whatever the crossover was being used for, and not purely when refuging a train.